# Strategic Marketing Planning

This book provides a uniquely practical approach to strategic marketing planning. Combining a comprehensive overview of theory with practice, each chapter takes the reader step by step through the strategic marketing process. Beginning with situation analysis, it moves on to marketing strategy (targeting and brand positioning) and finally details the overall implementation and creation of customer values.

This second edition has been fully updated to integrate both sustainability and digitalization throughout the whole strategic planning process, covering analyzing consumer needs, setting goals, choosing a brand positioning, and marketing communication. Subjects such as big data, AI, online behavioral targeting, influencer marketing, and social media are explored, accompanied by plentiful examples. A unique feature is the full integration of sustainability within normal marketing, led by a new customer value model. *Strategic Marketing Planning* equips the reader with the necessary tools and techniques to develop and deliver a thorough and effective marketing strategy.

With a broad range of international case studies that bring the theory to life, this renowned text is vital reading for undergraduate and postgraduate students of marketing management and strategic marketing. It should also be of interest to marketing practitioners who want a clear overview to aid them in the planning process. Support materials include PowerPoint slides.

**Karel Jan Alsem** is Professor of Marketing at the Hanze University of Applied Sciences in Groningen, The Netherlands. In addition, he is Assistant Professor of Marketing at the Faculty of Economics and Business at the University of Groningen, The Netherlands. He is also a consultant in branding and health care marketing. His main research interests concern strategic brand management, marketing communications, and marketing planning. Alongside a number of books, he has published papers in journals such as the *International Journal of Research in Marketing, Applied Economics,* and the *Journal of Market Focused Management.*

# Strategic Marketing Planning

## A Step-by-Step Approach

Second Edition

Karel Jan Alsem

Routledge
Taylor & Francis Group

LONDON AND NEW YORK

Designed cover image: Ryan McVay / Getty Images

Second edition published 2024
by Routledge
4 Park Square, Milton Park, Abingdon, Oxon, OX14 4RN

and by Routledge
605 Third Avenue, New York, NY 10158

*Routledge is an imprint of the Taylor & Francis Group, an informa business*

© 2024 Karel Jan Alsem

First edition published by Routledge 2019

*British Library Cataloguing-in-Publication Data*
A catalogue record for this book is available from the British Library

*Library of Congress Cataloging-in-Publication Data*
Names: Alsem, K. J., author.
Title: Strategic marketing planning : a step-by-step approach / Karel Jan Alsem.
Description: Second edition. | Abingdon, Oxon ; New York, NY : Routledge, 2024. | First edition
    published by Routledge 2019. | Includes bibliographical references and index.
Identifiers: LCCN 2023022150 (print) | LCCN 2023022151 (ebook) | ISBN 9781032463933 (hardback) |
    ISBN 9781032463834 (paperback) | ISBN 9781003381488 (ebook)
Subjects: LCSH: Marketing—Management.
Classification: LCC HF5415.13 .A435313 2024 (print) | LCC HF5415.13 (ebook) |
    DDC 658.8—dc23/eng/20230720
LC record available at https://lccn.loc.gov/2023022150
LC ebook record available at https://lccn.loc.gov/2023022151

ISBN: 978-1-032-46393-3 (hbk)
ISBN: 978-1-032-46383-4 (pbk)
ISBN: 978-1-003-38148-8 (ebk)

DOI: 10.4324/9781003381488

Typeset in Times New Roman
by Apex CoVantage, LLC

Access the Support Material: www.routledge.com/9781032463834

# Contents

# Preface to the second edition

This second edition appears five years after the first edition. This does not seem to be a long period; however, the world has dramatically changed since then. The coronavirus, wars, #meetoo, and especially sustainability are more important than ever. Although climate change has already been known about for decades, it looks like only recently have humans realized that the Earth is not infinite in room for all of us. In 2023 the IPCC published alarming conclusions about the slow disaster coming to all of us.

What does this have to do with marketing? A lot. Marketing is the key discipline within organizations to influence consumer behavior, and this behavior should be more sustainable, just like the behavior of organizations themselves. So, I think brands should take the lead in this. Marketing can be helpful in this respect instead of having the image of stimulating too much unsustainable consumption. Both organizations who do regular business and now also have to be and act more sustainable as well as organizations who have stimulating sustainable consumer behavior as a main task (such as governmental organizations and NGOs) can and should use marketing to do this.

This second edition of *Strategic Marketing Planning* can help with this. It still is about regular strategic marketing planning but now with explicit attention to sustainability in all stages of marketing: culture, research, strategy, and tactics. It is my wish that in the end, this will also improve the image of marketing itself.

A number of adjustments have been made in this second edition without changing the structure. An overview of all adjustments can be found after the contents. As in the first edition, digital marketing is integrated in all phases. This also happens with sustainability in this edition. Chapter 1 discusses the specific characteristics and challenges of sustainable consumer behavior. Sustainability then recurs in many phases of this book, now including our Brand Benefitting Model, a model that plays an even more prominent role in this edition, based on an even clearer definition of customer value. Some specific new topics such as inclusive marketing and customer experience management are also covered. In the section on brand positioning, the models are arranged more logically. Simplifications have also been made, as with the internal analysis, which now consists of four steps. The topics of crisis communication and influencer marketing have been rewritten. In addition, the case material has been updated in this edition, and examples about corona have also been included.

## Preface for the first edition

This book describes the current thinking on strategic marketing from a how-to perspective. The theory of strategic marketing is presented in steps. Those steps can be followed to arrive at a strategic marketing plan. This book has a combination of five attributes that make it different from other marketing strategy books. First, it deals only with *strategic marketing*. Therefore, there are no separate chapters devoted to consumer behavior, market research, or each of the marketing instruments (the 4 P's are dealt with in two chapters). The second attribute is the *process approach*. The third attribute relates to what the author feels is important in marketing: customers and brands. A *customer and brand orientation* is followed throughout the book: in the analysis, in choosing options, in developing marketing strategy, and in implementation. The fourth attribute is that in many places in the book, *strategic guidelines* are given: what to do and what not to do in marketing practice. Finally, there is much attention to *tools and techniques* that can be helpful in the planning process. In summary, this book combines an academic and applied approach of strategic marketing planning.

The book is primarily targeted at students with a basic knowledge of marketing. Thus, the relevant target groups are undergraduates in the third or fourth year and some MBAs. The book can be used in, for example, courses in marketing strategy or marketing management. The book can also be used in executive teaching and by marketing practitioners who are looking for academic support for their daily decision making.

The book consists of four parts, including 14 chapters, with each chapter being a step in the strategic marketing planning process:

Part 1  Introduction and marketing planning

  1   The essence of marketing
  2   The strategic marketing planning process

Part 2  Situation analysis

  3   Mission, customer values, and market definition
  4   Internal analysis
  5   Customer analysis
  6   Industry analysis
  7   Competitor analysis
  8   Distribution and supplier analysis
  9   SWOT analysis

Part 3  Corporate decisions and marketing decisions

  10   Corporate objectives and strategies
  11   Marketing objectives and marketing strategies

Part 4  Implementation

  12   Choice of product/service, price, and channels
  13   Marketing communications
  14   Organization and execution of marketing

Each chapter starts with key points and an illustrative case with questions. Throughout the text, many examples are included, most of them in separate boxes, enabling readers to concentrate on the theory, the examples, or both. Each chapter ends with a summary.

This book tries to reduce the gap between strategic marketing theory and marketing practice. The main message is that you should ask yourself continuously what effect your company's behavior has on potential customers. For example, you might ask: How does my amusing commercial score on brand recall? Or: Do more brand extensions reduce or increase customers' confusion? Things like this have to do with the attitude of the manager and also with the way the planning process is done. Both aspects receive attention in this book. The content of the book is the result of continuously wondering whether strategic marketing issues are and should be applicable in marketing practice. However, there is no 'truth'. Science by definition is a matter of asking questions, and a field as young as marketing science is only at the beginning of the process of finding the 'truth'. It is my hope that the ideas in this book not only lead to better marketing decision making but also lead to the asking of better marketing questions.

I would greatly appreciate it if you, as my customer, make me part of your ongoing needs and perceptions with regard to this book.

*Karel Jan Alsem*
*Hanze University of Applied Sciences Groningen*
March 2023

# Acknowledgments

The book is an updated and revised version of its Dutch counterpart, which is now in its ninth edition. First, I thank my Dutch publisher, Noordhoff, for permitting me to do this international version.

Second, I owe many thanks to Erik Kostelijk for preparing the starting cases and questions. I thank my publisher, Routledge, for publishing the book. Finally, I would like to acknowledge the feedback I received from the following reviewers. Their thoughtful reviews are greatly appreciated:

- Dr. Scott Dacko
- Dr. Erica Brady
- Dr. Robert Essig
- Dr. Kathy-Ann Fletcher

Finally, I would like to thank our quartet Tom, Sophie, Anne, and Floor (aged 31, 31, 29, and 27, respectively) for keeping their father sharp and young. And, of course, I am extremely grateful to my cobrand Cato for being an infinite source of positive support.

*Karel Jan Alsem*
*Haren, March 2023*

# Part I

# Introduction and marketing planning

1    The essence of marketing
2    The strategic marketing planning process

*Strategic marketing planning* aims to bridge the gap between the theory and practice of strategic marketing. It describes how a company (or brand) can go through the strategic marketing planning process and how marketing decisions can be made from an analysis of the brand and the environment. We opt for a *step-by-step approach* description of the *activities* that a company must carry out in the context of strategic marketing. These activities can be divided into analysis, strategy, and tactics/implementation.

The applications of the marketing principles described are not limited to (commercial) markets for food; durable goods, such as cars; and services, such as banks. Precisely because marketing in general aims to improve the relationships between a provider and target groups, the process also applies to healthcare, charities, regions, and other less profit-oriented markets, for example.

This book consists of four parts and thus follows the central CAST model (marketing as Culture, Analysis, Strategy and Tactics). The introductory Part 1 describes the principles of marketing ('marketing as culture') and the marketing planning process. The marketing planning process is then discussed step by step: each step is a chapter: in 12 steps (Chapters 3 to 14), you develop a marketing plan.

Part 2 is devoted to strategic analyses. Our starting point here is that without thorough, systematic situation analysis, finding a successful strategy is more luck than wisdom. Part 3 is devoted to strategy formation, with a strong focus on branding and positioning decisions. Part 4 contains the translation (including communication) and implementation

DOI: 10.4324/9781003381488-1

of the strategic decisions in tactics. Parts 2, 3, and 4 correspond to the basic parts of a marketing plan:

- a 'marketing report' (analysis results; Part 2)
- a strategic marketing plan (long-term decisions; Part 3)
- a tactical (and operational) marketing plan (elaboration of the market instruments for one year; Part 4)

All marketing activities must be carried out with a purpose: to create (long-term) value for the customer and society with a recognizable brand image. Based on this goal (customer/ society and brand), not only are activities described, but practical advice is also given. The book can be used to develop a marketing plan but can also serve as a guide for taking a closer look at your own marketing policy.

Part 1 of this book contains an introduction. In Chapter 1, we first discuss the importance of marketing and what marketing actually entails. Chapter 2 outlines the entire strategic marketing planning process that a company can follow to arrive at a marketing plan. The planning process is the common thread running through the book.

# Chapter 1

# The essence of marketing

## Key points in this chapter

- Outline what marketing is and describe how marketing developed, along with new visions about consumer behavior.
- Introduce marketing (customer and brand) as the key to developing customers' relationship with a brand.
- Describe aggregation levels in organizations.
- Stress the importance of a sustainable competitive advantage.

## Introduction

This book covers the concept of strategic marketing from the customer and brand perspective. It is done step by step, leading to a marketing plan for a brand. Following the route, the reader will be confronted with different theories and models, each of them contributing to the marketing plan. There are no side paths, such as a separate chapter about consumer behavior.

This introductory chapter is devoted to the importance and content of marketing. We start with an outline of the context in which marketing exists, why marketing is increasingly important, and which important developments must be taken into account. Subsequently, in Section 1.2, we indicate what we actually mean by marketing. We also see the hierarchy and developments in the marketing concept, including the relevance of sustainability. Finally, in Section 1.3, we discuss some forms of marketing and the relationship of marketing with other business functions.

## 1.1 The changing landscape of marketing

In this section we describe types of trends in marketing, online behavior and digital marketing, and the marketing spiral. Then the unconscious consumer and the role of emotion are discussed, and we conclude with sustainability.

DOI: 10.4324/9781003381488-2

### 1.1.1  Types of trends

In anticipation of the next section, we first note that marketing is mainly about customer-oriented action based on a clear brand identity. Marketing is one discipline or 'function', as are finance, human resources management, and information and communication technology (ICT). All these business functions have to do with a dynamic environment. This is often referred to by the acronym VUCA: an environment that is *volatile, uncertain, complex,* and *ambiguous*. In this section, we outline several developments ('trends') that have (or have had) an influence on marketing. We distinguish three types of trends:

1   Trends initiated by 'providers'/organizations
2   Trends in consumer behavior (demand side)
3   Trends in research/knowledge

The first two types of trends strongly influence each other. As we'll see later in this book, consumers often don't know what they want and latent needs don't surface until they're 'invented' by a company.

We now outline the following developments/trends:

1   Online and digital marketing
2   The marketing spiral
3   The unconscious consumer
4   Sustainability

In addition to these trends, there have been all kinds of other developments, such as the coronavirus, international conflicts, more attention to diversity, more equal treatment of women (#metoo), and much more. These are part of the macro-environmental analysis and are not discussed here. We chose the previous because they are directly related to marketing.

### 1.1.2  Online behavior and digital marketing

The arrival and development of the online world (from the early 1990s) has undoubtedly been the most important groundbreaking development for marketing in the past 40 years. Consumers' search and choice behavior largely takes place online. But the internet has also produced many *new products and services*, such as new intermediaries between traditional providers and consumers, such as Booking.com, but also new services such as Uber (including taxi, delivery), Airbnb (accommodation), Takeaway (meal delivery), Picnic (online supermarket), Gorillas (speed delivery), and Check (sharing scooters). These intermediaries' can be regarded as new 'retailers'.

## Case 1.1 New online retailers

Uber extended its portfolio

Uber Eats is an online food ordering and delivery platform launched by Uber in 2014. Meals are delivered by couriers using cars, scooters, bikes, or on foot. It is operational in over 6,000 cities across 45 countries as of 2021.

With the advent of the internet, the *availability of information* has also increased enormously. More and more information about brands is becoming available to consumers. This mainly concerns experience data (i.e. reviews). Reviews often play an important role in purchasing decisions, and consumer reviews appear to be even more important than official reviews (Ghimire et al., 2022). Due to the arrival of social media, the *distribution of information* is also faster than ever: a (re)action by a consumer can be disseminated at lightning speed via, for example, Twitter. Much is written about social media. But what makes social media special? It ensures that people's opinions can be spread rapidly among large groups of other people. So it is, as it were, an extreme form of what has been known for decades as 'word of mouth'. If word of mouth in the past indeed had to go from mouth to mouth (singular), nowadays one interesting tweet from someone can quickly reach thousands of others. And if there are also journalists who find it interesting to report this in 'classical' media such as a newspaper, then it goes twice as fast. The consequence of this rapid form of word of mouth is that the power of consumers is increasing. Companies therefore have to watch out for reputation problems and will have to deal with customer wishes even more carefully than before.

The online behavior of consumers means that the position of retailers ('shops') is under pressure. It is said that retailers must provide more 'experience'.

Because the internet is so important, marketing related to it is often referred to as 'online marketing' or 'digital marketing'. We make three comments on this.

The first comment we make on these designations is that we believe that the use of online channels is a normal part of marketing. Actually, (separate) online marketing does not exist. This already applies to young people: they have been brought up online and therefore do not know anything else. Nevertheless, we consider it important to define the concept of online marketing at this point, because a lot of attention is paid to it in theory and practice nowadays. We see online marketing by definition as part or subset of 'ordinary' marketing. So what is it exactly? We now consider both parts of this concept: first the designation 'online' and then the designation 'marketing'.

Online means that you are active on the internet. However, for some 'online-like' applications, you don't always have to be online, for example, when using apps on your phone. In marketing, too, some activities, such as analyzing 'big data', are partly based on online behavior but not limited to that. Moreover, the analysis itself does not require the internet. That is why the term 'digital marketing' is often used, which is a slightly broader concept than online marketing and includes everything that has to do with online-related media and applications. Following the scientific literature, we also use the term 'digital marketing'.

Then the word 'marketing'. A well-known part of digital marketing is 'optimizing' a website so that it is found quickly (search engine optimization [SEO]). The use of social media, such as a YouTube channel, is another example. What is striking about examples of online marketing is that they often concern online *communication*. But the internet is not only a communication channel; it is increasingly also a sales channel ('e-commerce'). Products sold via the internet are both physical products (e.g. electronics) and services (e.g. holidays, hotel reservations). Which brings us to the definition of digital marketing. Digital marketing therefore encompasses much more than just online communication. In fact, all phases of marketing (research, marketing strategy, marketing tactics) have digital aspects and applications. Digital aspects therefore recur in many chapters in this book as part of (ordinary) marketing.

### 1.1.3 Marketing spiral

Even before the arrival of the internet, and certainly afterwards, there has been increasing competition between brands. This is visible in all four marketing instruments (4 Ps: product, price, place, and promotion): more products and services, more communication, more price competition, and more frequent use of multiple channels. As we show in the next section, an important starting point in marketing is to differentiate yourself from competitors. That is getting more and more difficult, especially since everyone is trying to do this. As a result of this competition, consumers see less and less differences between brands, after which brands communicate even more or come up with price offers or introduce product innovations, and so on. So there is a spiral. Figure 1.1 shows the communication spiral. All spirals together are called the marketing spiral by Nederstigt and Poiesz (2022) (Figure 1.2).

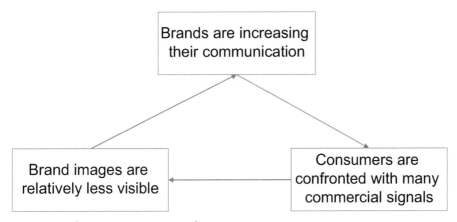

*Figure 1.1* The communication spiral

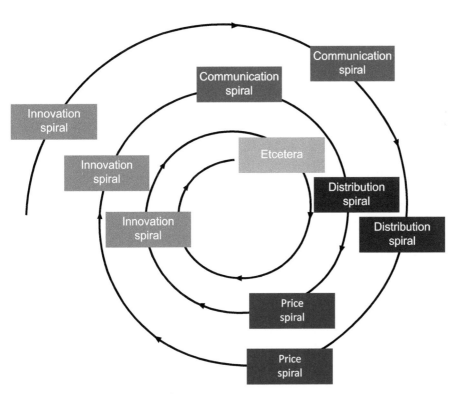

*Figure 1.2* The marketing spiral
Source: Nederstigt and Poiesz (2022)

## Case 1.2 The communication spiral

### Advertising offline still important

Although much attention in marketing is given to online channels, 'classical' offline communication such as outdoor or TV advertising is still important. All signals of brands unconsciously affect brand perception in consumers' minds.

With regard to the increasing range of products and services, you could say that this is good for consumers But how happy are you when you have to choose from 40 different detergents for a shelf in a store? Consumers do sometimes get tired of that, so much choice also creates uncertainty, and you have to make a lot of effort to find out everything. The phenomenon that 'more choice' leads to more doubt prompted Schwartz (2004) to write his book *The Paradox of Choice*: Whether we buy a pair of jeans or a cup of coffee, take out a telephone contract, or choose an education, everyday decisions are increasingly complex due to the overwhelming abundance of choices.

### 1.1.4 The unconscious consumer and the role of emotion

For years, the central principle in economics was that people act rationally. For example, if a consumer needs new shoes, he or she will collect information about possible brands, compare, choose, and buy. A classic consumer behavior model depicts these phases (Figure 1.3).

It has long been recognized in marketing theory that these phases are only completed when there is high involvement. *Involvement* in this context means how important a consumer finds it to make a good product choice. In practice, many marketers find their products very important and sometimes think that consumers do too. Unfortunately, for

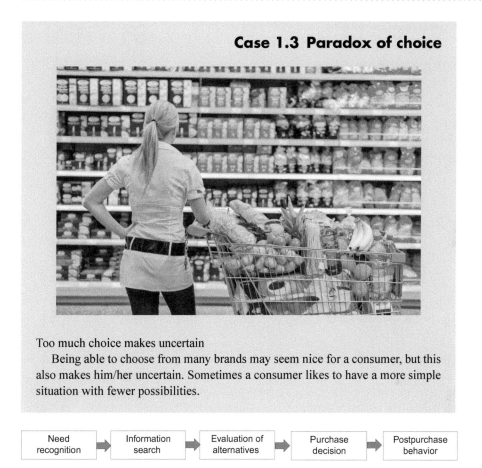

## Case 1.3 Paradox of choice

Too much choice makes uncertain

Being able to choose from many brands may seem nice for a consumer, but this also makes him/her uncertain. Sometimes a consumer likes to have a more simple situation with fewer possibilities.

| Need recognition | → | Information search | → | Evaluation of alternatives | → | Purchase decision | → | Postpurchase behavior |

*Figure 1.3* **Classic consumer behavior model**

ordinary people, products and brands are often not that important at all, so there is low involvement. People with low involvement make 'unconscious' decisions more often than with high involvement.

Much psychological and economic research therefore shows that people are largely driven by emotional and often unconscious motives instead of rational considerations. This has everything to do with the idea that people have two systems for making choices. Kahneman (2011) talks about two 'systems'; see Figure 1.4. *System 2* is the conscious system in which decisions are made in a rational manner.

But *system 1* is more the autonomous, unconscious choice process. With the latter, think about hearing your name in company without paying attention or going home on autopilot by bike. System 1 therefore seems to be becoming increasingly important. System 2 is especially good for long-term decisions and to counter (sometimes) overly spontaneous reactions.

In economics, this view is the core of *behavioral economics*, for which Richard Thaler was awarded a Nobel Prize some years ago. Psychology has always been important in marketing, and the role of emotion has always been recognized. However, coupled with

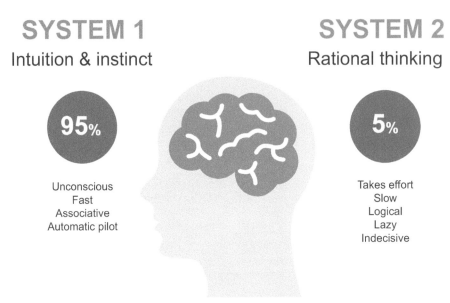

*Figure 1.4* **Systems 1 and 2**

the fact that consumer involvement in buying brands is often low and appears to be decreasing due to ever-increasing choice, the importance of emotion and subconscious behavior cannot be overemphasized. According to some authors, more than 95% of people's decisions are made unconsciously (Dijksterhuis, 2007). For marketers, this means, among other things, that brands must present themselves to customers in a consistent manner across the board.

### 1.1.5 Sustainability

Let's start with a definition of this concept. This is necessary since this term is – somewhat confusingly – used both for environmental issues ('planet') and for matters concerning the sustainable employability of personnel ('people'). In this book, we choose the designation 'sustainability' for matters relating to the environment. In Section 11.3.4, we relate this to the Sustainable Development Goals (SDGs).

There is worldwide agreement that the earth is experiencing a climate change that is already having far-reaching consequences and will have many more consequences. Major consequences are predicted for weather conditions, the water level, and the food supply ('shortages from 2050') and thus also for migration and stability in countries. In fact, the current generation of people is finding out that the Earth is finite. The average temperature on Earth has also been rising for 'only' ten years. About 50 years ago, for example, the Club of Rome already warned about this, but now that people are starting to feel the consequences (heat, rain, forest fires, energy shortages, etc.), sustainability is really starting to come to life. The challenge of dealing with this has also increased due to international conflicts from 2022 onwards. Energy prices then rose sharply, and even the availability of energy came under pressure.

## Case 1.4 The importance of sustainability

### Patagonia changes into a sustainable company

A half century after founding the outdoor apparel maker Patagonia, Yvon Chouinard, the eccentric rock climber who became a reluctant billionaire with his unconventional spin on capitalism, has given the company away.

Rather than selling the company or taking it public, Mr. Chouinard, his wife, and two adult children have transferred their ownership of Patagonia, valued at about $3 billion, to a specially designed trust and a nonprofit organization. They were created to preserve the company's independence and ensure that all of its profits – some $100 million a year – are used to combat climate change and protect undeveloped land around the globe.

The unusual move comes at a moment of growing scrutiny for billionaires and corporations, whose rhetoric about making the world a better place is often overshadowed by their contributions to the very problems they claim to want to solve.

At the same time, Mr. Chouinard's relinquishment of the family fortune is in keeping with his longstanding disregard for business norms and his lifelong love for the environment.

'Hopefully this will influence a new form of capitalism that doesn't end up with a few rich people and a bunch of poor people', Mr. Chouinard, 83, said in an exclusive interview. 'We are going to give away the maximum amount of money to people who are actively working on saving this planet'.

Source: www.nytimes.com/2022/09/14/climate/
patagonia-climate-philanthropy-chouinard.html

Sustainability is a global social issue that affects everyone and involves many business functions. The role of marketing in this is difficult. It is sometimes argued that marketing is a co-cause of unsustainable behavior, due to the supposed emphasis on (more) consumption and putting the interests of the company, the shareholder, and the manager (profit) first. In our view, however, that is not the core of marketing. Marketing is about relationships between organizations and stakeholders. And it is also important for long-term consequences and various interest groups. Marketing can actually play a positive role in stimulating sustainable behavior. This is important for organizations such as governments and interest groups but also for companies that will increasingly be held accountable for their sustainable behavior. Sustainability has also long been the subject of scientific marketing research. For a long time, the approach was to identify 'the green consumer' with terms such as 'green marketing'. But Kilbourne (1998) already indicated, some 25 years ago, partly on the basis of empirical research (including Kilbourne & Alsem, 1997), that a more macro perspective is needed to avert the ecological crisis. Kotler (2011) argued for 'reinventing marketing with sustainability in mind'. Whether this has actually happened now, we leave in the air. Here we discuss some important aspects of sustainable consumer behavior:

■  What is sustainable consumer behavior?
■  What is the problem with consumer behavior?
■  Which factors play a role in sustainable consumer behavior?

We base this largely on the state-of-the-art paper by White et al. (2019) entitled 'How to SHIFT Consumer Behaviors to Be More Sustainable: A Literature Review and Guiding Framework'.

### Definition of sustainable consumer behavior

Sustainable consumer behavior differs fundamentally from 'ordinary' consumer behavior in a number of respects. Two dimensions are often mentioned, along which major differences exist. The first is short versus long term. The second is the target group perspective: is it the consumer him- or herself or also other stakeholders? In short, the core of sustainable consumer behavior is that it concerns consumption behavior that has *no* adverse consequences for others in the long term. So you should not burden others with the negative effects of your consumption behavior.

### Problem with sustainable consumer behavior

Many studies show that people find sustainability very important. But, unfortunately, there is a big gap in the behavior of these same people. Finding sustainability important does not always lead to sustainable behavior. Nederstigt and Poiesz (2022) also show the well-known consumer behavior triangle with 'motivation, capacity and opportunity' at the corners (Figure 1.5).

You could say that the motivation is there. Capacity has to do with one's own possibilities and with the opportunity to actually do something. There are limitations in both areas. It is often the case that sustainable alternatives are even more expensive than

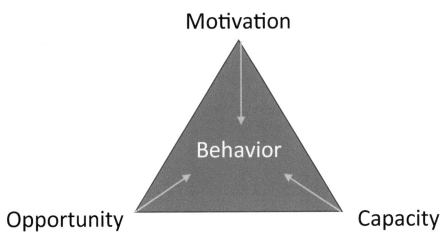

*Figure 1.5* **The consumer behavior triangle**

non-sustainable, for example, vegetarian food. And not everyone can afford to buy a heat pump or electric car. At the same time, everyone can take the bike more often for shorter distances instead of the car, take a shorter shower, or turn down the heating a bit. So there is more at play. We'll get into that now.

*Factors influencing sustainable consumption behavior*

In their study, White et al. (2019) developed the SHIFT model. According to this model, five categories of factors influence sustainable behavior:

1. Social influence: social norms, social identity, and social desirability.
2. Habit formation.
3. Individual self: 'self-concept, self-consistency, self-interest, self-efficacy, and personal norms'. For example, people who are younger, more liberal, or better educated are more likely to engage in environmentally friendly behavior.
4. Feelings and cognitions: two routes to action: more conscious or intuitive, cognitive or based on (negative and positive) emotions, learning and framing.
5. Tangibility: the problem with sustainable consumption is that people first feel the burden (e.g. higher costs), while the benefits are only realized in the long term, in the future. It is important to make these future benefits tangible in today's consumption.

According to the authors, the SHIFT model can be used to close the gap between attitude and behavior that often exists in sustainable contexts. If barriers lie mainly in the social factors, an opportunity is to communicate the behavior of others. Often there will be several obstacles, and combining 'interventions' will therefore be more effective. The extent to which an obstacle is important depends on the personal context of the citizen. Both personality aspects and social influences can play a role in this.

Because marketing and sustainability are closely linked, this book will include sustainability in all phases of marketing (culture, analysis, strategy, tactics).

## 1.2 What is marketing?

Many people think of marketing as advertising and sales. But that is not the core of marketing as we envision it. In this section we first show that the concept of marketing can be interpreted in three (related) ways (Section 1.2.1). We then describe the development of the concept of marketing to the present day. We distinguish three development phases in marketing: up to the 1990s (Section 1.2.2), between 1990 and 2010 (Section 1.2.3), and from 2010 (Section 1.2.4). We end in Section 1.2.5 with some conclusions.

### 1.2.1 The concept of marketing

The concept of marketing can be interpreted in different ways (Webster, 1992, 2005):

1   As a organizational culture (the marketing concept or vision): a set of beliefs that directs the organization in such a way that there is a commitment to meeting the needs of the customer in order to be profitable in the long term. In short: the customer comes first. Later in this chapter we argue that the brand identity should also be at the core of the marketing concept.
2   As a strategy: choosing target groups and positioning the products and services (STP: *segmenting, targeting, and positioning*). As input for strategy development, a Strengths, Weaknesses, Opportunities, Threats (SWOT) analysis is required: linking internal strengths and weaknesses to external opportunities and threats.
3   As tactics and activities: the daily activities around the four market instruments product development, pricing, distribution, and channel choice and around communication.

In this classification we therefore state that the handling of the four market instruments (the 4 Ps) is a tactical matter: short-term decisions for, say, a year. This is a simplification of reality, because we agree with Varadarajan (2010) that many 4P decisions can also be strategic and thus have consequences for several years. Despite the fact that Figure 1.6 does not accurately represent reality, the figure is very clear for educational purposes.

Figure 1.6 is called the CAST model (culture, analytics, strategy, tactics) and basically represents a hierarchy in marketing theory. The highest level (culture) describes the core of what marketing is concerned with: customers and brands. The three stages below are the three concrete steps that are taken in marketing. That's first: analytics and research. Next is a thorough choice of the (marketing) strategy: target group and positioning. The choice of marketing strategy determines the direction for step 3: the development of marketing as a tactic.

The three meanings of marketing are therefore logically in line with each other. The highest level of this, the marketing concept, has traditionally had the customer at its core. Now that marketing concept itself has undergone several developments over the years, partly prompted by increasing knowledge about consumer behavior. We distinguish the following phases (Kotler, 2011):

■   Marketing 1.0: customer wishes and competitive advantages
■   Marketing 2.0: relationships and emotions
■   Marketing 3.0: social and societal interests

For each of these forms of marketing, the new needs come in addition to the previous ones.

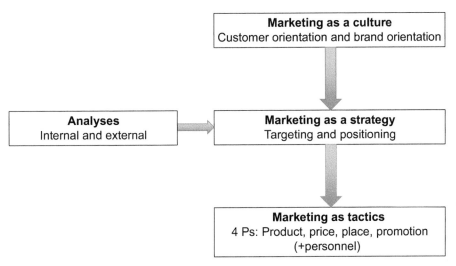

*Figure 1.6* **Marketing hierarchy (CAST model)**

## 1.2.2 Marketing 1.0: customer needs and competition

It is not entirely clear when marketing was 'invented'. The top journal *Journal of Marketing* was founded in 1936. In any case, marketing seems to have become more and more well known since the 1960s. One of the international founders of marketing science is Philip Kotler, who published the first edition of the standard work *Marketing Management* in 1967. As stated in Section 1.2.1, according to the 'classic' marketing concept, the customer is central. This external orientation is an important difference with many other business economic disciplines, such as finance, organizational science, human resources management, and business development. An important starting point of marketing is the needs of customers.

*Strategic marketing concept*

In the 1980s, the realization arose that customer orientation alone is not enough to be successful. It is also necessary to be better than the competition: only by achieving a sustainable competitive advantage can a company continue to operate profitably in the longer term. Competition was already increasing sharply at that time, partly due to less favorable economic developments in that period.

A well-known author who propagated the competitive idea was Porter (1980). All in all, a marketing concept emerged that can be referred to as the *strategic marketing concept* (Day & Wensley, 1983). The strategic marketing concept actually forms an extension of the classic marketing concept and states that a company must meet the following conditions:

■ The company must be *customer oriented.*
■ The company must focus on realizing *sustainable competitive advantages* of products in markets (for example: lower price, better service, better design).

- The organization must also have an eye for other target groups, especially retailers.
- In addition, it is important that the company make a profit in order to *survive in the long term.*

### Market orientation

The aforementioned points of attention largely correspond to what is referred to in the marketing literature as market orientation. Market orientation consists of the following components (Narver & Slater, 1990; Kohli & Jaworski, 1990):

- *Customer-oriented thinking (customer orientation).* Does the company make reasonable promises and keep them? Are customers treated as individuals? Are the wishes and opinions of the target group specifically explored by means of market research? And if so, does that have consequences for trading in the company?
- *Competitive thinking (competitor orientation).* Does the company have a lot of information about individual competitors? Is that information systematically analyzed and distributed throughout the organization? Does the company know when to respond to competitor actions and how to differentiate itself from competitors?
- *Interfunctional coordination (interfunctional orientation)* or integrated decision-making: Does the organization share information internally? Are the strategies for the various functional areas integrated? Are joint decisions made? Is the entire organization genuinely interested in customers?

Putting customer wishes first still applies and can still be improved in many organizations, say Verhoef and Lemon (2013), who introduce the concept of *customer value management* and introduce various ways, including the smart use of data, to make customer value really play a role.

## 1.2.3 Marketing 2.0: emotions, relationships, experiences, and brands

In the 1990s, two expansions of the marketing concept were introduced, mainly prompted by the realization that consumers do not only make decisions 'cognitively' but that emotions and subconscious decisions play a major role in them (see Section 1.1). This led to attention to *'experiences', relationships, customer loyalty,* and the *brand.* The logical connection between experiences (in a broad sense) and brand thinking is that a clear brand identity is necessary (but not sufficient) to build relationships with customers.

### Relationships

In this context it has been stated that it is no longer about (one-off) transaction-oriented marketing but about relationship marketing (Gummesson, 1987, 1999; Webster, 1992) or direct marketing (DM): obtaining and maintaining a structural, direct relationship between a supplier and the customer (Hoekstra, 2003). This also includes thinking in terms of customer satisfaction and *customer loyalty.* A frequently mentioned thought is that it is cheaper to focus on existing customers than on new customers (Reichheld, 1993, 1996). They differ in cost by a factor of five. Whether this factor is correct, we leave unexplored. However, it is logical to assume that someone who is already a customer, by definition, thinks more positively about the company than someone who is not a customer. Indeed, that makes it likely that customer retention is more efficient than new customer retention. A focus on customer retention can therefore be defended and is also in line with the marketing idea of customer focus. Of course, a company cannot do without attracting new customers, simply because customers are always disappearing.

Incidentally, there is a danger in relationship marketing, namely doing your best too intensively and therefore too intrusively trying to make a customer your 'friend'. Then it becomes 'sales' again.

Later, Vargo and Lusch (2004) came to an appropriate interpretation of the marketing concept by emphasizing the *service aspect* of marketing: every marketer should see him- or herself as a service provider and should therefore also be prepared to provide an appropriate service to customers instead of focusing too much on the product. In fact, this is about realizing a customer-oriented attitude. This can only be achieved by the people in the organization itself. Everyone in the organization must therefore be interested in the customer (Gummesson, 1991, 1998). The idea of service is thus very close to the idea of relationship marketing (Ravald & Grönroos, 1996).

### Experiences

Experiences are the experiences people have with brands. Brakus et al. (2009) define '*brand experience*' as 'subjective, internal consumer reactions and behavioral reactions, elicited by brand-related stimuli such as packaging, communication, environments and personal contacts'. The authors show that brand experience consists of four dimensions: sensory, affective, intellectual, and behavioral. Experience is therefore not necessarily about 'spectacular' experiences but simply about the total of impressions that a consumer experiences with a brand through all senses. Most clearly, 'experiences' play a role in stores, for example. When you walk through an Apple store, you 'experience' the brand in every way. But you also experience a brand through other channels, such as a video on YouTube. Verhoef et al. (2019) show in a review article that the sum total of all cognitive, affective, social, and physical experiences is important. And that brings us naturally to the brand and its positioning because they form the starting point of all those experiences. Figure 1.7 shows the relationships between the topics of this section.

### Brand thinking

Also in the 1990s, we saw the emergence of brand thinking in marketing. This has to do with three aspects:

1   *Emotions*. We already mentioned it: in humans, 'system 1' is often decisive. Brands will have to respond to this. In communication, for example, not only do physical product properties have to be emphasized, but emotional associations also have to be linked to the brand.

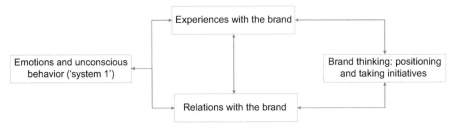

*Figure 1.7* **Emotions and the brand**

2 *Customers often don't know what new things they want.* In a video clip made at the end of the 1990s, people clearly state that they have no need for a mobile phone ('Then I'll write a letter'; 'Imagine being called on my bicycle, terrible'.) Ideas for innovations will therefore often have to come from a company itself. You could also say: companies must respond to the *latent* needs of consumers and therefore have a long-term vision.

3 *Customers may have wishes that do not fit the brand.* If there is a need for insurance from Unilever, should Unilever provide it? No, because that doesn't suit Unilever. This point has to do with the brand identity of a company. Day (1999) rightly warns that a company can be too customer oriented. This in turn has to do with the so-called *resource-based view* (Wernerfelt, 1984). Also according to this view, a strategy should mainly be based on what a company is good at, the *core competences* (Prahalad & Hamel, 1990; Srivastava et al., 1998). Hooley et al. (1998, 2004) are among the few authors who suggest combining the resource-based view with marketing. They call this *resource-based marketing*.

From the theory of the marketing hierarchy as described here, there is also an objection to a complete focus on the customer. Indeed, it would be inconsistent if the hierarchical model focused exclusively on the demand side at the highest level and the supply side was added at lower levels. So, also for logical reasons, marketing as a culture must also explicitly name the supply side. This is best done by including the brand identity in the core concept of marketing.

Attention to 'the brand' and 'branding' has been widely available in marketing literature, especially since the 1990s (Aaker, 1991, 1995; Keller, 1993; Keller & Swaminathan, 2019). But including the supply side through the brand in the *core concept of* marketing is unusual. In our opinion, organizations that subscribe to a marketing orientation ('culture') should focus on two things: customer needs and brand identity. An organization strives to deliver *customer value* and to build a strong brand. Alsem and Kostelijk (2008) introduced this and referred to it as identity marketing, but it is in fact 'ordinary' marketing (see Figure 1.8).

In practice, things often go wrong on two sides of Figure 1.8:

■ There is too little attention for the customer: does it really make him or her happy? Fournier et al. (1998) refer in this context to the 'end of relationship marketing'.

■ Too little attention is paid to brand identity: do we make choices that fit well with our identity, and are we consistent?

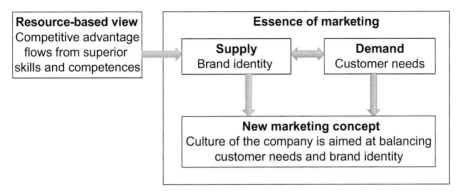

*Figure 1.8* New marketing paradigm according to Alsem, Kostelijk (2008)

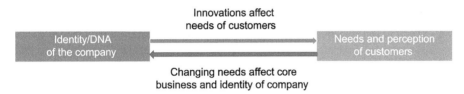

*Figure 1.9* Identity and needs

## The identity of a brand versus the wishes of customers

The identity of a brand and the wishes of customers have been described as separate constructs, but it is important to note that they can reinforce and influence each other.

The mutual reinforcement lies in the fact that if a brand is recognizable to customers, a form of *trust* can more easily arise. Also, according to Morgan and Hunt (1994), trust is an essential factor in relationship marketing. Relationships and brand identity therefore belong together.

There is also a dynamic relationship between customer wishes and brand identity (see Figure 1.9). This dynamic goes both ways. First, consumers learn from new products from companies. Apparently consumers sometimes don't even need certain products at all, but as soon as they are there, everyone wants them anyway! Earlier we mentioned the example of the mobile phone. It may have been Steve Jobs's strength that he 'sensed' what potential needs people had without them being aware of it. In short: there is an influence of a 'brand identity' (translated as products) on the wishes of consumers.

At the same time, there is an influence that runs in the opposite direction. New needs may arise that companies can respond to. It is said that people are increasingly in need of convenience. So organizations can try to make people's lives easier. A company like Kodak was too slow to respond to the growing need for digital photography (invented by them, after all). Philips, on the other hand, has regularly adapted and has even divested the activity with which this company once started (lightning).

## Studies: Sharp and the importance of brand awareness

The importance of the brand is also empirically supported. In some publications worth reading, Byron Sharp of the London Business School summarizes various studies he has done on brand choices based on many databases with actual purchase data (Sharp, 2010; Romaniuk & Sharp, 2015). The most important conclusion from all these studies is the great importance of brand awareness. Sharp shows that consumers have a strong preference for well-known brands. Moreover, it appears that information about, for example, quality plays much less of a role. For example, Sharp shows that brands that are similar in the perception of consumers compete with each other much less directly than you would expect on the basis of those perceptions. The size of a brand plays a dominant role in the preferred position a brand has in the minds of consumers. Not only is the mental availability of a brand (communication) important, so is its physical availability (distribution).

One explanation for the findings of Sharp et al. lies in the low level of involvement that consumers generally have when purchasing products. We already mentioned this in Section 1.1: people usually do not get very involved in brands. Seen in this way, it is logical that consumers are mainly guided in their choice of a brand by the simple fact that they know a brand: in other words, brand awareness, probably with the thought: I know that brand, in any case, and if it is so well known, it is probably good. A good example of such a brand is Heineken. As a beer brand, Heineken will probably have a high brand awareness worldwide, almost 100% in many countries. However, the question is how this brand is doing with 'unique associations'. The point is that Heineken has had quite a variety of advertising campaigns in recent decades. Some campaigns were also quite generic, with slogans such as 'Biertje? Heineken!' So the question is how consistent and unique Heineken is in its brand communication. Nevertheless, Heineken is the global market leader in beer. One reason for this may be that it is 'simply the tastiest beer'. Certainly for the beer category, however, it has been shown that emotion is much more decisive for brand choices than the actual product characteristics. A simple blind test ('do this at home!') will be able to demonstrate this: with a brand name, completely different preferences emerge than without a brand name. The explanation is probably that Heineken has both a high recognition and yet also evokes a 'good feeling', which is the result of all visible behavior of the brand. That good feeling apparently ties in with the subconscious choices consumers make when choosing brands.

While the findings of Sharp et al. seem logical, there is an academic debate about the importance of brand image at this point. In an award-winning paper, Pauwels and Ewijk (2013) show that both 'soft' metrics that measure attitude (i.e. the strength of associations) and 'hard' data about consumer online behavior are good predictors of final sales. So brand image, which goes beyond brand awareness, does matter. Hanssens (2015) shows that the average advertising elasticity is only about 0.1, which does not indicate that strong media pressure has a major influence on sales.

Our conclusion from this dispute about the relevance of image is that both brand awareness and brand image are important.

## 1.2.4 Marketing 3.0: society and other interest groups

We have already considered the challenges of sustainability. Since roughly 2010, increasing attention has been paid to this problem in marketing. Kotler (2011) wrote an intro about this in a special issue of the *Journal of Marketing*. Interestingly enough, it is precisely this famous Kotler who much earlier (around 1971) introduced so-called 'social marketing' ('the societal marketing concept') and 'demarketing'. *Social marketing* involves the marketing of an idea (e.g. anti-smoking campaigns) or charity (e.g. nature conservation) or other socially relevant 'products'. In the context of sustainability, it is of course about the environment but also about personnel policy, although in this book, as mentioned earlier, we focus on sustainability with regard to the environment. *Demarketing* is understood to mean encouraging a *reduction* in the question of what is or can be applied (flying?) in the context of, for example, energy consumption and other environmentally harmful behavior.

Social marketing therefore automatically involves many more target groups than just consumers. Hillebrand et al. (2015) speak of stakeholder marketing in this context. Porter and Kramer (2011) introduced the concept of *shareholder value*: companies should expand their business model by providing value to society.

So you could say that the foundations for 'marketing 3.0' were laid a long time ago but have only emerged strongly since 2010 and more recently since 2022. In a special issue of the *Journal of Marketing*, Kumar (2018) and other authors rightly state that the implementation of marketing will have to change significantly. Kumar uses the term 'transformative marketing' for this. Another term is 'purpose marketing'. But just as with 'digital marketing', sustainability must also be part of 'ordinary marketing'. We will therefore not use a new term for this ourselves. Digitization and sustainability are simply part of marketing.

## 1.2.5 Conclusion and marketing as an activity

Figure 1.10 summarizes the developments in the marketing concept.

For the aforementioned developments in marketing, matters do not *replace* the foregoing but are *added*. In concrete terms, this means that in 2023 *the core of the marketing concept* can be defined as follows:

*Organizations that follow marketing as a culture in the organization are concerned with meeting (latent) functional, emotional and social needs of target groups, better than competitors, based on a strong brand identity. True customer focus and brand thinking are leading. Value must be delivered for the company, the customer, and society* (Figure 1.11).

We have presented marketing as culture (umbrella concept), strategy, and tactics. We also indicated that analyses and research form the basis for strategic decisions (CAST model). To be as concrete as possible about what marketing practically entails, it is good to indicate which *activities* fall under marketing. These are three steps (the 'AST' from the CAST model):

1   Perform analyses/research
2   Marketing strategic choices
3   Marketing tactics

| Period | Assumption about consumer behavior | Marketing concept | Emphasis on: |
|---|---|---|---|
| Until about 1990 | Functional needs | Marketing 1.0: Classic and strategic marketing | Customer needs Competitive advantages |
| 1990-2010 | Emotional consumer | Marketing 2.0: Relationship marketing and identity marketing | Relationships Experiences Brands |
| 2010-present | Sustainable consumer | Marketing 3.0: Social or transformative marketing | Social and societal challenges Other interest groups |

*Figure 1.10* **Developments in the marketing concept**

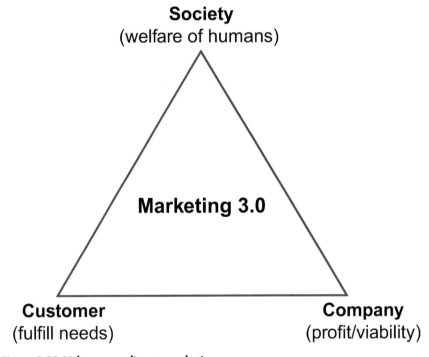

*Figure 1.11* **Values according to marketing**

We then define marketing as an *activity* as follows:

*Marketing is, based on careful analyses of the market and one's own organization, choosing a distinctive range of products/services that meet the needs of customers, partners, and society and marketing those products/services through brand-oriented choices of prices, communication, and channels and through brand-oriented management of the personnel.*

Figure 1.12 summarizes the core of marketing. The interests of society are now subsumed under those of customers, in accordance with the Brand Benefitting Model to be discussed later in this book.

The American Marketing Association (AMA), a very reputable marketing institute, defines marketing as: *Marketing is the activity, set of institutions, and processes for creating, communicating, delivering, and exchanging offerings that have value for customers, clients, partners, and society at large.*

All in all, four 'stakeholders' are important in marketing:

1    the organization itself: a suitable identity
2    customer groups: delivering customer values
3    society: no burden for future generations
4    personnel: social policy

For these target groups, the first two form the core of marketing, but the third always plays a role. With regard to personnel, the *human resources management business function* is primarily responsible for this.

## 1.3 Marketing in organizations

Given the content of marketing outlined previously, several conclusions can be drawn about the relationships with other parts of the organization and also about the application of marketing in markets.

### 1.3.1 Marketing and other functions in the organization

The decisions made show that strategic marketing planning is a very important part of strategic management. In particular, the choice of the *markets* in which it wishes to be active is a very important decision for a company, which therefore forms the core of the company's strategy. The proposals for and information about these decisions are provided by the marketing functional area.

It also appears that the aforementioned components of strategic marketing have implications for other functional areas. The field of strategic marketing is therefore not separate from other functional areas. In fact, due to the aforementioned environmental developments, not only marketing itself but also the internal coordination of marketing with other functions within the company is becoming increasingly important.

Figure 1.13 shows which relationships between marketing and other parts of the company have become more important in recent years.

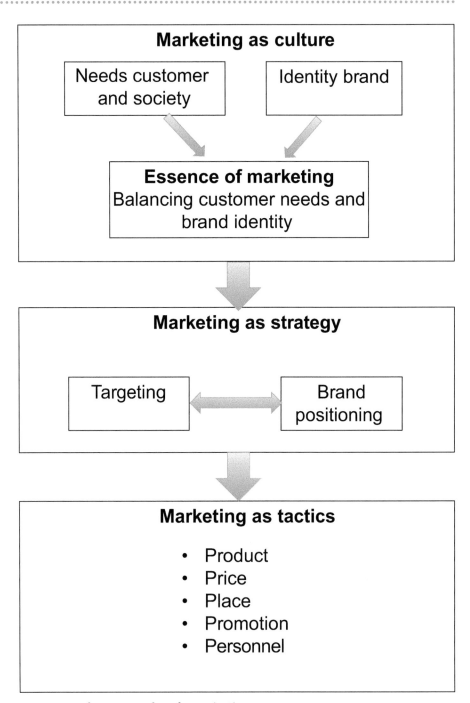

*Figure 1.12* The essence of marketing (3.0)

*Figure 1.13* **Marketing and other functions**

First of all, there is the relationship between marketing and *research and develop-ment* (R&D). This concerns the importance of innovation. Due to increasing customer demands and competition, creating, and maintaining a competitive advantage is becoming increasingly important, so innovation is important. Companies must constantly consider whether the product and service offering cannot be improved and renewed. Much research also shows a positive relationship between innovation and performance (see, for example: Damanpour et al., 1989; Zahra et al., 1988; Han et al., 1998).

A second important relationship between marketing and another functional area is that with *human resources management* (HRM, the human resources department). The point here is that the people in the organization ultimately determine the external image of the organization and that without well-motivated staff, the implementation of chosen strategies is at risk (Foster et al., 2010). This is the principle of *internal branding*, which means that companies must ensure that all employees are sufficiently aware of the company positioning and also behave as such. Gummesson (1991) introduced the term 'part-time marketers' in this context to indicate that all employees should be customer oriented.

A third marketing relationship that we would like to highlight is that of the *Finance Department*. In marketing practice and science, there is a noticeable trend of growing interest in the financial aspects of marketing: does marketing really pay for itself? This logical question is referred to as the question of the *accountability* of marketing (Verhoef & Leeflang, 2009). There are also journals that focus on this issue, such as the *Journal of Accounting and Marketing*. Van Helden and Alsem (2016) state in this journal that marketing performance should be measured with much more than financial metrics.

## 1.3.2 Forms of marketing

The increasing importance of marketing is also reflected in the fact that marketing is being applied in more and more industries where it was not used before (see also Kotler, 2004). Examples:

- *Business marketing*. Business marketing is defined as marketing from organization to organization, so not directly to the final consumer, but to another company. This form of marketing is not new at all, but it receives less attention in books than *consumer marketing*. It can also be noted that in practice, business marketing pays a lot of attention to sales (personal sales) because establishing relationships (*customer relation management* [CRM]) and bringing in customers through personal contacts is in practice an important part of business marketing. However, it is important to realize that business marketing also consists of building strong brands, because ultimately buyers ('customers') are also people who are sensitive to branding activities.

■ *Health care marketing*. The government's policy is to achieve an increase in quality and cost reduction in healthcare by introducing (regulated) competition. Due to this increasing competition in healthcare markets, the importance of customer relationships and brand positioning is becoming increasingly important (Alsem & Klein Koerkamp, 2016).

■ *Energy branding*. The use and above all the responsible use of energy increasingly require marketing and therefore also the 'branding' (positioning) of energy brands. A difficult but necessary challenge.

■ *Place marketing*. Regions (cities, municipalities, [parts of] provinces, countries) are increasingly competing for the favors of three target groups: visitors (tourists), residents, and businesses. A clear positioning then becomes increasingly important and therefore also regional marketing (also known as city marketing or destination branding) (Anholt, 2010).

■ *Cultural marketing*. This concerns a variety of services, such as museums (Tobelem, 1997), visual arts, performing arts, music, and film. Not all of these services were originally set up to be financed from the market; in fact, even with a large influx of visitors to a museum attraction (a so-called blockbuster), the income usually still does not cover the expenditure. But despite that, interest in culture is increasingly viewed critically. The aim of cultural marketing is, then, to draw more attention to the different forms of culture.

## Summary

Due to various environmental trends, thinking from target groups (customer focus) is becoming important for more and more organizations. The core of marketing theory (the marketing concept) has evolved along the notions of what customers' needs actually are: primarily functional needs (marketing 1.0) but also good experiences and relationships with brands (emotional needs, marketing 2.0) and in the last few years also an interest in sustainability (marketing 3.0). Marketing as a culture nowadays also means that companies must deliver value to customers and the society that fits their own brand identity: 'What can I do for you?', taking into account the long-term interests of customers and society.

Marketing itself is carried out in three steps. The first step consists of an analysis of the internal and external environment, in which research among customers forms the core. The second step is to determine the marketing strategy: choosing target groups and your own (brand) positioning. The third step is that form and content are given to the four market instruments (product, price, place, and communication) plus personnel from the marketing strategy.

So the difference between marketing and communication is that communication is one of the market instruments, next to product, price, and place (and personnel). Marketing also includes doing research and determining a strategy. In our view, marketing is actually 'market-oriented business'.

Recent developments, such as opportunities for digital marketing and an increasing importance of sustainability, have a major influence on an organization's marketing decisions. Partly for this reason, marketing should not be isolated: cooperation with other functional areas is of great importance. Examples are: strong alignment with strategic management, pricing and accountability with finance, internal branding with HRM, and innovation with R&D.

## Will the engine of the rock continue to rock?

*For decades, the style and the sound of the Fender Stratocaster had a strong influence on rock 'n'roll. But the American guitar company is facing an uncertain future. Because of the developments in music, electronics are increasingly replacing the guitar.*

In 1948, radio repair man Leo Fender took a piece of wood, screwed another piece of wood to it, and added an electric system. You have heard the rest of the story, even if you do not know it. You've heard it in the guitar riffs of Buddy Holly, Jimi Hendrix, George Harrison, Keith Richards, Eric Clapton, Pete Townsend, Bruce Springsteen, Mark Knopfler, Kurt Cobain, and so on. It is the sound of the electric Fender guitar.

The Fender company, in full Fender Musical Instruments, is the world's largest manufacturer of guitars. The Stratocaster, which came on the market in 1954, is still one of the most sold guitars. The cutting sound of the Strat stands for everything that is rock and roll. But in 2022 the heart of rock is no longer beating as it once did.

A Stratocaster is expensive; it is just not one of the first necessities in life for most people. But Fender suffers from more than its price alone. The company is also plagued by the powerful guys that make the money move on Wall Street. In 2012, almost half of Fender was in the hands of the venture capitalist Weston Presidio, who wanted to sell his share for a nice price. The economy was in bad shape, and he hoped to get some of his investment back. However, the IPO went no further: investors were not convinced by the possibilities that the Fender brand could offer. After the withdrawal of the public offering, Weston Presidio sold its stock to the private equity arm of Hawaiian automotive retailer Servco Pacific, which in turn sold a portion of its stake to San Francisco's TPG Growth. With all these changes in ownership, the company experienced a rough ride and tries to look for some stability now.

In the past years, Fender has made some ballsy moves. First, Fender made the move to let customers order direct from their website. In 2015, Fender launched a division called Fender Digital to focus on apps, websites, platforms, and tools. The company debuted Mod Shop, an online customization site where customers can design their own colorful guitar or bass. While the digital move is currently only limited to 'custom-configurable' guitars, it probably still left a bad taste in the mouths of many of the company's dealers. Then in 2016, the company released Fender Tune, a free app that helps players tune their guitars. It is the first in what is to be a line of teaching devices the company plans to launch over the next years, according to CEO Andy Mooney.

But even now, with the currently booming economy, uncertainty about the future is what makes life hard for Fender. Times have changed. In the fifties, sixties, and seventies, guitars were the engine behind all developments in pop and rock music. And the real rock 'n' roll enthusiast still wants this. Take Rick Barrio Dill. He is bassist of the soul and rock band Vintage Trouble and went crazy when his specially made Fender Reissue Precision bass guitar was stolen when he was on tour with the Cranberries. 'I felt like someone had just died; I was a complete wreck', says Dill. He reported the theft via Twitter. Before he knew it he got a message from Gibson Guitars, the big rival of Fender. The company offered him a new guitar. Dill rejected the offer. But a similar bid that Fender made him shortly after, he grabbed it with both hands. 'Fender is flowing through my veins', says Dill. The guitarist also collects vintage Fenders. In 1999 he bought a Tobacco sunburst Fender Jazz Bass from 1969 for 900 euros. Four years later he sold the instrument for 2,000 euros. 'Now I try to find one again and I have to pay at least 5,000 euros for it'.

However, these enthusiasts are fewer and fewer. For most musicians, even the average enthusiast, the guitars of that time have been replaced by electric turntables, drum computers, and synthesizers. Hip hoppers and rappers do not need a guitar to hit the charts.

The guitars that are still sold are the lower-priced ones. The instruments are made in China and cost a fraction of the more than €1,200 that you quickly spend on a Fender 'Eric Clapton' Stratocaster. But with such a cheaper guitar, you can also 'make a nice piece of music'. Fender has already outsourced part of its production to low-wage countries and, like many other guitar builders, is building simple guitars. But the profit margins on those instruments are much lower than on the showpieces of the past.

The American Guitar Center, the largest musical instrument store in the world, is also experiencing difficult times, with the market turning more and more towards online shops. According to analysts, Guitar Center is crucial for Fender. No less than a sixth of the guitars that Fender sells are purchased at that instrument store.

One of the big problems that Fender has to deal with, ironically enough, is Fender itself. When Fender first released its classic Stratocaster and Telecaster guitars in the 1950s, it became one of the first electric guitar manufacturers in the United States. Since then, the company has developed a reputation for high quality among professional musicians. The guitars that were produced in the sixties and seventies are much more beloved than the instruments that the company produces nowadays. Whether it is true or not, musicians have the idea that the classic Fenders have a different, more beautiful sound and are qualitatively better than the guitars that are produced nowadays. Modern techniques might make the sound of new instruments more perfect than ever, but it is the imperfections that create the classic sounds so much loved by real musicians.

How to proceed with Fender is the big question. According to one of the shareholders of the company: 'I love Fender. It is the most beautiful company in the world. We are in it for the long term and we will do what is right for Fender'. But whether the right thing is the old-fashioned guitar, the internet, or even guitar education is a question that remains unanswered.

## Questions

1  Which trends affect the Fender brand?
2  The book discusses a hierarchy in marketing: the CAST model. Illustrate this marketing hierarchy for Fender.
3  Discuss whether the strategic marketing concept can be used by Fender.
4  Illustrate the resource-based view by using the information about Fender in this case.
5  Identity marketing tries to find a balance between customer needs on the one hand and brand identity on the other. Show how this 'tension' between supply and demand is relevant for Fender.
6  Digital marketing is becoming increasingly relevant for any kind of business. Illustrate this for Fender.
7  At first sight, corporate social responsibility may not seem to be of immediate concern to a brand like Fender. How could Fender profile itself with marketing 3.0 and thus appeal to the responsible consumer?
8  Give strategic marketing advice for Fender based on the information in this case.

# Chapter 2

# The strategic marketing planning process

## Key points in this chapter

- To know different levels in a company and the content of strategy at these levels
- To know the essence of marketing strategy
- To know the different steps in the marketing planning process

## Introduction

The previous chapter explained what marketing entails. It starts with the realization that a company must act in a customer- and brand-oriented way (culture). This requires a clear choice in target group and positioning (strategy). The strategy is then translated into an application of the four Ps (tactics). Crucial in this process is a sound choice of marketing strategy. The basis for this is laid in the internal and external analysis.

In this chapter we show how to go through the entire strategic marketing planning process. But first we will discuss the different levels that exist in (large) companies (Section 2.1). We then focus on the concept of sustainable competitive advantage as part of the marketing strategy (Section 2.2). Then the phases of the planning process are discussed (Section 2.3). We conclude the chapter in Section 2.4 with a description of the various components of the marketing plan.

## 2.1 Levels and types of decisions in a company

Several 'levels' can be distinguished within a (large) company, and different types of decisions are taken at each level. There are companies that limit their activities to one

DOI: 10.4324/9781003381488-3

market, for example, a car manufacturer that only makes small cars for a target group. Many smaller and/or start-up companies also focus on one market. However, many companies are active in more than one market. For example, Procter & Gamble is active in baby care (e.g. Pampers), fabric care (e.g. Ariel, Dreft), grooming (e.g. Braun, Gillette), hair care (e.g. Pantene, Head & Shoulders), oral care (e.g. Oral-B), and skin care (e.g. Olay, Old Spice).

But even a small business like a local restaurant can distinguish different markets, such as room rental, catering, and dinners on site.

To achieve clarity in the marketing planning process about what should be analyzed and what should be decided upon, it is important to understand the levels within a company. Three levels may be distinguished (see Figure 2.1):

1  the corporate level (Section 2.1.1)
2  the division and Strategic Business Unit (SBU) level (Section 2.1.2)
3  the product and market instrument level (Section 2.1.3)

## 2.1.1 The company level

The company level is the top level, also known as the 'corporate level'. This concerns the company as a whole. All the different products that a company releases on the different markets are collectively referred to as the product mix or the range.

## 2.1.2 The division and SBU level

A division is a more or less autonomously operating unit within a company. A division can contain different product groups. A product group (also called product line, product category, or simply *category*) comprises a group of related products. Examples of product groups are: snacks, internal transport, consultancy, foot care products, and men's clothing. In practice, a product group is often used as a market definition, for example, the health insurance market. Although the product group is only one of the three dimensions of a market definition (the other two are customer groups and customer functions; see Section 3.1.2), this means that product groups often correspond to markets. We will therefore regularly make this connection in this book.

A strategic business unit (also known as strategic product group) is concentrated around a product group (and therefore usually also a market). Many companies operate with SBUs, which in turn are sometimes grouped into divisions (see Case 2.1).

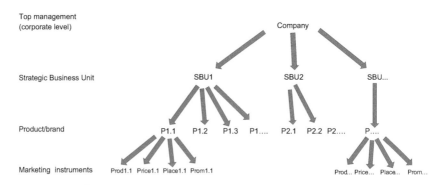

*Figure 2.1* **Levels in a company**

## Case 2.1 Many companies have several brands in different SBUs

### L'Oréal has four groups of brands

The L'Oréal product mix includes consumer products (including through the L'Oréal Paris and Garnier brands), professional products (for example, for hairdressers), luxury products (including Lancôme and Cacharel), 'active cosmetics', and finally the Body Shop brand.

Although there is often a difference between the division and the SBU level, we will not make a distinction between the two levels in the rest of this book. The reason for this is that a division level can be considered a corporate level, but one step lower.

In practice, divisions are often also smaller companies within a large company. Therefore, what is said about corporate objectives and strategies can also apply to divisional objectives and strategies. For example, the corporate strategy determines which financial resources are available for SBUs. When there is a divisional level between the corporate and SBU levels, the divisional strategy defines the allocation of resources across SBUs.

Incidentally, in a company that is active in one market, the company level and the SBU level coincide, and the range is limited to one product group.

### 2.1.3 The product level and marketing mix level

A product is something (good or service) that is concretely offered on a market. A product can be intended for different target groups. A combination of a product and a target group is usually called a product-market combination (PMC). Different *varieties of* a product are sometimes marketed; for example, there may be differences in sizes or packets and flavors. A company often brings individual products to a market, supported by the use of market instruments. Typically four categories of market instruments are distinguished: product (composition, packaging), price, distribution (channels), and communication (such as advertising and promotions). Because market instruments are filled in for products, the market instrument level corresponds to the product level.

## 2.1.4 The position of the brand

A company uses a brand to distinguish its products from competing products. A brand consists of a word, name, symbol, letter, or sign (or combination of these). A brand is the bearer of a reputation or image. Reasoned from the point of view of the supplier, a brand is, as it were, the identity made visible that the product must radiate.

At what levels do brands play a role? The most obvious is the product level. A product is almost always offered under a brand name. Examples of products are Pampers diapers, ABN AMRO student account, LG Television. The designation brand is traditionally associated with products. In fast-moving consumer goods markets, brand names are also most visible at product level: each product has its own brand name. Yet this is a limited view of the importance of brands. Brand names play a role not only at the product level but at all three levels in a company. Although companies like Unilever and Procter & Gamble make little or no use of the name of the company for consumers, Unilever is nevertheless a brand, for example, in the labor and financial markets. We also find brands at the intermediate division level: producers Van den Bergh Nederland and Iglo-Ola are also brands. In markets of services and consumer durables, the brand name at the product level sometimes corresponds to that at company level (e.g. Philips, BMW). We will take a closer look at brands and brand levels in Chapter 11.

## 2.1.5 Strategic, tactical, and operational decisions

In the literature, a distinction is often made between strategic, tactical, and operational decisions. This concerns the long, medium, and short term, respectively. However, the distinction in that 'term' is not always clear. What is medium? In this book we define the difference between those three based on the *content* of the decisions. *Strategic decisions* are decisions at the corporate and SBU level and, in terms of marketing, relate to target group choices and positioning. *Tactical (marketing) decisions* relate to the resources and concern the four market instruments. In our opinion, *operational decisions* relate to the implementation of the plans: who does what, and when? In this book we will not go into this operational level. In practice, strategic decisions will last for several years and tactical decisions for about a year. But this is not absolute, because communication decisions (tactics/tools) can also be recorded for several years.

## 2.2 Core of the marketing strategy

It is important to distinguish between:

- the corporate strategy (Section 2.2.1)
- the marketing strategy (Section 2.2.2)

## 2.2.1 Corporate strategy: growth direction and value strategy

At each of the levels described in the previous section, decisions are made and strategies are outlined. The content of those decisions differs per level. For example, a chairperson of a board of directors (*corporate level*) will not be concerned with advertising decisions (*product level*). Conversely, a margarine brand product manager (*product* level) will not be concerned with the decision to invest more in diaper sales; the latter is a matter for top management (*corporate level*).

A clear connection can be made with strategic marketing decisions and the levels from Section 2.1 This connection is summarized in Figure 2.2. *Three types of decisions* need to be made at each of these levels:

1   **Where** will we compete: in which markets and with which target groups?
2   **How** will we compete: with what distinction do we profile ourselves in the chosen markets?
3   **Who** are we going to compete with: with whom do we want to work?

These kinds of decisions are interrelated. For example, the choice of a market (where?) is especially useful if you can gain a competitive advantage there (how?). And the choice for a partner (with whom) is partly determined by what you are good at and also less good at (how?).

The elaboration on the three questions depends on the level. At the corporate level, the question 'Where will the company compete?' is that the management of a company or division is (among other things) concerned with determining the desired positions (for example, desired growth) of product groups and brands. This will have to be done in such a way that the desired business objectives (such as a certain growth in turnover) can be achieved with all products together. Growth can be achieved:

■   with existing products and brands, but also with new ones
■   with existing customers and target groups, but also with new ones

The *times* at which the goals must be achieved are also a matter for top management. From the desired goals to be achieved with the various brands, top managers will also have to determine the available resources. Ambitious plans require a lot of money.

| Level | Where to compete? | How to compete? (competitive advantage choice) | With whom? |
|---|---|---|---|
| Corporate strategy | Determining the composition and desired positions of product groups and brands (growth directions) | Choice of corporate identity | Choice partners |
| Marketing strategy | Target group determination | Brand positioning | |
| Market instrument strategies | – | Elaboration of positioning | |

*Figure 2.2* **Types of strategies and levels**

In practice, making choices about goals and investments is not a one-sided top-down matter. Objectives and budgets at lower levels are *negotiated* between top and lower management. Product managers or *brand managers* will have to try to sell their ambitious plans to the management. A convincing plan gets more money.

At the corporate level, the question 'How are we going to compete?' relates to the choice of the so-called *value* strategy. Does the company want to position itself towards customers through leadership in quality and innovations, through efficiency and low prices, or through relationship building? The corporate strategy also specifies whether the company wants to grow on its own or with the help of others ('With whom?': cooperation, acquisition, merger).

## 2.2.2 Marketing strategy: target group and positioning

At the level of the marketing strategy, a distinction can also be made between *where* and *how*. The *where* question involves a more detailed description of the target group. The *how* question of the marketing strategy involves the distinguishing power or competitive advantage. What reason should a customer buy your brand and not another brand? That competitive advantage should be sustainable as well.

The concept of a *sustainable competitive advantage* has become central to the literature on competitive analysis and strategies since the early 1980s (Porter, 1980, 1985). Simply put, a sustainable competitive advantage means that a brand:

■ is good at something (strong point),
■ in which its competitors are not good (and also difficult to become good at: sustainable),
■ and is important to the customers.

Three 'parties' (the three Cs) thus play the most important role in the choice of competitive advantage:

1 the *company*: the company or the brand itself
2 the *customers*: the buyers
3 the *competitors*: the competitors

Analysis of these three Cs is therefore essential.

Companies that have a competitive advantage will be able to achieve the best financial results in the industry. Therefore, every company should strive to gain a sustainable competitive advantage from its products.

The definition of the term 'sustainable competitive advantage' shows that there is an important difference between a strength of a company and a sustainable competitive advantage. Not every strength leads to a sustainable competitive advantage. This is only the case if the following two conditions are met (see also Figure 2.3):

1 The competitors do not have that strong point: it is therefore a *relatively* strength.
2 The strong point is relevant: it matters to customers.

So a company can be good at something, but if it is not relevant to the customers that the company is so good at it or if the competitors also have that strong point, it will not yield anything. An example of the latter is airline safety. Because (almost) every

*Figure 2.3* **The sustainable competitive advantage**

company is safe (this is also an absolute necessity), safety is not a sustainable competitive advantage. If a company has a particular strength, it is imperative to check whether its competitors have the same strength (this is determined in the competitor analysis; see Chapter 7). After that, the strength must be converted into an advantage for the buyers, for example, in the form of better quality or a lower price. This advantage must also be communicated to the customers (for example, by means of advertising).

The next question is whether the competitive advantage is also sustainable in the sense of defensible (see Case 2.1). For example, a company with a technological advantage that is easy to imitate will probably soon lose that advantage. If the competition is able to use an even better technology, the initial advantage can even turn into a disadvantage (leapfrog or *leapfrogging*). In practice, the defensibility of competitive advantages is the biggest problem. Virtually every advantage can be and is quickly followed. Research also shows that followers sometimes manage to achieve higher market shares than innovators (Kerin et al., 1992; Bowman & Gatignon, 1996). Pioneers will therefore have to adopt a flexible attitude and also try to learn from the experiences of the followers (Christen, 2000). In order to understand the defensibility of the competitive advantage, the company can try to predict what the competition will do. This is one of the objectives of the competitor analysis.

## 2.3 Content of the strategic marketing planning process

We start this section with the importance of an environmental analysis.

### 2.3.1 Importance of an environmental analysis

A manager who has a problem can arrive at a solution in two ways: quickly and with little substantiation or somewhat less quickly and well substantiated (see Figure 2.5). Sometimes the first way is very successful.

## Case 2.2 Sustainable competitive advantage

## Volvo is safety

Although all cars are basically quite safe, there are differences. Ever since its founding in 1927, Volvo has been committed to making the safest car ever. In 1959, Volvo invented the three-point seat belt, and today every car has it. But also the layered windscreen, crumple zones, and certain forms of side protection, all things that are now also in other cars.

Defensibility is difficult, but through continuous innovation, Volvo remains the safest.

The idea of a sustainable competitive advantage is closely linked to the concept of positioning. Positioning means determining the place of a brand in the minds of customers in relation to the products of competitors. What image or what associations does a company want to give to the brand? Ries and Trout (1981) have called this: 'positioning, the battle for your mind'. Positioning is about choosing those brand associations that will:

- be relevant to the customers
- be unique to the brand

Moreover, if a brand succeeds in communicating the desired associations in such a way that those brand associations are strongly anchored in the target group, then three important requirements for a successful brand are met: *strong, relevant*, and *unique*. Keller (2019) also mentions high brand awareness as a requirement (Figure 2.4).

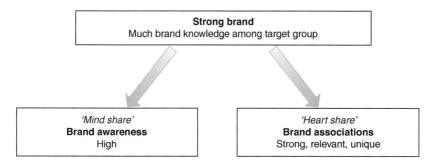

*Figure 2.4* **Strong brand equity according to Keller and Swaminathan (2019)**

In Figure 2.4 we make a distinction between *mind share* and *heart share*. We do this because brands have both a functional/informative side and a more emotional one. The brand personality and the values that the brand represents play a role in the latter. A brand must therefore appeal to someone's head and heart. Brand awareness is mainly focused on mind share because it is about whether someone has heard of the brand. People's associations with brands can potentially lead to a more emotional relationship with the brand. Good positioning therefore requires an in-depth knowledge of the psychology of the customer.

Another important requirement for positioning is focusing: daring to opt for targeted positioning. A wide choice is not a choice, is often said. The search process often boils down to searching for a word on which a brand can distinguish itself.

The choice of that word is difficult, essential, and subtle. *Difficult*, because with general characteristics such as quality, young, dynamic, and reliable, a brand is usually not distinctive, while many brands want to be just that. It is also difficult because companies often do not dare to choose. With a central message, 'so many other good things are not being said'. *Essential*, because in fact it talks about the central choice of the brand identity. Everything must be controlled from that identity. *Subtle*, because it requires a lot of creativity and empathy with the customer and other parties in the environment to come up with the 'right' word. Brands that have made a clear choice in 2023 (and before) are, for example, IKEA (affordable home furnishings), Red Bull ('gives you wings'), Volvo (safety), and Pampers (best for the baby).

The concept of positioning is sometimes associated exclusively with communication. It would then mainly be about the slogan or simply about 'what fun stories we are going to tell in the campaign this year'. Brand positioning, however, goes much further: it controls all activities related to the brand, that is, production, personnel, purchasing, all market instruments, and so on. After all, the positioning is the promise to the customer, and that promise must be kept. This is only possible if everything is aimed at getting it done. It starts with the people who answer the phone, and it 'ends' with how satisfied a customer is with the product. Brand positioning therefore not only has an external function (promise to the customer) but also an internal one: towards the employees. Communicating the brand positioning to internal target groups is called *internal branding* (see also Chapter 14).

Incidentally, in our view, the concept of positioning is not essentially different from concepts such as (desired) reputation, identity, vision, or competitive advantage. Because brands exist at different levels in an company, positioning also exists at multiple levels: at the corporate and product level. At company level, this concerns the reputation of the company, also known as *corporate identity* or simply reputation. At Philips, the brand name is the same as most of its product names, so the corporate identity is consistent with that of all of its products.

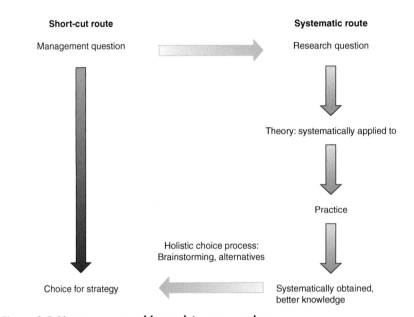

*Figure 2.5* **Management problem-solving approaches**

A manager does not have to be an analyst to achieve success. In this book, however, we take a different approach. We believe that with better substantiation, the chance of success is greater. The 'better' lies in using a good *system* and the right tools based on a (marketing) theory and more and better knowledge because all parties in the company's environment are analyzed. The explicit formulation of alternatives is also part of the better (more scientific) approach to practical management problems.

A 'more scientific' approach to a marketing problem does not mean that the result becomes less practical. The final choice of a solution requires a more holistic approach: *creativity*, *innovation*, and *market awareness*. Good homework forms the 'input' for this. How a company should do its homework and then translate it into goals and strategies is the content of the strategic marketing planning process.

In Section 2.3.2, we first provide an overview and global structure of the process. We then discuss the phases of the process in Section 2.3.3. Finally, we conclude with some remarks about the course of the process (Section 2.3.4).

## Case 2.3 Evidence-based marketing

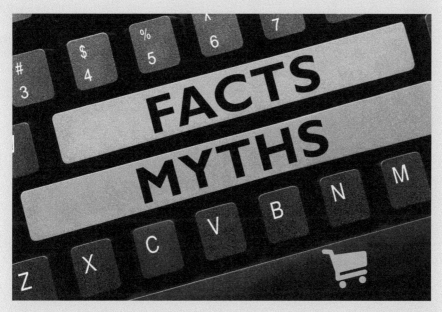

Medicine is all about being 'evidence based'. Doctors will base their decisions on evidence-based knowledge and on a thorough analysis of the patient. And that is normal. Now try this exercise: replace the word 'medicine' with the word 'marketing' and 'doctors' with 'marketers', and you have an uncanny reflection of what is happening in our industry today. The sad fact is that even we marketers, the supposed experts in positioning, branding, and communication, have become suckers for the sales patter of Google, Facebook, and various industry 'gurus'. Instead of spotting hucksterism for what it is, our bias towards the new and the novel stymies us. In fact, we love new and exciting things, even when they are vastly inferior to old ideas. Snapchat strategies versus television campaigns, anyone? I am not alone. Only in the past few weeks, I met representatives of an international airline who believed that their core customer base was millennials, whereas the analysis showed that few people under the age of 40 flew with them. So, what to do? Let's start with some simple basics: don't fall into the traps that various vendors and slick agencies tell us. Stop the nonsense such as 'Facebook marketing', 'inbound marketing', 'content marketing' – these are fake names invented to brand something that has been around for years. Remember: it is essential to adopt the practices and mindset of evidence-based marketing. Why? So then we can see the forest, the trees, and everything in between. Let's make it even easier and have this as our mantra: tools change, tactics occasionally change, strategies can change, but marketing principles never change.

Source: Colin Lewis, *Marketing Week*, 9 May 2018

## 2.3.2 Overview of the process

In the (marketing) literature, various authors (see, for example, Leeflang, 2003; Ferrell & Hartline, 2010; Aaker, 2013) outline the various steps that a company can take to arrive at a strategy. The way in which this process is worked out is not the same for all authors. In Figure 2.5, we show the steps that we believe a company could take in the planning process. In this subsection, we will explain the figure globally. We will go into more detail in Section 2.3.3.

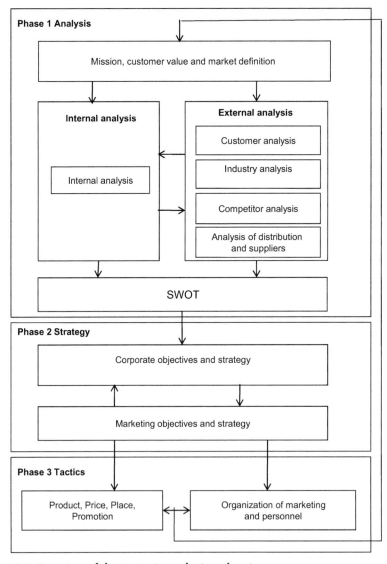

*Figure 2.6* **Overview of the strategic marketing planning process**

The overall design of the process is that a combination of a internal analysis (analysis of the company and the brand itself) and a external analysis (analysis of the environment) forms the basis for the formulation of marketing objectives and strategies and then of the marketing tactics (implementation). The combination of strengths, weaknesses, opportunities, and threats forms the input for the phase in which a strategy is chosen. The goal of the external analysis is to gain insight into the opportunities and threats (*opportunities* and *threats*) that are to be expected.

### Situation analysis (Part 2)

Part 2 follows the internal analysis (at all levels) and the various phases of the external analysis (mainly SBU and product level). These two parts together form the situation analysis. The order of the phases within the situation analysis can differ per author. We start with the internal analysis, because that includes the evaluation of the results (*control*). We consider the strengths and weaknesses of the *company* and the brand more or less as preconditions within which the strategy must be developed. After all, financial characteristics, management culture, corporate mission, and so on cannot be changed quickly. Within the external analysis, something similar applies to the competitor and industry analysis: these can also be regarded as preconditions. This does not apply to the most important target group: the customer.

Marketing is ideally suited to 'teach something' to target groups. In principle, the customer can be easily influenced. Because in theory and practice a lot of attention is paid to achieving value for the customer, the external analysis therefore starts with the customers. In our view, insight should be obtained on a continuous basis into the wishes, satisfaction, and perceptions of customers and non-customers. This customer analysis forms the source of a variety of information in other analysis phases. Then the other parts of the external analysis take place: first an overview of the entire industry and then specific analyses of the competitors, distributors (or other intermediaries), and suppliers. Finally, a separate SWOT analysis follows, in which results from the internal and external analysis are linked. The first blocks are the analytical part of the planning process.

### Corporate and marketing strategies (Part 3)

After the analytical part, business objectives and corporate strategy are chosen; these mainly answer the question of where and when to compete. Because the analyses are often performed for SBUs (markets), and a company often operates in several markets, different situational analyses will form the basis of the company strategy. If the company strategy opts for a new market, a new analysis must be carried out.

Subsequently, the marketing objectives and marketing strategies are chosen. This concerns sales goals and target group and brand decisions. These decisions mainly determine 'how the company will compete'.

### Implementation (Part 4)

The market instruments are determined on the basis of the marketing strategy. This is the marketing tactics. The marketing tactics can be regarded as part of the marketing implementation. After the decisions have been recorded in a marketing plan, implementation takes place. In addition to the organization of marketing and communication, attention to employees is also of great importance. Proper execution is impossible without good internal management.

## 2.3.3 Description of the phases

We now describe the stages of the marketing planning process.

### Mission, customer value, and market definition (Chapter 3)

A situational analysis of a brand and a market cannot be carried out until the situation we are talking about is known: how is the market defined? Without *market definition*, for example, no market share can be calculated. Is Coca-Cola active in the soft drinks or 'colas' market? This makes quite a difference to the size of the market share and also to the number of competitors. To find out, the *mission* of the company must first be studied. Within this, statements are normally made about the markets. This is a precondition for the development of the marketing strategy.

From the point of view of positioning (the core of the marketing strategy), it is also important to know which *customer value* focuses on the company: the main line along which the company competes with other companies (see also Chapter 3). The brand positioning should not conflict with this. Finally, the current product-market combinations are mapped out and the market is specifically defined in terms of customer needs. This concerns the determination of the current market: the market in which one is currently active (*what business are we in?*).

### Internal analysis (Chapter 4)

The internal analysis starts with the question: what have been the results so far? This forms the *control*: an evaluation of the results achieved. For other authors, such as Kotler and Keller (2016), control is the very last phase of the planning process (*analysis, planning, implementation, control*). At the same time, control always forms the starting point of a new planning phase: it is a cyclical process. We choose to start with a 'look back'.

The *desired results* or *objectives* must be analyzed. We start Chapter 4 with a brief explanation of objectives. The results of the strategy (and goals) can be measured in profit, sales, market share, and so on; the choice of measurement unit depends on how the objectives are formulated. In addition to financial criteria, customer-oriented standards are also used, such as customer satisfaction (the *balanced scorecard* [BSC]) and sustainability goals. This step gives a first impression of where any problems lie. The analysis is carried out as disaggregated as possible, so not only at the product and instrument level but also within these – if possible – by regions, customer groups (segments), varieties, and retailers.

Finally, the internal factors that are important in finding a (new) strategy are examined. To this end, the strengths and weaknesses of the company, the SBU, the product, and the market instruments are determined. This is done through the eyes of the target group as much as possible. The strengths and weaknesses are compared (at a later stage) with those of the competitors. If the strengths can be translated into added value of products for customers, they provide starting points for sustainable competitive advantages. The weaknesses – if they threaten to create strategic problems – must be improved. The latter can take place through in-house development or through collaboration with competitors.

The internal analysis is also called the micro-analysis. The external analysis then consists of a meso analysis (regarding the industry, the market, the competitors, and the customers) and a macro analysis (trends outside the industry). In this book, we do not use this classification, and we also combine a part of the meso analysis (industry) with the macro analysis.

Chapters 5 through 8 deal with the *external analysis*.

## Customer analysis (Chapter 5)

The central premise of this book is that a company's policy should be aimed at creating optimal value for the customer, matching the brand identity. Continuous contact with the target group is therefore essential. A manager responsible for a brand must have an ongoing knowledge of the 'psychology of the customer'. A good customer analysis (including potential customers) provides for this.

More specific objectives of the customer analysis are: gaining insight into their characteristics (who are the customers, can segments be distinguished, which customers are the most profitable?), their needs (the importance of concrete and abstract product characteristics), their perceptions (how do they view their own product and competitors?) and their behavior (information search behavior, buying behavior).

The customer analysis is performed for an entire market (SBU level) and for individual segments and products (product level). The customer analysis also forms a source of data for other phases in the situation analysis and is therefore the core of the situation analysis. For example, there are direct lines to the competitor analysis (competitor identification, success factors, and competitive strengths and weaknesses), the distribution analysis (brand position with retailers), the industry analysis (expected market growth), and the internal analysis (brand strengths and weaknesses).

## Industry analysis (Chapter 6)

After the customer analysis, the process moves from macro to micro. First there is an analysis of the entire industry, and then a closer look is taken at some of the interest groups within it: competitors, distributors, and suppliers. A first goal of the industry analysis is to find possible opportunities and threats, especially from the macro environment. A second goal is to gain a summary insight into the attractiveness of the market. To this end, the industry structure is analyzed, among other things.

The market attractiveness mainly influences the objectives/investments that are determined per SBU. The industry analysis analyzes the following three categories of factors:

1   macro-environmental factors, such as socio-cultural and political developments
2   aggregated market factors, for example, market size and market growth
3   industry structure factors, such as the intensity of competition and the power of retailers

Because it is particularly important to gain insight into the *future* attractiveness of the market, the company should try to make predictions. Given the great uncertainty that exists in a company's environment, it is advisable to define scenarios, for example, scenarios about macro-environmental factors such as the business cycle. The industry analysis primarily takes place at the SBU level, that is, for the entire market. In addition, a company can also investigate the attractiveness of market segments.

### Competitor analysis (Chapter 7)

The aim of the competitor analysis is to gain insight into the future behavior and the strengths and weaknesses of the company's main competitors. The future behavior of competitors provides insight into potential opportunities and threats. A company that is aware of the strengths and weaknesses of its competitors is able to assess its own relative formulate strengths and weaknesses (see Figure 2.3). A competitor analysis also provides insight that can be used to find potential *collaboration partners*.

A competitor analysis can be performed at all levels. At the product level, the most important competitors are the providers that target the same target group as their own company. The competitor analysis is fed on a number of points from the customer analysis (identification of competitors, strengths, and weaknesses of competitors).

### Distribution and supplier analysis (Chapter 8)

After analyzing the customers and the competitors, the other parties (interest groups) in the industry are subjected to a critical analysis.

As we explained in the strategic marketing concept (see Section 1.2.2), *distributors* are an increasingly important interest group for manufacturers due to their increasing power.

A distribution analysis takes place on three levels. At the macro level, it concerns the distribution structure in which online channels are evidently growing. At the meso level, it concerns the distribution of power within a group of distributors (such as retailers). And at the micro level, the behavior of individual distributors is analyzed, such as that of Delhaize. From the customer analysis, information about purchasing behavior at and satisfaction with retailers can be included in this phase.

A final interest group that deserves further analysis is the *suppliers*. A good relationship with suppliers means that purchasing can take place in a more efficient, effective, and sustainable manner. Certainly the latter (sustainability) is becoming increasingly important.

### SWOT analysis (Chapter 9)

The SWOT analysis forms the connecting link between the various analyses and the strategy phases. First, it is important to weigh up the possibilities for the value strategies. Based on a selection of strengths, weaknesses, opportunities, and threats, ideas for the marketing strategy are then brainstormed. 'Facts' are thus creatively translated into 'ideas'. In the SWOT analysis, some alternative directions are finally indicated (options). Finally, by confronting the options with a number of selection criteria and preconditions, the product manager will come to a decision about the desired strategy. It is important to reiterate that this is where the creative process begins. A strategy can never be 'calculated' or 'derived' from points in the SWOT. In this book, therefore, no scoring and weighting system is linked to the SWOT. The SWOT is the inspiration and basis for strategic choices.

### Corporate objectives and strategies (Chapter 10)

A first step in this respect is a reassessment of the company mission: should the company's business be changed? The objectives of the company are also laid down. Subsequently, a portfolio analysis can be performed. In a portfolio analysis, the expected incoming and outgoing cash flows of different SBUs or brands are compared with each other. Such an analysis can also be done during the internal analysis. Based on this, it can be decided in which SBUs or brands the company wishes to invest more and in which less. Partly on this basis, the company strategy is formulated. The corporate strategy involves a choice of positions of and investments in SBUs and brands.

Finally, the company must choose the competitive growth strategy (either through self-development or through collaboration).

All components of corporate strategy commit resources and people for an extended period of time and are therefore unlikely to be significantly changed from year to year. Usually there will be adjustment. We also emphasize the interaction with the marketing plans: the business decisions will largely be fed by the SBUs. That is why feedback is indicated from the next planning step in the planning process (see Figure 2.6).

### Marketing objectives and marketing strategies (Chapter 11)

After the formulation of the business decisions, the marketing objectives and marketing strategies are chosen. *Marketing* objectives are formulated per product, for example, growth of the market share of product Y to 34% in one year. The marketing strategy is the choice of the target group (including segmentation) and the desired positioning of the brand. We also include decisions about the brand elements brand name, design, and logo. The marketing strategy is the link between the business strategy and the market instrument decisions and is therefore of crucial importance. Without an explicit implementation of the marketing strategy, the various market instruments are out of control. The specific choice of brand identity is a multi-year matter that must be propagated for a long time consistently.

### Market instrument decisions (Chapters 12 and 13)

The marketing strategy is then translated into marketing tactics: decisions regarding the market instruments (the four Ps) product, price, place (distribution), and promotion (marketing communication). Incidentally, for the product market instrument, an important part of the strategic decisions has already been determined by the implementation of the business and marketing strategy (such as brand decisions). Because of the important role of marketing communication, including various digital possibilities, we discuss this market instrument in a separate chapter (Chapter 13).

### Organization of marketing and personnel (Chapter 14)

Finally, the plans must be converted into actions: implementation. In many companies, the implementation often goes wrong. An organization geared to the customer is important: bring the customer in-house through customer managers. All communication must be aligned with the identity and preferably directed by a 'reputation manager'. The principle of the 'part-time marketer' is also relevant: especially in service organizations, but also in retail, customer orientation and behavior according to the core values are everyone's business, and the importance of good staff is therefore evident.

We conclude Chapter 14 with some planning tips.

## 2.3.4 Properties of the planning process

At the end of this section, we would like to review the planning process described from two dimensions:

■ the importance of analysis and creativity
■ the breadth of the process

### Analysis and creativity

Analytical thinking is usually convergent thinking: the homework should lead to a solution. Creativity requires divergent thinking: coming up with ideas outside the existing frames of mind. Looking at the planning process, the first part is clearly analytical: the homework must be done accurately and using the right methods. From the SWOT onwards, the creative approach becomes increasingly important: appropriate positioning must be applied, and the chosen core values must then be communicated in a clear and often creative manner via online and offline media channels. To stay ahead of the competition, standard solutions are often not enough.

### Width of the process

In terms of scope, the SWOT starts broad: all possible internal and external aspects are included. Although the analysis is limited to one market, various interesting issues can play a role in and around that market, which can also lead to innovations. But during and after the SWOT, a different mindset is needed. First, within the SWOT, the most important issues should be identified. Subsequently, a positioning must be established that also requires focus. After the marketing strategy has been determined, the process will broaden again because the chosen message must be widely disseminated from all activities of the company. This is necessary because without clear (and perhaps somewhat 'exaggerated') communication, no position in the mindset of the target group is reached. This ties in with Sharp's studies mentioned previously, which have shown that 'presence' has a strong influence on purchase.

In this way, a hourglass view of the planning process is created (see Figure 2.7).

## 2.4 Structure of a marketing plan

Figure 2.8 contains an overview of the components of a marketing plan. The various components largely parallel the structure of the strategic marketing planning process. A marketing plan does not develop company objectives or company strategies.

A marketing plan is essentially developed for a single brand. In the figure, we also give an indication of the length of the various parts. Without attachments, a marketing plan will be around 25 pages. In practice, it can be observed that marketing plans are not always completely written out in 'report form'. Sometimes the headlines of all parts in a (PowerPoint) presentation will suffice. That presentation is then the marketing plan itself. There is nothing bad about that in itself. The length indications in Figure 2.8 relate to the number of pages or sheets in the presentation.

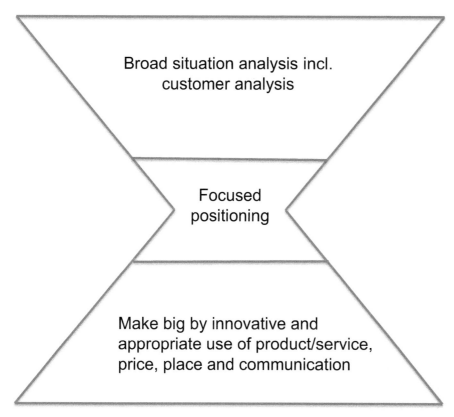

*Figure 2.7* Hourglass schedule

**1 Management summary**

The summary makes it possible for top management to take in the most important points of the plan in a very short space of time. The management summary shows the main conclusions from the SWOT analysis, the goals set in the plan, the chosen strategies, and the financial expectations. In the summary, the *arguments* that people have for the chosen strategy are also very important. Although the summary should be short, it should also be very concrete.

**2 Introduction and background**

The 'introduction and background' section serves as a general introduction to the marketing plan and as a framework within which decisions are made. The following points are included:

- First of all, it contains a statement of the company's mission and objectives, as well as the SBU objectives. It can be assumed that these must be regarded as given for the product/brand.
- Subsequently, the specific market for the product is defined on the basis of the dimensions mentioned in Chapter 3. Without this designation, it is unclear what

| Part | Number of pages |
|---|---|
| 1 Executive summary | 1-2 |
| 2  Introduction and background | 2-3 |
| •   Corporate mission and corporate objectives, SBU objectives | |
| •   Market definition and product brand background | |
| •   Results evaluation | |
| 3  Situation analysis | 6-10 |
| •   Internal analysis | |
| •   Customer analysis | |
| •   Industry analysis | |
| •   Competitor analysis | |
| •   Distribution analysis | |
| 4  SWOT analysis | 2-3 |
| •   Key issues ( SWOTs ), environmental vision and core problem | |
| •   Value strategy | |
| •   Marketing strategy options plus choice option | |
| 5  Marketing objectives/expected results | 1 |
| 6  Marketing strategy | 2-4 |
| •   Target groups | |
| •   Brand positioning | |
| •   Brand name and design | |
| 7  Market instrument decisions ( *marketing programs* ) | 6-10 |
| •   Instrument objectives | |
| •   Instrument decisions | |
| 8  Financial indicators and budgets | 1-2 |
| 9  Evaluation criteria | 1 |
| 10       Attachments | 10+ |
| •   Any further market data and data on past marketing activities | |
| •   Possible explanations of situation analysis | |
| •   Scenario analysis and *contingency plans* | |
| •   Time and activity schedules | |
| •   References | |

*Figure 2.8* **Content of a marketing plan for a product/brand**
Source: Based on Dibb et al. (2003)

the plan refers to. You can also choose to display the results of the identification of the competition here (first step competitor analysis). The advantage of this is that a picture of the market is already created at the beginning of this section. Some background information is also provided with the product/brand. After all, not every reader of the marketing plan is fully aware of the situation to which the marketing plan relates.

■ Finally, the problem conclusion is given. This forms the starting point for the plan and is therefore placed at the beginning. In the planning process itself, the problem conclusion will not be addressed until later (see Section 9.3).

Any time series of various variables of interest (such as market shares and advertising expenditure) can be used as *product facts* and be included in an appendix.

### 3  Situation analysis

Situational analysis is discussed extensively in this book. For the various components, predictions and/or assumptions (*planning assumptions*) of variables can also be displayed. This involves forecasts of variables such as macro-environmental factors, market data, and competitive behavior. For variables that have not been forecast, assumptions about future developments must be made. These assumptions (as well as the objectives) should be as specific as possible, for example, the expectations 'no response from competitor G' and 'a 5% growth in market demand'.

The explicit presentation of the assumptions is of great importance when choosing objectives and when evaluating the results later (in the internal analysis). If the predicted results are not achieved, this may be due to an assumption that turns out not to have been met, for example, a reaction from a competitor. In such a case, the company may have to choose an alternative strategy (this is shown in Section 10 – the appendices – of the marketing plan).

In practice, the competitor and industry analysis are often presented together.

### 4  SWOT analysis

The SWOT analysis forms a summary of the situation analysis and provides starting points for strategies.

### 5  Marketing objectives/expected results

The results to be achieved in terms of sales, turnover and market share are an important reason why a certain strategy is chosen. Objectives are usually specified for several years, for example, for three years.

### 6  Marketing strategy

A brief description of the marketing strategy is not sufficient. Elements such as target groups, brand personality, and type of positioning must be detailed. The argument for the choice of strategy must also be presented here.

### 7 Market instrument decisions

The plans must be translated in detail into *concrete action programs for the coming year* (annual plans). Four questions need to be answered:

1 *What* exactly will happen?
2 *When* will it happen?
3 *Who* does it?
4 *How much* does it cost?

These decisions are tactical and operational. Detailed interpretation and division of tasks are important for proper implementation. This section contains both tactical and operational decisions.

### 8 Financial indicators and budgets

Financial insight is a very important part of the marketing plan. The following financial indicators must be included here:

- the necessary budgets: budgets for sales promotion, sales costs, research, product development, and so on
- the predicted costs, revenues, cash flow, and profit: these predictions have already been used in the shareholder value analysis

This part is of great importance for higher management. It gives them insight into the investments required and the extent to which the plan will contribute to the company's financial objectives. The financial part thus forms the starting point for the negotiations between the manager submitting the plan and top management. In order to gain insight into the *risks*, the 'financial picture' will always be assessed by top management in relation to the assumptions. An expected high profit is attractive, but high uncertainty about this is a major drawback. Top management will also try to estimate the payback period, which is determined, among other things, by when a profit will be made. If this moment is too far in the future, the plan will be considered unattractive.

### 9 Evaluation criteria

In order to verify during the course of the year whether the plan will achieve its objectives, the 'evaluation metrics' section (also known as *performance indicators*) must include two things:

1 First, the objectives and budgets must be translated (disaggregated) into regions, varieties, distribution channels, and periods within the year (e.g. for each month or quarter). For example: with the introduction of a new brand X, the aim is to achieve a market share of 5% in a year (marketing objective). This target is now translated as follows: a share of 2% must be achieved on 1 April, 3% on 1 July, 4% on 1 October, and 5% on 31 December.
2 Subsequently, it must be indicated which information is required for the progress check. In other words: what standards will be used for the audit and how will they be measured? These measures depend on the objectives. For example: monitoring of progress takes place on the basis of Nielsen (scanning) data.

**10 Attachments**

Particularly in a highly dynamic environment, it may be desirable to have *alternative strategies* ready in case something 'unexpected' happens (a *contingency*), such as the introduction of a competing product. These unexpected events may have already been analyzed in the scenario analysis. A *contingency plan* can be based on a previously considered but abandoned strategy. In an appendix to the marketing plan, it can be described in which scenario which option should be chosen. In addition, one must indicate as specifically as possible *when* a certain scenario becomes current, for example, 'if sales are more than 10% below the targets' or 'if the weighted distribution does not exceed 70%'.

For the sake of clarity and for ex-post control, it is important to include schedules of planned activities in the *annexes*. For the sake of clarity, for example, time bars can be used.

# Summary

Three levels can play a role within a company: the corporate level (top management), SBUs (product groups), and products. In a small company, these levels will coincide. Brands play a role at all levels. In order to achieve customer loyalty, brand reputation is important in addition to satisfaction. The choice of brand positioning (desired brand associations) should be based on the balance between customer needs and a brand's unique strengths. Daring to choose is important. Essentially, the essence of the marketing strategy is to answer the question: why should a customer choose my brand and not the competitor's? In order to make the best marketing decisions for a brand, a systematic approach to knowledge gathering is preferable.

This book covers the strategic marketing planning process. Based on the chosen market definition and results evaluation, a situation analysis is performed: an internal analysis and an external analysis (ABCD: buyers, industry, competitors, and distributors/ suppliers). The data obtained in this way is further analyzed with a number of strategic analysis methods. Creativity is important in the translation process into strategies and ultimately a marketing plan. Finally, the plan must be implemented. Based on interim measurements, the implementation and the results are checked. The results of the evaluations form the input for a new planning process. Attention to digital and sustainable aspects is important in all phases of the marketing planning process.

Marketing planning goes from broad (situation analysis) to narrow (focus in positioning) to broad again (magnifying message). A marketer must have analytical skills and be creative.

## Experience Disneyland Paris

Disneyland Paris is part of the Walt Disney Company. The park opened in 1992. Since then, the park has become the largest theme park in Europe. During the record-breaking year 2012, 11.2 million people visited the famous amusement park. In that year, Disneyland Paris celebrated its twentieth anniversary. This twentieth anniversary, with new attractions, major renovations in the parks and hotels, and great media attention, contributed to this high number of visitors. This proved difficult to surpass. In the years after 2012, partly due to the poor economic situation, the number of visitors gradually decreased. However, this decline seemed to be slowing: the number of visitors increased to a total of around 10 million people in 2018 and 2019, but then the COVID pandemic had a huge impact on visitor numbers. In the lockdown year 2020, there were only 2.6 million visitors, slowly increasing to 3.5 million visitors in 2021.

Disneyland Paris is becoming less and less dependent on French visitors alone. According to Disney, the company's new pricing policy – fewer promotions, discounts, and last minutes – is the reason that the number of French visitors has fallen in recent years.

With the increasing number of visitors in the years before COVID, the company's turnover also increased. However, this increase was also caused by visitors spending more money during their visit to Disneyland Paris: the average guest spending in parks has been increasing in recent years. According to Disneyland Paris, this increase is caused by continuous investments in 'customer experience'. These investments fit in well with the mission of the Walt Disney Company:

> The mission of The Walt Disney Company is to be one of the world's leading producers and providers of entertainment and information. Using our portfolio of brands to differentiate our content, services and consumer products,

we seek to develop the most creative, innovative and profitable entertainment experiences and related products in the world.

The Walt Disney Company is an international company that specializes in family entertainment. The company consists of four elements:

- Parks, Experiences, and Products. In addition to Disneyland Paris, these include the Disneyland Resorts in Los Angeles, Florida, Tokyo and Shanghai.

  Disney Parks, Experiences and Products brings the magic of Disney stories and franchises to life through theme parks, resorts, cruise ships, unique vacation experiences, consumer products and more around the world. With experiences created by Walt Disney Imagineering, beloved characters come to life for guests and consumers of all ages.

- Studio Entertainment, responsible for the production of the Disney films.
- Media Networks: the television channels and streaming services of the Disney Media Group. This includes Disney+.
- Direct-to-Consumer and International, with a focus on high-quality entertainment through games, social media, and other digital platforms.

Disneyland Paris consists of two parts. On the one hand, there are the theme parks of the resort: Disneyland Park (including Fantasyland, Frontier Land, and Main Street USA) and the more television and film-oriented Walt Disney Studios Park. These parks host well-known attractions such as Big Thunder Mountain and Pirates of the Caribbean. The revenues in these parks are driven by two factors: the number of visitors and the spending per visitor (on food and drinks, admission prices, and merchandise). Next to the parks are the hotels and Disney Village. Visitors to Disneyland Paris can stay overnight here, but the hotels are also used for the organization of events and conferences.

Disneyland Paris aims to increase sales and profitability in the future through increasing visitor numbers and increasing average spending per visitor. To achieve this, the company continues to invest in the 'experience' that Disney offers its visitors. After all, if expectations of the visitors are exceeded, this leads to repeat visits and positive word-of-mouth advertising. Continued investment is also necessary: the competition in the market is constantly growing, and the competitors are not sitting still either.

An interview with Président Tom Wolber, adapted from the annual report of Disneyland Paris in 2015,[1] illustrates the confidence with which Disneyland Paris faces the future:

**How do you see the 2015 fiscal year?**
Throughout the year we increased our efforts to enhance the guest experience and to make our resort something truly special. We launched an ambitious program to renovate ten of our iconic attractions, including the emblematic

Space Mountain: Mission 2, and Mystères de Nautilus. These major innovations are starting to bear fruit. Revenue was up 7.3%, thanks to increases in theme park attendance, hotel occupancy rates, and average spending per guest. Disneyland Paris welcomed 600,000 additional guests this year, and average spending reached a record level of €53.8 per guest – an increase of 6%.

**How do these results reflect your strategy?**
These results demonstrate the positive impact of our long-term strategy to improve the quality of the guest experience and to increase guest satisfaction. This strategy is part of our constant drive for excellence, which is vital because our future lies in providing the very best quality. Continuous investments are necessary if we want to stay ahead of the competition and secure the future of Disneyland Paris. We operate in an increasingly competitive environment, as the leisure sector in Europe offers an ever-widening range of products and alternatives. We need to stand out to maintain our position as the sector leader.

**What is the key to the success of Disneyland Paris?**
Over the years, Disneyland Paris has strengthened its position as Europe's leading tourist attraction. Our success is first and foremost the result of the commitment of our employees. Their talent, creativity, and enthusiasm bring the Disney magic to life every day for millions of guests. We are increasing our creative efforts to enchant our guests, drawing on the heritage of the Disney brand. Our brand represents the values of sincerity and excellence, as well as the importance of dreams, and is one of the pillars of our success.

**What are your priorities for the coming years?**
We continue our renovation efforts in our parks and hotels, and we continue to offer new experiences to our guests. This work is part of our constant drive for excellence, and is also part of the build-up to our 25th anniversary in 2017. For this symbolic date, we want our resort to be even more attractive, more magical, and more welcoming than ever. As Europe's leading tourist destination, we should continue to do everything in our power to set an example in all areas, not only in our efforts to offer an experience but also in our HR policy or in our social and environmental responsibilities.

Providing a family experience is what made Disney great. Visitors come mainly to meet the Disney characters in person. Disney offers a unique opportunity to get a cuddle from Mickey Mouse or to take a photo together with Donald Duck. These are memories and experiences that people really remember, that lead to a second or third visit, and that cost relatively little money in terms of investment. Celebrations accompanied by parades, festivities, and more shows to permanently enrich the Disney feeling will continue to play a major role in the parks.

## Questions

1 Three levels can be distinguished in a company. Illustrate these three levels for the Walt Disney Company.

2 Does Disneyland Paris have a sustainable competitive advantage? If yes, which one? Please explain your answer.

3 Define the marketing objective for Disneyland Paris, based on the information in the case.

4 Define the corporate strategy, the marketing strategy, and the market instrument strategies for Disneyland Paris. Use information from the case where possible.

5 a In the external analysis, several specific analyses have to be performed. Which analyses are these?

   b Provide, for each of these analyses, an example of information that is of interest to Disneyland Paris. Use information from the case where possible.

6 Disneyland Paris offers a real-life experience where people go to meet their favorite Disney figure or to enjoy a ride in one of the attractions in the park. It is not an online experience. Does this mean that digital marketing is not relevant for Disneyland Paris? Why (not)?

1 Disneyland Paris was an independent company until 2017, which was registered with the name Euro Disney S.C.A. In 2017 it was taken over completely by the Walt Disney Company. Since then, annual reports for Disneyland Paris were no longer publicly available. The optimism, of course, remained.

# Part 2

# Situation analysis

Part 2 discusses the various components of the situation analysis. A thorough situation analysis lays the foundation for well-considered objectives and strategies. We start the situation analysis with the definition of the market, which must fall within the mission of a company (Chapter 3). The first real analysis step is then the internal analysis (Chapter 4), including a review of the results to date. The external analysis starts with the customers (Chapter 5). With this, we want to express how important it is to have insight into the wishes and perceptions of the target group. After the customer analysis, an overview of the entire industry is first given in Chapter 6. We then take a closer look at some of the parties involved. Chapter 7 deals with competitor analysis. In Chapter 8 we look at the distributors (channels) and suppliers. We conclude this part with the SWOT analysis (Chapter 9).

DOI: 10.4324/9781003381488-4

# Chapter 3

# Mission, customer values, and market definition

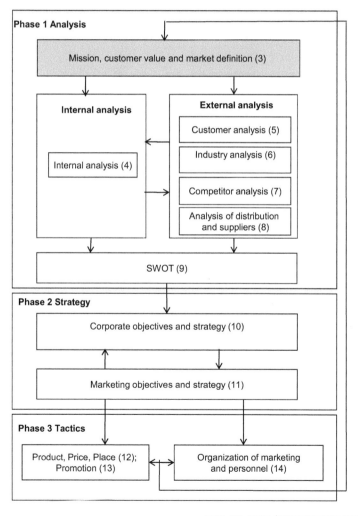

Phase 1 Analysis

- Mission, customer value and market definition (3)
  - Internal analysis
    - Internal analysis (4)
  - External analysis
    - Customer analysis (5)
    - Industry analysis (6)
    - Competitor analysis (7)
    - Analysis of distribution and suppliers (8)
  - SWOT (9)

Phase 2 Strategy

- Corporate objectives and strategy (10)
- Marketing objectives and strategy (11)

Phase 3 Tactics

- Product, Price, Place (12); Promotion (13)
- Organization of marketing and personnel (14)

DOI: 10.4324/9781003381488-5

### Key points in this chapter

- Know the function and components of a mission and a vision
- Know the essence of customer value and the different values that exist
- Know how to define a market: components and guidelines

## Introduction

The first step in the process of creating a marketing plan is to define the market. No analyses can be carried out without a market definition. A market definition for a brand must always fall within the mission of a company. First, the mission must be clear. That is why we discuss the company's mission and vision in Section 3.1. Within the vision, the choice of customer values (Section 3.2) plays a major role: which customer needs does the company want to meet? In Section 3.3, we indicate how a market definition takes place. We describe this on different levels, and we end with some guidelines.

## 3.1 Developing a customer-oriented vision

In this section we first look at the functions of the mission (Section 3.1.1). We then discuss the components of the mission in Section 3.1.2 and then come to corporate social responsibility (CSR). Finally, in Section 3.1.3, we discuss the vision of a company.

### 3.1.1 Functions of a mission

Many organizations have a *mission statement*. But just as these missions are often vague, so is the literature about what exactly a mission entails and what elements it should contain. Based on a survey of 59 large companies in the United Kingdom, Klemm et al. (1991) come to four different types of missions:

1. *The pure mission.* This is a reflection of the company's long-term goals, based on the philosophies of top management. For a publisher, for example: 'We want to make a growing contribution to the provision of information and opinion-forming in Dutch society'.
2. *Strategic objectives.* This is a rough representation of the desired direction and positions. For example: 'Our mission is to establish Sony Ericsson as the most attractive and innovative global brand in the mobile phone market'.
3. *Quantified planning objectives.* These are the concrete objectives for a certain period. For example: 'We want to achieve a 10% higher profit next year than this year'.
4. *Market definition (business definition).* This is a demarcation of the breadth and activities of a company. For example: 'We publish newspapers and magazines'.

This summary shows that the missions formulated by companies vary from very broad to very limited. The goal of a mission is threefold:

1   First of all, formulating a mission forces a company to *reflect on its activities* ('What business are we in?'). It is thus an important part of the strategic planning process. Particularly in companies that are not very market oriented, it can be a good starting point in the planning process to first try to get the existing activities on paper.

2   The second function of a mission is an *internal function*: it helps to motivate the staff. Thus, a mission must contain elements of objectives that can be pursued by the employees.

3   A third function of a mission is to create a certain image to the outside world (*external function*). To this end, the identity of the company can be included in the mission, as well as, for example, social objectives.

According to the research of Klemm et al. (1991), the internal function is most important: the main purpose of the mission is to sell the philosophies and ideas (values) of the top management to the employees. From the point of view of implementation and management, a mission is therefore an important instrument. An example of a very short, but at the same time extremely motivating, mission comes from a Japanese car manufacturer whose mission for quite some time was 'Beat Benz'. The research by Klemm et al. also shows that a change in management is the most important reason for changing the mission. 'Changes in market conditions' are mentioned less often as a reason to change the mission.

Research by Hooley et al. (1992) shows that there is a need to separate mission and vision. According to these authors, it is essential to formulate a short motivational vision about what the organization wants to achieve in the future. This is also called *strategic intent* (Hamel & Prahalad, 1989). On this basis, we can therefore say that a mission only fulfills an essential function if it motivates. Since this is often not the case in practice, it is argued that companies should formulate not so much mission statements but *ambition statements*.

A mission is what the company is and does now; a vision is what the company wants to achieve in the future. That vision is motivating. We agree with these definitions and show in Figure 3.1 which choices should form the basis of a strategic business plan. We choose to first have the mission defined in order to indicate what the company wishes to achieve in the future (vision). We will discuss each of the components listed in Figure 3.1 in more detail in Sections 3.1.2 and 3.1.3.

**The mission: what do we do now?**

•   Definition of activities

•   Societal mission (external and internal) and other dimensions of corporate image

**The vision/ambition: what do we want to achieve in the future?**

•   Belief: belief about what is important

•   Identity and positioning of the organization: value strategy

•   Long-term goals

*Figure 3.1* **Mission and vision of an organization**

## 3.1.2 Two types of missions and sustainability

The mission consists of the following components:

■  the economic-technical mission
■  the social mission

### Economic-technical mission

The economic-technical component concerns the demarcation of the current activities: *what business are we in?* Markets can be defined in several ways. The most obvious way is to define markets based on products. A market then consists of all suppliers who bring a certain product to the market. For example, companies may be active in the beer market, the car market, the coffee market, the air travel market, or the personal computer market.

A disadvantage of defining markets on the basis of products is that this only concerns the supply side: it does not show who the products are intended for or who the buyers are. The market definition should therefore also include the buyers. For example, a company can manufacture beer for home consumption or for use in the hospitality industry (or for both). Personal computers can be intended for individuals, schools, or companies. It is also possible to give a geographical demarcation of the buyers. Do you only serve the domestic market or also abroad? And in the latter case: which countries? In short, in addition to the products, one must also indicate who the customers are.

Another important point of criticism of the use of the product dimension is that it does not look at the functions that the products fulfill for the customers. In other words: the underlying needs of the customers for whom the products are intended are not considered. There is then a danger that you will overlook competitors who fulfill the same function for the customers (i.e. who meet the same needs) but with completely different products. For example, a petrol company can use the product-oriented market definition 'we sell petrol' but also the customer-oriented definition 'we supply energy'. In the latter case, you keep the option open to also supply other products that cover the same need, such as gas.

Some authors (Abell & Hammond, 1979; Abell, 1980) therefore argue that a market definition should not only be formulated in terms of products but also in terms of customer functions.

A classic example of a product-oriented mission are Swiss watch manufacturers, which for years used as a market definition: hand-made precision movements. Due to the advent of chip technology, they were overtaken by foreign manufacturers who could deliver the same quality at considerably lower prices (digital watches). It was only when sales of Swiss watches fell dramatically that the market definition was reformulated based on consumers' need to 'know what time it is'. Subsequently, new production methods were also used and cheaper watches were produced (Swatch).

All in all, we conclude that a market definition can contain the following dimensions (similar to Abell [1980]: customer technologies, customer groups, customer functions):

■  *Products* (customer technologies): 'We design systems that link customer needs to the supply of information'.
■  *Customer* groups (segments): 'Our target groups are private individuals and companies in the Netherlands'.

- *Customer functions* (needs): 'We help our customers to find information on the Internet more effectively and efficiently'.

### Societal mission: sustainability

The other component of the mission is of a social nature. For example, external social goals relate to climate, internal goals to matters such as the working atmosphere, employment, and fringe benefits. This has everything to do with the aforementioned sustainability, also known as the 'three Ps': companies should not only have an eye for Profit but also for People and the Planet. Nowadays, every company should consider corporate social responsibility of paramount importance.

The term CSR is also used with different meanings. We can distinguish the following facets of CSR, two external and one internal:

- *Sustainability*, that is, doing business in an environmentally friendly manner. As indicated in Chapter 1, this has become a very important issue worldwide in recent years.
- *Social projects*. These can be various 'charities'.
- *Internal social policy*. This is in fact *sustainable human resources management* and is related, for example, to a positive action policy for immigrants, women returning to work, or the elderly. A partial aspect of this is the combination of work and care. There seems to be an increasing focus by employees on a more balanced work-life balance. By responding to this, companies can retain their people for longer.

CSR therefore means that in addition to *profit*, there is also attention for *people* (external and internal) and *planet*, the well-known trilogy people, planet, profit. The term 'sustainability' is therefore (as mentioned earlier) used for both the P for Planet and the P for People. In this book we use the term sustainability for the 'planet' side of sustainability. So, as indicated in Chapter 1, *acting sustainably* is acting in such a way that future generations are not saddled with the social 'costs'. We regard personnel as another issue.

## 3.1.3 Vision of a company

The vision is the entrepreneur's dream. It is the view of the current top management of a company about the function of existing and new products in the future and about the role that the company can play in providing them. In our opinion, the most important part of the vision is to indicate what the company wants to mean to the customer: what value does the company want to provide? The vision (see Figure 3.2) largely stems from the existing core competencies: what are we best at?

Figure 3.2 shows that a vision contains the following components:

- Opinions about what the company considers important in the environment and especially among the target group. ('We believe that over the next five years there will be a strong consumer demand for local products'.)
- The identity of the company as it is translated to the customer ('Our aim is to be the most locally oriented manufacturer of food within five years'). The company will often base this on its core competencies or *core competences*.

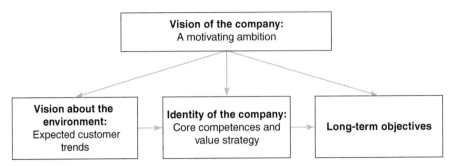

*Figure 3.2* **Components of the vision of a company**

■ The company's long-term goals ('We want to become the largest provider of local food').

It is important that the vision contains a *clear motivational aim*, which the entire staff within a company can agree with. The latter is also important: a vision should not be imposed on the staff as a forced straitjacket. It is important that support be created for this. Being able to formulate a clear and challenging ambition is an important requirement for a leader. A clear ambition is a strong tool for creating teams. In practice, however, many organizations lack challenging visions, and when they do exist, they are not always sufficiently shared with the workforce. We will come back to this in Chapter 14.

At the end of this introduction we make a comment on the place of the vision in the planning process. Can the formulation of a vision take place prior to the situation analysis? Can an organization make decisions about the future without an extensive situation analysis? We choose to initially consider the vision more or less as given in the marketing planning process. This has to do with the level at which these matters operate: formulating a vision is a matter for top management ('the leader'); the strategic marketing planning process concerns individual markets and SBUs. For example, if a company has not chosen a clear value strategy, it will still have to do so after the situation analysis. We will come back to this in the SWOT analysis in Chapter 9.

## 3.2 Customer values

In Chapter 1, we indicated that having a competitive advantage is essential. Different 'models' can be used for the choice of such an advantage. In this section we present some important ones. But first, let's take a look at what 'customer value' actually is.

### 3.2.1 What is customer value?

Customer value is defined as the utility that a customer derives from a product, where we define utility as the difference between revenue (in the broad sense) and cost (in the broad sense). In short:

Customer value = 'Revenue' product – 'Cost' product

## Case 3.1 A vision should be motivating

### The vision of Ikea

'**To create a better everyday life for the many people**'. This vision goes beyond home furnishing. We want to have a positive impact on the world – from the communities where we source our raw materials to the way our products help our customers live a more sustainable life at home. If you've ever visited IKEA, you'll have probably worked out what our business idea is – '**to offer a wide range of well-designed, functional home furnishing products at prices so low that as many people as possible will be able to afford them**'.

This equation should not be interpreted as a mathematical expression. The matters that we (will) discuss here cannot (in principle) be expressed in numbers. It's about the thought behind it.

We already mentioned in Chapter 1 that products are not only about the 'real', functional 'returns' but that emotional aspects – the associations with a brand – also play a role. An advantage that lies somewhat in the middle between functional and emotional benefits is the degree of *customer friendliness* that a customer experiences with a provider: how you feel treated and how 'nice' they are to you. The polite customer friendliness of a provider has several advantages for a customer. First, of course, emotionally: it just feels nice when people are nice to you, for example, in the hospitality industry when you go out for dinner, but also when you are being treated by a doctor. Customer friendliness also has practical advantages: if they know you, they already know what your preferences are, and it is easier to buy something, for example, in a clothing store.

Costs are not just about monetary costs but about 'sacrifices' in a broad sense, so, for example, also the effort to be able to buy the product somewhere. Finally, 'costs' also include societal costs, such as the ecological footprint. So:

> Customer value = (Functional and emotional benefits) + (Customer friendliness) –
> (Price and customer sacrifices and societal sacrifices)

## 3.2.2 The Brand Benefitting Model

Based on the aforementioned definition of customer values, a company can therefore choose from various options to satisfy customers. In other words: to make a choice from the brand promises. That is the basis for the Brand Benefitting Model developed by us (Figure 3.3).

On the left side of the model are the revenues for the customer; on the right side are the 'costs'.

There are three types of revenue (benefits):

1   *The highest quality (in the narrow sense).* This applies to products that score best in tests or services that are delivered with a high degree of professionalism. Things like innovation and creative listening to the customer are of great importance.

2   *Service and customer orientation.* These two concepts belong together: a company that handles complaints properly, for example, offers good (aftersales) service on

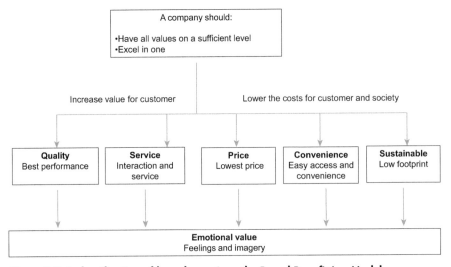

*Figure 3.3* **A classification of brand promises: the Brand Benefitting Model**

this point and is customer oriented. We do not count getting 'customized' advice that is done online as part of this benefit. We mean real customer attention and service (see Case 3.3).

3  *Strong emotional associations.* We have placed this at the bottom of the model because, in our opinion, brands should always create emotional associations.

Companies can also be best at lowering the sacrifices. These are:

1  The lowest price.
2  Convenience. There are two forms of convenience:
   ■  easy *access* to product or service, for example, short waiting times and quick accessibility;
   ■  ease of *use*: products that are simple or services that are clear
3  Socially responsible, so very sustainable and no 'future costs' for society.

If a company scores sufficiently on all benefits, it must then also enable the link to the customer's feelings by adding emotional values to the product or service. These are therefore at the bottom of the model. By competing both instrumentally and emotionally, a company applies so-called two-way positioning (see Section 11.3.3). In our opinion, a *combination* of instrumental and emotional positioning has two main advantages:

■  It provides better opportunities for finding distinctive core values because competing on quality alone, for example, is not distinctive.
■  It offers the strongest opportunities to build a relationship with the customer because the customer is addressed at both 'the head' and 'the heart'.

If we make a link with the content of the core of marketing, then it can be said that the Brand Benefitting Model lays the foundation for the search for that promise that forms the best fit between the strengths of the company and the wishes of the target group.

The model can also be used in the internal analysis to determine how strong the company is on the various brand promises. The same can be done with the competitor analysis.

In anticipation of the models discussed in the following, it also applies to the Brand Benefitting Model that companies must first 'score' on all five benefits and then try to excel in one benefit. For example, it is obvious to expect that in the very near future, all brands will have to have a certain degree of sustainability as a precondition to be purchased. That does not necessarily mean that you are top at it as a brand, but it does mean that you are sufficient.

## 3.2.3 The value strategies of Treacy and Wiersema

In the much-cited article 'Customer Intimacy and Other Value Disciplines', Treacy and Wiersema (1993) (T&W) present three possible value disciplines (or value strategies):

1  *product leadership*
2  *operational excellence* or leading in low cost for the customer
3  *customer intimacy* or an individual customer approach

### 1 Product leadership

Product leadership is the development of innovative, value-added products. This strategy is used, for example, by Procter & Gamble, which, in all markets in which it operates, maintains that Procter brands are the highest quality in the category and best serve the consumer need for which the product is made. Other examples of companies that seem to opt for product leadership are technologically strong companies such as Apple, Microsoft, Philips, and Sony (see Case 3.2).

### 2 Operational excellence

Operational excellence means to excel in the proper and efficient execution of all business processes. An 'excellent production process' must lead to the customer having to incur as few 'costs' as possible. In addition, a low price is the most obvious way to meet

## Case 3.2 Sony: innovation in technology and entertainment

Sony's business falls into technology and entertainment (such as the PlayStation and Sony Pictures [movies]) – so basically 'hardware' and 'software'. Sony's mission is to inspire and 'fulfill your curiosity'. Sony says it has an unlimited passion for technology, content, and services, and, through its continuous innovation, for delivering new exciting entertainment, creating unique new cultures and experiences. 'Everything we do is to move you emotionally'.

a customer need. Incidentally, this is not necessary: 'costs' can also be non-financial, such as the effort to buy the product (*convenience*). 'Always delivering on time' can also be part of it. Important in this value strategy for a company is standardization and the achievement of economies of scale. This strategy is chosen, for example, by the airline easyJet, which saves costs in as many areas as possible (including the 'service' en route: food is only provided for an extra fee) and is therefore able to compete at very low prices. Other companies that excel in operational excellence are McDonald's (see Case 3.3), Aldi, IKEA, and, in the United States, Wal-Mart. This value strategy is explicitly about excelling in efficiency. In principle, every company will of course try to keep its own costs as low as possible and to have the internal processes run as smoothly as possible, but that does not mean that these companies excel in low costs for the customer.

### 3 Customer intimacy

Customer intimacy means an individual customer approach (customer leadership or the best in relationship marketing). Obtaining 'intimate' relationships with the customer

## Case 3.3 Operational excellence

### McDonald's manages to keep costs low through uniform choices

McDonald's is a good example of an unambiguous global formula. By applying a 'global strategy', McDonald's is able to achieve enormous cost advantages. It seems that for fast food, it doesn't make much difference which culture you operate in. In this case, perhaps you can also turn it around: McDonald's has created the fast food culture itself in various cultures. That, too, is part of marketing: teaching consumers something instead of just following them.

through the provision of customized products and/or through a policy that is completely focused on attention to the individual customer and customer loyalty is paramount. Many online providers, such as Amazon, Netflix, and bol, but also small and medium-sized enterprises (SMEs), seem to choose this strategy because they know exactly what people's preferences are. Based on this, they can make recommendations and offers. But this is not 'true customer focus'. Customer intimacy is also normal in business markets: personal contacts and products and services tailored to individual customers (companies) are common in industrial markets. In small and medium-sized companies, a truly personal, individual customer strategy also seems to be applicable. There are also opportunities for implementing customer intimacy in service markets and consumer retail. In marketing practice, however, many service providers in the Netherlands are more concerned with sales than with building relationships. Few providers excel in this strategy in other industries as well. There are companies that pay attention to individual customer retention (such as KLM). But that doesn't mean the company excels at it. Customer intimacy therefore seems to be able to offer a competitive advantage in many industries in the future.

T&W argue that every company must make a basic choice of excelling in one of three disciplines: what value does the company want to best provide? This choice determines the entire business: production, personnel, marketing, and so on. In addition, the other two value disciplines must also be at a sufficient level. This last condition is sometimes forgotten in the description of T&W. This addition is very important, because T&W state that a company can only excel in one of the three if, for example, a minimum level of quality of internal processes (operational excellence) has been achieved (see Figure 3.4). So, in fact, a company can only excel in one discipline when all three disciplines are at

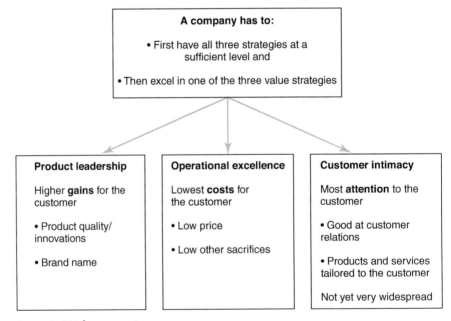

*Figure 3.4* **Value strategies**

a decent level. A company must therefore first get things 'right' in terms of innovation, efficiency, and customer focus before it can achieve excellence.

Incidentally, due to the growth of the internet, the distinction between the value strategies has become blurred. This is especially true of the difference between operational excellence and customer intimacy, which can be remarkably almost the same online, because in the online examples mentioned, the online technology provides a 'customized' advice or loyalty program, respectively. This gives the customer the feeling that something is being done especially for them. But this has essentially nothing to do with personal customer relationships, because no one at the provider is involved! There are, however, more comments to be made about the classification of T&W. That's not how brand thinking works, and sustainability plays no role. It is also the case that the value strategies are not really defined in terms of customer needs: they say more about the internal processes of a company. Our Brand Benefitting Model does meet those requirements. At the same time, T&W's supply orientation is also an advantage: it makes it easier to categorize the activities of companies.

### 3.2.4 Format of Porter

The classification of T&W shows similarities with the generic competitive strategies of Porter (1980). Porter lists three ways in which a company can distinguish itself:

1   *differentiation:* distinguishing itself from the competition
2   *cost leadership:* striving for the lowest cost level in the industry
3   *a focus strategy:* focusing on one segment or niche

Porter also mentions a fourth strategy: 'stuck in the middle'. This means that no clear choice has been made. According to Porter, strong profitability is never achieved with this. We agree with the latter. However, Porter's classification itself is not very telling. After all, differentiation must follow each provider (competitive advantage). The question is mainly what. Lowest cost says little about customer needs, and focus is a targeting strategy and says little about where the company excels.

### 3.2.5 Conclusions about the classifications

We draw the following conclusions about the classifications of strategies:

1   A general conclusion that applies to all classifications is that a provider must make a choice about what it wants to excel in. This corresponds to one of the 'brand laws' to be covered later in this book, namely 'focus'. At the same time, the provider must score sufficiently on other customer values.
2   For all classifications, the question is also justified whether they relate to the entire company: can different customer values be chosen within a company? Hendry (1990) states in his article 'The Problem with Porter's Generic Strategies' that Porter's concept should be involved at the SBU level. If we extend this to the classification of T&W, we see that a value strategy must be chosen within an SBU but that different value strategies are possible between SBUs. The clearest is a value strategy for an

entire company, but if there are more or less autonomously functioning divisions or SBUs within a company, then differences in value strategies are conceivable.

3  Porter's and T&W's classifications are not both based on customer needs and therefore lack consistency. The relationship with the internet is also difficult to explain.

All in all, the Brand Benefitting Model is best suited to really think in terms of customer values. T&W can be used to look at the internal processes of companies. These must then be translated into customer values, which is the subject of the Brand Benefitting Model.

## 3.3 Market definition

In this section, we will successively discuss:

- market definition at the SBU level (Section 3.3.1)
- market definition at the product-brand level (Section 3.3.2)
- market definition and new activities (Section 3.3.3)
- the importance and danger of the market definition (Section 3.3.4)

### 3.3.1 Market definition at the SBU level

For convenience, we defined a strategic business unit around a specific market or product category in Chapter 2, for example, the SBUs salad dressing, children's clothing, student accounts, and travel insurance. This definition implies that an SBU is not always clearly visible as an organizational unit in a company.

A market definition at the level of an SBU takes place in a similar way to the mission: on the basis of the dimensions products, target groups, and needs. There are differences between the corporate level and the SBU level:

- Since marketing plans are drawn up at the SBU level, the market definition at the SBU level should be as concrete as possible, while somewhat vaguer terms can be used in the mission statement.
- An SBU's market will by definition be narrower than that of the company; the sum of all the SBUs market definitions will, in theory, correspond to the company-wide market definition.

Defining the customer's need has a direct influence on the breadth of the competition. A competitor is, by definition, a provider that can meet the same customer needs. The way in which the need is defined therefore determines the competition. So not only are instrumental needs important but also properties derived from products, such as prestige and status. These values can also be used in the market definition.

We illustrate the use of the dimensions at the level of an SBU with an example (see Figure 3.5). A manufacturer's SBU 'jam' examines the possibilities in three different dimensions:

1  customer function
2  customer groups
3  customer technology

The need that is being addressed is defined instrumentally in this example and is the need for spreads. Alternative needs are pie filling and dessert components.

Possible customer groups are home users, catering, healthcare, and canteens in companies. Alternative customer technologies (corresponding to the need for sandwich fillings) are peanut butter, sprinkles, sandwich spread, cheese spread, cheese, and meat products. Within these dimensions, the following market definition has been chosen: 'We meet the need for spreads among home users by making jam'. Incidentally, we should note with regard to Figure 3.5 that it is in principle constructed for the level of the final customers (consumers).

The use of the three dimensions mentioned is not only important for defining the current market but also makes it possible to think about possible growth directions in a structured manner when making business decisions. In particular, the well-known four growth strategies of Ansoff (1957; see also Section 10.3.2) can be directly linked to the axes in Figure 3.5. The relationships between the market definition dimensions and Ansoff 's growth strategies are shown in Figure 3.6.

Figure 3.6 shows which growth strategy is applicable for a particular combination of changes in market dimensions. For example, if one wishes to grow within the existing three dimensions, there is market penetration. This is also the case if only the customer function dimension is changed. Growth along only the customer group dimension implies market development, while growth with only expansions of the product dimension (i.e. for the same needs and customers) is called product development. Change in both the customer groups and products dimension means diversification. If these are related products that cover the same needs, then there is related diversification. If other needs are also met, then there is unrelated diversification.

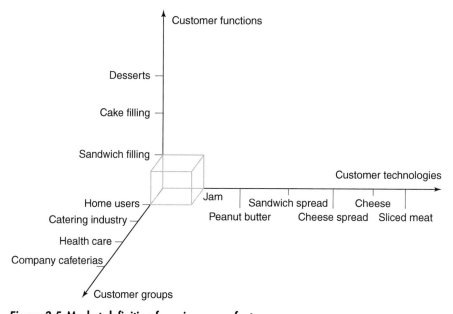

*Figure 3.5* **Market definition for a jam manufacturer**

| Customer function | Customer groups | Buyer technology (producer) | Growth strategy according to Ansoff | Example jam manufacturer |
|---|---|---|---|---|
| – | – | – | Market penetration | Price reduction jam |
| × | – | – | Market penetration | Emphasize another application: jam as pie filling |
| – | × | – | Market development | Selling jam to the catering industry or abroad |
| – | – | × | Product development | Manufacturing peanut butter for consumers |
| – | × | × | Related diversification | Sell peanut butter abroad |
| | × | × | Unrelated diversification | Fruit juices or ready-made pizza fabrication |

*Figure 3.6* **Market dimensions and growth strategies; – or × means: no or change of this dimension**

Figure 3.6 can serve as a checklist when generating growth options. Generation of options is covered in the SWOT analysis in Chapter 9.

Final decisions on growth directions are made after the situational analysis accompanying the corporate strategy. That is why we return to growth strategies in Chapters 10 and 11.

## 3.3.2 Market definition at product-brand level

In addition to a market definition at the SBU level, a more detailed definition can be helpful for brands in further analyses. In concrete terms, this could involve a division of two of the three dimensions mentioned above: target groups and products/services. Then the following three steps must be taken:

1   First, all products are listed. For companies that produce goods, this can probably be done quickly. This is already a lot more difficult for providers of services: what are the products of a bank?
2   Then the various (customer) target groups of the organization are described. An obvious division is the distinction between private individuals (final customers) and companies (business markets). But of course it is possible to segment within these groups according to various (segmentation) variables that range from general background characteristics (age, type of company, retail chain, etc.) to more product-related variables, such as heavy versus light 'users' or price buyers versus quality seekers.
3   Finally, it must be indicated which combinations of products and target groups are current for the organization.

Figure 3.7 contains some fill-in schemes that can be used for this. An advantage of overviews such as those in Figure 3.7 is that they can be the starting point for later analyses.

Case 3.4 is an example of market dimensions in sports markets.

| Description of products (and varieties) | |
| --- | --- |
| Products 1 | |
| Products 2 | |
| Products 3 | |
| Products 4 | |
| Product ... | |
| **Description target groups** | |
| Target group 1 | |
| Target group 2 | |
| Target group 3 | |
| Target group 4 | |
| Target audience ... | |

| Matrix of product- target group combinations * | | | | | |
| --- | --- | --- | --- | --- | --- |
| | Target group 1 | Target group 2 | Target group 3 | Target group 4 | Target audience ... |
| Item 1 | | | | | |
| Products 2 | | | | | |
| Products 3 | | | | | |
| Products 4 | | | | | |
| Product ... | | | | | |

*Figure 3.7* Worksheets for defining product-market combinations. Mark each section with an 'x' if that combination exists for the organization

### 3.3.3 Market definition and new activities

Defining the market (at the company, SBU, and product level) for the situation analysis seems to imply that the definition is not influenced by the outcomes of the situation analysis. In practice, this influence does exist. If, for example, the market for newspapers and magazines on which a publisher is active develops very unfavorably, this may be a reason to adjust the publisher's mission (for example, to be active in the consumer market of the press) and to become active as well in information provision for companies. In that case, the question becomes *what should our business be?* (information provision for companies), answered differently than the question *what business are we in?* (consumer market press). Here the relationship with the vision becomes clear again: the vision is the difference between the current and the desired market.

A difference in the field of activities now and what is planned does mean that this new field (in the example, news offerings via the internet) must also be analyzed to determine whether this new market is attractive.

## Case 3.4 Offering several markets

## Market dimensions in sport markets

Organizations in sports markets (clubs, associations, stadiums, etc.) deal with two target groups: spectators/viewers and advertisers (sponsors). The definition of the 'product' sport is 'battle'.

The special thing about this product is that it is not stable. Its course and outcome are always uncertain. There are two forms of sports marketing: marketing of sports and marketing through sports (sponsorship). Organizations dealing with the marketing of 'struggle' (sports) can apply the planning concepts described in this book. It is about selling your own product as well as possible to viewers and advertisers and building relationships with these target groups. Marketing through sports is mainly about communication.

Sponsors can use the medium of sports organizations to achieve brand objectives (familiarity, image) and to build their own relationships (e.g. invite customers to skyboxes).

Paris Saint-Germain is an example of a club/brand that has consciously worked on its image since its acquisition in 2011 by Qatar Sport Investments, going from a relatively unknown brand, sometimes associated with lower social classes, to 'the one and only Parisian football club' with a different logo (a stylized Eiffel Tower) and investments in top players who themselves possess considerable 'brand equity' such as Neymar, Messi and Ibrahimovic. The result is also entrance tickets are extremely expensive.

Finally, one may wonder whether ideas for new activities emerge if one analyzes only the existing markets from the existing SBUs. In this regard, we note that both the SWOT analysis and the reconsideration of the mission should explicitly pay attention to signals that point to opportunities outside the current activities.

Summarizing the foregoing, we can indicate the following four steps in defining the market and formulating the mission:

1   Start from a definition of the market in which one is currently active.
2   Perform an external analysis of the environment. Also analyze opportunities and threats outside the existing market.
3   Based on the external (and internal) analysis, analyze whether there is reason to become active outside the existing market. In other words: define the desired market.
4   If yes, perform a new external analysis with the changed market definition. This is necessary because with a different market definition, there is also a different competitive situation, different market growth, and so on. In the case of a broader definition, the number of competitors will be higher.

After conducting another external analysis, the company must then ask itself whether it still finds the chosen market attractive. If so, the planning process continues. We have summarized this in Figure 3.8.

In short, the phases 'definition of the (current) market', 'external analysis', and 'formulation of business decisions: definition of the desired market' are completed when there is no reason to change the market definition. Incidentally, we should note that in practice these steps are usually completed only once or at most twice: first for the current market and then for a more broadly defined market (see Case 3.5).

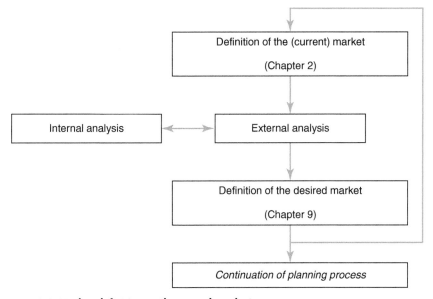

*Figure 3.8* **Market definition and external analysis**

## Case 3.5 Market definition

### Board games or online games

Suppose a manufacturer uses the current market definition/mission: 'manufacturing board games'. An analysis of the board game market now shows that sales are declining. An important cause of this seems to be the rise of online games. Based on this observation, the manufacturer must make an important choice: not to change the mission and try to maintain sales of board games through marketing efforts or to adjust the mission and decide to also enter the online gaming market. The choice of whether to adjust the mission depends, among other things, on the situation in the online games market. The manufacturer therefore carries out an additional external analysis, namely of the online games market. This shows that there is very strong competition in this market and that completely different know-how is needed to gain a strong position in that market. On this basis, the manufacturer decides not to adjust its mission but to try to restore its sales of board games by focusing more on the use of board games around the holidays.

In practice, repeating a situation analysis is also often carried out when the company is considering becoming active abroad. In that case, the market abroad must be analyzed in the second round.

### 3.3.4 Importance and danger of the market definition

In an article that has become a classic entitled 'Marketing Myopia', Levitt (1960) warned against an overly supply-oriented definition of a market. In the mission, we already mentioned the example of the too-narrow, product-oriented market definition of Swiss watch manufacturers (Section 3.1.2). It is of great strategic importance how broadly or narrowly a manager defines the market. After all, if a company defines the market broadly, there will be many competitors. However, if a company starts from a niche (or segment), the number of competitors is by definition limited. There is therefore a direct relationship between the market definition and the number of competitors: market definition can be regarded as 'defining the competitive set' (Lehmann & Winer, 2008). This implies that there is also a direct relationship with the concept of market share. Because the market share is calculated over the defined market, a narrow market definition (for example, the market of health yogurts) implies a higher market share than a broad market definition (the market of yogurts). It is not uncommon for us to see in practice that equities are calculated on sub-markets instead of entire markets.

In this context, Lehmann and Winer distinguish four levels of competition:

1   *Product form* competition: Competition between brands targeting the same market segment, such as Pepsi Light versus Coke Light.
2   *Product category* competition: competition between products with similar properties, such as different soft drinks.
3   *Generic competition*: products that meet the same consumer needs, such as beverages.
4   *Budget* competition: competition for consumer money, such as food and entertainment.

Market definitions in annual marketing planning are usually based on product form or product category competition. In Chapter 7, we discuss these forms of competition in more detail in the identification of competitors.

## Summary

In order to carry out a situation analysis, it must first be known in which market the company is active and what customer value the company is pursuing. These are important preconditions within which the marketing strategy must be developed. The market definition has to do with the mission of the company and the customer value with the vision. Studying these two should lead to the identification of the market and customer value.

Organizations are best managed when there is a clear mission and a common vision. A mission concerns a demarcation of the current activities and possible social goals. A vision refers to the future. Which development in the target group does top management consider important? What identity should the organization have (value strategy choice)? And what are (other) long-term goals?

A choice for a customer value is very important: a company that does not specialize in anything will achieve low profitability on average. In principle, companies can choose from the following promises: best product quality, best service and customer attention, lowest price, highest convenience, best durability. In addition, emotional positioning is important. Incidentally, specialization is only possible after the company has reached a sufficient level in terms of innovation, quality of processes and customer focus.

The market for the organization is defined in the mission statement. At the level of the SBU, a further market definition takes place on the basis of the dimensions products, needs, and target groups. The market definition chosen at that level forms the starting point of the situation analysis. At product or brand level, the target groups dimension can often be broken down even further in order to obtain a more detailed definition of product-market combinations. It is important to use a demand-driven market definition that is not too narrow, because otherwise a company overlooks competitors and runs the risk of being overtaken by an unexpected angle.

## Coffee is an experience

It happens millions of times a week – a customer receives a drink from a Starbucks barista – yet it's unique every time. It's a snapshot: a hand reaching over the counter to pass a cup of coffee to another outstretched hand, a name on a Starbucks cup, a brief break with a latte. But every contact with a customer also creates a connection.

Starbucks is committed to honoring that connection in everything they do – from striving for the best-quality coffee to working with partners and suppliers to conduct business responsibly – and has been since the beginning of the company.

## The beginning – and why conquering the heart of coffee culture took so long

In 1971, when the first Starbucks coffee shop opened in Seattle's old Pike Place Market, it was just a one-shop business. Starbucks sold a selection of the world's best freshly roasted coffee beans from this small shop. The name, inspired by the story of Moby Dick, evoked the romance of the early days of coffee in the 18th and 19th centuries.

In the years that followed, Starbucks increasingly focused on the romance of the coffee experience. The Italian coffee house tradition was copied: a place for conversation and a sense of togetherness. A sense of home. Starbucks grew in the 1980s and 1990s and successfully internationalized as well. Starbucks set foot in several European countries. However, the expansion to Italy was long delayed. For good reason – food touches the heart of Italian culture, and Italians don't take it easy on American corporations trying to change their culture. Large American corporations like Ben and Jerry's and Häagen-Dazs, for instance, tried to sell ice cream in the Italian market, with mixed results, to say the least. When Ben and Jerry's opened a shop in the touristic Piazza del Duomo in Florence years ago, they were shunned by the Italians, who regarded the hard American ice cream as an insult to Italy's wonderfully soft gelato, as well as the American tourists, who didn't travel all the way across the Atlantic for ice cream they could get back home. The shop closed after about two years. Häagen-Dazs was another American brand that met the same fate in Florence.

If there is any culture in the world that takes its coffee seriously, it's the Italian. Coffee is part of Italian culture, a ritual engrained in people's habits. People start the day with an espresso that they drink standing at the counter of one of the tens of thousands coffee bars that you can find in even the smallest villages. The Starbucks way of imitating – and Americanizing – Italian coffee culture can be considered an insult by Italians.

Therefore, the introduction had to be planned carefully. The first Italian Starbucks opened in Milano in 2018. Starbucks picked Milan as its entry point, a city that matches tradition with a modern global lifestyle, and also a city of fashion and finance. This contrasts with Naples and Rome, where the espresso culture is much more sacred. Located in a trendy square near some of Milan's top tourist attractions, the 25,000-square-foot building is outfitted in Tuscan marble and gleaming copper, featuring extravagances such as a 500-pound in-house coffee roaster, augmented reality (AR)-configured walls, an aperitivo bar, and a liquid nitrogen affogato station. Old mixed with new at Starbucks Milan, a perfect metaphor for the meeting of American and Italian coffee cultures. The marble floor of the store was constructed in a traditional Palladian style, while the ceiling was built using the latest technology. The building's facade is an imposing structure that used to be the city's historic post office. Starting in 2018, Starbucks gradually expanded to around 20 stores in northern and central Italy, with the first Starbucks finally opening in Rome in 2022.

## Starbucks changes – step by step

Starbucks has become a global success. Since its beginning, the company changed gradually to what it has become now.

Nowadays, in addition to good coffee, Starbucks also serves all kinds of trendy drinks. This started with taking over The Coffee Connection in 1994, including the 'Frappuccino' that has since been for sale at all Starbucks locations. This was followed by further changes in the offerings, like adding cheesecake and a number of other snacks. In addition to coffee, you can also get tea at Starbucks. Starbucks has hosted the tea brand Tazo since 1999.

Another milestone was the introduction of the sub-brand 'Starbucks Reserve': exclusive, premium coffee, available at selected Starbucks locations. The largest stores in cities such as New York and Chicago got a special Starbucks Reserve corner, where a real barista prepared the special coffees. Due to the success of

Starbucks Reserve, Starbucks decided to open its first Starbucks Reserve Roastery in Seattle. These 'coffee theme parks' are heaven for coffee lovers. Coffee beans are roasted on site and transported through transparent tubes to the coffee bars. Each Starbucks Reserve Roastery has its own style, combining industrial with luxury. You can also drink coffee cocktails or buy Starbucks coffee with a whiskey flavor. Starbucks is an experience, and sometimes even more than that. For some people it even replaces the workplace. In addition, for many, Starbucks remains a short stopover for a coffee to go and a quick snack.

The most important thing for Starbucks is that customers do not consider themselves a customer but a kind of family friend. When you place your order, you will first be asked what your name is. They you hear someone shouting 'one latte for Roger'. And then it's 'Roger, your latte is ready'. And when you leave: 'Bye, Roger'. It gives the feeling 'they know me here; they like me'. The feeling of home is further enhanced by the relaxed chairs and the tables littered with newspapers, comic books, and magazines. The free Wi-Fi makes the coffee store the perfect place to work or meet your friends in a homey atmosphere.

Starbucks has become a real status symbol in many countries in Europe. In the Netherlands, for example, you can see that after people have finished their Starbucks cup, they continue to carry their cup for a long time. Starbucks is a strong brand, but something else plays a role in the Netherlands. 'For us, the memory of America is also very much attached to it', according to Dutch communications advisor Marc Pos.

> When you walk into Starbucks, your mind is in New York. Any Dutch person who has been to America remembers his Starbucks visit there. The memory is what makes Starbucks so much fun. You feel like a cosmopolitan, and at the same time it feels familiar.

The Dutch are real coffee drinkers, but much has changed in this country in less than 20 years. The Dutch used to drink a cup from one large pot of coffee, shared with all family members. But now it's all about variation, surprise, and experience. 'There is an evolution in coffee going on', according to the commercial director of Starbucks Netherlands. 'Not so long ago it was "do you want coffee?", now it is "what coffee do you want?" Everyone has their own preferences, their own tastes'. Young shoppers and millennials are looking for variety and surprise. Their expectations regarding coffee flavors, coffee experience, and brands are formed in the out-of-home coffee world. In addition, it also has to be top-quality coffee from the best arabica beans and prepared with real milk. Starbucks is the brand that has not only made coffee trendy, it is certainly the brand that continues to surprise with new flavors and blends.

An important strategic step for Starbucks was its introduction in supermarkets in the years following 2010. From then on, coffee with the Starbucks logo was also available in European supermarkets. This made it possible for consumers to make Starbucks coffee at home. In Europe, the sale of coffee products in supermarkets is the result of a collaboration with the Swiss food giant Nestlé. The whole coffee beans and roasted and ground coffee of Starbucks are combined with capsules (cups) developed with the technologies behind Nespresso and Nescafé Dolce Gusto. These capsules can be used in machines that also make Nespresso and Nescafé coffee.

Starbucks was not afraid that the brand would be perceived as less special by consumers if it were available everywhere. The company sees the arrival of the new products as a reinforcement of the brand. Retail experts agree: 'In a coffee store you experience drinking a cup of Starbucks coffee very differently than at home on the couch. People are willing to pay extra for the Starbucks experience. Coffee is emotion'.

A final development for Starbucks was stimulated by the coronavirus pandemic. Before, almost all sales were in Starbucks stores and retail, but due to COVID-19, delivery boomed. People order Starbucks coffee from their home or workplace, sometimes several times a day. One might think, why order coffee and have it delivered? But Starbucks lovers do because of the unique brand experience.

## The view of a Starbucks general manager

Bas Rietveld is general manager of Starbucks Netherlands. He emphasizes the importance of experience. 'We have a Reserve Bar in our Amsterdam Starbucks location', says Rietveld, pointing to a bar with an immense coffee machine.

> We offer coffees that are not available anywhere else in continental Europe. Single blends, hand roasted, truly unique. Some of our guests have a coffee passport. It lists the unique coffees they have tasted. Very nice, those are the real enthusiasts.

'We always refer to our employees as partners', says Rietveld.

> They are professionals, baristas, they know coffee. They share the coffee experience with our guests. When we have a meeting with each other, at the store or at the head office, we always start with a coffee tasting. All the time. In addition, people are trained several times a year, everything to keep coffee knowledge updated.

According to Rietveld, sustainability is also an important theme. For example, Starbucks stopped serving its Frappuccino in transparent cups in 2023. 'That doesn't seem that much of a strategic challenge, but it is. Our iced coffees are "Instagrammable" in a transparent cup. You see them regularly on social media. So we have to come up with an alternative'.' Reducing the environmental impact of the cups coincides with two other efforts: developing solutions for recyclable cups and dramatically increasing the use of reusable cups by Starbucks customers. Rietveld says: 'For example, we encourage Starbucks customers to use their own reusable mugs or cups for their drinks'.

## Starbucks: mission and core values

www.starbucks.com describes the mission and core values extensively:

From the beginning, Starbucks set out to be a different kind of company. One that not only celebrated coffee but also connection. We're a neighborhood gathering place, a part of your daily routine. Get to know us and you'll see: we are so much more than what we brew. We call our employees partners because we are all partners in shared success. We make sure everything we do is through the lens of humanity – from our commitment to the highest-quality coffee in the world, to the way we engage with our customers and communities to do business responsibly.

**Our Mission**
To inspire and nurture the human spirit – one person, one cup and one neighborhood at a time.

**Our Values**
With our partners, our coffee and our customers at our core, we live these values:

■ Creating a culture of warmth and belonging, where everyone is welcome.
■ Delivering our very best in all we do, holding ourselves accountable for results.
■ Acting with courage, challenging the status quo and finding new ways to grow our company and each other.
■ Being present, connecting with transparency, dignity and respect.

**A culture of inclusion**
We're committed to upholding a culture where inclusion, diversity, equity and accessibility are valued and respected. Your entire experience – starting with your application – is designed to be the beginning of an inspirational journey, where you are treated warmly and with transparency, dignity and respect. We actively hire individuals with disabilities and provide reasonable accommodations and assistive technologies that enable people to do their jobs. Starbucks is committed to offering reasonable accommodation for job applicants with disabilities.

## Corporate social responsibility at Starbucks

Starbucks's commitment is reflected in the actions that Starbucks and coffee farmers around the world are taking to ensure the future of coffee remains sustainable and strong. Starbucks.com lists six examples:

1   Sustainable purchasing and cultivation. Starbucks coffee is 99% ethically sourced, and the company is on a mission to make coffee the world's first

sustainably sourced agricultural product. Starbucks buys coffee verified by C.A.F.E. (Coffee and Farmer Equity Practices). Developed in conjunction with Conservation International, these guidelines provide comprehensive social, environmental, and economic criteria to help sustain and strengthen coffee communities.

2   Open source agronomy. Starbucks Farmer Support Centers in Hacienda Alsacia in Costa Rica and in eight other coffee countries around the world bring together agronomists, researchers, and farmers to make coffee more sustainable and profitable.

3   Climate-resistant coffee trees. Starbucks has donated more than 31 million climate-resilient coffee trees. Farmers, whether they grow coffee for Starbucks or not, can use these trees to replace diseased or old trees. Starbucks aims to supply 100 million trees to farmers by 2025.

4   Loans for farmers. The Starbucks Global Farmer Fund has invested €41 million in coffee-producing countries around the world, funds that farmers can use to renovate and strengthen their farms and farming practices to be even more productive and sustainable.

5   Support in difficult times. Starbucks is using the Farmer Support Centers to share information and supplies during the difficult COVID-19 period. In addition, the Starbucks Foundation donated $1 million to support education, communications, supplies, and materials aimed at helping prevent COVID-19 in coffee, tea, and cocoa farming communities.

6   Invest in a variety of high-quality coffee. Starbucks also sources high-quality coffee grown by smaller coffee growers from a wide variety of places around the world. Female coffee growers also receive special attention.

*Inspired by www.starbucks.com, consulted on September 6, 2022, and the Forbes article 'Why It Took Starbucks 47 Years to Open a Store in Italy', September 13, 2018. The interview quotes with Bas Rietveld are based on an article in Move-On Magazine (www.moveonmagazine.nl/koffie-thuis-laten-deliver-yes-do-that-starbucks-fans) also accessed September 6, 2022.*

## Questions

1   Treacy and Wiersema distinguish three value disciplines.
    a   Which value discipline was chosen by Starbucks? Please explain your answer.
    b   Explain whether the T&W model is fully applicable to Starbucks.

2   Which brand promise is central to Starbucks according to the Brand Benefitting Model? Explain your answer.

3   Create a 'three-dimensional' representation of the market definition for Starbucks at the consumer level.

4   The book distinguishes four levels of competition. Identify potential competitors of Starbucks for each of these levels

5   Assess the mission statement of Starbucks. To what extent does this mission statement fit in with the components and objectives of a mission as defined in the book?
6   The book distinguishes three components of corporate social responsibility. Give examples of each component for Starbucks.
7   The case describes Starbucks's step-by-step transition process. Name the most important changes and indicate which growth strategy from Ansoff's matrix each change corresponds to.

# Chapter 4

# Internal analysis

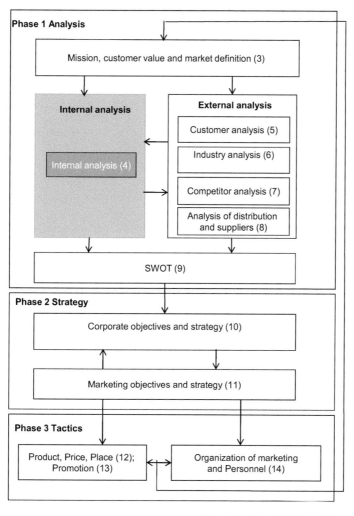

Phase 1 Analysis

Mission, customer value and market definition (3)

**Internal analysis**

Internal analysis (4)

**External analysis**

Customer analysis (5)

Industry analysis (6)

Competitor analysis (7)

Analysis of distribution and suppliers (8)

SWOT (9)

Phase 2 Strategy

Corporate objectives and strategy (10)

Marketing objectives and strategy (11)

Phase 3 Tactics

Product, Price, Place (12); Promotion (13)

Organization of marketing and Personnel (14)

DOI: 10.4324/9781003381488-6

## Key points in this chapter

- Know how to define objectives for a company
- Recognize the importance of sustainability and the trade-off with growth objectives
- Be capable of analyzing a brand's strengths and weaknesses
- Use the customer perspective in the internal analysis

## Introduction

In Chapter 3 we defined the market. Chapters 4 to 8 map out the company's internal and external environment. Within that environment, the analysis of (potential) customers is the most important. Customer wishes can change the fastest and can best be influenced by the company. All other components of the situation analysis generally change less quickly and are much less easily influenced by marketing policy. This applies not only to competitive behavior and industry trends, for example, but also to many internal matters, such as management culture or financial position. In short: many parts of the situation analysis can be regarded as *preconditions* for marketing strategy formation, while customer behavior can best be influenced and offers the most opportunities.

With regard to the order of the elements of the situation analysis, we choose – for practical reasons – to start with the company itself.

Most of the data is available from the company itself. Starting with the company also offers the opportunity to first look back at what has been achieved so far and to see where any problems lie. The external analysis then takes place in Chapters 5 to 8, starting with the most important group: the (potential) customers.

This chapter has two goals: an evaluation of the results so far and an analysis of its own strengths and weaknesses. It is important to determine what makes the company unique. When one's own strengths and weaknesses are compared to those of the competitors, insight is gained into the relative strengths and weaknesses relative to the competition. These relative strengths and weaknesses are compared to the opportunities and threats in Chapter 9.

We start in Section 4.1 with a brief consideration of how objectives should be formulated and what their role is in the planning cycle. The first step is then a reassessment of the company objectives (*balanced scorecard*). This place in the planning process therefore involves a reassessment of the goals; new goals are set after the SWOT. Section 4.2 discusses the application of the balanced scorecard. Section 4.3 outlines a design for an evaluation of the 'other results' (*control*). Sections 4.4 and 4.5 show how the internal analysis can be carried out further, at the company and brand levels, respectively.

## 4.1 Objectives and the PDCA cycle

Goals and planning go hand in hand. We will first explain this on the basis of requirements for goals and the so-called PDCA cycle.

### 4.1.1 Requirements for objectives

Formulating an objective has two functions. First, the objective within the company serves as a guideline for what one wants to achieve. An objective, therefore, has, among other things, a communicative and a motivational function: everyone knows what is being worked towards. A second function of an objective is that the goal is an instrument in the planning process: a goal is a standard for answering the question of whether a strategy is successful. If the objective is achieved, the company can be satisfied (and perhaps continue on the same footing); if the goal is not achieved, the strategy probably needs to be changed.

Based on the aforementioned functions, an objective should meet *five requirements*, summarized in the acronym SMART (originally introduced by Doran, 1981):

1  Specific
2  Measurable
3  Ambitious
4  Realistic
5  Timed

*Specific* means that it must be clear what the objective is about.

*Measurability* means that it can actually be registered whether the objective has been achieved. The objective must therefore be expressed in measurable variables and preferably be quantitative: expressed in numbers. In practice, objectives are often used that are not quantitative, for example, 'achieving a high market share', 'a reasonable profit', 'being able to continuously offer high-quality products', or 'a good working atmosphere'. Although it is not in itself objectionable that a company has such qualitative objectives, it should be realized that they cannot play a role in the planning process. At most, they have a motivating effect, but the question is ultimately whether the management has achieved the goals: for example, is there a good working atmosphere now?

*Ambitious* or challenging means that one should not start from objectives that are too 'low'. Choosing an aspiration level that is too low results in a decrease in motivation to perform.

However, the objective must be *realistic*. It must be reasonably possible to achieve the goal. Although a target such as 'a doubling of the market share in one year' is challenging and ambitious, it is generally not feasible. This then leads to the unnecessary situation that virtually every strategy will fail.

*Timebound* means that an objective must be defined for a specific time period. If this does not happen, then one cannot determine the moment at which it can be verified that the goal has been achieved. If the planning horizon is longer than one year (for example, three years), it is wise to indicate a time frame so that interim evaluations are possible. For example: we want to achieve the following market share development with the new product X over the next three years: 10 % in year 1, 12% in year 2, and finally 14% in year 3.

In summary, therefore, an objective is preferably expressed in numbers, contains a time indication, and is motivating and achievable.

## 4.1.2 The PDCA cycle

Measuring results and therefore data is only meaningful if something is done with it in a meaningful way. Verhoef et al. (2016) state that the analysis of (big) data should always lead to better ways to deliver *customer value* and ultimately to *value for the company*. Measuring outcomes is directly related to goal setting. The so-called PDCA cycle is often cited in this context: Plan, Do, Check, Act (see Figure 4.1)

'Plan' refers to making plans, for example, a marketing or business plan, including measurable objectives. 'Do' is then the actual implementation, for example, the marketing of a new printing technique, including all kinds of related communication. 'Check' is to see whether the objective (e.g. a desired turnover in year 1) has been achieved. And 'Act' refers to adjusting the execution if necessary.

The results evaluation referred to in this section corresponds to the check phase. If a company wants to check whether goals have been achieved, the relevant goals must be measured.

The (continuous) measurement of results is part of *marketing intelligence*. Marketing intelligence means that a company collects and analyzes all information necessary for marketing decisions. Part of this is measuring those variables that play a role in checking outcomes. This then concerns the choice of *metrics*. Metrics are the variables that a company wants to measure quantitatively. The development of metrics receives a lot of attention in marketing science. This is important for companies because metrics can be used for control, such as in the PDCA cycle.

Some companies already do a lot of research and measurements themselves as manufacturers of fast-moving consumer goods (FMCGs). But also in healthcare, everything and anything is measured. Healthcare institutions are also obliged to do so by the government and health insurers. On the other hand, there are companies that measure virtually nothing, for example, many small and medium-sized enterprises that do not (or do not think they have) the time and money for it.

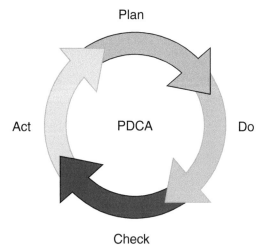

*Figure 4.1* **PDCA cycle**

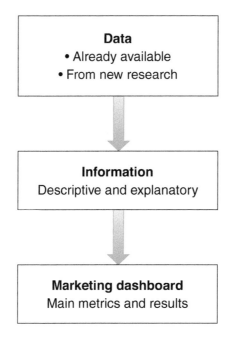

*Figure 4.2* **Purpose of marketing intelligence**

A first step in marketing intelligence is to look at what is already available, for example, the results of customer satisfaction studies, or everything that becomes available online. The second step is to see if more is needed, for example, about the competition or about your own image. The third step is to convert data into *information through analysis*. A distinction can be made between descriptive methods and explanatory methods. Descriptive methods summarize developments and show them in a compact way. Explanatory methods try to establish relationships between developments, for example, differences between young and older consumers or the relationship between image and loyalty. The most important results can be summarized in a 'marketing dashboard', which provides an overview of the most important metrics (variables) and their interpretation. Figure 4.2 summarizes this.

## 4.2 Step 1: application of the balanced scorecard

The method of the balanced scorecard developed by Kaplan and Norton (1992, 1993) can be helpful in choosing goals. This method means that in joint consultation between lower, middle, and higher management, measurable goals are set for four fields – finance, customer satisfaction, efficiency, and innovation:

1   financial goals
2   customer-oriented goals

3    internal and social goals
4    innovation goals

From around 2000, a discussion has started whether, and if so how, goals related to 'sustainability' should be added to these four categories (see, among others, Figge et al., 2002; Kalender & Vayvay, 2016; Hansen & Schaltegger, 2018; Jassem et al., 2022). After a systematic review of relevant literature, the latter concluded that there are two views on the role of sustainability in relation to the BSC:

1    In each of the four fields, separate attention is given to the effect on sustainable goals.
2    There is a fifth pillar needed: sustainable goals.

Some authors believe that sustainability should not be included separately in the BSC. They view sustainability as part of the strategy and argue that the BSC is not a strategy framework. In fact, they say that the 'theory' does not need to be adjusted but that sustainability can play a role from all goals. This view ties in with our view in Chapter 1 and that of Kotler (2011) that (in our case) there is no need to change marketing theory per se but that sustainability can, and perhaps should, play a role in all planning stages. Nevertheless, in the context of making sustainability initiatives visible and stimulating, we consider it justifiable to choose the other perspective, namely to make it visible separately. So, given the enormous importance of sustainability, we add a fifth 'pillar' to the BSC (Figure 4.3): 5 sustainability goals.

## 4.2.1 Financial goals

Almost every company will set financial goals for itself. These goals can be set in terms of profit, gross margin, cash flow, share price, and so on. Some financial measures can be measured in absolute terms, others in relative terms, for example, in relation to turnover (profit margin) or in relation to capital employed (*return on investment*; ROI). For a more extensive treatment of financial indicators, it suffices to note that the literature on this subject can be studied.

Setting financial goals is obvious but at the same time one-sided. Kaplan and Norton state that it is important to also set goals with regard to the building blocks of, for example, profit. Those building blocks include costs and revenues. Revenues, in turn, are influenced by customer perceptions of the quality and degree of innovativeness of the company's products. By also formulating goals with regard to costs, customer-oriented standards, and innovation, according to Kaplan and Norton, a more balanced interpretation of the goals is given.

## 4.2.2 Customer-oriented goals

In addition to financial goals, goals can be set that relate to (potential) customers. Such goals are also called marketing objectives. This includes:

■    'hard' goals such as sales, turnover, and market share
■    more underlying ('softer') goals, such as:

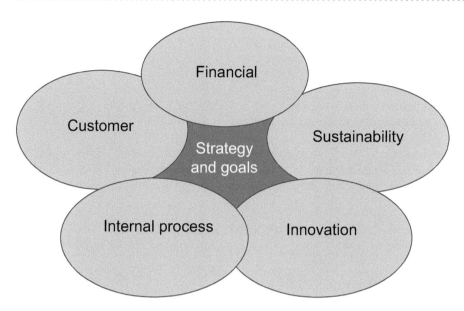

*Figure 4.3* **Sustainability and the balanced scorecard**

- ☐ *customer* satisfaction
- ☐ customer *loyalty* or brand *loyalty*, to be measured on the basis of interviews and/or analysis of data on purchasing *patterns*
- ☐ perceived quality or other image aspects of the brand: 'How does the buyer view his own product and the competing products?'
- ☐ quantity and content of complaints

*Customer satisfaction* and *customer loyalty* are closely related, but they are not the same (Oliver, 1999). The pursuit of customer satisfaction and customer loyalty is currently receiving a lot of attention, which can be explained by the focus on value management. Customer loyalty has two dimensions: a behavioral dimension (measured, for example, as the share of the brand/company in the customer's category purchases: the customer's 'market share') and an emotional dimension (the customer's attitude towards the brand, to be measured via questionnaires).

## 4.2.3 Internal and social goals

Internal and social goals are about internal effective and efficient functioning. The goals here relate to efficiency and personnel. Measures for efficiency are, for example:

- ■ turnover compared to investments
- ■ turnover rate
- ■ debtor term
- ■ liquidity
- ■ overhead costs

Measures for satisfaction of staff are:

- working atmosphere and morale
- personal development
- employee turnover
- sick leave
- turnover per employee

The personnel-oriented goals have everything to do with the P of People and its 'sustainability': social goals, in other words. Dealing well with personnel is essential, also in order to be able to attract new personnel to the labor market (see Case 4.1). For

## Case 4.1 The importance of good personnel management

### The millennial

It seems more and more that young people in 2023 want a different work balance than generations before them. Private life and sufficient freedom are considered essential. That, together with the emergence of major staff shortages after the coronavirus in 2022, makes the importance of being an attractive employer even more important. For all these reasons, you increasingly see employers making provisions for staff to be able to relax sufficiently in between. Ping-pong tables at work are typical facilities for millennials, it is said.

that reason, following Kalender and Vayvay (2016), we have supplemented the designation 'internal goals' with 'social'.

### 4.2.4 Innovation goals

Innovation is the basis of success. Only companies that regularly introduce new products are relatively successful. The extent to which the company learns from past experiences also plays a role here. Measures for this are, for example, the percentage of successful product introductions, the turnover from new products, or the number of concrete new product plans in progress.

### 4.2.5 Sustainability goals

Every organization will have to deal with the climate. We have already mentioned the good example of Unilever. As stated, we choose to make sustainability goals visible separately. Elaboration into criteria can be emissions, waste, use of materials, and so on (Figge et al., 2002).

Figure 4.4 shows a elaboration of the BSC. The vision formulates long-term goals for financial growth, customer satisfaction, costs, sustainability, and innovation. If top management considers driving customer focus and brand building important and also recognizes that this entails additional investments, the financial goals can be set somewhat lower and the customer-oriented goals higher. The long-term goals are then made more concrete for the short term. For example, 'strong improvement in customer satisfaction' is translated into 'improvement of brand image', 'increase in frequency of use', and 'increase in customer satisfaction'. Subsequently, each of these factors is described as how it is measured. For example, improvement of the brand image is measured by the percentage of people in the target group who associate the brand with the identity characteristic 'cheeky'. Sustainability can be measured by $CO_2$ emission. Finally, the numerical goals themselves are indicated. The latter takes place in consultation with top management and middle management, with the goals being assigned to specific managers.

The BSC has the advantage of a comprehensive planning and control process. Formulating joint measurable goals can also strengthen team spirit, but that depends on how the goals were achieved. If this is done top-down, this is unlikely to lead to an increase in motivation and team spirit. If it can be embedded in a process that actually leaves responsibilities to lower management, it can be helpful.

### 4.2.6 Economy versus sustainability

Especially with the addition of sustainability goals, it is clear that there is an interdependence between the five types of goals. We are referring in particular to the tension between economic and sustainability goals. The tendency of many managers is to want to grow economically. Given the sustainability challenges mentioned, the question is whether this is still wise. Case 4.2 elaborates on this further.

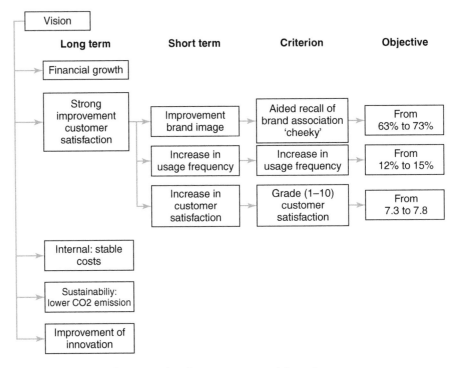

*Figure 4.4* Balanced scorecard with customer part elaboration

## 4.3 Step 2: evaluation of the results

In the evaluation of results, we are talking about analysis of quantitative data ('data'). The first step has been outlined for this: a review of the five main objectives. But there is a lot more data, and, as we mentioned earlier, more and more data is coming. That is why we take a closer look at measures of customer-oriented variables (Section 4.2.2).

Two types of customer-oriented data can be distinguished:

■ own collected data from research by means of, for example, questionnaires or registration of purchases
■ data on customer online behavior, such as search and information behavior, but also purchasing behavior and after-sales behavior such as expressions of (dis)satisfaction

We now focus on the first category. Additional online analyses are discussed in the next chapter.

Each organization measures its own sales and turnover. These are examples of customer-oriented variables. In many cases the analysis of this data can go deeper. The level of detail in the analysis of customer data depends on the availability of data.

## Case 4.2 To grow or not to grow: that is the question

### Is Black Friday still relevant today?

*Black Friday:* consumers can buy all kinds of things at special prices, very handy also during the holidays. A great opportunity for an entrepreneur to get some extra turnover, right?

Black Friday comes from the United States and has now grown into a *Black Friday week* (Amazon) or in some cases two weeks. Yet some entrepreneurs do not participate.

IKEA does something different: *Bring Back Friday*: to make it more sustainable, you can bring your second-hand furniture to IKEA and get money in return. And retailer Dille & Kamille started in 2018 together with Trees for All Green Friday and in 2022, on the same 'Black' November 25, 2022, they even closed completely, and staff did volunteer work! These companies realize that they can benefit from these great promotions in the longer term because their reputation, read: their brand, is strengthened, justly, because in this time of environmental degradation, it is becoming increasingly clear that things can only be saved if we no longer assume 'growth, growth, growth' and therefore also 'buy, buy, buy'. For an entrepreneur, the message is clear: think about your long-term brand reputation. Fair and sustainable are the future. In this way, as entrepreneurs, we may teach our customers, read: 'the people', that things can be done differently.

Most of the data is available for food markets (Nielsen, IRI, and GfK retail panels). We first discuss analyses that may be performed with this data. We then conclude with a few remarks on industries other than those of daily consumer goods (fast-moving consumers goods).

For the food markets, the following sales developments may be analyzed:

1   market developments: sales developments for the total market and market segments (varieties)
2   manufacturer's brands:
   a   developments per brand in total and by packaging units
   b   regional differences in brand developments
3   competitors:
   a   identify biggest competitors
   b   developments and sales of competing manufacturers
4   position of manufacturers' brands and competitors in the various retail organizations plus development over time (sales and distribution analyses)
5   sales developments at retailers with and without promotions (provides indicative insight into the effects of promotions)

If the company also has data from household panels (GfK) or customer sales figures from its own databases, sales analyses can also be carried out that are broken down into target groups. Such detailed analyses are necessary because it is difficult to identify causes from aggregated figures. For example, a slight increase in sales may seem like a good result, but this may be the result of strong growth in region A and a stabilization or even a decline in region B. This then leads to the conclusion that there are problems in region B, for example, a disappointing distribution.

An accurate analysis of the market share can also give indications of problems (Hulbert & Toy, 1977). Is there a decrease or an increase? Incidentally, the market definition is crucial in a market share analysis (see Section 3.3). With a smaller market, the share automatically becomes larger. An instrument that can be helpful in the market share analysis is the *Parfitt & Collins analysis*. The market share of a brand is split into (the product of) three components:

1   *Degree of penetration*. This is the percentage of households that have ever bought the product.
2   *The percentage of repeat purchases*: The extent to which the same brand is bought again after purchasing a brand.
3   *The usage intensity index*. This is the degree to which buyers of the brand use more or less of the relevant product group.

For example, if these three components assume the values 10% (penetration), 40% (repeat purchases), and 1.5% (consumption), the market share will be 6%. The development of these individual components provides a better insight into potential problems than does the progress of the market share as a whole.

The Parfitt & Collins analysis is often used in combination with awareness measures. The following indicators are then relevant:

1 *Awareness* (spontaneous or assisted): percentage of people who know the brand
2 *Consideration set*: percentage of people who are considering the brand
3 *Trial*: percentage of trial purchases
4 *Repeat*: percentage of repeat purchases

For online analysis, variants are often devised such as: 'awareness, engagement, conversion, loyalty'. This is in fact the same.

The size of the various percentages, and in particular the differences between them, are an important starting point when formulating market instrument objectives. This leads to low awareness and a (relatively) high *trial*, concluding that communication should be intensified. A low *trial* may be related to too high a price or too limited distribution. A low *repeat* has more to do with the performance of the product itself.

Accurate analyses are also possible in other industries, although they are less detailed. The main data limitation outside FMCG markets is that data is often not collected centrally and therefore no (hard) sales data from competitors is available. But every company can register its own sales in detail and also have customer research carried out (by research agencies). It is important to ensure that the registration of results takes place over a long period of time and consistently. As long as market shares are not used, but with their own sales data or customer satisfaction measurements, many organizations can measure and analyze results in detail.

## 4.4 Step 3: internal analysis at company level

Various models are available that are helpful in the strength-weakness analysis. Figure 4.5 contains an overview. In this section we discuss the methods at the corporate level. We will not yet discuss portfolio analysis here: it is so closely linked to corporate strategy that we will discuss it in Chapter 10. The brand level is discussed in Section 4.5.

| Method | Source of data | Result |
|---|---|---|
| *Company level* | | |
| Customer Values | Management | Main direction of competitive advantage |
| Checklist functional areas | Management | Judgment per functional area |
| Marketing audit | Management | Marketing orientation |
| Portfolio Analysis (Chapter 10) | Management | Overview and strength current activities |
| *Brand level* | | |
| Customer perception research | Customers | Customizable judgments |
| Four or five Ps | Customers | Judge (functional) brand performance |
| Checklist brand values and brand personality | Management or customers | Scores brand values or brand personality traits |

*Figure 4.5* **Methods for the internal analysis**

| Brand benefit | Current level | Desired level |
|---|---|---|
| Quality | 6 | 7 |
| Service | 7 | 8 |
| Price | 6 | 6 |
| Convenience | 7 | 7 |
| Sustainability | 4 | 6 |
| Emotion | 7 | 8 |

*Figure 4.6* Possible outcome of a management discussion about the current and desired brand benefits

### 4.4.1 Brand benefits as an analysis model

In the previous chapter, we discussed customer values. Managers can give themselves marks for each of the brand benefits and then indicate the desired improvements in the strategic choices. Figure 4.6 contains an example of the outcome of a management discussion based on the Brand Benefitting Model ('brand benefits'). This can be very helpful in discussions about the brand positioning.

### 4.4.2 Management's assessment of functional areas

At the company level, strengths relate especially to functional areas. The core skills of a company are often referred to as *core competencies* (Prahalad & Hamel, 1990). A checklist can be used to analyze strengths and weaknesses at the company level. Figure 4.7 provides a more specific checklist. This list concerns possible strengths and weaknesses of the various functional areas in a company:

■ *innovation*: technological skills, R&D expenditure, patents, and so on; also the eco-logical footprint can be seen as part of innovation
■ *production*: added value, capacity, and so on
■ *financing* options: short term, long term, possibility to finance from the parent company, and so on
■ *management and organization*: quality of (top) management, organizational struc-ture, corporate culture, and so on
■ *personnel*: motivation and customer focus
■ *marketing*: staff customer focus, product quality, digital maturity, online presence, strength of advertising (agency), and so on

The strengths and weaknesses mentioned in Figure 4.7 are not independent of one another. For example, the attitude and motivation of the staff strongly depend on the

## Innovation

- Technical product superiority
- Ecological footprint
- New product capabilities
- Research & development
- Technologies
- Patents
- Digital maturity

## Production

- Cost structure
- Flexibility in production
- Means of production (machinery, etc.)
- Access to raw materials
- Vertical integration
- Production capacity

## Financing options

- From the operational activities
- From resources available in the short term
- Opportunities for raising equity and loan capital
- Willingness of the parent company to finance

## Management and organization

- Quality of top and middle management
- Leadership
- Knowledge of the market
- Company culture
- Organizational structure
- Strategic objectives and plans
- Entrepreneurial qualities
- Planning system
- Staff turnover
- Quality of strategic decision making

*Figure 4.7* **Possible strengths and weaknesses (sources of benefits) at the corporate level**
Source: Based on Aaker (2013)

---

## Staff

■ Staff attitude and motivation
■ Customer orientation

## Marketing

■ Product quality
■ Width of the product line
■ Segmentation
■ Distribution
■ Relationship with distributors
■ Quality of sales promotion
■ Digital marketing
■ Representatives
■ Services

---

***Figure 4.7* (Continued)**

quality of top management and the organizational structure, while the same motivation in turn influences the creativity and innovative capacity of the company.

With regard to the analysis of the financial position of the product and the company, we note that the (known) financial ratios can be calculated and analyzed. These relate to:

■ *liquidity:* the extent to which a company can meet its current financial obligations, measured, for example, by the current ratio (current assets/current liabilities)
■ *the financial structure (solvency):* to be measured, for example, by the debt ratio (loan capital/total invested capital)
■ *the activities:* for example, the turnover rate of the stock (turnover/stock) and the *average credit term* of creditors (average amount due/turnover × 365 days)
■ *profitability:* to be measured, for example, by the gross or net profit margin or the return on equity (net profit/equity)

Another model often used for firm-level strength-weakness analysis is McKinsey's rather elaborate *7S model*, which consists of:

■ shared values
■ strategy
■ structure
■ systems
■ staff
■ style of management
■ key skills

### 4.4.3 Marketing audit

Measuring the quality of the marketing (department) is the subject of a marketing audit. A *marketing audit* is an independent review of all marketing activities in the company or in the SBU. This concerns:

- An evaluation of the extent to which a company operates in a market-oriented way:
  - ☐ Are there clearly formulated objectives and strategies?
  - ☐ Do the objectives and strategies explicitly take environmental factors into account?
  - ☐ Do the strategies actually match the environmental factors?
  - ☐ How do customers view the company and its products?
  - ☐ And so on.
- The knowledge that a company has of the environment:
  - ☐ What is known about macro-environmental developments, industry structure factors, competitors, and customers?
  - ☐ And so on.
- The analysis that the company has made of the environment:
  - ☐ Is market research being carried out?
  - ☐ Are predictions made?
  - ☐ Does a strategy evaluation take place regularly?
  - ☐ Is there a marketing information system?
  - ☐ Is big data used?

A checklist must be used to carry out a marketing audit. Figure 4.8 shows such a checklist developed by Kotler (see, for example, McDonald, 1995; Kotler & Keller, 2016). This checklist contains 15 questions with a maximum score of two points for each question.

#### Customer vision

1 Does management consider it important to organize the company in such a way that customer needs are properly met?
2 Does the company develop different products and marketing plans for different segments?
3 Does the company consider marketing important throughout the organization?

#### Integrated marketing organization

4 Is marketing coordinated and directed high up in the organization?
5 Does marketing work well with research, production, purchasing, logistics and financing?
6 How well is new product development organized?

*Figure 4.8* **Marketing effectiveness review instrument**

## Adequate marketing information

7    When were the latest market research studies, environmental analyses, distribution analyzes and competitive analyzes carried out?
8    How well informed is the company about the potential profitability of segments, customers, territories, products, channels and sales orders?
9    What efforts are being made to measure and improve the cost-effectiveness of marketing?

## Strategic orientation

10   To what extent is formal marketing planning done?
11   How clear and innovative is the current marketing strategy?
12   To what extent are setbacks and scenarios taken into account in the planning?

## Operational efficiency

13   How well is the marketing strategy communicated and executed?
14   Does management effectively use the marketing tools?
15   Does management show that it responds quickly and decisively to new developments?

**Figure 4.8 (Continued)**

The total number of points is a measure of the effectiveness of marketing in the company. It is also assumed that each item has the same weight.

Digital aspects could be added for various aspects to the somewhat outdated instrument in Figure 4.8. For example, with marketing information: 'To what extent does the company use digital analyses/big data?' And with strategic orientation: 'How digital is the marketing strategy developed?'

# 4.5 Step 4: internal analysis at brand level

The methods described previously provide insights at the company level. It is also essential to assess the strengths and weaknesses at brand level. Insight into strengths and weaknesses at the brand level is largely obtained by a manager from the customer analysis. It is about knowing how the customer views the brand (*attitudes*). In the context of value thinking, it is relevant to use a customer perspective in the strengths-weaknesses analysis. What the customer thinks is the truth the manager is dealing with. The performance of customer analyses is discussed in Chapter 5. Various methods are provided there that are helpful, in particular for measurements of perceptions. Perceptions or associations determine the brand image, and brand associations should be strong, unique and relevant.

Checklists can be used when measuring customer perceptions, for example, the Brand Benefitting Model. Another simple model that can be used is one that measures performance around the marketing instruments. It is then advisable to add the P for personnel as the fifth. The market instruments in themselves say little about how

| Marketing instrument | Benchmark |
|---|---|
| Product | Quality |
| Price | Price perception, 'value' |
| Place (channels, locations) | Availability, findability |
| Communication | Communication style, clarity, attitude towards ads |
| Staff | Expertise, customer focus, service |

*Figure 4.9* Measuring the functional brand strengths

customers perceive them. That is why we translate them into customer-oriented measures (Figure 4.9).

The 5P model emphasizes the functional properties of a brand. But brands also have emotional properties. A distinction can be made between personality characteristics (such as a masculine brand) and end values (such as freedom). In this book we discuss various models that can be used for this, such as:

- the means-end chain of meanings (Chapter 5)
- Jennifer Aaker's Brand Personality Scale (Chapter 11)
- the Value Compass (Chapter 11)

It is therefore important for a manager who performs an internal analysis not only to determine what the functional core competencies are but also to determine the emotional characteristics. As a result of the internal analysis, it must be clear, among other things, what the DNA of the company or brand is.

## Summary

An internal analysis aims to evaluate the results and to make a strength-weakness analysis. There are four steps:

1   During the evaluation, an inventory is made of which objectives are available at the various levels and whether the objectives set have been achieved. The principle of the balanced scorecard says that in addition to financial goals, other – underlying – goals should also be measured and reassessed: measures of innovation, customer satisfaction, and social and societal goals.
2   Subsequently, the customer-oriented standards in particular are subjected to a detailed analysis in order to gain insight into any problem areas.
3   Strengths and weaknesses are examined at organizational and brand level. At the organizational level, strengths or weaknesses can be identified through self-assessment of strengths and weaknesses in the different functional areas and by conducting a marketing audit that also considers digital skills.
4   At the brand level, both functional and emotional strengths should be considered, examining the entire palette of brand attributes. In practice, knowledge of customer perceptions will also form the basis of an internal analysis.

## How Wal-Mart found its footing in the Amazon era

This is not a story about rebranding. Although the US's largest retailer has evolved its marketing, product mix, private-label offerings, agency and vendor relationships, strategy, and more, Wal-Mart insists that there's no fundamental change in how the company operates. 'As business and technology advance and customer habits continue to change, it requires any brand to pause and refresh or redefine as necessary', according to Wal-Mart's management.

That adaptability has helped Wal-Mart reverse the streak of sales declines that marked 2013 and 2014. Today, despite hiccups during the COVID-19 period, the company boasts continuous sales growth. To survive the retail carnage that pushed Sears and Kmart toward irrelevance and dragged down success stories like Target and Kroger, the $485-billion giant remade itself as a unified online-offline proposition. It has rolled out drive-thru pickup of grocery orders and has installed automated kiosks where people can collect orders inside. It's using technology more smartly to maximize checkout orders at walmart.com. For customers who shop in person, the chain has improved its quality with revamped produce sections and higher-end exclusive or private-label apparel, food, and nonfood items.

But through all of this, Wal-Mart hasn't lost sight of its signature low-price proposition. Although the old slogan 'everyday low prices' has been transformed into 'We don't just save you money, we allow you to live better', the slogan is the fundamental tenet of a cult masquerading as a company. Over the years, Wal-Mart has relentlessly wrung tens of billions of dollars in cost efficiencies out of the retail supply chain, passing the larger part of the savings along to shoppers as bargain prices. In the United States, wherever Wal-Mart competes, average grocery prices are 14% lower than elsewhere.

Needless to say that part of these savings have also been realized by continuous pressure on the already low wages for Wal-Mart sales clerks. Wal-Mart's huge advantages in buying power and efficiency force many rivals to close. For every Wal-Mart supercenter that opens, two other supermarkets will close. As the number of supermarkets shrinks, more shoppers will have to travel farther from home. Meanwhile, the failure of hundreds of stores will cost their owners dearly and put thousands out of work, only some of whom will find jobs at Wal-Mart. Most likely at lower pay: Wal-Mart is blamed sometimes for the sorry state of retail wages in America. On average, Wal-Mart sales clerks – 'associates' in Wal-Mart terminology – earn an average of around $13.90 an hour, or around $28,000 a year. As a comparison, the federal poverty line for a family of four in 2022 was $27,750.

The low-cost strategy is obvious, but what might most separate it from its competitors is that Wal-Mart knows change is expensive, and sometimes you have to lose money to make it. Wal-Mart management recognizes that the big retailers of the past made decisions to preserve the models they created. Wal-Mart has decided it wants to be a retailer for the long haul, even if that means being a little suboptimal in its returns. Wal-Mart is [also] willing to invest in a new business model, even one that it's kind of bad at and will take them 'a while to get good at'.

## Save money. Live better

Wal-Mart's vaunted lower prices have made life harder for such rivals as Target, Kroger and Dollar General, even if the primary intended targets were Amazon and hard discounters like Aldi and Lidl. A Wal-Mart marketing manager once emphasized this point as: 'None of our marketing efforts matter unless we have price leadership. We're always maniacal about not letting people get distracted from price'.

But price is a game no retailer wins all the time. Avoiding the fate of failed retailers rests at least as heavily on delivering the second half of Wal-Mart's slogan, 'Save Money. Live Better', with a bigger focus on convenience and quality. Nowadays, it's not only price. Over the past years, convenience is increasingly becoming a driver for consumer behavior. That's partially based on expectations raised by online shopping and other digital services. But the demand for more shopping convenience also stems from sobering factors specific to the United States: both parents working in 60% of two-parent households, people working an average of five hours longer a month than a few years ago, and people tethered to work via smartphones, which put them in contact with their jobs on average 13.5 hours a day, or, as the marketing manager puts it, 'nearly all their waking hours'.

Wal-Mart reaches every demographic in the United States, but to win on convenience, the retailer is focusing more on a segment it calls 'busy families'. They're the most intense combination of being busy and money challenged. Busy families have the highest bar in terms of delivering on price, quality, and convenience.

Wal-Mart believes that if they can deliver on this segment, they can probably deliver on everybody.

This group is a little higher income than Wal-Mart defined their customers in the past. But that doesn't mean Wal-Mart is going upscale as much as it's targeting a segment that's more suburban and multicultural than its prior core.

'They've found the right balance between promotion and everyday low price', according to a consultant. The company has removed some of the clutter of bargain-bin store-floor displays, for example, but hasn't done away with them entirely. Most shoppers give Wal-Mart credit for having the lowest prices most of the time, the consultant says – or at least being close enough that it's not worth the effort to shop around.

In combination with the emphasis on convenience, the company also gives more significance to the store experience. So there is a focus on making sure checkout lines aren't longer than three deep and generally keeping the store experience 'clean, fast and friendly'. Wal-Mart has improved customer satisfaction as a result, according to its own measures and external sources such as the American Customer Satisfaction Index, which tracked a major lift this year.

Add to clean-fast-friendly the three-legged stool of price-convenience-quality. Winning on those last three is key for Wal-Mart to succeed across the biggest customer base in America. Just based on trading area, Wal-Mart skews a lot more Middle American or red state than its more coastal, blue-state competitors Amazon and Costco. But Wal-Mart's demographics look pretty much the same as America's. According to Wal-Mart, there are three very different groups of shoppers who are particularly interested in Wal-Mart's defining proposition of saving money:

- people living paycheck to paycheck
- people scrimping on basics to pay for high-end purchases such as iPhones
- well-off consumers who got that way in part by frugality

## Linking online and offline

Amazon is on track to pass Wal-Mart as the biggest US retailer: between 2021 and 2026, Amazon stands to grow its US retail market share from 10.8% to 14.9%, whereas Wal-Mart's share will shrink from 13.2% to 12.7%. But Wal-Mart's e-commerce is growing as well.

Winning in e-commerce is crucial for all segments of shoppers, who all want convenience. To try to buttress an online presence still dwarfed by Amazon, Wal-Mart has enlisted its huge portfolio of stores. Wal-Mart finally appears to be breaking through in making 'bricks and clicks' work together in a way that meaningfully affects online sales growth. Free two-day delivery on millions of items without an Amazon Prime-like annual fee was one key to sparking a surge in e-commerce sales. Discounts for store delivery on nearly a million items are also helping. And the chain put advertising weight usually reserved for the brick-and-mortar stores behind the online sales efforts.

Wal-Mart is also using tech to tweak its pricing strategy. Under Wal-Mart former e-commerce chief Marc Lore, who was CEO of online retailer Jet.com before Wal-Mart acquired it in September 2016, the retailer started experimenting with bringing Jet's more complex pricing model, which bestows steeper discounts on larger orders. Shoppers might get a lower price on Wal-Mart.com, for example, by adding baby wipes to a basket that includes diapers.

The whole variety of inducements looks to be working, with a stimulating effect on Wal-Mart's online presence.

## Mixing up the product mix

With rivals like Aldi, Lidl, and Costco competing largely based on their private-label programs, Wal-Mart is putting more resources into its own brands, too, and not just the lowest-cost tiers but also higher-end products.

Consequently, Wal-Mart sells private-label products aimed not just at the biggest mass brands but also emerging players such as L'Oréal USA's Matrix salon brand. 'Aspirational products at disruptive prices' was how Wal-Mart described its product development effort. This includes some Wal-Mart 'exclusives', such as a Keurig K-Cup coffee maker hitting stores now priced at $59 – $30 or more below prices elsewhere – and Yankee Candles priced around $10 less than they sell for elsewhere.

As an example, Wal-Mart has significantly staffed up development for its own baby-care brands, focusing on everything from pouch meals to baby wipes and strollers, with products priced 25% to 50% below branded rivals. Winning in packaged goods is key to winning online and offline with those 'busy families'. And families with newborns are among the busiest. They eat at home more and buy more of just about everything as they establish households. 'Wal-Mart.com was built on big-ticket purchases like TVs', according to a Wal-Mart official 'What's happening now is a much more balanced approach where consumables play a much bigger role in customer acquisition'.

## Everyday low supplier pricing?

While Wal-Mart has seldom hesitated to throw its weight around to get better prices, it's starting to use its power in new ways. One example was in what appears to be a first for the retail industry: Wal-Mart recently conducted a review to streamline the army of third-party field merchandisers that help place displays and products in its stores, culling the firms involved to 5 from more than 30. It was an audacious move because outside marketers, such as P&G and Unilever, pay the firms for their efforts, not Wal-Mart. But Wal-Mart was able to engineer a roster that made the process more efficient in its stores, a spokesman says. It also ensured that each supplier had an in-store marketing force dedicated specifically to the chain. The expectation is that the resulting supply-chain savings get passed back to Wal-Mart.

But it also meant forcing big suppliers like Unilever to switch vendors. 'Right now they're in a fairly enviable position in that they're indispensable for shoppers and suppliers', according to Wal-Mart. 'Suppliers may not be happy with how they do business in every case, but they can't walk away. '

Wal-Mart acknowledges that the efforts to get more efficient may mean some added tension with suppliers. Then again, suppliers have plenty of grumbles about other retailers.

## Wal-Mart as startup

Even as Wal-Mart wields its bigness in new ways, it's playing with small flanker brands in e-commerce. Counting Jet.com, it has acquired a number of small e-commerce players whose customers often weren't big on Wal-Mart, including Hayneedle, Shoebuy, ModCloth, Moosejaw, and Bonobos.

Perhaps one true sign of a shift is that Wal-Mart says it's not imposing itself on these brands. Wal-Mart describes this approach to the newly acquired online retailers this way: 'Imagine if you get purchased by the world's largest company and you have access to those resources, and yet they aren't really going to change you. All they want is for you to be better versions of yourselves'.'

Whatever you call it – reinvention or something else – Wal-Mart is 'not going down the path of generational decline like Sears and Kmart', as the marketing manager of Wal-Mart puts it. But that doesn't mean that the work is done.

## Questions

1   Which brand promise (Brand Benefitting Model) has been chosen by Wal-Mart?
2   'The second-worst thing a manufacturer can do is sign a contract with Wal-Mart. The worst? Not sign one'. Explain this expression.
3   a   Use the information in the case to identify strengths and weaknesses for Wal-Mart.
    b   Use your analysis of strengths and weaknesses to determine the DNA of Wal-Mart.
4   Illustrate with an example how Wal-Mart could use big data to finetune its operations.
5   Create a means-end chain for Wal-Mart by using the information in the case.
6   What is the relation between key success factors and the competitive advantage of an organization? Illustrate this relation for Wal-Mart.
7   Define objectives for Wal-Mart. Use the balanced scorecard. Use the information from the case, but make your own assumptions wherever necessary.
8   According to marketing theory, a strategy can only be developed after an extensive situation analysis. But some organizations seem to focus initially on their own core competencies, without adapting the strategy to the (external) environment. Which choice did Wal-Mart make here? Explain briefly.

# Chapter 5

# Customer analysis

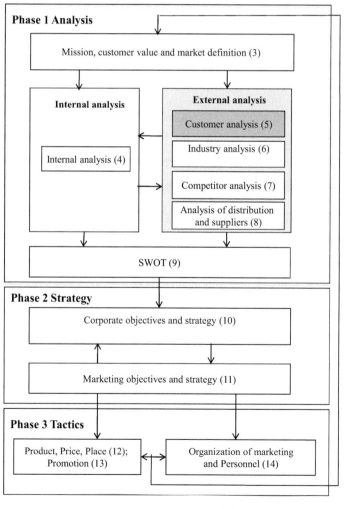

**Phase 1 Analysis**

Mission, customer value and market definition (3)

**Internal analysis**

Internal analysis (4)

**External analysis**

Customer analysis (5)

Industry analysis (6)

Competitor analysis (7)

Analysis of distribution and suppliers (8)

SWOT (9)

**Phase 2 Strategy**

Corporate objectives and strategy (10)

Marketing objectives and strategy (11)

**Phase 3 Tactics**

Product, Price, Place (12); Promotion (13)

Organization of marketing and Personnel (14)

DOI: 10.4324/9781003381488-7

## Key points in this chapter

- Be able to apply segmentation based on data
- Know the most important consumer behavior models
- Know how to measure needs and perceptions of customers
- Know how to measure brand image
- Be able to deal with primary and secondary sources of customer data

# Introduction

Marketing is about customers and brands. That is why we start the external analysis with an analysis of the (potential) customers and the brand image. In this chapter we refer to customer analysis as an indication for any form of research in which information is collected from (potential) customers. This is also referred to as market research, which is not only quantitative (often questionnaires) but can also be qualitative.

Section 5.1 outlines the goals of a customer analysis. Section 5.2 then discusses segmentation. In Section 5.3, we discuss some (simple) models of customer values. Sections 5.4 and 5.5 are devoted to research into customer wishes and perceptions, respectively. Section 5.6 specifically discusses measuring brand strength. In Section 5.7, we discuss individual customer data that has become increasingly available as a result of digital developments. Section 5.8 provides some basic guidelines for primary research, broken down into qualitative and quantitative research.

# 5.1 Goals of the customer analysis

An important common thread in this book is the starting point that in practice a company must strive for customer satisfaction and for the alignment of the brand identity and brand image. The question, then, is how a brand can achieve this. To find out, it is essential to 'talk' to those customers. What do they want (wants) and what do they think of you (perceptions)? This chapter provides a further structure for a so-called customer analysis.

We already note that a customer analysis is not the only source for insight into customer wishes. The biggest problem with market research is that it is difficult for people to indicate what they would like (in the future). Future needs are usually underestimated by people. Therefore, data from a buyer analysis cannot always be used as direct or sole guidance for trading but must be interpreted and then combined with other sources. With this caveat in mind, we now move on to what can be called the most important phase in the situation analysis.

Customer research can be used for various purposes. Malhotra et al. (2017) distinguish between three methods of research:

- *explorative*: qualitative research
- *descriptive*: quantitative research (survey and observation)
- *causal/explanatory*: quantitative research supplemented with
  - □ experiments and/or
  - □ statistical correlation study

This classification is clear but does not yet establish a relationship with the required data.

Ferrell and Hartline (2010) classify the customer analysis according to the *six Ws*:

1 Who are our current and potential customers?
2 What do our customers do with our products (including use situations)?
3 Where do our customers purchase our products?
4 When do our customers purchase our products?
5 Why (and how) do our customers choose our products (including perceptions of brands/products and needs)?
6 Why do potential customers not purchase our products?

Although Ferell and Hartline's classification can be used very well, it has the limitation that no distinction is made between the different (strategic) goals of the customer analysis. A customer analysis itself actually has different use situations, where different information has to be collected in one situation than in another. In our view, there are four use cases or goals of the buyer analysis:

1 use for segmentation and target group selection (Chapter 11)
2 use as a basis for strengths-weaknesses research (Chapter 4) and brand positioning decisions (Chapter 11)
3 use for checking results achieved (Chapter 4) and measuring the effect of market instruments (Chapter 13)
4 use in competitor identification (Chapter 7)

| Goal of customer analysis: information for the benefit of | Required data from primary research | Type of research | Research discussed in |
|---|---|---|---|
| 1 Segmentation and target group selection | Who, what, where, when, why? | Quantitative | Section 5.2 |
| 2 Positioning and strengths and weaknesses | Value hierarchy and customer satisfaction: why, why not? | Qualitative and quantitative | Section 5.3 |
| 3 Results analysis (control) and effect study | Why, why not: brand awareness, brand associations, customer satisfaction, among others | Quantitative | Section 5.3 and 13.10 |
| 4 Competitive analysis | Who, what, why, why not: chosen brand and competitors | Quantitative | Section 7.2 |

*Figure 5.1* Goals of the customer analysis

Each of these goals requires specific information (division by questions) and a specific research approach (division by research method). Figure 5.1 summarizes this. The first three of these goals are discussed in detail in this chapter.

## 5.2 Segmentation research

### 5.2.1 Requirements for segments

A segment means: a group of (potential) customers. Segmentation research ties into the first dimension of marketing strategy: the choice of target audience (*targeting*). In this context, the STP trilogy is often referred to: *segmenting, targeting, positioning*. Segmentation is research. *Targeting* (and positioning) is strategy and therefore making choices (see Chapter 11).

The core idea of segmentation is that people often have different needs and that it is more profitable to approach people differently with your marketing (for example, with different products) instead of everyone in the same way.

A group of customers can be considered a segment if the following *segmentation requirements* are met:

1   *Homogeneity/heterogeneity*. Within a segment, the response to a marketing activity should be as homogeneous as possible and between segments as heterogeneous as possible.
2   *Sufficient size*. Segments that are so small that profitable operation is impossible do not make sense.
3   *Measurable/identifiable*. It must be possible to identify the customers in segments in some way so that results and strategies can be linked to concretely described segments. Moreover, without identification, it is difficult to estimate the size of the segment.
4   *Accessible*. To use market instruments, in particular distribution and communication instruments, it is necessary to be able to reach the segment.

Only quantitative research can provide insight into these conditions. This type of research entails collecting a large amount of data from a large number of people and then attempting to identify groups of consumers that meet these requirements (segments).

### 5.2.2 Steps and methods

A segmentation analysis is divided into three phases:

1   Collecting of the data
2   Analysis of the data
3   Description of the segments (personas)

#### 1 Collecting the data

First, by means of, for example, in-depth interviews and group discussions with customers, attempts are made to gain as much insight as possible into the motivations, attitudes, and behavior of the customers. This knowledge is used to draw up a questionnaire that is administered to a large group of customers. For consumer markets, data must be collected on three categories of segmentation variables: *personal* variables, *category-specific* variables, and brand-related variables (see Figure 5.2). The last two collectively become *behavioral* variables because these variables relate to consumer behavior. Part of the category-related variables is the *customer journey*, both offline and online. Figure 5.3 contains an overview of segmentation variables for business markets (industrial markets).

The data mentioned in Figures 5.2 and 5.3 can be considered the minimum background data collected from target groups.

## 2 Analysis of the data

Segments must be distilled from the collected data. In principle, the following paths can be followed (see Figure 5.4):

■ *Forward segmentation*, also known as *a priori segmentation*. The buyers are classified on the basis of general characteristics (for consumer markets, the

| Category | Subcategory | Variables |
|---|---|---|
| A  Personal (customer characteristics) | 1  Geographically | • Region/province/zip code area<br>• Urbanization degree |
| | 2  Demographic and socio-economic | • Age<br>• Gender<br>• Family phase<br>• Family size<br>• Income<br>• Occupation<br>• Education<br>• Welfare class |
| | 3  Psychographic | • Lifestyle<br>• (Final) values<br>• Personality |
| B  Product (category) | 1  Benefits | • Importance of product properties (relevance associations) |
| | 2  Buying behavior (customer journey) | • Role in decision process (Initiator, Influencer, Decision maker)<br>• Search behavior (offline and online)<br>• Buying/shoppingbehavior (offline and online) |
| | 3  Usage Behavior | • (Product) involvement and usage amount (light, moderate, heavy user)<br>• Use situations<br>• Usage status |
| C  Brand | 1  Brand awareness | • Compared to 'own' brand/phase in the buying process (degree of awareness, whether or not a buyer)<br>• Compared to competing brands: consideration set |
| | 2  Brand associations | • 'Own' brand (strength, relevance, uniqueness)<br>• Competing brands |
| | 3  Brand loyalty | • Behavioral loyalty (*share of wallet*, switching behaviour)<br>• Emotional (recommended, brand ambassador) |

*Figure 5.2* **Most important segmentation variables for consumer markets**

| Demographic | • Industry |
| | • Business size |
| | • Location |
| Usage variables | • Technology (required technology at customer) |
| | • Usage status (heavy user, light user, no user) |
| | • Customer capabilities (need for service) |
| Purchasing approach | • Purchasing organization (central, decentralized) |
| | • Power structure (technical, financial, etc. ) |
| | • Type of relationships (strong, weak) |
| | • Purchasing policy (leasing, service, systems, etc. ) |
| | • Purchasing criteria (quality, service, price, etc. ) |
| | • Purchasing process (customer journey, offline, online) |
| Situational factors | • Urgency of delivery |
| | • Applications of delivered product |
| | • Order size |
| Personal characteristics | • Degree of similarity with supplying company |
| | • Risk attitude |
| | • Supplier loyalty |

*Figure 5.3* **Segmentation variables for business markets**

Source: Adaptation of Bonoma and Shapiro (1983)

category A variables in Figure 5.2), and then whether there are differences in behavioral characteristics (product and brand-related variables) between the groups is examined.

■ *Backward segmentation*, or segmentation based on behavioral differences (product category or brand variables). It starts from groups of buyers that show different behavior towards the product and then looks for general characteristics on the basis of which the groups can be described. The behavioral analysis is often based on differences in the importance that customers attach to certain product attributes (benefits: specific product-related variables). This form of segmentation is therefore called *benefit segmentation*. The major advantage of benefit segmentation is that – if segments are found – the requirement of homogeneity/heterogeneity is always met: there is a direct relationship with purchasing behavior. This means that different products/varieties can be developed for the different benefit segments. For this reason, researchers are increasingly using benefit segmentation in practice. Benefit segmentation usually uses two statistical analysis techniques: factor analysis to reduce the data set to fewer factors if necessary and then cluster analysis to create segments that differ as much as possible. The researcher must indicate which behavioral variables should be used to search for clusters.

## Case 5.1 Research into buying behavior

### Women play major role in partner's clothing choice

Only a third of Dutch men between the ages of 25 and 65 enjoy buying clothes, and new clothes are mainly bought out of necessity. The role of female partners in the purchasing process should not be underestimated. For example, four out of five Dutch women indicate that they play a role in their husband's or boyfriend's clothing purchases. This is the conclusion of research carried out by menswear store Jac Hensen and market research bureau Markteffect among more than 2,000 respondents.

Source: *Adformatie*, October 18, 2022

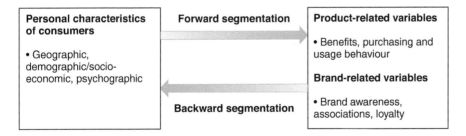

*Figure 5.4* Approaches to segmentation

### 3 Describing the segments

A profile is then drawn up for each segment found on the basis of the scores on the variables studied. We look for the most characteristic properties of the segments. The segments are named for identification. This then leads to a *persona* (Figure 5.5). This is often a rather subjective matter.

Some market research agencies have developed their own general segmentation separate from products. A frequently used example is that of Motivaction (Case 5.2).

## Case 5.2 Segmenting consumers

### Motivaction segmentation and personas

Based on a large study of various background characteristics and lifestyle variables, Motivaction has divided Dutch people into mentality segments or 'personas' (referred to as 'environments' by the bureau):

1   *Traditional bourgeoisie*: lower to middle class, strongly conservative, family is central, woman does the housework.
2   *Modern bourgeoisie:* somewhat more modern than the traditional bourgeoisie, more focused on owning and pampering, family is important but also status, low education, all income classes.

3   *Post-materialists*: middle to upper class, post-modern, non-materialistic, need for reflection and culture, idealism, more women than men.

4   *Convenience oriented*: lower class, modern, very fond of convenience and entertainment, more women, less elderly.

5   *Cosmopolitans*: critical world citizens, highest social class, modern to post-modern, pampering, impulsive.

6   *Postmodern hedonists*: pioneers of the experience culture, more young and highly educated, independent.

7   *New conservatives*: liberal-conservative, politically interested, especially higher educated, older men.

8   *Upwardly mobile*: career-oriented individualists, international orientation, traditional, many young people, especially men.

An assumption in general segmentation methods is that segments have different needs for all products and services. That is of course not the case. For example, age can play a role in beer preferences, but not in cars. Another disadvantage of ready-made, 'own' methods of agencies is that the data and methodology are not disclosed. The realization is therefore a black box.

It is therefore recommended to apply your own segmentation for your own specific category.

## 5.2.3 Guidelines for segmentation

Segmentation is an important topic in marketing literature, primarily because of its strategic importance but also because it is a quantitative topic that can therefore be subject to a great deal of empirical methodical research. It would go too far to go further into (statistical) methods for segmentation here, but we can indicate that the methods used are becoming increasingly flexible. For example, it can be taken into account that a person ends up in not one but two segments. This is in line with the fact that people can have different preferences at different times. There are also more and more methods that make it possible to segment despite missing data, for example, if people have not completed a questionnaire completely (for an application in a political context, see Paap et al., 2005).

A general finding seems to be that segmenting based on product-related variables gives better results than based on people's background characteristics, such as age. Reasons for this can be:

■   People show less and less predictable behavior.
■   People's preferences can differ greatly per usage situation.
■   Within households, individual members can have very different preferences.

Overall, the backward segmentation method is preferable. In all cases it is necessary to collect data on behavioral and background characteristics from a large number of (potential) customers. With the growth of digital consumer behavior, this has only become easier.

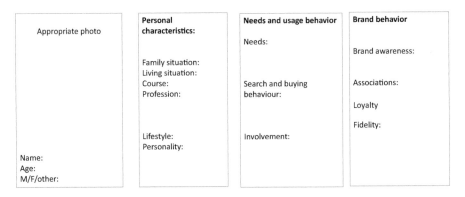

*Figure 5.5* Way to describe a persona

Segmentation therefore 'ends' with a representation of the different groups of customers:

- their properties (personal variables)
- their needs (category variables)
- their perceptions (brand specific variables)
- preferably a summary name per segment: persona (see Figure 5.5)

This forms the input for the target group choice, as discussed in Section 11.2.

## 5.3 Models of consumer behavior

This book does not contain a chapter on consumer behavior. For detailed information on this, we refer in general to the literature. However, this chapter is about how you can investigate that behavior. Some well-known models from the literature can be used for this. That is why we cover some of them here.

We start with a/the basic model of consumer behavior (Section 5.3.1).

Then we go into:

- the multi attribute attitude model (Section 5.3.2)
- the means-end chain of meanings (Section 5.3.3)
- for service markets the SERVQUAL model (Section 5.3.4)

### 5.3.1 The standard consumer behavior model

Figure 5.6 shows a basic model of consumer behavior described in many books (a.o. Kotler & Armstrong, 2021).

At the bottom is the consumer's purchasing decision process, already referred to in Chapter 1. He/she encounters a 'problem' ('need'), collects information (googling, for example), evaluates various options, makes a decision, uses the product or service, evaluates the experience, and may relinquish it (waste).

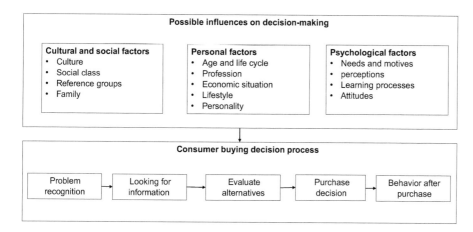

**Figure 5.6** Basic consumer behavior model

Source: Based on Kotler and Armstrong (2021)

Three kinds of factors influence this process. Cultural and social influences, such as family and friends; personal factors such as age, income, lifestyle, and personality (risk aversion, for example); and psychological factors such as motives, perceptions (how he/she views products), learning, and attitudes.

This model is not directly a model that can be easily translated into market research. It mainly serves as a general model to understand how consumer decisions can be made and what influences them. The models we discuss in the following deal with partial aspects of consumer behavior and form easier starting points for market research methods.

## 5.3.2 The multi-attribute attitude model

The name of the multi-attribute attitude model seems more complex than the model itself (see Figure 5.7). The model simply shows that the customer value (utility) that a customer derives from a product is determined, on the one hand, by the *importance* that the customer attaches to certain product characteristics (for example, he attaches great importance to the price). The interest can then be interpreted as the customer's need: for example, he wants a low price because he considers it important. On the other hand, the customer value of a product is determined by *a brand's score* on those product characteristics (a high price therefore leads to little realized value).

The name also simply means a combination of many characteristics that lead to a total judgment (*attitude*). From a 'mathematical' point of view, we could say that if the importance of all properties is combined (multiplied) by the scores on all those properties, a kind of total value of the product is obtained. The calculation example in Figure 5.8 shows this: the total score ('usefulness') that the shop in question earns from the consumer in question is 6.7.

An important insight provided by the multi-attribute attitude model is that the question 'Why does a customer buy my product?' involves a combination of two completely different variables: category needs and brand perceptions.

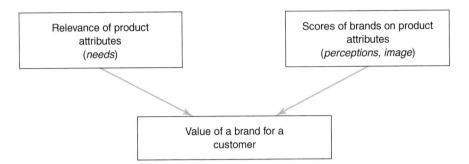

*Figure 5.7* **Multi-attribute attitude model**

| Characteristic | Importance (in %) | Score shop A | Importance × score |
|---|---|---|---|
| Price level | 40% | 7 | 2.8 |
| Broadness range | 20% | 8 | 1.6 |
| Friendliness of staff | 20% | 5 | 1.0 |
| Freshness products | 10% | 6 | 0.6 |
| Store cleanliness | 10% | 7 | 0.7 |
| Total | 100% | | 6.7 |

*Figure 5.8* **Calculation example with the multi-attribute attitude model**

The multi-attribute attitude model does assume that a product can be divided into separate properties and that these properties can also be properly named. In practice, this is not always easy:

■ Emotional (brand) characteristics in particular are difficult to include in the model.
■ The importance that people attach to characteristics strongly depends on their underlying motives and the situation of use, as Woodruff (1997) also argues. For example, a consumer may find the price more important for daily shopping than for Christmas shopping.

The model in the next subsection meets this need.

## 5.3.3 Means-end chain

The essence of the means-end chain is that people's motivation to buy products often lies deeper than just the direct benefit. For example, a customer can buy a yoghurt dessert because it contains less fat (characteristic). The customer finds this important because eating less fat makes him look good (consequence), which in turn is important because it fits better with his personality ('looks good') whereby he feels valued in his environment (final value). Properties of products therefore lead to consequences that match someone's personality and final values (see Figure 5.9 and Case 5.3). The name of the model comes from the idea that the physical properties of a product are a 'means' to achieve higher 'goals' (values).

The higher motivations to buy a product (i.e. the means-end chain) can differ for a consumer depending on the situation in which the product or service is used. The aforementioned yoghurt dessert can be bought in the summer because of its fresh taste. Then there is a difference in motive, depending on the season.

The higher values are often the basis for adding emotional attributes to brands through communication. The means-goal chain is hierarchical: 'lower' benefits serve to satisfy 'higher' goals. Woodruff (1997) also argues that consumers can receive customer value at three levels: at the level of product features, consequences, and goals. We divide the 'goals' into two levels: personality and final values.

To find out the deeper values of consumers, the *laddering* technique can be used. Consumers are then continuously asked why they bought a product and why it is important ('And why do you think eating less fat is important?').

## 5.3.4 The SERVQUAL model

The essence of a service is that it is intangible and transitory. But, just like with products, it is simply about delivering added value for the customer. In the case of services, the staff is very important, because they have contact with the customer. The service is delivered in interaction with the customer. Measured in terms of production value, services form a larger category in the Netherlands than (physical) products. The models from Sections 5.3.1 and 4.5.2 are in themselves suitable for use in service contexts. But a well-

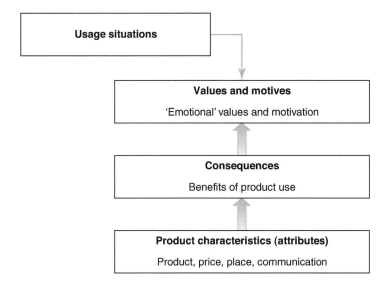

*Figure 5.9* **Means-end chain**

## Case 5.3 Emotional motives

**VanMoofs immensely popular, especially in Amsterdam**

Since 2019, the e-bike has been the most sold new bicycle. Meanwhile, more and more people seem to hate e-bikes, as with many products that become popular in a short time. Anti-social, lazy, energy hungry; if you have one maybe you shouldn't put it in front of the door. A brand that is doing very well is VanMoof. Since 2017, the turnover of this Dutch brand has increased tenfold. Despite bad reviews, everyone, especially in Amsterdam, wants such a thing. Design, being seen with it, 'being the boss on the road': that's what you want. A textbook example of emotional positioning, where down-to-earth competitors Batavus and Gazelle are bought by people who just want a good sturdy e-bike instead of one of those trendy VanMoofs. Despite this success the brand went bankrupt in 2023, due to their system of repair which could only be done by VanMoof themselves, leading to a endless queue of waiting and unsatisfied customers.

Source: NRC, 6 June 2022 and 28 July 2023

known model of service quality has also been developed specifically intended for service situations (Parasuraman et al., 1985). This SERVQUAL model (short for SERVice + QUALity) is shown in Figure 5.10.

Central to this model is that the quality of service is defined as the difference between the expected and the actual (perceived) service. If there is a gap between the two, there is no optimum quality. So giving the customer what he wants is the idea of the model. If there is a gap, it can have various causes. The model explores this by showing a number

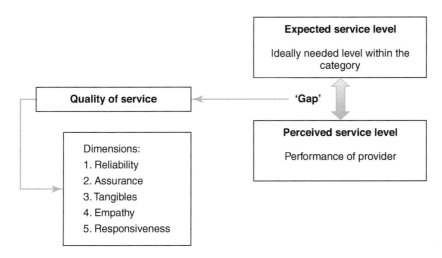

*Figure 5.10* **The SERVQUAL model of quality of service**

of other gaps (not shown in Figure 5.10), such as a difference between what management thinks the customer wants and what the customer really wants.

Empirical research using the SERVQUAL model has revealed a number of dimensions of service quality:

1   *Reliability:* the extent to which the provider keeps its promises.
2   *Certainty:* how certain is a customer about whether her expectations will come true (confidence in the provider).
3   *Tangibles:* all tangibles of the service, such as folders and atmosphere in a bank.
4   *Empathy:* the extent to which the provider puts himself in the position of the customer.
5   *Responsiveness:* the willingness of the provider to listen to the customer and do what she wants.

Measuring service quality can be done by measuring both customer expectation and realization. This is done per dimension. Per dimension, different sub-aspects can be questioned. Expectation is measured as what a customer ideally wants, independent of the specific provider. Example: a customer attaches great importance to a provider of financial services showing that they know the customer (aspect of empathy).

The two components expectation and performance show that the basis of the model stems from the multi-attribute attitude model. There, too, there is a requirement (general interest in the category) and a score (of the specific brand).

Finally, we note that the demands people place on brands and the performance of those brands are not separate from each other. As customers have more and longer good experiences, the requirements increase. This is a tricky point, because it means that customers' wishes are never stable and that they have to be 'taught' all the time what they can and cannot expect. This also emphasizes the importance of innovation. People are used to something new at a certain point, and then something new has to come.

## 5.4 Measuring the importance of product properties

The multi-attribute attitude model thus says that the 'usefulness' of a product for a consumer consists of a combination of:

■  The importance of product properties
■  The 'score' of the product on those properties

And all this in the eyes of the consumer. In this section we examine the 'importance' or 'relevance' of a product characteristic for a consumer.

### 5.4.1 Direct method: Likert scale

One way to investigate the importance of dimensions is to ask *directly* about the importance, with or without a scaling technique, for example, a 5-point scale (*Likert scale*) from 'very important' to 'unimportant'. For instance:

Rate the importance of the following smartphone features to you:

|  | Not important at all | Fairly unimportant | More or less important | Important | Very important |
|---|---|---|---|---|---|
| Price |  |  |  |  |  |
| Brand |  |  |  |  |  |
| Camera function |  |  |  |  |  |
| . . . |  |  |  |  |  |

A direct way of asking about importance has two disadvantages:

■  Customers often indicate that they find everything important. With a direct method, they are not forced to take into account the interaction between product properties (e.g. quality and price).
■  Customers tend to think instrumentally: concrete product features are often referred to as important, while abstract image aspects are often decisive in reality.

For these reasons, indirect methods such as conjoint analysis can also be used.

### 5.4.2 Conjoint analysis

Conjoint analysis is a method to determine the importance of product properties. This is not done by asking but by deducing it from the choices consumers make in a simple experiment. Figure 5.11 shows how this works.

The starting point is that a product consists of a bundle of characteristics. For example: the value (the 'usefulness') of a cake to someone is determined by five properties (*step 1*). For each of those properties, possible levels are determined for the experiment that are

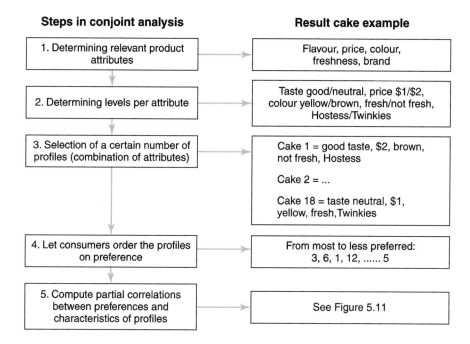

**Steps in conjoint analysis**

1. Determining relevant product attributes

2. Determining levels per attribute

3. Selection of a certain number of profiles (combination of attributes)

4. Let consumers order the profiles on preference

5. Compute partial correlations between preferences and characteristics of profiles

**Result cake example**

Flavour, price, colour, freshness, brand

Taste good/neutral, price $1/$2, colour yellow/brown, fresh/not fresh, Hostess/Twinkies

Cake 1 = good taste, $2, brown, not fresh, Hostess

Cake 2 = ...

Cake 18 = taste neutral, $1, yellow, fresh, Twinkies

From most to less preferred: 3, 6, 1, 12, ...... 5

See Figure 5.11

*Figure 5.11* Setup of a conjoint analysis

realistic in practice (*step 2*). For example: the taste (tasty, neutral), the price (€1 or €2), the color (yellow or brown), the freshness (fresh or not fresh), and the brand name (Hostess or Twinkies). With conjoint measurement, a manager wants to find out how important those properties are. New properties can also be included. If the analyses are done on a large number of people, differences between groups of consumers can also be looked at (*benefit segmentation*).

Subsequently, a number of so-called products are defined, where each product is defined as a combination of properties (*step 3*). For example: cake 1: has a good taste, has a high price, is brown, is not fresh, and is from Hostess. Cake 2: is averagely tasty, has a low price, is yellow, is fresh, and is from Hostess. And so on up to a certain number of cakes, for example, 18. It is not necessary to use all possible combinations (in the example, there would be 32), but a selection can be made using specially developed schemes. This concerns so-called *fractional designs* or fractional factor designs: overviews of combinations of profiles given a number of attributes and levels per attribute. All the consumer has to do is sort the cakes by preference (*step 4*). It can be useful to put each product on a card, with or without a suitable picture. The consumer can then arrange the cards in order. For example, in SPSS (a program used for statistical purposes), the preferences of the respondents are statistically explained from the composition of the profiles. For each respondent (or groups of respondents), it is then calculated how important the consumer considered each of the properties, for example, taste: 45%, price 27%, color 5%, freshness 9%, brand 14% (see Figure 5.12 for a possible outcome).

| | Taste | | Price | | Colour | | Freshness | | Brand name | |
|---|---|---|---|---|---|---|---|---|---|---|
| | *Level* | *Utility* | *Level* | *Utility* | *Level* | *Utility* | *Level* | *Utility* | *Level* | *Utility* |
| | Yummy | 60* | €1 | 40 | Yellow | 10 | Fresh | 25 | Hostess | 30 |
| | Neutral | 10 | €2 | 10 | Brown | 5 | Not fresh | 15 | Twinkies | 15 |
| Difference between highest and lowest | | 50 | | 30 | | 5 | | 10 | | 15 |
| Importance | | 45%** | | 27% | | 5% | | 9% | | 14% |

*Figure 5.12* **Possible outcome of conjoint analysis for cakes for one respondent**

\* This means that level 'nice' of attribute 'taste' gives a utility of 60 units. The scaling or measurement unit is not directly important; it is about relative differences between levels.

\*\* This is calculated by dividing 50 by the total of all differences (110).

Data from larger groups of consumers can be used for segmentation, product decisions, and pricing decisions. Advantages of conjoint analysis are:

- the simple questioning: the customer's selection process is simulated
- the fact that the interaction between characteristics is taken into account: respondents must implicitly consider which characteristics they find most important

Conjoint analysis is a commonly used method in marketing practice and theory and has various applications (Cattin & Wittink, 1982).

We note that the results of a conjoint analysis or of the direct inquiry into needs provide an excellent basis for segmentation. After all, it is precisely in this phase that insight is gained into what customers find important (see also Section 5.2).

When choosing respondents, the question is whether research should be carried out exclusively among customers or also among potential customers. There is something to be said for both choices. Investigating exclusively the preferences of existing customers fits in with the pursuit of relationships with customers. On the other hand, a brand cannot ignore the fact that new customers must always be attracted. So research among potential customers is also important.

Conducting research among one's own customers has the advantage that the preferences of the customers can be accommodated in a customer information system. If someone has been a customer for a long time, the importance of values can often be deduced from the purchasing behavior of users.

## 5.5 Measuring perceptions and associations

How well or poorly do we provide the desired product properties? This question can be examined qualitatively as well as quantitatively: how do we and our competitors score on properties and consequences?

In fact, *brand perceptions are* measured here. At this point a comparison is in order with the measurement of what Keller (1993) calls *brand equity*. According to Keller, brand awareness and brand associations are the sources of brand equity. These sources should lead to results in the form of satisfaction, brand loyalty, market share, and so on. To know if a brand is successful and why, it is therefore important to measure the sources and results of brand equity. Measuring brand associations can be done qualitatively or quantitatively.

## 5.5.1 Qualitative methods

Qualitative methods are:

- The *direct association method*. What do you associate brand A with?
- *Projective techniques*. Indirect methods, such as having matching photos indicated or describing the brand as a person with character. The latter method is very suitable for measuring psychosocial (abstract) properties of a brand and provides important information for the choice of brand positioning.

Another part of the qualitative analysis is gaining insight into consumer satisfaction and especially into the underlying causes of the level of satisfaction. Talking to consumers about what they think of the brand and why is often a big eye-opener for managers.

As we will see in Section 5.7, qualitative research does not require very many respondents to get a fairly complete picture of what is going on with customers (and non-customers). Even if one decides not to conduct quantitative research, qualitative research is already extremely valuable and can be used individually for strategic decisions.

## 5.5.2 Likert scales and spider diagrams

Also with quantitative methods, we can distinguish between direct and indirect methods. For example, direct methods use statements, where the respondent is asked to rate their level of agreement on a ranking scale (Likert scales). The rule of thumb for a Likert scale is that at least 5 categories are required to interpret the ordinal scale as an interval or ratio scale, that is, to calculate averages. For instance:

To what extent do you agree with the following statements about the iPhone 14?

|  | Totally disagree | Disagree | More or less agree | At sometime | Totally agree |
|---|---|---|---|---|---|
| An iPhone 14 is expensive |  |  |  |  |  |
| An iPhone 14 is a good brand |  |  |  |  |  |
| An iPhone 14 has a good camera function |  |  |  |  |  |
| . . . |  |  |  |  |  |

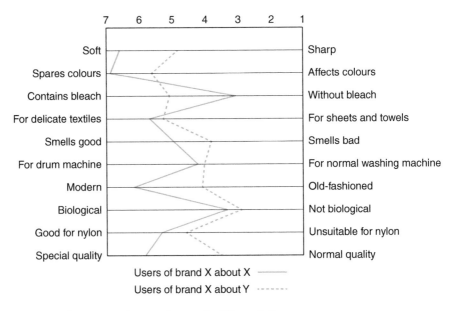

*Figure 5.13* **Detergent images (semantic differential)**

Scores from such a table can be displayed in two ways: with percentages of people who (totally) agree/disagree, and so on, or with scores where scores 1 to 5 can be chosen in the table and thus an average over respondents can be calculated, for example, a 4.1 on the statement 'An iPhone is expensive'.

A simple instrument that clearly displays both instrumental and abstract brand properties is the *semantic differential*: a graphical representation of brands' scores on properties. Figure 5.13 contains an example.

Another way to represent brand scores is in a *spider chart*, where, for example, eight properties are shown in a circle. Figure 5.14 contains an example of scores on values for users and non-users of a mustard brand. Both the semantic differential and the spider diagram can show comparisons between, for example, two brands (Figure 5.13) or two target groups (Figure 5.14).

## 5.5.3 Perceptual mapping

Indirect quantitative methods to measure brand perceptions are methods for the benefit of *perceptual mapping*. Perceptual maps are certainly important and easy-to-understand research methods for positioning and communication decisions. In this technique, brands are placed in axes; for example, the axes say something about conservative/dynamic, tough/feminine, or other brand personality traits (see also the overviews of brand values in Section 11.4). Sometimes groups of consumers (segments) are also placed in such images.

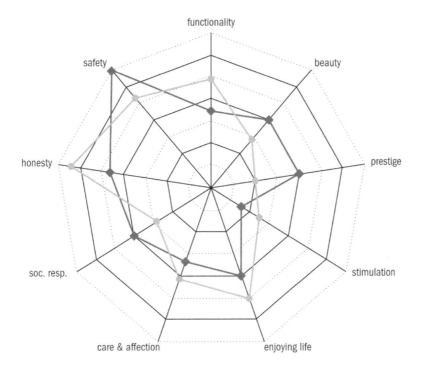

*Figure 5.14* Spider diagram: scores on values for users and non-users of mustard brand

A valid way in which perceptual maps can be obtained is with the technique of multidimensional scale analysis. With MDS, brands, properties, and ideal points (wishes) of users are clearly placed in a figure using a statistical method, using simple questions to respondents. Figure 5.15 contains an example of a *joint space* (brand space) for the roll-your-own tobacco market.

A brand's score on a characteristic is obtained by drawing a perpendicular line from the brand to a characteristic. Figure 5.15 shows, for example, that tobacco brands C and F score highest on the characteristic dark, while brand A has a young and feminine image. The image of A is very similar to that of B. If A wants to grow at the expense of B, it must position itself differently, for example, as a somewhat stronger shag, that is, to the right (higher score on characteristic 9). Another advantage of this is that there is a segment of smokers that needs a strong and cozy brand (segment III), but such a brand does not exist.

Some important advantages of MDS as a research method are:

■ The results of MDS (graphic displays of brand positions) are easy to understand and as such an excellent communication tool for positioning decisions.
■ MDS makes it possible to use more than two dimensions. The dimensions on which people rate brands are placed as vectors in the figure.
■ The positions of the brands in space are 'hard'; that is, they are calculated according to a quantitative method. This distinguishes MDS from commonly used qualitative

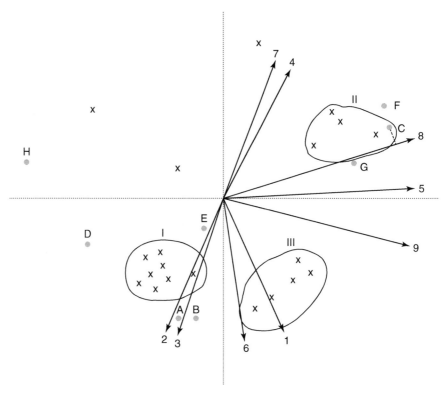

Explanation: A to H are the brands, 1 to 9 are the attributes,
X is the ideal point of a consumer, I, II and III are segments.

Attributes: 1 = pleasant, 2 = for young people, 3 = for women, 4 = bitter, 5 = tar,
6 = smells good, 7 = difficult to get used to, 8 = dark, 9 = smells strong.

*Figure 5.15* **Example of a joint space with features: tobacco brands**

ways of placing brands in spaces.
■ The method of data collection at MDS follows a true-to-nature approach: respondents are asked to compare brands as a whole (as well as in the store, for example) and only afterwards are the properties placed in the figure. This makes MDS an indirect method in which respondents do not have to indicate what they consider important but which can be determined by the researcher afterwards on the basis of the results.

Reliable results of MDS can already be achieved with a small number of respondents. These results also lend themselves well to segmentation into, for example, use versus non-use.

Taking measurements as described in this section provides insight into the strengths and weaknesses of the brand. That is why there is a link between the customer analysis and internal analysis. It is very important here to distinguish between customers and potential customers. Potential customers (i.e. non-customers) often view a brand differently than customers (see Case 5.4). An answer to the question 'Why don't potential customers buy our product?' is important for winning new customers.

## Case 5.4 Difference in perceptions between customers and noncustomers

## Will New Zealand remain a green and pleasant land?

'100 per cent pure New Zealand': Tourism New Zealand's catchphrase used since 1999. Why mess with a good thing? The notion of a country blessed with pristine land, water, and air appeals not only to visitors; it goes to the core of what the country means to New Zealanders themselves. So the slogan has the 'authenticity' such expressions always call for.

But there is a problem. New Zealanders are growing unsure about their country's 100% pure image. One issue comes from the sheer numbers of tourists themselves. Another comes from the back end of a cow. Some of the most popular tourist places are getting 'hammered'. Another problem is fragile landscapes ravaged to make way for cows, such as in the Mackenzie district, a dry upland rich in endemic plant and animal species that has been completely changed by irrigation. Conservationists are appalled that a rare ecology has been destroyed. Indeed, water gets to the heart of New Zealanders' concerns. Dairy cattle need a lot of it and produce copious excrement and urine in return. This pollutes watercourses and fills lakes with algal blooms, despite new requirements to fence streams off from livestock. Some rivers have become too polluted to swim in.

With images like that, it can't be long before visitors notice there's a problem in this pure, unsullied land.

Source: *The Economist*, 21 September 2017

## 5.6 Measuring brand strength

In this section we will discuss brand power and brand value, the brand equity pyramid, the net promoter score, the brand power questionnaire, and the indirect measurement of the importance of product properties.

### 5.6.1 Brand strength and brand value

Measuring brand strength: a brand is an important part of a company's assets. The fact that people know a brand and have certain associations with it is 'worth money'. For various reasons, it can be important to know how strong a brand actually is. Namely:

- for the benefit of strategy formation and (adjustment of) the marketing policy
- due to mergers and/or acquisitions
- due to a financial valuation on the balance sheet (and/or due to possible damage due to crisis situations)

The method by which the value of a brand must be measured depends strongly on which of the aforementioned motives plays a role. In the case of the latter two reasons, a manager will want to know the financial value of the brand. But when it comes to day-to-day strategy-making, one number is of little use to a manager because one number does not provide any insight into the strengths and weaknesses of a brand. For strategic marketing purposes, several separate dimensions of a brand will have to be mapped. In this context, Keller and Swaminathan (2019) compare a brand to an aircraft: a pilot will never rely on one 'meter' but on a multitude of them.

We distinguish between two types of brand strengths:

1  Brand power: the power of the brand in the eyes of the customer. This involves different dimensions of the brand, such as the reputation and the image.
2  Brand value: the financial value of the brand for the company.

There is, of course, a connection between these two concepts: a brand with stronger brand power (more brand knowledge) will also be worth more money (Figure 5.16).

In this book, we focus on brand power. We agree with Keller (1993), who uses the term *customer-based brand equity* to indicate that brand strength is measured from the perspective of customers. Measuring the financial value of a brand is not easy and is often done by agencies. A well-known method is that of agency Interbrand. This estimates the annual future cash flow of a brand and multiplies it by a factor that depends on the brand strength of the brand. For more insight into methods to measure the financial value of a brand, we refer to the literature. All methods require a fair degree of subjectivity. Agencies often keep parts of the methodology secret. This makes it impossible to validate a method.

We will now discuss in Sections 5.6.2 and 5.6.3 two commonly used models: Keller's brand equity model and the net promoter score. Next, we present a way to measure brand

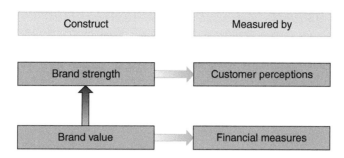

*Figure 5.16* **Measuring brand strength**

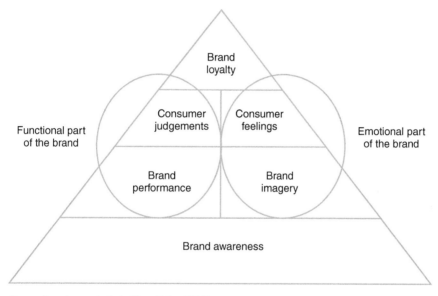

Source: Based on and adapted from Keller (2013).

*Figure 5.17* **Customer-based brand equity: Keller's pyramid**

power with a comprehensive questionnaire: the brand power scale (Section 5.6.4).

## 5.6.2 Brand Equity Pyramid

Keller (2019) outlines the so-called brand equity pyramid (Figure 5.17 shows a modified version), which he later renamed the brand resonance model. The hierarchical model states that a brand must first achieve *brand salience* (brand awareness): a brand must acquire a prominent position in the minds of customers. The importance of familiarity ties in with Sharp's aforementioned findings (see Chapter 1). The second level relates to brand performance. This concerns the rational performance (left side) and the more emotional performance (right side). The third level concerns how the customer responds to the characteristics of the brand: what does he think of it, and what kind of feelings does the brand evoke? The highest level is about brand loyalty (*brand resonance*), which involves not only buying behavior (such as repeat purchases), but also emotional loyalty or even customer ambassadorship. The latter can occur if a customer feels actively involved with a brand. Reactions on social media are often an expression of this.

For market research, Keller's model means that all six boxes should be measured to know how strong a brand is.

### 5.6.3 Net Promoter Score

Ideally, customers are very loyal to a brand and even show involvement. In practice this rarely happens. Nevertheless, it is important for a brand to know how loyal customers are. There are two types of brand loyalty:

- *emotional brand loyalty*: a customer is a real 'fan' of your brand
- *behavioral* brand loyalty: a customer always buys your brand: repeat purchases

Brand loyalty in terms of behavior seems to be the most important for a brand because it generates sales. Yet that is not entirely true. Repeat purchases can also come from habit and convenience without true, emotional brand loyalty. The risk is that customers then easily walk away if, for example, a competitor has a better offer. Naturally, a brand prefers to have customers who are emotionally and behaviorally loyal. We mentioned earlier that Sharp discovered that even real brand fans occasionally buy another brand, a form of 'infidelity', so to speak.

One way to measure emotional brand preference is to ask about the likelihood that you would recommend the brand to others: the degree of 'customer ambassadorship'. The question is then: 'Please indicate on a scale of 0 to 10 how likely it is that you would recommend the brand to friends and family'.

The interpretation of this scale is subjective. For example, the 'report mark' of 7 or 8 seems quite high. However, people are often rather indifferent about brands, so a figure of 8 does not mean that customers are actually active ambassadors and, for example, will spontaneously say in social media that they are so happy with their iPhone. It is often assumed

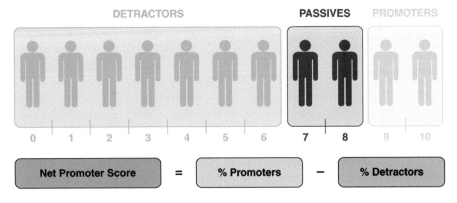

*Figure 5.18* Net promoter score scale

that people already have to score a 9 or 10 before they are active ambassadors. That is why Veldhoen and Van Slooten (2010) state that 9+ *experiences* must be created! Conversely, a 'report mark' of 6 does not necessarily mean that a customer is sufficiently satisfied.

All these considerations led to the so-called net promoter score, a measure developed by Reichheld (2003). On this scale, the respondents are divided into promoters (scores of 9–10), passives (scores of 7–8), and 'runaways' (6 and below) (see Figure 5.18).

Then the percentage of runaways is subtracted from the percentage of promoters. This yields the net promoter score (NPS). A percentage of 75 or higher is considered high. An NPS can also be negative: more scores of '6 and below' than '9 and above'. This does not necessarily mean that the brand is performing poorly. In many categories, NPS scores are low on average simply because engagement is low. NPS scores also vary by country. While there is no academic evidence that this measure is 'better' than other measures (Keiningham et al., 2007), measuring the degree of recommendation itself is an interesting thought that is close to expected behavior. Incidentally, no clear scientific conclusion has yet been drawn about the extent to which the NPS is or is not a good predictor of a company's profit. The NPS is particularly interesting as a benchmark for comparison.

## 5.6.4 Brand strength scale

For marketing-strategic goals, it is recommended to measure the brand strength on the basis of a number of dimensions (the aforementioned 'meters from an airplane'). The question then is which 'meters' are needed and how the scores are arrived at. We use some parts from the aforementioned models, apply some changes, and arrive at the following dimensions:

1    category involvement
2    importance of properties
3    brand awareness
4    functional brand associations
5    emotional brand associations
6    uniqueness brand
7    brand preference and loyalty
8    customer properties

The main differences from Keller's pyramid are that variables are ordered differently and category involvement and customer attributes are added. The eight types of variables correspond to the three types of variables covered in segmentation: categorized variables (1 and 2), branded variables (3 through 7), and customer characteristics (8). Figure 5.19 shows an example of a detailed questionnaire. The questionnaire also contains some items from a scale developed by Yoo and Donthu (2001). Specific scales can be used for the emotional associations, such as the brand personality scale or the value compass, both of which are discussed in Chapter 11. In Figure 5.19, we assume that management itself has chosen some specific associations with which it wants to be associated: the identity.

The power of measurements often lies in comparisons. The measuring instrument outlined here (or variants thereof) is particularly valuable if the measurements are repeated regularly (*monitoring* or *tracking*) so that changes can be observed. Comparisons

1 Category involvement

- ☐ How often do you buy deodorant?
- ☐ How important is buying deodorant to you?

2 Relevance of attributes
Let me tell you some attributes of deodorant products in general.
Would you indicate how important those qualities are to you?

- ☐ Price
- ☐ Fragrance
- ☐ How long it works
- ☐ Ease of use
- ☐ Appearance product
- ☐ Feeling on the skin
- ☐ Environmental friendliness
- ☐ General quality

3 Brand awareness

- ☐ I am familiar with Ax .
- ☐ I can easily recognize Ax from other brands.
- ☐ I can easily recall some of Ax 's features.

4 Functional brand associations
The following questions are related to Ax .
Please indicate to what extent you agree with the statements.

- ☐ Ax is cheap.
- ☐ Ax smells good.
- ☐ When I use Ax it helps for a long period of time.
- ☐ Ax is easy to use.
- ☐ The Ax products look nice.
- ☐ Ax feels nice on my skin.
- ☐ Ax is environmentally friendly.
- ☐ Ax is of high quality.

5 Emotional brand associations
Please indicate to what extent you think that the mentioned characteristics fit Ax .

- ☐ Young
- ☐ Fun
- ☐ Daring
- ☐ Male
- ☐ Temptation
- ☐ Reliable

*Figure 5.19* **Example of a detailed questionnaire to measure brand strength: brand strength scale (BSS)**

6   Brand uniqueness

☐   If you weren't buying Ax deodorant, what brand of deodorant would you choose?
☐   To what extent do you find Ax clearly different from other deodorant brands?

7   Brand Use and Preference

☐   Do you currently own Ax?
☐   How often do you buy Ax?

Please indicate the extent to which you agree with the following statements.

☐   Ax is my first choice in deodorant.
☐   I would recommend Ax to my friends (brand ambassadorship).
☐   If another brand is as good as Axe, I would buy Axe .

8   Customer Properties

☐   Are you male/female/none?
☐   What is your age?
☐   What is your highest completed education?
☐   What class does your gross annual salary fall into ?[#brief]

**Figure 5.19 (Continued)**

between groups of customers (segmentation) are also interesting.

## 5.6.5 Indirectly measuring the importance of product properties

We mentioned the difference between the importance of product features and the brand's score on them. With the method of conjoint measurement described in Section 5.4.2, we also mentioned that asking about importance often gives less reliable answers and that it may therefore be better to find out the importance by means of, for example, conjoint measurement.

The brand strength scale offers a simpler way to derive importance scores indirectly by asking for and combining two types of data:

■   the scores on (functional and emotional) characteristics
■   a performance measure such as brand ambassadorship

When the brand performance is explained by means of a simple regression from the scores, it is found which associations have the strongest influence on the final brand assessment. This implicitly 'calculates' the importance of those associations (see Figure 5.20). A concrete result is, for example, the price sensitivity. That is the influence of people's opinion about 'whether Ax is cheap' on brand preference.

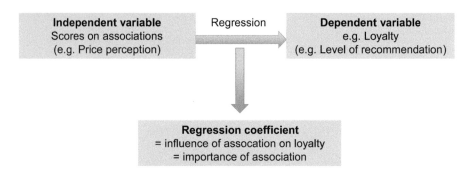

*Figure 5.20* **Estimating the importance of associations retrospectively**

## 5.7 Individual customer data

In this section, we will successively discuss the possibilities of individual customer data, especially online data, and the selection of customers.

### 5.7.1 Possibilities of online data

With the enormous growth of online behavior (of both customers and companies), individual data is 'on the street'. This is a break with the previous century, in which obtaining data per customer was very difficult for manufacturers, and only retailers with, for example, a customer card had data per customer.

There is now enough data, it seems. But is that true? What data is currently available online and what kind of information does that provide? Online data relates to:

- Communication behavior: what do consumers do on social media?
- Search behavior: how do consumers search online (keywords, which sites, etc.)?
- Click behavior: which sites (and pages) have the most clicks?
- Buying behavior: what do consumers buy online?

The big advantage of this data is that it concerns actual behavior. This is in contrast to research with questionnaires. But this is where a limitation immediately comes into play: online data provides hardly any insight into the 'why question'.

What is also unknown are demographic and psychographic characteristics of consumers. The question is, incidentally, to what extent the latter is serious. Background characteristics of consumers are normally important for media accessibility. But consumer targeting can be done without that background data. Online consumers can easily be followed on the basis of their online behavior. If someone texts their family that they went to the dentist, don't be surprised if they see a banner for toothpaste next. Another way to reach customers online is to send targeted messages to specific locations (mobile marketing or location marketing). By capturing the signal from smartphones, mobile providers know where people are. If someone approaches a drugstore, the offer of that drugstore can 'coincidentally' come across on the smartphone.

We mention a few more pluses and minuses of online data. A plus is that online is ideal for experiments. For example, testing different websites or Facebook messages and seeing what the differences are in responses. This is called *A/B testing*. Limitations are that online consumers are not necessarily representative of all customers of a brand. In addition, online purchases still make up a limited portion of all sales.

In addition, the rules regarding privacy have become stricter. In practice, there are two 'systems' for protecting the use of individual customer data: *opt-in* and *opt-out*. Opt-in means choosing to participate and that people must give explicit permission for the use of data (active permission, for example, with a loyalty card). Opt-out means choosing to 'opt out' and implies that it is tacitly assumed that individual data may be used unless objected to (passive consent, e.g. responding to a coupon promotion). Opt-in is becoming more important. This is also friendlier from a customer-oriented point of view. This is also referred to as *permission marketing*: you can only enter into a direct relationship with a customer if she has given explicit permission for this.

In contrast to self-collected data, online data is often unstructured (Balducci & Marinova, 2018). To extract the right information from the large amounts of 'unstructured data', specific research methods are needed (Wedel & Kannan, 2016). For example, it may concern textual information from consumer reviews and discussions, which therefore requires textual analysis methods (Humphreys & Wang, 2018). But it also concerns artificial intelligence (AI). Because there currently (2023) is a lot of attention on artificial intelligence, we make some extra remarks about AI.

The reason for growing attention to AI is probably that new, appealing applications of AI have been introduced, such as ChatGPT: an application that can produce impressive texts by simply providing some keywords. Some people think that AI is quite new. That is not true. It was 'invented' in 1950. And in marketing, 'big data' has existed since the invention of 'scanner data' in the 1980s and after the World Wide Web in the 1990s. Since then, market researchers have used statistical software to analyze this data. The central idea of AI is no more or less than to find patterns in data. The data can be hard data (numbers, texts) but also soft data such as sound and the relation between the data (e.g. speech recognition). A related method is machine learning: a specific form of AI aimed at enabling software to improve itself by 'learning and doing'. Applications of AI are: self-driving Teslas, Google Home (or Nest), Siri, apps to make a drawing from text, and (thus) ChatGPT. For sure, new applications of AI will be developed in the future. The final question is how useful AI is for marketing. In our view, AI is helpful in the stage of analysis.

## 5.7.2 Selecting customers

Companies that are able to obtain data on purchasing behavior at the customer level have various tools at their disposal to analyze that data. Of these we cover:

- the customer pyramid
- the customer portfolio analysis

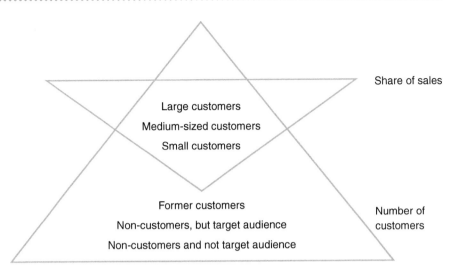

*Figure 5.21* **The customer pyramid**

## Customer pyramid

The customer pyramid (see Figure 5.21) is a diagram that ranks (potential) custom-ers. This ordering can be done, for example, on the basis of the annual turnover (per customer). It is plausible that a similar 80/20 rule exists for customers as for products: 20% of the customers could be good for 80% of the turnover. Of course this is a fairly arbitrary rule of thumb, and a different ratio may just as well apply, but the meaning is clear: a small number of customers are responsible for a large part of the turnover.

Further down the pyramid, we find the medium and small customers, former custom-ers, non-target customers, and finally the non-target people. Once an order of customers has been made, the next question is what characteristics the various groups have. Why is a large customer big and a small customer small? Why have customers left? Why are some audience members not customers at all?

Figure 5.21 can be an aid to target group selection and value strategy. In theory, the best strategy seems to be the one with the strongest possible flow from bottom to top. There are several options for this:

■ turn a non-customer into a customer
■ retain customers
■ increase customer turnover

Each of these strategies requires a different approach. In the context of relationship mar-keting, it is often said that retaining customers is four times cheaper than making new ones. On the other hand, it is difficult to completely ignore new customers. Without growth, the customer base will shrink.

Customer selection is also called customer discrimination. This may suggest an unethical principle, but is simply part of targeting.

*Customer portfolio analysis*

Another tool that can be helpful in this context is the customer portfolio analysis. Each customer is classified according to two characteristics:

1   the extent to which the customer is a 'heavy user' in the product category: the (potential) size of the customer
2   the share of the brand turnover in the customer's category purchases, or the customer's market share

The first criterion says something about the potential/expected attractiveness of a customer, the second about the current attractiveness. A concept that is often used in this context is the *customer lifetime value*: the value of a customer to a company, measured over the customer's entire life, including the effect of recommendations the customer makes to others (ambassadorship). This concept shows that customer loyalty is essential for a company, because a customer who walks away can make a big difference in future revenue. There is a lot of scientific literature on measuring customer lifetime value (Gupta et al., 2006; Borle et al., 2008; Blattberg et al., 2009), which means that the use of this concept is also possible in practice.

## 5.8 Primary research: tips and pitfalls

Primary data is data that an organization itself collects through fieldwork (market research). For an extensive treatment of market research, we refer to the literature on this topic (Malhotra et al., 2017; Cooper & Schindler, 2014). We cover a few points here. In market research, the following three choices must be made:

1   *Choice of target group (who?)*. Among which target group or target groups should the research be conducted? This question is to a large extent decisive for the further design.
2   *Desired information and choice of quantitative or qualitative research (what?)*. We will consider this question in Section 5.8.1.
3   *Design (how?)*:

   ■   data collection
   ■   sample
   ■   method of questioning

### 5.8.1 Quantitative or qualitative research

As always with market research, there are two basic types of research possible:

1   quantitative study
2   qualitative research

## 1 Quantitative research

Quantitative research is by definition conducted among larger numbers of people. Due to the large-scale approach, 'harder' conclusions can be drawn than with qualitative research: after all, results are obtained in percentages. Another advantage is that differences between sub-target groups (segments) can be made visible, for example, differences in satisfaction between young people and older people or between different types of companies (an 'explanatory' goal).

Because the type of fieldwork in quantitative research (online, written, or telephone) requires a structured approach, such a method is best suited for 'factual' research, especially descriptive. Quantitative research is not primarily intended to provide insight into the 'why' of certain results.

## 2 Qualitative research

Qualitative research consists of personal (face-to-face) interviews with individuals (in-depth interviews) or groups (group discussion, focus groups).

Qualitative research can be used as an independent resource to find out how people view the brand and what its strengths and weaknesses are. It can also be performed prior to quantitative research: as a source of inspiration for and/or pre-testing a questionnaire.

The choice of a quantitative or qualitative approach should not be taken primarily on the basis of the impression that quantitative research is by definition more reliable than qualitative research. Of greater importance is the question of what kind of information one wants to obtain. If the organization wishes to gain insight into the percentages of people from the target group who are or are not satisfied with the product in the context of customer satisfaction survey and how the relationship is with the composition and backgrounds of the target group, then a quantitative approach is required. It should be realized, however, that such a survey cannot reveal the *cause of any dissatisfaction*. Information about these causes is often best obtained by looking at the comments added by respondents (e.g. at the end of a questionnaire). In this way, the biggest complaints emerge in a questionnaire.

However, this concerns an incidental inventory of problems, which moreover is actually qualitative in nature. If one especially wants to know why there is dissatisfaction and what an organization can do about it, then a qualitative approach is more obvious.

Figure 5.22 shows the ideal choice on this point: first qualitatively, then possibly quantitatively and then again qualitatively. Customer research will always start with qualitative research, whereby an initial inventory is obtained of possible problems and information that is relevant for setting up a quantitative study is collected. Such research can then be followed by quantitative research to provide insight into whether goals have been achieved, the extent to which certain problems occur, and differences between groups. Subsequently, a deeper qualitative analysis can be carried out among target groups to find out what causes any problems, and possible solutions can possibly be presented to respondents.

Of course, the method described here is only possible with sufficient resources. With limited resources, at least some qualitative research will almost always be required,

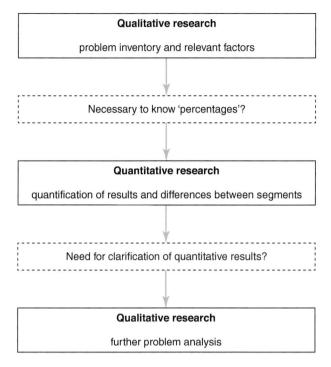

*Figure 5.22* **Research phases**

because a small number of conversations with customers already provide insight into problems and possible solutions. Examples:

■ By talking to only a few customers, a large telecom company discovered that customers did not find the various subscriptions as simple as the managers themselves thought.
■ At a bank, the website, which was made with a lot of technical ingenuity, was given a try by customers. They turned out not to understand many terms at all: the website was made far too much by the company and much less by the customer.

After the company has decided on the most appropriate type of study, decisions must be made on the further design and on the size and composition of the sample. We first elaborate on these topics for qualitative research (Section 5.8.2). Subsequently, in Section 5.8.3, we will discuss two specific examples of qualitative research. Finally, in Section 5.8.4, we discuss the quantitative research.

## 5.8.2 Qualitative research: tips

We will give only a few short guidelines (for a more extensive treatment, we refer to Malhotra et al., 2017 and Cooper & Schindler, 2014). In qualitative research, one has to make a choice between individual conversations/interviews or interviews in groups. In general, it can be said that if people are interested in their own individual behavior (such as choice processes, usage behavior) of people, individual conversations are preferable. If the researcher is mainly interested in gaining insight into how 'people' think about the organization and its products, a group discussion can be chosen. A group discussion has the advantage that more issues and ideas emerge through the interaction within the group.

Subsequently, the *size and composition of the sample* must be determined. The most crucial is the latter: the respondents must be carefully selected according to the relative composition of the entire target group. Suppose, for example, that the target group consists of 30% women over the age of 60. In that case, 6 women over the age of 60 should be included in a research group of 20 people. If respondents are selected in the 'correct' manner, the representativeness of qualitative research is, in principle, sufficiently guaranteed.

A related point is the sample size. An important criticism of qualitative research is that a survey of a few people can never be the basis for strategic decisions of an organization. However, research shows that if approximately 15 to 25 respondents from a group are questioned, then virtually no new cases will emerge. After about 20 interviews, the researcher will therefore know 'what's going on'. Usually she even has a reasonable impression of the extent to which the target group is aware of this.

In group discussions it is usually recommended to interview more or less homogeneous groups. Think of a few groups of customers, as well as one or more groups of non-customers (potential customers) and perhaps former customers. A common pitfall in market research is that only customers are interviewed. The results of such research are by definition not representative of the entire potential target group, because existing customers on average think more positively about the organization than customers who are with competitors. If we assume that every organization not only exists for its own customers but is also interested in potential new customers, this means that non-customers must also be questioned.

With regard to group discussions, a group size of six to eight people is considered appropriate in most cases. We also note that the 15 to 25 respondents mentioned apply to each group to be studied about which the researcher wishes to make statements. If a researcher wishes to investigate the differences between, for example, male customers, female customers and non-customers, the standard therefore applies three times. If the minimum of about 15 people per group is assumed and group discussions of about 8 people are chosen at a time, then a minimum of six group discussions should be organized in this example.

With regard to the method of data collection, there are open questions, in which it is the task of the interviewer to monitor whether all topics are covered. We do point out the danger of interviewer bias: inaccurate answers as a result of influences by the interviewer. Face-to-face examinations require expert questioning in order to collect information that is as pure as possible. The strength of good qualitative research lies in 'creative listening'.

In principle, two methods can be used to process interviews:

1   The researcher summarizes the results in a short summary text.
2   Having recorded interviews (online) transcribed into text, highlighting words and having them analyzed with text analysis software such as Atlas.TI.

### 5.8.3 Customer journey mapping and neuromarketing

In this subsection we discuss two specific qualitative research methods: *customer journey research* and neuromarketing.

#### Customer journey mapping

A popular tool in qualitative research is mapping the 'customer journey '. This means that a researcher maps out the experiences of contact moments for individual customers from the very first contact to the last and everything in between. This is close to the decision-making and buying process as depicted in the basic consumer behavior model in Figure 5.23. This involves looking at how the customer has experienced the contact and how the organization can improve on it. So a hospital could map the *patient journey* by analyzing all contact moments on the patient's experiences from the patient's arrival at the reception up to and including discharge after surgery. In the literature, attention to the customer journey coincides with the attention to customer experiences (see, among others, Lemon & Verhoef, 2016).

Figure 5.23 provides a schematic view that can be used in customer journey research.

1  An organization should first list all phases with contact moments.
2  Customer satisfaction is examined for each phase.
3  The outcomes are analyzed per phase by looking at what the organization itself has done.
4  The results are used as input in internal discussions with staff.

#### Neuromarketing

As we mentioned earlier in Chapter 1, the majority of customer choices are driven by unconscious drivers. It is therefore logical that researchers would like to look literally

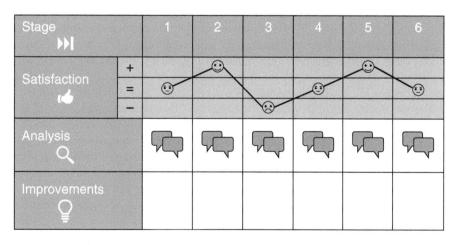

*Figure 5.23* **Schematic view of customer journey research**

inside the head of that consumer. For example, researchers borrow techniques from the medical sciences and put respondents under a scanner and then make brain scans while a respondent sees an advertisement. At most, this provides an impression of the emotions of respondents to certain stimuli. But there are important caveats to note.

First of all, the name 'neuromarketing' suggests all kinds of incorrect things, namely that there would be separate marketing based on 'the functioning of the brain'. This misconception may also lead to marketing being seen as unethical because it 'sneaky try to mislead us'. Neuromarketing therefore does not exist and can be better called neuromarket research, for example.

A limitation of neuromarket research is that the link with behavior is often difficult to draw. Instead of trying to delve deeper into the mind of the consumer, a researcher could actually go less deep and put more emphasis on measuring behavior. The latter is also increasingly happening in much experimental psychological research.

### 5.8.4 Quantitative research: tips

Quantitative research using questionnaires is now largely conducted online. It also happens by mail. The advantage of a written survey is the possibility of a longer questionnaire and the relative simplicity of reaching a very large number of people. On the other hand, the response is often very low (in consumer research, often no higher than 15%). Quantitative research involves a fully pre-structured multiple-choice questionnaire, because otherwise no quantitative analyses can be performed. Because an error or ambiguity in a questionnaire that has been sent out cannot be reversed, it is essential that the questionnaire be tested in advance until no ambiguities are indicated by the test persons (after being explicitly asked for).

A model like the one described in this chapter can be used when constructing a questionnaire, but it is always good to also study other studies (including scientific studies) that have investigated similar problems. If relationships need to be explored, a conceptual model can form the basis for the format of the questionnaire. Studying literature also applies to the use of scales (items to measure constructs). There are even publications with entire overviews of scales in marketing and consumer behavior (*Handbook of Marketing Scales*). The method of asking questions and thus the use of items determines, among other things, the *validity*: are you measuring what you want to measure? For constructs in which several items (i.e. a scale) are used, the validity of the items can be checked afterwards by seeing whether they correlate sufficiently (Cronbach's alpha).

For the sample size, the larger it is, the greater the (statistical) reliability of the results. But this relation is not linear (it is a 'root function'). Without going into formulas that can be used to calculate the reliability margins of answers, we can say that a rule of thumb is that at least 100 respondents must be reached per target group to be researched. Assuming an expected non-response of, for example, 20%, a minimum of 500 questionnaires would have to be sent per group in the case of a written survey.

*More important than the sample size is the sample composition.* If the composition of the group of people who participated on characteristics relevant to the research does not correspond to the entire target group (is not representative), the results are unreliable. It is therefore very important to check afterwards whether the requirement of representativeness has been met. If the response group deviates from the target group, additional respondents must be obtained or so-called reweightings must be applied in the analysis.

It is sometimes said that a study was representative because of its large sample size (or, conversely, unrepresentative because of its small size). This statement is nonsensical, because *representativeness is not related to sample size*. In well-known tables on statistical margins, numbers of approximately 380 respondents correspond to a confidence level of 5% in the results. These numbers are correct in themselves but say nothing about the representativeness. A representative group of 100 respondents may give more valuable results than a non-representative group of 1,000 respondents!

With regard to reporting on quantitative research, it is advisable to make your own short summary tables or figures and not include SPSS output in the body of the report or even in the appendices.

In conclusion:

1   Never automatically fall into the urge to create and administer questionnaires. Think carefully about the purpose of your research and then see what kind of information and therefore research is needed.
2   When you create a questionnaire, study other studies first. Use existing scales as much as possible and use a conceptual model for explanatory research.
3   In quantitative research, representativeness, that is, the composition of the sample, is more important than the size of the sample. A minimum of 380 respondents, for example, is therefore nonsensical.
4   Preferably use theory and a conceptual model to draw up a questionnaire.

## Summary

Customer analysis is divided into primary research (market research) and secondary research (using existing sources, such as online data).

A first application is to substantiate segmentation. Segment identification takes place by analyzing, on the basis of large-scale quantitative research, which groups of consumers or customers display similar preferences or comparable usage behavior and then describing these groups on the basis of the most characteristic features. The segments found are the basis for *targeting decisions to be made later*.

A second goal of customer research is to provide the necessary information for making positioning decisions. To this end, one must gain insight into two different dimensions: what is important to customers, and how does the brand perform on the desired properties? Various models and methods can be used, each with its own specific utility. For example, conjoint analysis is suitable for finding out the importance of properties. The means-goal chain is an argument for digging deeper into motivations. Measuring brand perceptions can be done with Likert scales. Keller's brand equity pyramid is part of the basis of the brand power questionnaire that has been presented. Eight dimensions are reflected in that list: category involvement, importance of attributes, brand awareness, functional brand associations, emotional brand associations, brand loyalty and ambassadorship, uniqueness, and consumer characteristics. These dimensions should be measured at least annually, allowing comparisons over time.

The amount of online data, often not collected yourself, is increasing enormously. This data has the great advantage that it concerns actual communication, search, and purchasing behavior of consumers. Analyzing it requires specific methods (e.g. artificial intelligence). The internet is ideal for experimental research. Online data provides little insight into why consumers do or do not buy products. Stricter privacy rules also place restrictions on the use of individual data.

A combination of qualitative and quantitative primary and secondary research provides the most complete picture of the profile and the wishes, perceptions, and behavior of (potential) customers.

## Kia in the UK: from 'budget' to premium

Kia certainly didn't pull any punches when it came to describing how British consumers might see the brand. 'Low value', 'budget', and 'small' were just some of the words that Kia's marketing director David Hilbert singled out. But that is all changing with the South Korean manufacturer investing in its ambitious plan to go premium and going full speed ahead in electric cars.

The car brand has been in the UK for around 30 years, so Hilbert claims it is still 'quite a new brand', which is one of the reasons people on the street who know Kia but don't own one 'still have the perception that we do low-value or budget cars'. In recent years, however, Kia has set out to change perceptions by releasing more premium cars, such as its Sportage and Sorento models. Its flagship in the electric and hybrid car segment, the Kia Niro, has become one of the leading cars in that segment. Another crown jewel in Kia's lineup is the Stinger. It is the result of nearly 10 years worth of design and engineering, and a model Hilbert, who joined the brand in 2016 to drive the transformation, argues redefines Kia as a 'luxury performance' brand.

'The launch of the Stinger is a way to challenge those perceptions of the Kia brand. Over the past few years you can see how we've developed our product range to really move away from that initial small car status we had in the UK', he says. 'Our newer models are quite polarizing in their design, and that makes them stand out from the crowd'.

As Kia has become a top 10 seller in the UK over the years, it no longer sees itself as a challenger brand but as a mainstream competitor, going up against brands such as Nissan, Hyundai, Renault, and Peugeot. Moving upmarket, however, does mean it will have to face off against a new set of brands. Hilbert believes its focus on tech, including safety features like a heads-up display, will set it apart from rivals. Features such as this will be added to its other models in future.

'With the Stinger, you don't have direct competitors, it's mainly premium ranges of mainstream brands, like Vauxhall's Insignia series or the high-end Ford or Volkswagen models. But we also touch on competing with premium brands, such as the Audi A5 and A4 series', he explains. 'With those premium brands you have to pay for the extras and added spec. But you get that as standard with the Kia Stinger. From a branding point of view, you could argue manufacturers like Audi are more premium than mainstream, but ultimately people buy cars on the exterior styling, and we believe we have a great looking car that will turn heads'.

## Shift in marketing

The move to attract a more premium audience has also led to a change of approach in marketing. With its target audience – mostly men who are 'successful in their careers' – being hard to reach and time poor, the brand decided to have multiple strands to the Stinger's launch campaign.

The introduction campaign of the Stinger involved a 'hero' TV ad and digital activity. A major part of the campaign also included an out-of-home takeover at Waterloo Station in London where passersby can see, touch, and feel the car. 'The best way to shift perceptions is by people seeing and physically touching the car, and to see how far we've come in terms of quality and design', according to Hilbert.

A lot of promotional attention was focused around the Six Nations Championship over two major rugby weekends, when the English team took on Wales and Scotland. The brand doesn't sponsor the tournament, but it wants to be associated with sporting events such as this. Sport has always been a 'crucial ingredient' of Kia's marketing strategy. It has previously rolled out global sponsorship deals around football and invested heavily in cricket on a local level. 'Sports helps us build Kia's personality. As we are a relatively new brand we need to develop a personality and sports provides a good way of doing so', he says.

Yet the brand's head of communications, Jane Fenn, insists it isn't looking to become an official sponsor of rugby events just yet. 'Obviously we have associations with football and cricket already, and rugby isn't something that we've sponsored. At the moment that's not our intention, it's around trying to best reach our audience and knowing that the audience's passion points are around sports', she says.

## The challenge of turning a brand around

Kia is undoubtedly keen to attract a new demographic, as well as to keep its appeal among its existing customer base. When asked if there is a risk of alienating consumers by trying to appeal to too many different audience segments, Fenn quickly refutes this claim. 'The fact we've got such a diverse product portfolio means the future for us is very much around being a brand that sticks at every single life stage. It's about making sure we have models that fit into what people are looking for at any stage. I don't see it being an issue', she says.

The car brand also claims to be realistic about turning its image around, and is taking a 'long-term approach'. Hilbert says the UK car industry is 'arguably one of the most competitive environments in the world', due to the nation's historic affection for cars. But a regional design office in Germany helps the Korean brand create new products for European tastes.

He concludes: 'If you think about where we were about 20 years ago compared to where we are now, we've gone from selling 10,000 cars a year to 100,000 in 2022. This is phenomenal growth and proves we are changing people's perceptions. Models like the Stinger and the Niro inject even more passion into that and push the boundaries'.

Source: Marketingweek.com, Feb. 5, 2018

## Questions

1   'Kia is undoubtedly keen to attract a new demographic'. Do you agree that demographics are the most relevant segmentation variable for Kia? Explain your answer.

2   Use the multi-attribute attitude model to determine how Kia is perceived, as compared to two competing brands: Toyota and Ford. You decide the characteristics based on which you compare the brands and investigate by talking to at least five (potential) car owners.

3   Use laddering to define customer values with respect to cars:
    a   Invite a car owner for an interview
    b   Define the usage situation on which you wish to focus during the interview (motivation for using the car: commute, leisure, etc.)
    c   Identify the benefits associated with using the car in that usage situation
    d   Finally, define the underlying values for this car owner

4   Create a means-end chain for a premium car brand such as the Kia Stinger.

5   Create a persona for the Kia Stinger. Use the information in the case, but add on with your own desk research or by talking with car owners.

6   Kia focused its promotion around two rugby events. On which dimension(s) of brand equity do you expect this promotion to focus: awareness, identity, image, or resonance? Explain your answer.

7   Do you personally feel that the image associated with rugby matches with the brand image desired by Kia? Explain briefly.

8   Suppose Kia would like to measure whether rugby matches the brand image of Kia.
    a   Would you advice qualitative or quantitative research? Or a combination? Explain your answer
    b   Create an appropriate research design

9   Suppose Kia would like to use MDS to determine its position in the market. Which steps should be executed to do this analysis?

10  Measure the net promoter score for Kia by conducting a small survey among a number of car owners.

# Chapter 6

# Industry analysis

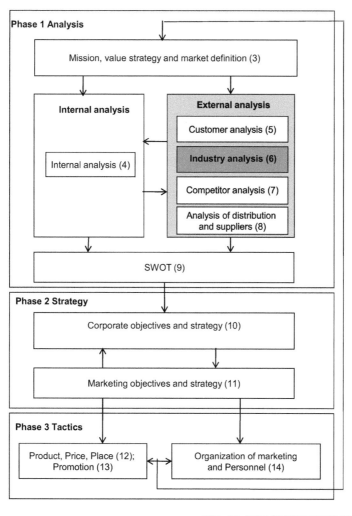

Phase 1 Analysis

Mission, value strategy and market definition (3)

Internal analysis

Internal analysis (4)

External analysis

Customer analysis (5)

Industry analysis (6)

Competitor analysis (7)

Analysis of distribution and suppliers (8)

SWOT (9)

Phase 2 Strategy

Corporate objectives and strategy (10)

Marketing objectives and strategy (11)

Phase 3 Tactics

Product, Price, Place (12); Promotion (13)

Organization of marketing and Personnel (14)

DOI: 10.4324/9781003381488-8

## Key points in this chapter

■ Know the differences between and the goals of an industry analysis and a competitor analysis.
■ Know the components of an industry analysis.
■ Realize that a Porter analysis is only part of an industry analysis, which in turn is part of an external analysis.
■ Be able to perform a macro-environmental analysis for a company.
■ Know how to assess the attractiveness of a market.

## Introduction

This chapter will review the industry analysis. The most important goal of this type of analysis is to gain insight into opportunities and threats from the perspective of the industry and the macroenvironment as well as insight into the attractiveness of the market in which the organization operates. Insight into the attractiveness of the market is important in regard to issues such as determining the investment level. Section 6.1 discusses the concept of industry analysis in relation to the concept of competitor analysis; these two concepts are strongly related. In Section 6.2, the goal and structure of an industry analysis are outlined. We then review the various phases of the industry analysis. Section 6.3 focuses on the analysis of the macroenvironment. The so-called aggregated market factors (including the product life cycle) are reviewed in Section 6.4. In Section 6.5, the factors related to industry structure (including the five competitive forces identified by Porter) receive attention. Finally, Section 6.6 explains how the results of the entire industry analysis can be summarized into conclusions about market attractiveness.

Because an industry analysis reviews not just the existing suppliers but also potential ones as well as parties that are not operating in the market directly, this chapter uses the term *industry analysis*. In this regard we are giving a broader meaning to that concept than is done in daily usage, where it typically refers to a group of businesses that produce or trade strongly related products, such as the house construction industry, the garment industry, and the shoe industry.

## 6.1 Competitive analysis: industry and competitors

The question 'What is competition?' seems redundant. After all, everyone knows the answer. Nevertheless, we will briefly consider this, because in recent years in particular in the literature there has been a tendency to shift more and more cases and parties under the designation of competition and competitive analysis. Two meanings can be given to the term 'competition':

1   The *degree of competition* (rivalry, competitive struggle in a market): how strong is the competition in a market for the favor of customers? In other words, how intense is the competition?
2   Competitors: the collective name for all the company's competitors.

Because of these two different meanings of the concept of competition, a *competition analysis* consists of two parts (Alsem, 1991):

1   An analysis of the intensity of competition in a market. This part of the competitive analysis falls under the *industry analysis*.
2   An analysis of the behavior of individual competitors. We refer to this as a *competitor analysis*.

The following differences exist between the two parts:

■   The main difference is that competitor analysis looks at *individual* competitors, while industry analysis looks at competition as a whole (see Figure 6.1). In other words, the industry analysis is a macro-level competitive analysis, while the competitor analysis can be seen as a micro and meso competitive analysis (strategic groups).
■   Another difference is that completely different facets of competition are studied. The competitor analysis involves analysis and prediction of the behavior and reactions of competitor A, B, and so on. To this end, the strengths and weaknesses of the competitors are mapped out, among other things. Industry analysis looks at the competitive forces in a market, for example, the distribution of power among suppliers or the bargaining power of suppliers. Porter's (1980) five forces model (see Section 6.5.2) is often used for this.

In this chapter, we discuss industry analysis. Chapter 7 is devoted to competitor analysis.

## 6.2 Purpose and structure of the industry analysis

One of the parts of a industry analysis is looking at the market structure, for example: How big are the different providers? Is there a strong concentration of power? And are the products very similar or are there important differences in the eyes of the buyers?

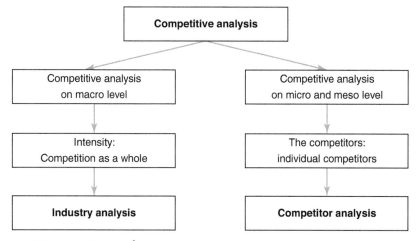

*Figure 6.1* Competitive analysis

Although all such questions are interesting in their own right, one has to wonder what should be done with the answers to these questions. If no clear goal of the analysis is established, there is a danger that all sorts of things will be sorted out without a clear relationship to strategy formation. And that would mean that the 'homework' has been done for nothing.

## 6.2.1 Purpose of the industry analysis

With regard to the industry analysis, two objectives are explicitly set.
We want to gain insight into:

1   the attractiveness of the market
2   industry opportunities and threats (such as from macro-environmental factors)

The market attractiveness conclusions are particularly important for formulating growth strategies and marketing objectives for the market for which the analysis is being performed. For example, the finding that a market is relatively attractive (for example, because of expected growth) leads to a decision to invest and to the formulation of ambitious growth targets sooner than in a market that is found to be unattractive (for example, saturated). This shows that an industry analysis has a strong relationship with a portfolio analysis (see Section 10.2). After all, the portfolio analysis also aims to determine the investments per product-market combination.

Gaining insight into possible opportunities and threats is a logical part of the SWOT analysis (see Chapter 9). The opportunities and threats are compared to the strengths and weaknesses at a later stage so that the company can then formulate possible strategies.

## 6.2.2 Structure of the industry analysis

An industry analysis examines all possible factors that influence market attractiveness. We can classify these factors as follows (originally taken from Lehmann & Winer, 2008):

1   Macro-environmental factors: factors from outside the market over which the various providers in a market have little or no influence but which do influence the market, for example, government decisions.
2   Aggregated market factors: factors related to market demand that directly determine the attractiveness of a market, such as market growth.
3   Industry structure factors: factors that determine the intensity of competition in a market, for example, the distribution of 'power' in a market: the concentration.

We have summarized these factors in Figure 6.2.
The combination of the three categories of factors listed in Figure 6.2 determines the attractiveness of a market. When analyzing it, the main thing is to identify changes over time and preferably to make a forecast.

**Macro-environmental factors**

- Demographic
- Economical
- Socio-cultural
- Technological
- Ecological
- Political-legal (government)

**Market factors**

- Market size
- Market growth and stage in product life cycle
- Economic and seasonal sensitivity

**Industry structure factors**

- Profitability
- Threat of new entrants
- Bargaining power of buyers
- Negotiating power of suppliers
- Intensity of competition
- Threat of substitute products

*Figure 6.2* **Components of the industry analysis**

# 6.3 Macro-environment analysis

We include here among the macro-environmental variables the variables that are difficult or impossible to control for the company and the other providers in a market. In Figure 6.2, we have listed the categories of factors that can be distinguished, the so-called *DESTEP* factors: demographic, economic, socio-cultural, technological, ecological, and political-legal. In the context of an industry analysis, these factors are important because they:

- affect all companies in an industry in most cases
- have a direct influence on the market size and thus on the market attractiveness
- can also affect other functional areas in a company, such as personnel and production

With regard to the aforementioned classification of macro-environmental factors, we can also note that there can be a mutual influence between the various categories of factors. For example, political decisions about income distribution can lead to changes in economic factors. A socio-cultural development such as growing environmental awareness goes hand in hand with a stricter environmental policy and with technological developments aimed at more environmentally friendly products, for example.

For each factor, the company must first determine what influence it has had in the past. For factors that can be quantified, such as economic and demographic developments, use can be made of causal models (see Section 13.10.3). The manager must then indicate what influence she expects to have in the future. For the latter, the macro-environmental factor itself must first be predicted. Various prediction methods can be used for this (see Section 9.1.2). For each category to be discussed (see Sections 6.3.1 to 6.3.6), we discuss content, data sources, and predictability. Finally, in Section 6.3.7, we provide some general points for attention in the macro-environmental analysis.

## 6.3.1 Demographic factors

Demography literally means description of the people. Demographic factors therefore concern characteristics of the population and, in particular, developments therein. This explicitly does not concern developments in a brand's target group, for example, the number of beer drinkers. Such developments are part of the market factors. Examples of demographic factors are:

- the size of the population in a given area
- the age structure of the population
- the number and size of households
- the degree of urbanization of the population in a certain area
- the composition of the population

A well-known example of a demographic development in many modern countries is the aging of the population: an increase in the percentage of elderly people (see Case 6.1). This has negative consequences for companies that market products for babies, such as diapers. However, a positive influence exists for markets for the elderly, such as trips for older people and magazines aimed at the elderly.

Other demographic developments in some countries include a decrease in population growth and decreasing household size. In most countries there are central statistical agencies that maintain detailed data, which is accessible online, regarding both past and predicted demographic developments. Although demographic developments are important issues for marketing, their effects appear gradually and in the long term.

## 6.3.2 Economic factors

Economic factors are important to many companies because these variables influence the extent to which consumers are likely to purchase certain products. Examples of these variables are consumer purchasing power, consumer confidence, the price level (inflation), and energy prices.

The government and politics (see subsequently) have a strong influence on economic developments.

## Case 6.1 Ageing

### 'Brands should stop seeing age as a defining feature of the over-50s'

New research conducted by Gransnet and Mumsnet among 1,028 of their users finds 78% of those aged 50 or over feel under-represented or misrepresented by advertising. This is worse for technology brands, cited by 87% of those questioned, followed by fashion brands (84%) and the entertainment industry (79%).

Nearly two-thirds (62%) believe they are ignored because advertisers are too young to understand the demographic, with 88% saying brands and agencies should employ more older people. Some 93% think advertisers need to start asking what over-50s want rather than assuming, while 92% want advertisers to acknowledge their spending power.

This has consequences for brands. Almost half (49%) of those questioned say they actively avoid brands who ignore them, while 69% suggest that if advertising were more representative of their age group, they would be more receptive to the brand behind it.

Gransnet editor Lara Crisp says: 'If advertisers want to talk to the over-50s, who have more disposable income than any other age group, they need to start by listening to them. It's just plain odd for marketers to assume that there's an upper age-limit when it comes to having an interest in technology, fashion or blockbuster films'.

Source: *Marketing Week*, 15 October 2018

## Case 6.2 Economic factors

### The crises from 2022: consumer confidence hits rock bottom

Energy crisis, housing shortages, staff shortages, nitrogen crises, angry farmers, political instability: the relief after the coronavirus quickly gave way to a less rosy feeling in some countries. If the economy had held up well during corona, a completely different perspective is expected after 2022. The fact is that energy prices have skyrocketed and consumers have to spend hundreds of euros more on energy. At the same time, (other) products and services have also become more expensive. It all doesn't look good. Consumer confidence therefore fell to an all-time low in the summer of 2022. After 2022, a recovery was visible, so the long-term effects might be limited, but no one knows for sure.

The influence of economic variables on market demand varies with the market. In general, due to their greater luxury character, consumer durables will be more sensitive to changes in economic developments than consumer non-durables. Although economic developments will often not have a significant impact on market demand for non-durable consumer goods, a shift in demand may occur. For example, an economic recession will have a favorable effect on cheaper brands, such as private label brands.

Detailed information about economic developments in the past are available at national agencies that collect statistical data. In contrast to government-related factors, economic variables are normally fairly predictable in the not too distant future. The reason is that these are often long-term trends that do not change strongly at one point in time. However, corona in 2020 and the East European war that started in 2022 show that the economy can also change quite fast.

### 6.3.3 Socio-cultural factors

Social-cultural factors relate to issues such as people's way of life, opinions, and standards and values in a society. They includes a large number of divergent developments, such as:

- an increasing awareness of climate change
- changes in media use (online)
- social changes within the family household, such as:
  - marrying later in life
  - an increase in the role of women in the labor process
  - an increase in the role of men in the household
  - delay in having children
  - changes in the upbringing of children
- the increase and revaluation of free time (work-life balance)
- a growing focus on health (eating habits, sports)
- a growth of subcultures

Clearly, these factors can have important marketing implications. The 'S' in DESTEP offers perhaps the best starting points for marketing. This creates new/growing markets for environmentally friendly products, leisure articles, quick meals, 'healthy' food, and so on.

Socio-cultural trends are important not only in product development but also in communication; just look at online behavior. The implication of this is that it will not always be easy for a company to actually convert a certain socio-cultural development into an opportunity.

Information about socio-cultural factors (past and future) is available online. Newspapers and magazines also often signal socio-cultural trends at an early stage. Furthermore, some (market) research agencies are explicitly involved in collecting information about living habits in the Netherlands. It appears that the corona pandemic has some consequences for people's behavior and thus for socio-cultural trends (see Case 6.3).

### 6.3.4 Technological factors

Technological developments can have far-reaching consequences. The most radical thing in recent years has undoubtedly been the arrival of computers and then the Internet, followed by the explosion of mobile phones, which has now become mobile online behavior in a broader sense. But less far-reaching developments, such as the introduction of dry soup, instant coffee, and compact washing powder, can also present important opportunities or threats. Technological developments are not only important from a marketing point of view. Technological developments are also important for other functional areas in the company, such as production, logistics, and information processing. In the context of marketing applications, it is often stated that a new technological invention (*technological push*) is only interesting if it is accompanied by sufficient interest from the market (*market pull*).

## Case 6.3 More from home after corona

Since the corona pandemic, people have been staying at home more often. We are still working at home more than twice as much as before the pandemic. We also order groceries, food, and clothing online more often.

That may not seem like much, but a majority of workers cannot work from home. This is because they have a job on location, such as train conductor or construction worker. As a result, the number of hours for people who can work from home is a lot higher. In the long term, these home workers expect to go to the office a little more often. But in the end, most people say that they plan to work from home one or two days a week on a structural basis.

Furthermore, after the pandemic, people also prefer to do other things at home than outside the home. For example, the number of people who (almost) never go away for a day has grown considerably. In addition, people shop online more often.

Incidentally, people have all boarded the plane again after corona, so the lasting effects of corona seem to be mainly in things that consumers like. Such as working at home.

Technological developments have accelerated in recent years, which means that the life cycles of products are also decreasing: the time for the development of a new, better product is getting shorter and shorter. Partly because fundamental technological research usually costs a lot of money, it is increasingly important for companies to be the first to come up with a product. Only then will there be enough time and market potential left to recoup the development costs of the product. When a competitor is earlier, part of the market has already been anticipated and one does not have the important image of being 'first'.

In contrast with other macro-environmental factors, a company can partly influence technological developments by itself, for example, through a strong research and development program. Influencing the other macro-environmental factors is generally not possible.

Information sources about technological developments are, for example, specialized sites or magazines.

## 6.3.5 Ecological factors

This category of variables has become dominant in the last few years: virtually the entire world recognizes that climate change is a major threat and that the Earth is running out of resources. Fossil fuels, but also eating meat, for example, must be replaced. And there are many more consequences, including for transport, production of companies, including agriculture (nitrogen), and so on. The term 'climate crisis' is appropriate. A related development is the level of energy prices, which we consider an economic factor.

Ecological issues also include the spread of (animal) diseases, such as swine flu, BSE (mad cow disease), and foot-and-mouth disease. With the worldwide corona epidemic since 2020, another 'human disease' has also been added (see also Case 6.3). These diseases obviously have a direct influence on people's consumption habits, but they also indirectly lead to increased attention to health. Case 6.3 shows that corona has partly changed our consumer behavior.

## 6.3.6 Political-legal factors (government)

Factors such as environmental policy, media policy, subsidy schemes, employment policy, monetary policy, and political developments abroad (war) can entail both direct and indirect threats or opportunities for a company. This influence can be limited but can also mean a 'trend break' in the development of a market. Two examples of 'sudden' shifts in the late 2010s are Trump's election as US president, which led to (more) instability, and Britain's decision to leave the European Union (Brexit, realized January 2020). The year 2022 gave some rest after corona but was quickly disrupted by the war in Ukraine. All of these events have a global impact. In some countries, legislative regulations are, of course, also important for companies themselves, such as those relating to smoking, 'vaping', (un)healthy eating, and gambling (Example 6.1).

## 6.3.7 Points of interest for macro-environmental factors

The following points of attention should be central to the analysis of all the macro-environmental factors mentioned previously:

- opportunity or threat
- continuous analysis
- forecasting and scenarios

## Example 6.1 More restrictive legislation needed

## Advertising for gambling restricted

After online gambling was declared legally free in the Netherlands in October 2021, gambling brands and advertisements sprang up like mushrooms. Many celebrities acted in humorous films with the message that you can easily get rich. According to researchers, this has contributed to a sharp increase in gambling and gambling addiction among young people, a serious matter. After the industry as a collective did not address this and therefore continued to opt for money, the rules for gambling advertising were tightened, like no famous athletes. But does this help enough? Pleas for a surcharge on the price of meat have not yet been implemented by the liberal government. It is not for nothing that Greenpeace is running a campaign in 2022 with the ultimate goal of a complete European ban on advertising and sponsorship for the fossil fuel industry. Maybe more regulation is a good idea after all.

An obvious sources of information about government decisions is Google. As for the ability to predict government decisions: tricky.

### Opportunity or threat

The influence of an environmental factor on the company depends on the company's ability to respond to a development, that is, on its own relative strengths and weaknesses. It cannot therefore be said a priori that a particular development constitutes an opportunity or a threat. For one company it can be an opportunity, for another a threat. In the latter case, a company can try to convert the threat into an opportunity: by deploying as many resources as possible, it can still try to respond to the development. For example, a publisher of youth magazines should not see dejuvenation and aging as a threat if they are able to market a magazine for the elderly.

In the SWOT analysis, we define opportunities and threats from the situation of an unchanged policy of a company.

## Continuous analysis

Due to the great importance of responding to macro-environmental developments in a timely manner – and preferably first if possible – it is important to be constantly open to signals from the macro-environment that indicate that a new trend is starting. In this context we sometimes speak of *environmental scanning*: the continuous scanning of the environment. Particularly for larger companies, it may be advisable to entrust someone specifically with this task.

Incidentally, the company must limit itself to relevant factors in environmental scanning. A complete macro-environmental analysis is impossible and unnecessary. In this context, Aaker (2013) argues that so-called *information need areas* must be designated: the most important factors in the external environment about which information must be collected continuously. A manager must identify these factors not only for macro-environmental analysis (e.g., demographic trend A, economic trend B, government factor C) but also for customer analysis (e.g., segments A and B) and competitor analysis (e.g., competitor A and potential competitor B).

## Forecasting and scenarios

Many macro-environmental developments are very difficult to predict. In practice, many predictions turn out not to come true or happen many years later – or earlier. Specialized agencies also regularly come up with new forecasts. In order to deal with this uncertainty in the planning process, it is possible to define scenarios around the most important factors. A scenario is a description of a possible environmental situation, for example, a disappointing economic climate or (for a beverage manufacturer) a total ban on advertising for alcoholic beverages. Incidentally, a scenario can also be defined with regard to the competition: for example, the competitor reacts or does not react.

In practice, usually no more than two scenarios are defined: a pessimistic scenario and a most likely scenario. In addition to a pessimistic variant, one should also define an optimistic scenario. After all, it can be bad, but it can also be good. And if things go well, the planned strategy may also need to be adjusted. In practice, optimistic scenarios are often omitted out of caution.

Defining a scenario is only meaningful if a manager also indicates how the company should respond in such a situation. To this end, an alternative plan can be described in an appendix to the marketing plan that corresponds, for example, to the pessimistic scenario. Such an alternative plan is called a *contingency plan*: it is accompanied by 'standards' (limiting values of variables) that indicate when such a plan becomes current. The most likely scenario then forms the basis for the marketing plan itself.

All scenarios must be realistic. A pessimistic scenario is not the same as assuming that everything is against you. For example, it is extremely unlikely that, in addition to disappointing economic growth, the competitor will come up with new, better products while at the same time energy prices are rising sharply and the government is imposing important online restrictions.

We have argued that macro-environmental factors can have a direct impact on total market demand. In Section 6.4, we discuss the aggregated market factors in more detail.

# 6.4 Aggregated market factors

Section 6.3 discussed the various categories of macro-environmental factors: the DESTEP factors. We have stated that every organization should try to keep abreast of developments in these variables. Any possible change or trend can represent an opportunity or threat. Macro-environmental developments can have an important influence on the attractiveness of a market. This influence is largely via the total market demand. In this way we arrive at an analysis of the aggregated market factors.

*Aggregated market factors* are variables defined around the total market demand (the primary demand or the size of the market). This involves the following variables:

■ The (potential) market size.
■ The (expected) market growth and (the stage in) the product life cycle.
■ Sensitivity to economic and seasonal trends.

## 6.4.1 Market size

The *size of the market* is important first of all because larger markets are in themselves more *attractive* than small markets. After all, large markets offer more sales opportunities, making it easier to recover the costs of investments. In addition, a larger market offers more opportunities for segmentation (such as searching for niches). Larger markets also attract more competitors, which adversely affects attractiveness.

Another reason for determining the market size is that it can indicate the *significance* of a certain market share. For example, a market share of 1% in the laundry detergents market generates a lot more turnover than the same market share in the liquid detergents market. The latter implies that it is important to clearly define a market: without an exact *market definition*, it is unclear what exactly the various analyses in the strategic marketing planning process relate to (see Chapter 3). In this regard, a manager may choose to define the market broadly or narrowly. In the first case, the market share will be relatively low and the number of competitors large. In the case of a narrow market definition, the reverse is true. This gives the impression that a manager can freely 'manipulate' market share by choosing a different market definition. That is, of course, not the case. The market is defined on the basis of strategic choices: which customer groups does the company serve, and who are its main competitors?

The analysis of the market size also involves trends and market segments. For example, a total market can shrink, but if certain submarkets grow, a company can focus more on that.

When analyzing the size of the market, the company must distinguish between:

- the *market served*: the current market
- the *potential market*: what would be the maximum feasible, for example, a 100% distribution of the product and strong sales promotion

Determining the potential market requires the application of *forecasting methods*. Data on the total market demand for food is collected by agencies such as Nielsen, GfK, and IRI. For other markets, a manager can use data from, for example, trade associations.

## 6.4.2 Market and submarket growth and the product life cycle

Market growth is also an important criterion for the attractiveness of a market. Within a market, the development of submarkets must also be considered. For example, a certain market (for example, the beer market) can stabilize or even decline, while certain submarkets (for example, non-alcoholic beer) can grow in the meantime.

Market growth is so important that it has been included as the market characteristic in the Boston Consulting Group's portfolio analysis (see Section 10.2.2). In addition to the current market growth, *expected* market growth is important. Thus, market growth predictions need to be made.

In making forecasts, the concept of the product life cycle can be used. The phase in the life cycle in which the market finds itself partly determines the expected development in the future.

Many products have a life cycle. After an introduction and a growth in sales, a stabilization follows and finally a decline. An important cause of such a cycle is that, over time, other, better products come onto the market, after which sales of the 'old' product start to decline. The life cycle of a product is usually visualized by means of a graph that shows the development of sales over time. It is often assumed that this curve is S-shaped and that four phases can be distinguished (see Figure 6.3):

1   In the *introduction* phase, sales are growing slowly: there are few consumers who know or use the product, and distribution is limited.
2   In the *growth* phase, sales are growing faster and faster: the product is catching on, distribution is increasing, and more and more consumers are buying it.
3   In the *maturity* phase, sales are still growing, but this growth is decreasing: there are not many 'new' consumers and later on sales are slowly declining.
4   Finally, in the *decline* phase, sales will fall sharply. In this phase, the function of the product is taken over by other products.

The product life cycle concept can be applied to product groups, brands, or varieties. In this case we talk about the life cycle of a product group, for example, laptops. It is about a market as a whole. The implementation of the market instruments will then differ per phase. For example, in the growth phase of a market, brands will be able to grow by focusing on the market potential, while in the saturation phase, growth must be sought in taking sales away from competitors (increase in market share) or through innovation.

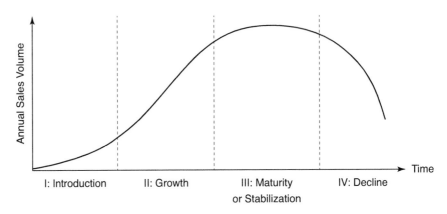

*Figure 6.3* **Example of an S-shaped product life cycle curve**

Brands and varieties can also have a life cycle, for example, Colgate toothpaste or Ariel Liquid. It is sometimes argued that in the introduction phase of a brand, the brand values to be communicated should mainly be instrumental, while in later phases the emphasis can be more on derivative, emotional properties.

The strategic implications of the life cycle concept are not always clear. A market in the growth phase seems attractive but attracts competitors. It is not uncommon for the number of providers in growth markets to become too large in relation to the ultimate market size. This irrevocably leads to the downfall of some of them. A product in the maturity or saturation phase seems less attractive, but in these phases there may be segments that still show growth. By choosing the right segmentation strategy, growth of the sales of the own brand is still possible. The latter illustrates that one should not take the life cycle of a product (or brand) as given but that one can influence and extend this cycle oneself. By choosing a good marketing strategy, a product (or brand) in the saturation phase can still offer many opportunities to remain profitable or become profitable again.

### 6.4.3 Cyclical and seasonal sensitivity

Markets in which sales are highly cyclical or seasonally sensitive are less attractive than markets in which this is not the case. After all, more uncertainty about sales and/or greater fluctuations means that a large degree of flexibility must exist in the company. Cycle sensitivity mainly occurs in luxury goods; these are often consumer durables. Sales fluctuations within a year due to seasonality (see Case 6.4) can occur for many products, such as beverages, travel, and sporting goods. A company that is active in several markets can try to reduce the uncertainty about total sales by making a well-considered choice of product-market combinations (portfolio decision).

## 6.5 Factors related to industry structure

Factors related to industry structure determine the intensity of competition in a market. An analysis of the intensity of the competition is important because a market is less attractive to the extent that the competition is more intense. Strong competition leads to

## Case 6.4 Economic sensitivity

### Traveling sensitivity to economy and news

The travel sector stays very sensitive to bad news in countries. Clearly, traveling was physically impossible during the pandemic. But after that, it recovered quickly. Disasters in countries also strongly affect the image of a country and thus the interest of tourists. The sector is also dependent on the development of private consumption. A shortage of personnel is a challenge, as is the growth of tourism in areas where the quality of life is under pressure as a result. Consumers are increasingly opting for convenience and are willing to pay for a unique experience. Collecting data is important for tourism providers in order to use it to provide added value to your guests.

increased marketing activity (promotional campaigns, high advertising efforts) and thus increases costs. As a result, the average profitability of companies is relatively low.

Because the profitability of companies is ultimately central to the industry structure analysis, it is important to first gain more insight into profitability (Section 6.5.1). Subsequently, the factors influencing average profitability must be examined. To this end, the firm can use Porter's (1980) industry model (Section 6.5.2).

### 6.5.1 Profitability

In a market, there can be important differences between the profitability of the various brands. Moreover, there are usually large differences in profitability between markets. Factors that determine this are, for example, the production process, the cost structure, and the competition. In an industry structure analysis, it is important to obtain the best possible insight into the profitability. The *variability* of profitability is also important: the extent to which profitability fluctuates over time. The latter is an indication of the risks present in a particular market. In markets with relatively high fixed costs, a drop in demand leads to a greater drop in profit than in markets with relatively low fixed costs.

In practice, it is not easy to gain insight into the average profitability in a market. It is true that companies publish data on costs and revenues in annual reports, but this data is never broken down into products and/or markets. The average profitability in a market must therefore often be estimated on the basis of impressions.

## 6.5.2 Industry structure according to Porter

In his well-known book *Competitive Strategy*, Porter (1980) establishes a relationship between the industry structure and competitive strategies. He argues that five factors (*competitive forces*) influence the competitive structure in an industry (Figure 6.4). In Porter's model, the central industry factor is the intensity of competition between existing suppliers in a market. The intensity of competition is determined by external and internal factors. We discuss these in the following.

### External factors

Figure 6.4 shows the external factors displayed. This concerns the threat of new competitors, such as:

1. the threat of new (potential) providers
2. the threat of substitute products
3. the bargaining power of suppliers
4. the bargaining power of customers (distributors and final customers)

If these 'threats' are strong, the intensity of competition will be relatively strong and the average profitability of companies will be relatively low. The threat posed by each of these four factors depends on a number of underlying factors, which are discussed in the following.

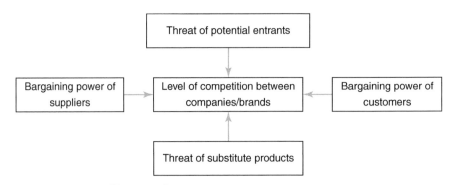

***Figure 6.4*** **Forces affecting industry structure**

The *threat from new providers* is strong if:

- the barriers to entry are low, for example, due to:
  - the absence of economies of scale
  - limited communication intensity
- there is little product differentiation
- there is easy access to the distribution channels

In many markets for consumer goods, there is indeed little (physical) product differentiation, but partly because of this, there are also intense communication efforts. A new product or brand can then only be successful if a corresponding communication budget is available. The latter also facilitates access to distribution channels: retailers prefer brands that are intensively promoted by the manufacturer.

The *threat of substitute products* depends on the breadth of the market definition used in the analysis. If one assumes a narrow market definition, there are relatively many substitute products.

The *power of suppliers and/or buyers (distributors)* is strong if:

- their power is highly concentrated
- they are not very price sensitive
- there is little product differentiation (presence of alternatives)

In the food industry in some countries, buyers (retailers) have considerable power because of their concentration. As a result of various mergers and acquisitions, only a few purchasing combinations are responsible for a large part of the turnover in the food industry. In other countries, that power is much smaller. Especially in less developed grocery markets (for example, in southern Europe), there are many smaller distributors and therefore these buyers have less power.

It is clear that for manufacturers, buyer power is an important factor. The increased concentration in some countries has led to the development of the account management system among manufacturers and a greater emphasis on collaboration with distributors.

This demonstrates that in the context of Porter's model, it is important to analyze the *distribution structure*. The market structure of the distribution chain determines the power of the distributor and thus the influence of this factor on market attractiveness.

In addition to the power of distributors, the power of final customers (consumers) is also increasing as a result of the use of the internet. We mentioned earlier that social media can, among other things, be extremely fast word of mouth, so that one complaint can turn into a serious reputation crisis, especially if journalists pick it up.

### Internal factors: the supply structure

Apart from the external factors, the intensity of competition between existing suppliers in a market is determined by a number of underlying *internal* factors. These are factors that directly determine the *supply structure* of the market. These factors are not shown in Figure 6.4 but will be discussed in the following. First, we discuss four elements that determine the supply structure itself: the number of providers, the degree of product differentiation (together these two dimensions determine the market form), concentration, and collaboration.

1    *The number of providers.* A larger number of providers in principle leads to a greater degree of competition.

2    *Degree of product differentiation.* This is the extent to which suppliers and products differ from one other. In this respect, competition is fiercer when, in the eyes of consumers, there are few differences between the products offered. With the ever-faster technological developments, products in many markets are increasingly similar.

3    *The degree of concentration of the suppliers.* With a strong concentration, market agreements can be made more easily and competition will generally be less intense; this also applies if the number of competitors decreases. This relationship does not always apply. If a company merges with a competitor (which increases the concentration), the larger company can throw more resources into the (competitive) battle. The relationship between concentration and competition is therefore not unequivocal and depends, among other things, on the company performing the analysis. For example, in the event of a merger, competition will by definition decrease for the merging partners, while competition may increase for the remaining providers.

The degree of concentration can be read, for example, by calculating the collective market share (concentration ratio) of the largest two (CR2) or four companies (CR4) and analyzing it over time. An increasing concentration ratio indicates a more one-sided distribution of power within the market.

Partly because of the importance of internationalization, concentration is increasing in various markets, for example, in banking, insurance, and aviation sectors. Concentration also plays a role in the healthcare sector, especially for health insurers, which still have a strong regional function. According to some, this somewhat hinders the functioning of the market.

4    *Collaboration within a market.* The existence of agreements or other forms of cooperation between competitors influences the organization of the market and therefore also the degree of competition.

Figure 6.5 provides an overview of the possible market forms.

| Homogeneity of the products | Number of providers | | |
|---|---|---|---|
| | A lot | Few | One |
| **Homogeneous** | Full competition | Homogeneous oligopoly | Monopoly |
| **Heterogeneous** | Monopolistic competition | Heterogeneous oligopoly | Monopoly |

*Figure 6.5* Market forms

The dimensions mentioned previously constitute the supply structure of the market. In addition, several other elements have an influence on the competitive behavior of suppliers:

■ *The development of the primary demand (market size).* In a shrinking market, growth in sales can only be achieved at the expense of competitors. Many markets are saturated, so this factor generally causes strong competition.
■ *The strategic effort of companies.* If a company carries out its main activity in a certain industry, it will be more competitive than a company that only carries out secondary activities in the same industry.
■ *The exit barriers.* This refers to all factors that make it difficult for companies to exit loss-making activities: the higher the exit barriers, the longer companies continue with loss-making activities and the fiercer the competition. Exit barriers can be:
  ■ *social factors*: the legal procedures for collective redundancies and the resistance of workers at risk of losing their job are very important barriers to exit
  ■ *highly specialized assets*: the liquidation value of a highly specialized machine is often considerably lower than its value in use
  ■ the *connection of a certain product with other products*, for example, due to the joint use of fixed means of production (buildings, machines, etc.), the desire to carry a complete range, or because of the company's image (withdrawing a product from the market will affect the share price negatively)
  ■ *emotional factors*, such as attachment to a product

For a company considering entering a market, one of the factors deserves special attention: *entrance barriers*. An analysis of entrance barriers is not only important to be able to determine the threat of potential suppliers but also to be able to determine which obstacles you have to overcome yourself in order to be able to enter a market. For a company considering entering a market, high barriers to entry are obviously a negative factor. In contrast, for companies that are already active in a market, high barriers to entry are a positive factor because they limit the threat of new entrants.

## 6.6 Determination of the market attractiveness

Conducting an industry analysis has the following goals:

■ obtain insight into opportunities and threats from the perspective of the industry
■ obtain insight into the attractiveness of the market

To summarize an industry analysis, first the identified opportunities and threats are listed.

Once a manager has examined the attractiveness of the market through the factors listed in Figure 6.1, it may be difficult to reach summary conclusions. After all, what is the conclusion if some factors are valued positively and others negatively? This problem is solved using the assumption that a high score on one factor can compensate for a low score on another. With this assumption, a summary 'score' can then be calculated using a weighted factor scoring method.

Suppose an ice cream manufacturer is considering producing candy bars. In order to investigate the attractiveness of the candy bar market, the manufacturer studies the factors listed in Figure 6.6.

Management gives a score for each factor on a scale of 1 (very unattractive) to 5 (very attractive). In the example, there is a large market. This leads to a score of 5 on the market size factor. On the other hand, there is also fierce competition. This factor is therefore given a score of 1. Subsequently, a weight is assigned to each factor on the basis of the importance (as estimated by management) of the factor for the attractiveness of the relevant market. Because different success-determining factors exist in different markets, this weighting can differ per market. The weighting also depends on how important the management itself considers a factor. For example, one company may find growth important, while the other considers profitability the most important. In this example, the market growth factor is considered the most important (weight 0.20). When all scores are multiplied by the weighting factors and added together, an attractiveness score of 2.95 is obtained.

The next issue is how this score should be interpreted. Is 2.95 high or low? The interpretation depends, among other things, on whether the company performing the analysis is active in the relevant market. A company that is already active in the market could compare its results with a previous period. This answers the question of whether the market is becoming more or less attractive and why.

A potential entrant could compare the results with another market, for example, the sandwich spread market: the market with the highest score is the most attractive for entry. In addition, the potential entrant must weigh the score against the height of the barriers to entry: what problems must be overcome to enter the market? Another market with a lower attractiveness score but also with lower barriers to entry may be preferable. After all, barriers to entry can be seen as the 'price' that must be paid to enter a particular market.

Obviously, the factor scoring method described here is subjective. The biggest challenge is determining the weights for the individual factors. Moreover, it is assumed that a

| Factor | Weight | Assessment | Score* | Value |
|--------|--------|------------|--------|-------|
| *Aggregate market factors* | | | | |
| Market size | 0.15 | Big | 5 | 0.75 |
| Market growth/product life cycle stage | 0.20 | Saturated | 2 | 0.40 |
| Seasonal and cyclical sensitivity | 0.05 | Limited | 4 | 0.20 |
| *Industry structure factors* | | | | |
| Margin of profit | 0.15 | Rather high | 4 | 0.60 |
| Threat of new entrants | 0.05 | Limited | 5 | 0.25 |
| Bargaining power of buyers | 0.10 | Strong | 2 | 0.20 |
| Negotiating power of suppliers | 0.05 | Limited | 4 | 0.20 |
| Intensity of competition | 0.20 | Very violent | 1 | 0.20 |
| Threat of substitute products | 0.05 | Pretty strong | 3 | 0.15 |
| *Total* | *1.0* | | | *2.95* |

*Figure 6.6 Example of calculating the attractiveness score of the candy bar market (1 = unattractive; 5 = very attractive)*

low score on one factor can be compensated by a high score on another factor. However, it is not unthinkable that a company require minimum values for certain factors, for example, a minimum required market growth.

An important advantage of applying the factor scoring method in the industry analysis is that the results of the entire analysis are clearly summarized. A systematically conducted and clearly presented industry analysis is of great importance not only for the benefit of our own analyses but also for internal communication within the company.

The example also shows that, compared to Figure 6.1, the macro-environmental factors have not been included in Figure 6.3. This is because they are factored into the assessment of market attractiveness through their impact on market size and growth.

Finally, we note that the way in which the industry analysis is summarized in Figure 6.3 allows for a direct link to the portfolio analyses in which several factors are taken into account (see Section 10.2). In the context of such 'multifactor portfolio analyses', analyses such as those in Figure 6.3 are very common.

The DESTEP analysis and Porter's model are very popular. These models are used in many theses at universities of applied sciences, for example, and sometimes it is even mandatory to use them. But we close this chapter with an important caveat.

An industry analysis is by definition at an aggregated level and provides general insights into market attractiveness and long-term developments therein (including via DESTEP). From a marketing perspective, this is of limited value. The DESTEP factors are usually long-term trends that many others also see coming and therefore offer little chance of gaining a competitive advantage. Porter's model shows the general competition but says nothing about specific competitors that you have to deal with as a manager. Most relevant in the industry analysis appear to be the market developments themselves and also those in submarkets. More or less, the whole industry analysis is interesting as background in a marketing plan, but the depth should come from customer and competitor analysis. And making any model compulsory is of course never a good idea: every research method and model should fit the research question. It is difficult to screw in screws with a hammer.

# **Summary**

The purpose of an industry analysis is to gain an impression of opportunities and threats from the industry and of (changes in) the attractiveness of the market and submarkets in which the organization operates. The attractiveness or expected profitability of a market is determined by the intensity of competition. The harder the fighting, the less attractive the market. The degree of competition, in turn, is determined by three categories of factors: macro-environmental developments (such as environmental and socio-cultural trends), aggregate market factors (such as market and submarket growth), and industry structure factors (such as retailer power). The macro-environmental analysis is an important source of opportunities. A company that can respond quickly to a socio-cultural development, for example, can gain a competitive advantage. As a result of various trends (such as climate change, online growth, political instability), important shifts in future consumption and information behavior can be expected. Given the large future uncertainties, a manager may choose to define scenarios around the most important trends.

The attractiveness of a market must be determined by making an assessment of the main underlying factors and calculating an attractiveness score based on this assessment. By weighting each of the examined factors and adding up the different values, one gets an attractiveness score that can be compared to the scores of other markets or to the score in a previous period. This information is especially important for determining the objectives and investment level of the organization in the relevant market (see Chapter 10). Information about opportunities and threats is also important for the marketing strategy. However, a more in-depth customer analysis and competitor analysis should be added.

## Aviation in trouble

Flying has become so cheap that it has changed our daily lives. Five days of work on a job in Poland, a bachelor party in Riga, or monthly up and down to the second house in Spain for a family from London: it's all possible. Yet the future doesn't look that bright for many airlines. The COVID pandemic changed everything for the airlines, and the outlook for aviation has not improved since then. Cut-throat competition continuously keeps airline ticket prices low, and increasing environmental awareness might impact our travel behavior, while fuel prices are rising due to the uncertain political situation and the war in Ukraine.

## Flying was the future

While airline ticket prices were going down continuously, the number of air passengers worldwide doubled between 2000 and 2010 to a total of 2.5 billion annually in 2010. The growth in passengers leveled off after that, but until the COVID pandemic in 2020, it was still growing in Europe at about 5% per year. However, a clear shift could be seen: 'traditional' airlines became less relevant and the low-cost airlines started taking the lead.

   The increase in passenger numbers was caused by a number of factors. Due to the low cost of flight tickets, flying became so cheap that people went to their holiday destinations by plane when they would otherwise have taken the car or train. However, the increase was not exclusively based on choosing another means of transport; low-cost carriers also expanded the market. Bachelor parties in

Latvia, a weekend in Ibiza, or shopping in Barcelona: without the low-cost carrier, this simply would never have existed. Flying became a commodity and mobility part of our lifestyle. We accepted the fact that flying is also very polluting.

Globalization, the emerging economies in Asia and South America, and European unification also contributed to increased mobility. Not only tourists were moving further and further away, business travelers also had more and more international contacts. And what about all those international students within Europe? Student exchanges created international friendships, and to maintain that, of course, one had to travel. The rise of social networking reinforced this: all those international friends on Facebook really had to be visited, if only to be tagged in even more photos.

## The trend reversed

And then COVID showed up. Much of Europe entered lockdown. Tourism became an illusion; business travel was replaced by Zoom and Microsoft Teams. Planes remained grounded, and aviation came to a standstill. For example, in the months of April and May 2020, there were only 700,000 air passengers in Britain, compared to more than 30 million in those two months the year before. Only freight transport increased, due to the sharp increase in online shopping during the lockdown period.

One would expect aviation to quickly return to its old level after the pandemic, and perhaps even more, with people wanting to make up for their missed holiday trips. However, this turned out not to be the case.

When European countries started to relax COVID regulations, tourism initially indeed quickly took off again. Airliner's profitable business classes, however, turned out to be much more difficult to fill: online meetings had become an excellent alternative to the expensive business trip. This shift was permanent: after the coronavirus pandemic, the number of business trips would never return to their former levels.

When corona finally disappeared from Europe, the sky seemed to clear for tourists. But then chaos at European airports appeared: long queues at all major airports in Europe. The reason: staff shortages. During the COVID crisis, tens of thousands of employees were laid off in the aviation sector: personnel who cannot simply be brought back. In addition, many airline employees were dissatisfied with the working conditions and the increased workload, resulting in strikes, which meant that flights had to be canceled again and travelers had to wait even longer to get their passports checked.

As a result, there were 373 million air passengers in the EU in 2021. This was an increase of 35% compared to 2020 but still well below the more than 1 billion passengers in the pre-COVID year 2019.

Improvement was in the air for 2022, but the Russian invasion of Ukraine created new uncertainties such as rapidly rising fuel prices, which initially made flying a lot more expensive, and then impacted overall purchasing power. Tourism is a luxury when a possible recession is looming and many people are struggling to pay their energy bills.

And with all that, global warming was becoming more and more a fact of life. The train to London has only 10% of the $CO_2$ emissions per passenger kilometer compared to the same journey by plane, and more and more people became aware of this. Even so, sustainability may be considered important by everyone these days, but that does not mean that we will immediately adjust our transportation behavior. Alternatives for flying are not always available either. After all, going on holiday by car is even more polluting, and the train is often hardly an alternative: Europe is hopelessly behind in terms of trains. A continental train journey can cost days, and hundreds of euros, due to differences in equipment and regulations. Despite a success like the Eurostar connection between London and Paris, a European network of high-speed trains connecting capitals is still a long way off. Nevertheless, opportunities for the train seem to arise. The European Union declared 2021 the European Year of Rail, and in time this may lead to new investments in railroad connections. In the meantime, the aviation industry is also aiming for more sustainability. With sustainable aviation fuel, flying on hydrogen, or electric flying on future generations of rechargeable mega-batteries, the aircraft of the future can become more sustainable. For now, however, this is still far away.

## Low-cost carriers

Revenues and margins were already under pressure in aviation before the COVID pandemic. For example, Air France-KLM saw passenger numbers rise by 2.8% to 101 million passengers in 2018, but profitability remained limited. Other national airlines did not perform much better. However, this was in stark contrast to the results of low-cost carriers. Ryanair, the European market leader for cheap flights, realized a profit of around 900 million euros in 2018, and the number of Ryanair passengers increased by 9% to more than 140 million.

Low-cost carriers such as Ryanair are also referred to as no-frills airlines. In Europe, they have emerged since the liberalization of the European aviation sector in the 1990s. Since April 1, 1997, airlines have been allowed to operate flights to and from any airport in Europe, regardless of the country in which they are established. The Irish Ryanair, the first low-cost carrier in Europe (founded in 1988), has grown since that date from 3 million passengers to 117 million in 2016. The low-cost model was replicated all over the world. The strategy is aimed at getting the plane as full as possible; after all, the airline doesn't earn anything from an empty plane seat. Extremely low prices well before the date of the flight ensure a high occupancy rate, and rapidly rising prices in the days before departure should bring in profit.

Low-cost carriers also aim to remove as many frills as possible. Regional airports, with much lower take-off and landing fees, are their base of operations. There are no free drinks and meals, and luggage has to be paid extra.

The efficiency of low-cost carriers is apparent from the following overview, which shows the number of passengers per employee (total number of passengers divided by the total number of employees of the company):

| Number of passengers per employee (based on annual reports from the airlines) | |
|---|---|
| Ryanair | 9,451 |
| EasyJet | 6,772 |
| British Airways | 735 |
| Air France\KLM | 715 |
| Lufthansa | 624 |

An increasing share of the European aviation industry is now in the hands of low-cost airlines. Ryanair is again the largest of these. In the pre-COVID years, national airlines had a much more difficult time than low-cost carriers, and they even started experimenting themselves with low-cost carriers. Air France-KLM's low-cost brand Transavia is an example.

Of course, COVID did not leave the no-frills airlines untouched. However, the following charts show that the low-cost carriers such as Ryanair initially recovered quicker than the national airlines (such as Lufthansa):

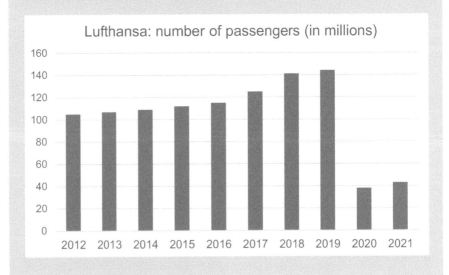

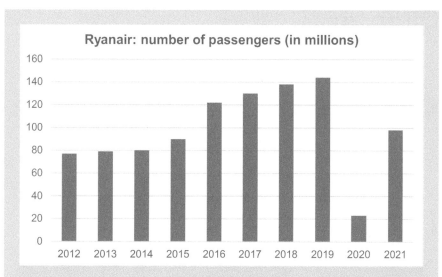

Ryanair: number of passengers (in millions)

The question is, of course, what will happen to European aviation in the future? Will the industry survive this crisis? And will low-cost carriers continue to outperform national airlines in the years to come, just as before?

## Questions

1   Which strategic groups can be distinguished in the European airline industry?
2   Make a macro-environment analysis of the European airline industry based on the information in this case.
3   The Brand Benefitting Model distinguishes a number of strategies to generate benefits for the customer. Which of these strategies has been chosen by Ryanair? Explain your answer.
4   In what stage of the product life cycle is the airline industry? Explain your answer.
5   a   Do you feel that the aviation industry is sensitive to economic fluctuations? Why (not)?
    b   Do you consider the aviation industry sensitive to seasonal trends? Why (not)?
6   a   Determine the attractiveness of the aviation industry, from the point of view of Ryanair, by using Porter's five-forces model.
    b   To what extent does this differ from the attractiveness from the viewpoint of AirFrance-KLM?
7   Give your own opinion:
    a   What is the future of the European airline industry?
    b   Who will be most successful in this future: the 'traditional' airlines or the low-cost carriers? Explain your answer

# Chapter 7

# Competitor analysis

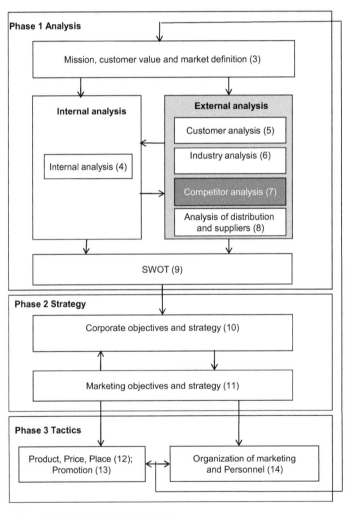

```
Phase 1 Analysis

    Mission, customer value and market definition (3)

    Internal analysis          External analysis

                               Customer analysis (5)

                               Industry analysis (6)

    Internal analysis (4)      Competitor analysis (7)

                               Analysis of distribution
                               and suppliers (8)

                    SWOT (9)

Phase 2 Strategy

    Corporate objectives and strategy (10)

    Marketing objectives and strategy (11)

Phase 3 Tactics

    Product, Price, Place (12);     Organization of marketing
    Promotion (13)                  and Personnel (14)
```

DOI: 10.4324/9781003381488-9

## Key points in this chapter

- Know the steps of a competitor analysis.
- Be able to identify competitors by using the appropriate methods.
- Assess competitors' strengths and weaknesses on the corporate and brand levels.
- Know which qualitative and quantitative data sources can be used in a competitor analysis.
- Put it all together in making a forecast of a competitor's strategy and reactions.

# Introduction

A competitor analysis can be thought of as a competition analysis at the micro level: The behavior of individual competitors is analyzed with the ultimate goal of predicting the competitors' actions and reactions. It is important to maintain a clear structure in a competitor analysis. Without structuring, the problem may arise, as it often does in practice, that large amounts of data are collected about competitors without deducing the relevant *information* from the data.

Section 7.1 describes the goal and structure of a competitor analysis. The first phase in a competitor analysis is identification of the competitors. Section 7.2 discusses the methods that may be useful in that process. Sections 7.3 through 7.6 outline the other phases of the competitor analysis. Section 7.7 reviews a number of data sources that may be used.

# 7.1 Goal and structure of the competitor analysis

## 7.1.1 Goal

A competitor analysis looks at individual competitors. A competitor analysis can therefore be regarded as a micro-level competitive analysis. Opportunities that the company can expect should mainly be sought in the weaknesses of the competitors. These offer starting points for our own competitive advantages. The extent to which competitors pose a threat to one's own company depends on their objectives and strategies. Comparatively less danger can be expected from a competitor who is satisfied with his position and has no new plans. However, a competitor that wants to grow and enters into an active competition with, for example, new products and high advertising efforts, poses a major threat to one's own company. Therefore, the objectives of a competitor analysis are:

1   gain insight into the strengths and weaknesses of competitors
2   gain insight into the future behavior (the expected strategies) of competitors

*Competitors' strengths and weaknesses* are compared to one's own strengths and weaknesses; this provides insight into the extent to which the brand is strong or weak *in relation to its competitors*. An own strong point has little strategic value if competitors also have that strong point. On the other hand, a weakness is less serious if all competitors have the same weakness. It is therefore about determining what the own *relative* strengths and weaknesses are.

Understanding the *expected behavior of competitors* provides indications of opportunities and threats posed by those competitors. Incidentally, with regard to the future behavior of competitors, a distinction can be made between:

- the expected 'autonomous' behavior of the competitors: what they intend on their own
- possible reactions of competitors to strategies of their own organization

## 7.1.2  Structure of the competitor analysis

When conducting a competitor analysis, the company can choose two angles: a rival approach and a partner approach.

1   A manager may regard competitors as rivals: other suppliers who compete for the favor of customers and who therefore have to be 'fought out'.
2   Competitors can also be considered possible cooperation partners. Collaboration can go so far as to involve a merger or acquisition.

For the practice of competitor analysis, this means that it should not only be aimed at looking for weaknesses in the opponent (in order to gain a competitive advantage yourself) but also at looking for starting points for cooperation. An opportunity arises when the competitor has an interesting strength in which its own company is weak and vice versa.

Example 7.1 is an example of a merger of two former competitors.

Five phases can be distinguished in a competitor analysis (see Figure 7.1):

1   identification and choice of competitors (Section 7.2)
2   competitors' objectives (Section 7.3)
3   current competitor strategies (Section 7.4)
4   identification of the success determinants and strengths and weaknesses of competitors (Section 7.5)
5   expected competitor strategies (Section 7.6)

Of the aforementioned phases, 4 and 5 provide the information we listed under the objectives of the competitor analysis: strengths and weaknesses, future behavior. Already we notice that the first four phases require a systematic and creative approach, while the last step (strategy prediction) above all requires important empathy with the 'psychology of the competitor'.

## Example 7.1 Huge merger at holiday parks

They announced it halfway through 2021, and at the end of 2022 it also seems to be coming around with the Authority for Consumers and Markets: the takeover of Landal Green Parks by Roompot. These two major providers of holiday parks want to join forces in order to gain an even stronger market position in Europe. Roompot is mainly active in Central and Southern Europe and Landal in Northern Europe, so the combination complements each other well. The investment company that owns Roompot sees opportunities to achieve a higher return. Whether Landal's beloved mascot Bolle and Koos Konijn from Roompot will both continue to exist is not yet certain.

Source: NRC, 18 June 2021, and www.parkvakanties.nl, consulted 13 October 2022

## 7.2 Identification and selection of competitors

A definition of what a competitor actually is can be: another provider that potentially meets the same needs of the target group. Based on this definition, the question of who the competitors are therefore depends on the definition of the need. The latter is related to the market definition. For example, do the top management of Coca-Cola think they are active in the 'colas' market or in the soft drinks market? Or even on the stimulant market?

We will discuss in turn:

■ levels of competition (Section 7.2.1)
■ methods to identify competitors (Section 7.2.2)

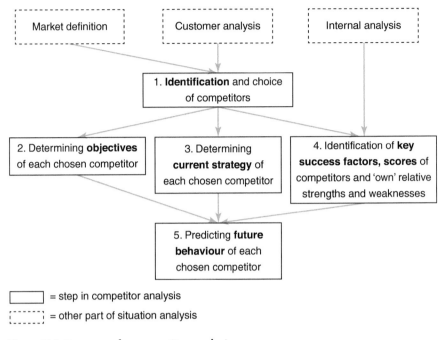

*Figure 7.1* **Structure of a competitor analysis**

■   the choice of identification method (Section 7.2.3)
■   the choice of which competitors are most important to the company (Section 7.2.4)

### 7.2.1 Competition levels

With regard to competition, we can distinguish four levels of competition:

1   *Product form* competition: competition between brands targeting the same market segment, such as Pepsi Light versus Coke Light.
2   *Product category* competition: competition between products with similar properties, such as different soft drinks.
3   *Generic competition*: products that meet the same consumer needs, such as beverages.
4   *Budget* competition: competition for consumer money, such as food and entertainment.

Figure 7.2 contains some other examples of competition at these four levels.

As one moves from product form to budget competition, the market definition becomes broader, and, as a result, the number of competitors increases. There is thus a direct interplay between the definition of the market and the identification of the competitors. As a result, there is also a relationship with marketing decisions: different product characteristics must be emphasized at the different levels of competition. If the manufacturer of low-priced TVs from Figure 7.1 chooses the product form level, then the

| Competition level | Low alcohol beer | Low-priced TV | Chinese restaurant |
|---|---|---|---|
| 1 Product form | Low alcohol/non-alcoholic beer | Low-priced TV | Chinese restaurants |
| 2 Product category | Beer | TVs | Restaurants |
| 3 Generic | Drinks | Equipment | Restaurants, eating at home |
| 4 Budget | Drinks, food, entertainment | Durable goods, vacations | Food, drink, entertainment |

*Figure 7.2* **Examples of competition levels**

competitors are other low-priced TVs, and he must emphasize why his TV is so much better than the other cheap TVs. If the manufacturer starts from the product category level, then he must position himself in relation to all other TV brands, for example, with the price. At the generic level, he must point out to the consumer the advantages of a TV over a computer, for example. At the budget level, he could communicate why a TV is so much more interesting than other leisure activities.

The choice of the level of competition is therefore clearly related to the market definition. The market definition in turn is determined by, among other things, two related factors:

- The *planning level* in the company: corporate, business unit, or product level
- The *planning term*: are these short-term plans (one year or less) or longer-term plans?

We show the relationship between this and the other in Figure 7.3.

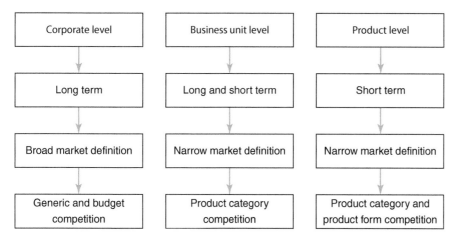

*Figure 7.3* **The relationship between corporate level, planning term, market definition, and level of competition**

As the level of aggregation in the company increases, the planning time generally becomes longer, the market definition broader, and the level of competition higher. For example, matters such as cooperation with potential partners play a role at the company level. This is a long-term matter that requires a broad market definition and therefore a high level of competition. After all, potential partners do not only have to be active in their own direct market but can also be active in adjacent markets. On the other hand, annual short-term planning is important at product level; this includes the day-to-day threat of directly competing products/brands (product category competition and product form competition).

## 7.2.2 Methods to identify competitors

The methods that can be used in the identification of competitors fall into:

1  competition-oriented methods
2  customer-oriented methods

### 1 Competition-oriented methods

In general, it can be said that the competition-oriented methods are especially suitable for determining competition at the *firm* level, while the buyer-oriented methods are suitable for identifying competing *products*. A competitive orientation means that one identifies the competition oneself on the basis of information about the competitors, for example, by checking which competitors follow a similar strategy to one's own company.

### 2 Customer-oriented methods

Customer-oriented (*customer-based*) methods use data on the demand side of the market: the competition is analyzed from the point of view of the customers. For example, customers can be asked which product/brand they would buy if the preferred product/brand were not available.

We first discuss two competition-oriented methods and then three customer-oriented methods. In Section 7.3, we briefly consider the advantages and disadvantages of both categories of methods.

### Competition-oriented methods

We can distinguish the following two competition-oriented methods:

1  management judgement
2  strategic groups

### 1 Management judgment

Based on her experience and market knowledge, a manager can sometimes reasonably estimate what the current and future competitors are (management judgement). If necessary, she can consult representatives, retailers or other internal experts. A tool she can use for this is to classify the competitors into companies and:

- whether or not to market the same *products*
- whether or not to serve the same *customers* (markets or segments)

The most direct competitors are companies that supply the same products to the same markets. More indirect competitors are companies with the same products that focus on a different market. Companies that serve the same market with different products can be seen as potential competitors.

### 2 Strategic groups

The second competition-oriented method involves dividing the suppliers in a market into strategic groups. A strategic group is a group of companies pursuing similar strategies. Insight into how these groups are composed can be obtained by examining which strategies the providers choose in a market, such as by looking at the choice of the target group and the positioning and the implementation of the market instruments: product quality, assortment, pricing, distribution spread, deployment of representatives, and the communication mix. In addition, the strategies with regard to other functional areas are also important, for example, the extent of R&D, production, purchasing, and finance. Example 7.2 contains an example of strategic groups in the Dutch banking market.

The concept of strategic groups simplifies competitive identification and choice, as it were. After all, competition will be strongest, especially within strategic groups. With a large number of competitors, the competitor analysis can then emphasize one's own strategic group. The other strategic groups can be analyzed as a whole. In practice, sometimes all (or groups of) 'small competitors' are defined as a strategic group, assuming that they apply more or less similar strategies (which is often not the case).

### Customer-oriented methods

We distinguish three customer-oriented methods:

1   direct identification research on customers
2   brand changes
3   positioning research

### 1 Direct identification research on customers

The most direct and simple method of identifying competition through buyers is to ask *directly* about competitors, for example, by asking questions such as: 'What other comparable products do you know?' or 'Which products have you also considered buying?' A researcher gains insight into the most direct competitor by asking, for example: 'Suppose your preferred brand were no longer available; which brand would you buy?' A disadvantage of such questions is that it is uncertain to what extent the opinion

## Example 7.2 Strategic group in the banking market: the 'neobanks'

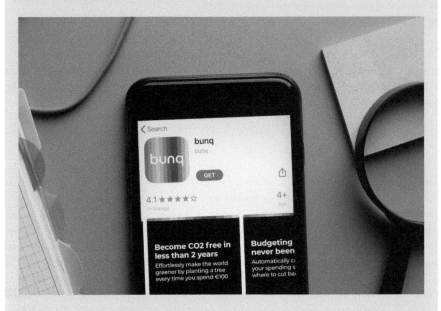

They are small, new, and what's more: digital. They promise a revolution in the banking world, with all their new services – for which you pay a little extra – and also by being more customer friendly. They do what the customer wants and not what a product can offer. Banks traditionally did it the other way around. The 'neobanks', such as Bunq and Knab, are doing their utmost to capture market share. Two problems. First, the big banks can imitate their trick. For example, the idea of an app to easily transfer money came from Bunq, but when ABN AMRO copied and distributed it a little later through its large network, the 'Tikkie app' took off. Second, it is still not possible in the Netherlands to transfer your bank account number to a new provider. 'Consumer organizations should take this up', says Bunq founder Ali Nikham.

Source: NRC, 16 November 2019

of the interviewee reflects their own behavior. The great simplicity of this method is an important advantage.

A variant of the direct question is to make a link with product use. Approaches via product use associations ask users of the product to name all use cases or applications. They are then asked to name suitable products for each application. Other product users are then asked to indicate how suitable each product is for each usage situation. Finally, the products can be clustered based on the equality of suitable applications. An advantage of this method is that it provides insight into less direct forms of competition, such as generic competition.

### 2 Brand changes

A more advanced customer-oriented identification method uses data on the extent to which customers switch between brands (*brand-switching data*). The advantage of this is that behavioral data is used. This data is usually collected through household panels. But online data can also be used when click and purchase behavior is analyzed per consumer.

### 3 Positioning investigation

Chapter 5 describes methods for mapping brand images. If this is done for different brands, it is possible to see which brands are 'close to each other'. The underlying distances can even be calculated exactly if the correct methods are used.

## 7.2.3 Selection of the identification method

In practice, competition-oriented methods are mainly used. This is also the simplest: one forms an opinion based on one's own market knowledge and does not have to carry out additional fieldwork.

However, competition-oriented methods have an important drawback: the question is whether what people think about the competitors actually corresponds with the perception of the customers. There is a risk that certain companies will be labeled competitors who are not actually perceived as such by customers, and vice versa. This danger is not present if one chooses a customer orientation when identifying the competition.

However, a customer orientation does have a number of *limitations*:

■   First, it is difficult to gain insight into potential competitors and indirect competitors. For example, customers only know the existing products; they are not aware of competitors who have not yet entered the market.
■   A second limitation is that buyer-oriented methods usually have to be implemented at the brand/product level. Customers often do not know the suppliers of products.

Both limitations imply that buyer-oriented methods are particularly suitable for short-term planning. After all, in the short term, it is unlikely that new competitors will enter, and the analyses can therefore be limited to the product-brand level.

However, for longer-term planning, one must also look at the company level and at possible potential competitors. The competition-oriented methods are especially suitable for this. We therefore conclude that it is advisable to choose both a customer and a competitive orientation when identifying competitors. In this way one puts into practice what Kotler (1984) so aptly formulated many years ago: 'learn how your customers view your competitors rather then how you view your competitors'.

## 7.2.4 Choosing the competitors

Once the competitors have been identified using the previous methods, the next question is whether a detailed behavioral analysis of all possible competitors should be carried out. In practice, this is not necessary and, moreover, generally unfeasible – let alone that a separate behavioral analysis can also be carried out of all possible potential competitors. Within the chosen market, the manager must make a choice of the competitors to receive the most attention. But who is most important? The biggest or the one most like us? And who will be important in the future? Because these questions will in principle be answered in the follow-up analysis, it seems impossible to make a choice in advance. A solution to this chicken-and-egg problem is to first perform a global competitor analysis and then take a closer look at a few competitors.

Two factors play an important role in the initial selection of competitors: *market share* and *similarity to one's own product/company*. It seems logical to always consider the largest competitors in terms of size, as well as those competitors that have similar products or target the same target group.

## 7.3 Objectives of competitors

In the second phase of competitor analysis, the company attempts to derive the objectives of its main competitors. This actually involves two aspects:

1   What does the competitor want?
2   How badly does she want that?

The first aspect relates to the competitor's growth direction: does the competitor want to maintain or increase market share? And if the latter is the case, does the competitor want to grow with the help of existing or new products and with existing or new customers? The second aspect is determined by the commitment of the competitor: the extent to which she feels involved in the product/market. Both aspects together determine the commitment and aggressiveness with which a competitor is active in a market. The greatest threat can be expected from a competitor that feels very involved in a market and wants to grow in that market. But a competitor that 'just' wants to keep its market share, but wants it very badly, also represents an important threat (see example 7.3).

Indications of what the competitor wants can be obtained in the following ways:

- *By comparing the competitor's objectives with current results.* A difference between, for example, desired and realized market share leads to an expected growth strategy.
- *By applying a portfolio analysis for the competitor.* Assuming that the competitor also applies a portfolio analysis itself, one can derive the most logical portfolio decision (investments and growth direction) on the basis of its own analysis of the position of the SBUs and products in a portfolio model.
- *By determining how important a product is to the competitor.* This can be measured in, for example, turnover, profit, or number of employees.
- *By studying the competitor's market instruments over time.* For example, a price reduction and an increase in advertising spending may indicate that the competitor is pursuing growth, which could pose a threat to its own product. On the other hand, minimizing marketing efforts could indicate a harvest strategy, that is, obtaining as much profit as possible. Less danger can usually be expected from such a competitor in the long term.

## Example 7.3 Apple and Samsung in fierce battle

In industries where technology is important, such as in the computer or mobile phone market, innovations are an important means of maintaining a competitive advantage. After all, large investments in research and development are often preceded. If a competitor can claim an innovation, it is very disadvantageous. The battle between companies like Apple and Samsung in the smartphone market is therefore fierce. Samsung attacks the competitor directly. For example, a commercial for the latest Samsung is introduced on purpose before the iPhone 14 comes on the market, and the voice-over literally says that 'the latest innovation does not come from an iPhone, but is already there, with the Samsung Flip Over'.

Source: www.imore.com

## 7.4 Current strategies of competitors

A company that wants to be able to indicate what strategy it expects from a competitor must first investigate what the competitor's current strategy is. This includes:

■  the marketing strategy: choice of target group (segments) and chosen positioning
■  the handling of market instruments

Insight into the marketing strategy is obtained through observation and analysis of the market instruments. You then first look at the market instruments of the competitors and derive the marketing strategy from this by asking yourself what the core message of the brand actually is. Insight into the competitive advantage that a competitor is seeking is provided, for example, by its advertising and all other offline and online communications. One can almost certainly assume that every company will communicate its (perceived) strength to its customers. A detailed analysis of the content of the competitor's communication is therefore of great importance.

You can gain insight into the target group targeted by the competitor through market research (who are the competitor's customers?) and indirectly, for example, via the competitor's communication channels (offline and online). The choice of distribution points also says something about the choice of target group. An analysis of the target groups that competitors have defined is important to avoid segments with intense competition, while segments with low competition represent an opportunity.

In Section 7.7, we discuss concrete data sources that the company can use in the competitor's strategy analysis.

## 7.5 Identification of success factors and competitive strengths and weaknesses

In the fourth phase of the competitor analysis, the company must answer three questions:

1  Which resources and skills in the market are important; in other words: what are the success-determining factors? (Section 7.5.1)
2  What are the strengths and weaknesses of the competitors? (Section 7.5.2)
3  What summary conclusions can we draw? (Section 7.5.3)

### 7.5.1 Identification of key success factors

In order not to have to identify all possible strengths and weaknesses in the strength-weakness analysis of the competitors, it makes sense to first determine which resources and skills are most important in a market. To this end, the success-determining factors in the market must be determined, that is, those resources or skills that have a major influence on the result of a company. 'Result' can refer to relative costs, customer loyalty, market share, profit, and so on (Day & Wensley, 1988). We can also say that these are the strengths that lead to an above-average result. A company that has these strengths has an advantage over competitors. Examples are: efficient physical distribution for food manufacturers, low labor costs for a television manufacturer, good relations with intermediaries for an insurance company, and so on.

To be able to operate successfully itself, knowledge of the success-determining factors is of great importance for a company. As a starting point for the identification of success-determining factors, one can use the same checklist as one that can be used for an internal analysis (see Figure 4.3). The question, then, is which factors from that checklist are most important. Aaker (2013) gives a number of questions that may be helpful:

1  Why are successful companies successful and unsuccessful companies unsuccessful?
2  What are the main motivations of customers? What do customers consider important?
3  Which phase in the production process produces the highest added value and which phase produces the highest costs?
4  What are the barriers to entry within the industry and between segments in the market?

#### 1 Comparison of successful and unsuccessful companies

A method that ties in with the first question is to compare successful and less successful companies. By comparing the characteristics of successful and less successful companies in one's own industry, one can gain insight into those characteristics that are responsible for success. We note that in order to reach reliable conclusions, sufficient data must be available. Because this is often not or only partly the case for a specific sector, such an analysis will often have to be carried out qualitatively, and the conclusions will be indicative.

### 2 Customer motivation

To answer the second question, a customer analysis must be performed. The aim is to find out what is important to people. The simplest method is to ask directly how important certain product properties (attributes) are considered. To prevent respondents from indicating that they find everything important, methods have been developed that take into account the *trade-off* between characteristics. A very suitable analysis method in this context is *conjoint analysis* (see Section 5.4). We will not discuss these and other methods in the context of this chapter.

### 3 Value chain

A method that ties in with the third question is an analysis of the value chain as it applies 'on average' in the industry. Activities that deliver the highest added value on average are potential success-determining factors. Furthermore, the phases in which the costs are highest are the most suitable for seeking cost benefits.

### 4 Barriers to entry

The fourth question implies that the barriers to entry should be analyzed. Factors that make it difficult for a potential supplier to enter the market (for example, obtaining the technology necessary to make the product, obtaining a high degree of distribution, or running an intensive advertising campaign) are generally also factors of great importance in the industry.

On the basis of previous analyses, the importance of each factor in the sector can be indicated (see first column of Figure 7.2).

## 7.5.2 Determining competitors' strengths and weaknesses

For each of the factors shown in Figure 7.4, it must then be determined to what extent the selected competitors are strong or weak in this respect. To this end, the company will have to collect a large amount of mostly qualitative data, in which discussions with various 'experts' (representatives, customers, researchers, etc.) will be an important source. Figure 7.4 provides a brief description and qualification for each of the competitor attributes.

## 7.5.3 Determining the relative strengths and weaknesses

In Chapter 4, we described different methods for the internal analysis. If those methods are also used for competitor analysis, a direct comparison can be made. For example,

| Characteristic | Importance in industry | Competitor A | Competitor B | Competitor C | Other competitors |
|---|---|---|---|---|---|
| **Marketing**<br>• Product quality<br>• Customer orientation and service<br>• Market knowledge<br>• Relationship with retailers<br>• Brand image<br>• Price level | | | | | |
| **Innovation**<br>• Technology<br>• Expenditure on R&D<br>• Patents | | | | | |
| **production**<br>• Raw materials<br>• Production resources | | | | | |
| **Sustainabiity**<br>• Footprint | | | | | |
| **Financing**<br>• Cash flow w<br>• Parent company<br>• Current position | | | | | |
| **Management**<br>• Flexibility<br>• Entrepreneurial quality<br>• Staff turnover | | | | | |

*Figure 7.4* **Potential success drivers in the industry and strengths and weaknesses of a company or brand**

the value strategies can also be determined for competitors, or image characteristics of competitors can be included in a perception study, so that you as a brand know whether you are perceived as 'younger' than competitor X.

A handy method for a *competitive* comparison is to draw up a table in which one's own organization is added as a comparison at the same time (see Figure 7.5: *a competitive grid*). One can limit oneself to the success-determining factors (factors of great importance in Figure 7.5). Comparison of competitors' strengths with own strengths provides insight into '*relative*' (*unique*) *strengths*.

| Success determining factor | Competitor A | Competitor B | Competitor C | Other competitors | Own organization |
|---|---|---|---|---|---|
| Innovative/new | 1* | 5 | 2 | 3 | 2 |
| perceived quality | 4 | 4 | 1 | 2 | 5 |
| Sustainability | 5 | 2 | 4 | 2 | 5 |
| Ambition top management | 2 | 2 | 5 | 4 | 1 |
| Distinctive image | 4 | 1 | 3 | 4 | 2 |

*Figure 7.5* **Competitive grid: scores on key success-determining factors of competitors and own organization:**

\* 1 = very weak; 5 = very strong

From Figure 7.3 we can deduce the following:

- The own organization is strongest in terms of high quality (5) and sustainability (5).
- Own relative strengths and weaknesses. Because A is also sustainable, this is not a relatively strong point for its own organization; the high quality is a relatively strong point and therefore a competitive advantage. The other points point to a lack of innovative management and (probably partly because of this) an unclear image.

Furthermore, Figure 7.5 can be used for an initial selection of future collaboration partners. For example, an own weak point is the quality of the R&D. Competitor B is particularly strong. Conversely, B's financial position is limited and that of its own organization is very good. So there seems to be a mutual interest in cooperation between the own organization and competitor B.

A more specific form of comparing one's own organization with its competitors is referred to as benchmarking. *Benchmarking* (sometimes referred to as 'copying') is best described as looking for best practice at other companies and then translating this into one's own company (Camp, 1995).

By comparing business processes within one's own company with those within other companies, one gains insight into one's own performance and thus into the starting points for improvement. These business processes can range from administration and production to comparing commercial performance. The comparison can be made with competitors but also with non-direct competitors. Research shows that benchmarking can be a good source of knowledge for finding a sustainable competitive advantage (Vorhies & Morgan, 2005). Case 7.1 is an example of benchmarking.

## 7.6 Expected strategies of competitors

In the previous stages of competitor analysis, we have answered the questions of who the main competitors are and what the objectives, current strategies, and strengths and weaknesses of those competitors are. In the final phase, the question of what the competitor will do in the future must be answered on the basis of the previous elements. At the same time, one should try to predict how competitors might respond to strategies formulated by the organization. It is therefore important at this stage

## Case 7.1 Competitive advantage

### Tenzing is really different from other drinks

Natural, sustainable, radically different: that is the energy drink Tenzing. No screaming like the big competitor Red Bull, but a sincere brand, based on the legendary Sherpa Jamling Tenzing, who has managed to climb Mount Everest many times. The brand started in England, is very successful there, and is now also for sale in the Netherlands. Tenzing: naturally energy.

to draw a kind of 'conclusion' from all the previous information about the expected behavior of the competitor. Good empathy for the position of the competitor is necessary.

It is not easy to arrive at concrete predictions in this last phase. Among other things, the company will have to use subjective forecasting methods: methods in which 'experts' in one way or another generate forecasts based on the available information. Concrete methods that can be used for this are a *Delphi study* (making a forecast in a number of rounds with experts in the company) and *role-playing*.

In a role play, people are assigned roles of market parties and each has to draw up a plan based on his own objectives (which are by definition conflicting: not everyone's market share can grow). The advantage of a role-playing game is that someone literally empathizes with the psychology of the competitor. Armstrong (2001, 2002) has shown that this forecasting method often produces good predictions of competitive behavior. As with the analysis of other environmental factors, it can also be useful here to define scenarios; for example, the competitor does not react or reacts to our strategy.

Finally, we make an important comment on the competitor analysis. Companies must be careful not to focus too much on the competition. Of course it is important to keep a close eye on the competition, but companies should be guided in their strategy primarily by the customer and not by the competitor. Research into price reactions by retailers in the United States shows that brands often 'overreact' to each other (Leeflang & Wittink, 1996 (they researched price reactions); Steenkamp et al., 2005 (they researched the reaction to promotions and commercial break)). This leads to unnecessary price reactions and reactions with other sales-promotion instruments that the providers themselves ultimately all lose.

## 7.7 Data sources

Collecting data about competitors is sometimes referred to as *competitive intelligence* (or *business intelligence*). In fact, this means nothing more than trying to collect as much data as possible about the competitors in the most inventive way possible. This can range from requesting university research reports to buying out a competitor's employee. How far creativity must and may go on this point, we leave unaddressed here.

In practice, several publicly available sources can be used. We can make a distinction between the following sources:

- What *other market parties* say about the competitor, for example, buyers, suppliers, their own representatives, and financial institutions.
- What competitors say about *themselves*, for example, in annual reports, online, lectures, press releases, job advertisements, advertisements, or via 'bought away' employees from competitors.
- What *third parties* say about the competitor, for example, online, articles in newspapers and magazines, consumer organizations (product testing), industry studies, research agencies, and universities.

For all data that a company collects about competitors, it is important to bring it together and make it accessible to others within the company. Only in this way can a coherent picture of the current and expected behavior of the competitors emerge.

To achieve this, the following conditions must be met:

- *Responsibility for competitor* analysis rests in one hand. This person can ensure that the correct analyses are carried out and that all data is collected.
- There is a well-functioning marketing information system. In such an automated system, not only must one's own data be stored but also that of competitors. Everyone in the company should be able to request the most recent data from the most important competitors and also to enter their own 'news'.

In addition to qualitative data, there are a number of *quantitative* data sources. In some countries there may be secondary data sources about the competitors. In Section 4.6, we discussed Nielsen, GfK, and IRI files that include data regarding sales, prices, and distribution of fast-moving consumer goods and some other product categories as well. Detailed data about advertising are collected in many countries by Nielsen Media Research.

A limitation of the quantitative data sources mentioned here is that they mainly relate to consumer markets of goods. This implies that conducting a competitive analysis in service or industrial markets requires greater inventiveness than in consumer markets.

Nevertheless, adequate competitor analysis is also possible in such markets by engaging the right people and collecting and processing data in a structured manner. For example, in Chapter 5, we showed how brand images can be measured. An organization can apply a similar method to itself and to its competitors.

## Summary

The purpose of competitor analysis is to understand the strengths and weaknesses of key competitors, as well as their anticipated strategies. The combination of both things, coupled with one's own strengths and weaknesses, determines whether the competitor should be seen as a rival or as a future partner. The question of how many competitors a company has depends on the level at which the target group competes: at the budget level, at the generic level, at the product category level, or at the product form level. The annual marketing plan usually looks at the last two levels. Within a chosen level, the most important competitors must then be determined. It is important to carry out this identification from the point of view of management and, moreover, to check how the target group views the competition (market research).

The current strategy and objectives are then determined for the most important competitors and what strengths and weaknesses they have. At the end of a competitor analysis, all collected information is introduced into, for example, a brainstorming or role-playing session, in which a forecast of the competitor's behavior is made from the perspective of the competitor. This also involves estimating the likelihood that the competitor will react to the future strategy of the company conducting the analysis.

Competitor data is largely qualitative in nature. For markets of non-durable consumer goods, a lot of quantitative data is also available from agencies such as Nielsen and GfK. But an organization's own market research can also contain information about competitors.

## McDonald's versus Burger King: concept or taste

You likely know more about the fast food industry than you realize. If you live in the United States – or pretty much anywhere else – it's everywhere. Off of every exit on the highway and at every rest stop. In the food court at the mall and on the commercial strips on the outskirts of town. In cities and at airports.

What you may not have noticed, though, is the changing dynamics within the industry. The last several years have seen an absolute explosion of diversity in both restaurant concepts and menu choices. This evolution reflects an industry that has been responsive to changing consumer tastes as well as entrepreneurs finding niche opportunities to profit, an industry that needs to be responsive as consumers become more and more critical about what they eat.

The fast food sector has been growing rapidly in the past decades due to the busy lifestyle of consumers. Hamburger giants, pizza chains, and sandwich restaurants all compete to favor the grazing consumer. But the growth has been slowing down over the past decade, partly due to the growing health consciousness of the consumer. The fast food market continues to be dominated by hamburger fast food restaurants in most countries. However that market share is sliding, and alternatives such as wok-to-go concepts have been gaining. Also, 'premium' fast food chains such as Five Guys claim to offer a better food or customer experience than the traditional chains. A recent trend is the rise of fast casual restaurants such as Shake Shack and Chipotle. These restaurants offer consumers freshly prepared, higher-quality food in an informal setting, with counter service to keep things speedy. Shake Shack, for instance, is a burger chain that is successful by offering a casual dining experience at a fast food pace.

*Figure 7.6* **Eating behavior**

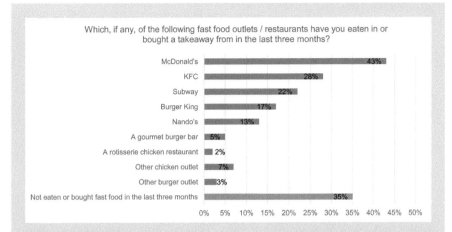

*Figure 7.7* **Restaurant usage**

Especially in the United States, these developments have led to price competition between McDonald's, BK, and other 'traditional' hamburger chains. But competition with 'dollar menus' not only leads to financial consequences; the brand equity also suffers.

McDonald's still is the global market leader. The golden arches not only symbolize Big Mac and Happy Meal but also a certain lifestyle. But there are negative associations as well. Especially in Europe, McDonald's is seen as an example of American imperialism, together with, for instance, Hollywood and Coca Cola.

The brand has to deal with growing health concerns as well as increasing competition. One of the causes is the growing diversity in the fast-food landscape. But there are also challenges in hamburger country itself. One of the competitors even claims to be king: the Burger King. Even though there are more McDonald's restaurants than Burger Kings worldwide (around 38,000 McDonald's restaurants against around 19,000 Burger King restaurants), both brands have established themselves firmly in the mindset of the customer.

The final word is up to the consumer: Does he love McDonald's or will he choose the BK way?

## McDonald's

The good thing of being a market leader is that free publicity comes more or less automatically.

The campaign 'I'm lovin' it' is, according to McDonald's, more than just a slogan. 'It's a way of thinking, with a central theme how McDonald's can satisfy the needs of every individual customer', according to the global chief marketing of McDonald's Corporation. The intention of this approach is to check whether the product range still matches the diversity of desires of the client. Store design and service will be adapted to the taste of the customer as well.

The McDonald's strategy is visible in the worldwide campaigns. In the commercials a variety of people are enjoying McDonald's products. At the start of the campaign reactions were mixed. Critics were surprised that McDonald's apparently had abandoned the 'think global-act local' approach. With this approach McDonald's had conquered the world and a unique image in each country of the world.

'The campaign is loaded with people enjoying themselves, individually. A boy is playing the drums with McDonald's straws, a businessman is swinging in the streets. Sometimes the fun has a cynical touch, like when a kickboxing girl kicks a milkshake out of someone's hands. This type of fun is typical for individualistic cultures like in Europe or North-America. In collectivistic cultures like in Southern Europe, Asia or Latin-America people have fun with each other', according to the criticism.

Another critic: 'This is a typical American feelgood-campaign. This might not work with a European audience. I also wonder whether it is smart to target young people. Especially in a number of European countries the brand is doing very well with families with children. McDonald's has to be careful not to lose this audience'.

Others, though, have more favorable opinions. A reaction is that the campaign fits a market leader.

> The campaign is superficial, but demonstrates a vision. Apparently McDonald's has no identifiable competitive advantage. That's why – like with a fashion brand – McDonald's uses a non-tangible appeal to make the brand relevant and valuable. If there would have been a distinctive advantage it would be a lot easier to make a nice commercial, which gives the consumer a hint of what they can find at McDonald's. But fastfood is not necessarily tasty or healthy. Whatever you say about it would not be believed by the consumer anyway. What remains is the ordinary, the day-to-day aspect of McDonald's. And because of this, McDonald's is part of our lives.

Even though the theme is global, execution of the campaign remains localized. A European marketing director of McDonald's highlights that: 'The specific contents will differ from country to country, especially because the strategy is focused at the individual consumer. The global strategy is localized in each country. In many countries in Europe, an important focus is on teenagers, young people, and families with children'.

## Burger King

The difference in positioning between Burger King and McDonald's was characterized once as 'concept versus taste' or 'brains versus belly'. The market leader, McDonald's, is communicating a lifestyle in its global campaign. Burger King, on the other hand, emphasizes its products. According to a marketing expert: 'I think that in the fastfood industry the best way is to communicate the product. Burger King has a distinctive way of making its products'. The preparation (grilled, meaning less fat) has been a unique selling proposition (USP) for BK for years.

The Burger King campaigns have a local approach, although the supporting slogan is global. For a long time, this slogan was 'Have It Your Way'. This slogan was based on the idea that Burger King offers a specific snack for each moment of the day. 'Nowadays, the consumer is changing its habits continuously', according to a marketing manager at Burger King. 'Grazing patterns and tastes change continuously'. Therefore, the slogan was changed in 2014 into 'Be Your Way'. In an interview, management of Burger King noted that 'Have It Your Way' focuses on only the purchase – the ability to customize a burger. By contrast, 'Be Your Way' is about making a connection with a person's greater lifestyle. 'We want to evolve from just being the functional side of things to having a much stronger emotional appeal', according to BK's brand management. In 2022, BK's customer focus was emphasized even more with the new slogan 'You Rule'.

Whether the new tag line can help Burger King's image over the long term remains to be seen. Real BK lovers know the slogan. These people appreciate BK for its quality, the flame grilling as a way of preparing the food, and the Whopper. But the slogan is almost unknown for most people. A marketing specialist observed that

> The problem is that people don't see themselves as living the Burger King lifestyle. You've got to be realistic with the place that your brand holds in real life. And it is not certain whether the consumer knows what the slogan 'You Rule' stands for.

The reply of BK's brand management to this criticism: 'We will communicate this more in the future. The slogan puts the customer in the middle. The customer decides on the size of the menu, and whether he wants ingredients like cheese, ketchup or bacon'.

Next to a new slogan, part of BK's strategy is to directly challenge McDonald's products. For instance, when McDonald's brought back the McRib sandwich, Burger King responded by unveiling a $1 BK BBQ Rib as a cheaper alternative.

Burger King management is clear about its value proposition. It is just as good as McDonald's, with the same products, just slightly more upscale and, possibly, cheaper. At the same time, Burger King is noted for its superior burgers. Therefore, Burger King remains aware of the importance of its flagship: the Whopper.

## Questions

1   Explain, based on the case about the fast food market, what the difference is between the industry analysis and the competitor analysis.
2   Which strategic groups can be identified in the fast food industry?
3   Four levels of competition can be distinguished. Define for each of these levels competitors for McDonald's.
4   According to the Brand Benefitting Model, a company has to choose for a specific brand promise in order to be successful. Which brand promise is

essential for fast food? Do you see any differences between Burger King and McDonald's? Explain.

5 The industry structure can be defined by using Porter's five-forces model. Execute this model for the fast food industry. Draw your conclusions about the attractiveness of this industry, from McDonald's point of view.

6 The case highlights the observation that 'McDonald's has no identifiable competitive advantage'. Do you agree with this observation? Explain your answer.

7 Suppose McDonald's would like to identify its most direct competitors by means of multidimensional scaling. Describe step by step what needs to be done to execute this analysis.

8 What would you favor in the fast food industry: a campaign focusing on the product (like the 'You Rule' slogan of Burger King) or a campaign focusing on the lifestyle you want to create with your brand (like McDonald's)? Explain your answer.

9 What do you consider the key success factors in the fast food industry?

10 a What is the competitive advantage of McDonald's, as compared to Burger King?
   b What is the competitive advantage of Burger King, as compared to McDonald's?

11 Imagine McDonald's asked you to analyze and predict the strategy of Burger King by performing a competitor analysis. Start with the information in the case, but do additional desk research where necessary.
   a Define the (marketing) objective of Burger King.
   b Identify the current marketing strategy (target group selection and positioning) of Burger King.
   c Determine the strengths and weaknesses of Burger King.
   d Predict the future strategy of Burger King: how do you expect Burger King to proceed in the near future?

12 Imagine Burger King asked you to analyze and predict the strategy of McDonald's by performing a competitor analysis. Start with the information in the case, but do additional desk research where necessary.
   a Define the (marketing) objective of McDonald's.
   b Identify the current marketing strategy (target group selection and positioning) of McDonald's.
   c Determine the strengths and weaknesses of McDonald's.
   d Predict the future strategy of McDonald's: how do you expect McDonald's to proceed in the near future?

# Chapter 8

# Distribution and supplier analysis

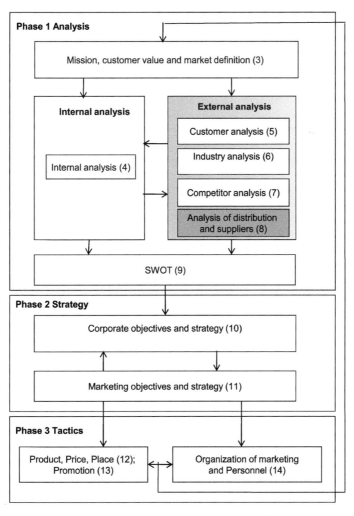

**Phase 1 Analysis**

Mission, customer value and market definition (3)

**Internal analysis**

Internal analysis (4)

**External analysis**

Customer analysis (5)

Industry analysis (6)

Competitor analysis (7)

Analysis of distribution and suppliers (8)

SWOT (9)

**Phase 2 Strategy**

Corporate objectives and strategy (10)

Marketing objectives and strategy (11)

**Phase 3 Tactics**

Product, Price, Place (12); Promotion (13)

Organization of marketing and Personnel (14)

DOI: 10.4324/9781003381488-10

## Key points in this chapter

- ■ Know aggregation levels in the distribution analysis.
- ■ Be able to analyze the distribution structure in an industry.
- ■ Assess the role of disintermediation.
- ■ Be able to analyze the distribution intensity by applying different criteria.
- ■ Know the steps in an individual distributor and supplier analysis.

## Introduction

A thorough distribution and supplier analysis is important because it offers the opportunity to build good relationships with these parties. Availability of your product has a strong influence on market share. A competitive advantage can then be achieved through a good channel strategy. And a good relationship with suppliers can be a basis for high quality or excellent sustainability. Of course, the growth of online sales means that more and more providers will follow a *multichannel* strategy: selling through multiple (for example, in-store and online) channels. But in all cases, a good distribution analysis is important.

Section 8.1 focuses on the structure of the distribution analysis, after which Sections 8.2 to 8.4 flesh out the distribution analysis on three levels: the macro, meso, and micro levels. Section 8.5 is devoted to supplier analysis.

## 8.1 Goal and structure of a distribution analysis

In preparation for Chapter 11, we note that three types of decisions must be made in the context of deploying the market instrument distribution (or channel strategy):

1 the choice of distribution intensity (target)
2 the choice of distribution channels
3 distribution channel management

In this chapter, we will not discuss these decisions, but we will focus on providing an analysis scheme with which the necessary information can be obtained in order to implement the said decisions in the most responsible manner possible. For the purposes of this book, we limit ourselves to a few key points.

A distribution analysis takes place at three levels of aggregation:

1 *Macro level*. This involves mapping the entire distribution column, both vertically (possible levels, long or short channel) and horizontally (different types of intermediaries within a level). So this is a global distribution structure.
2 *Meso level*. This analysis involves:
   - ■ the more specific distribution structure within one type of intermediary, for example, the distribution of power of retail chains within the type of supermarkets

■ the position of brands within one level and in particular within the group of retailers (analysis of distribution intensity)

3 *Micro level*. This concerns the strategies and wishes and desires of individual distributors (distributor analysis). Separate distributors here mainly refer to separate retail chains, such as Jumbo. It is therefore not about separate distribution points, because a chain consists of many stores. Some also consider this meso level; in this book we do not do that because it is about the relationship with individual companies, as well as competitor analysis.

The levels cannot be separated from each other. Thus, the distribution structure has a macro and a meso component. While this distinction makes analytical sense, both belong to the distribution structure. Furthermore, analysis of the distribution structure at the meso level (within one group of intermediaries) requires information on the market shares of individual retail chains. These data are obtained from the micro-level distribution analysis.

These three levels are discussed in turn in Sections 8.2 to 8.4.

## 8.2 Distribution analysis at the macro level

In this section we discuss the dimensions of the distribution analysis and the online channels.

### 8.2.1 Dimensions of the distribution analysis

The analysis of the distribution structure at the macro level involves two dimensions:

1 the number of levels in the distribution column (vertical: length of the channel)
2 the type of intermediary links within one level, such as the distinction within the group of retailers between supermarkets, discounters, convenience stores, specialist shops, or the 'grey circuit' of, for example, petrol stations (horizontal: width of the channel)

Insight into this is important for the choice of the type of intermediate links. There are two possibilities regarding the length of the channel: direct delivery and indirect delivery.

Direct delivery takes place to customers without the use of intermediaries; online delivery has of course grown enormously and is still growing. We will discuss this further in Section 8.2.2.

With indirect delivery, intermediaries are called in. Possible intermediaries between producer and consumer are agents, importers, wholesalers, and retailers. If one opts for delivery via retailers only, then we speak of a short channel. In all other cases one speaks of a long channel. Some of the selection criteria here are the number of (final) customers that the company wishes to serve and the type of product (including shelf life and complexity). Incidentally, it is not necessary to choose one channel. Companies are increasingly opting for a multichannel strategy, for example, by combining *bricks* (offline) and *clicks* (online: e-commerce).

## 8.2.2 Online channels

The internet makes it relatively easy to have direct contact with customers, and direct contact enables direct trade. Online shopping (e-commerce) has therefore expanded enormously. Direct delivery to customers by *producers* implies that intermediaries are 'cut out' (*disintermediation*). Such decisions in food are difficult, because the intermediaries are also customers and will not be happy if they are ignored.

Another challenge for online sales is to limit costs. The logistics require an entire organization and lead to additional costs, including the costs of returns (see Case 8.1). For example, consumers who buy clothing often seem to have many sizes and types delivered, a large number of which are then returned free of charge. It seems that there are also consumers who really wear a new suit, for example, for a special occasion and send it back the day after, sometimes with stains on it.

The arrival of online shopping has created a new kind of companies that do not provide their own products or services but help you as a customer to choose *'intermediaries'* between service providers and customers. Booking.com is well known (Case 8.2), but there are also plenty of airline ticket sites. The difference with 'product intermediaries' such as amazon.com is that no logistics device needs to be set up for these services: no products need to be physically transported. You buy someone else's service, just on another site. Very simple. The business model that these sites have is that they usually get a share of the turnover. As online shopping is becoming increasingly important, these new intermediaries are also becoming increasingly important, and employment at these organizations is also increasing. Because customer wishes and customer behavior plus ICT knowledge are essential, new marketing-ICT functions are emerging.

## 8.3 Distribution analysis at the meso level

### 8.3.1 Distribution structure at the meso level

In the previous section, an analysis was provided of the distribution structure at the macro level. However, more detailed information is needed to determine the optimal choice of a channel. We briefly describe the role of the *wholesaler* and then discuss the level of the individual *retailers* in more detail.

The *wholesaler* is positioned between the manufacturer and the retailer, and its core function is to tailor the supply and demand of goods in markets, both qualitatively and quantitatively. As a result of the enormous development in ICT, in which manufacturers and retailers increasingly coordinate their supply and demand with each other more easily and intensively via electronic data interchange (EDI), there is evidence that the wholesale trade is being eliminated. For a supplier, this means that an analysis of the added value that the wholesaler can offer is relevant.

Within a single level of intermediaries (e.g. retailers) or even within one type of intermediary links (e.g. supermarkets), it is important to understand the distribution of power (market shares) between individual companies and distributors. After all, this distribution also determines the importance of individual retail brands (in addition to volume and margin) and is therefore a guideline for the marketing efforts in this regard. When analyzing the distribution of power, the company must – of course – take into account

## Case 8.1 Costs of return

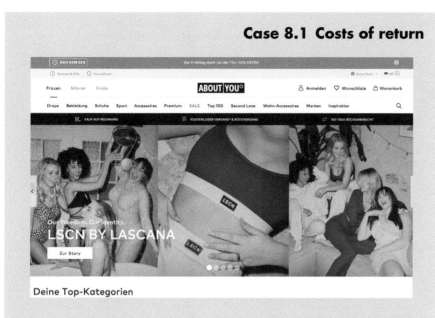

More than 200 billion dollars (~180 billion GBP) worth of merchandise was returned in 2021, according to a study by Appriss Retail and the National Retail Foundation, amounting to approximately 20% of total online sales.

In addition, according to a consumer survey, around 25% of customers believe they're returning between 5% and 15% of their purchases. A small percentage even said they return more than half of what they buy online. The numbers worsen during holidays like Christmas when it's estimated that two out of three consumers return a gift or purchase. It's especially the case with apparel, electronics, and jewelry items that return rates are high (the average eCommerce return rate for apparel is around 10%).

Returns cost businesses about 66% of the original item's price. Even if the item is returned in good condition, the entire returns process will still be costly because of the required labor, transport, and inspection (the business usually shoulders the return cost).

Source: lestbloom.com, 7 October 2022

the various forms of cooperation that exist between distributors (buying combinations, franchising, etc.). In some countries a tendency towards concentration has occurred in the food retail industry. For example, in the United States, Wal-Mart is by far the largest food retailer, with a share of more than 30% in some product categories.

### 8.3.2 Analysis of the distribution intensity of a brand

The distribution intensity of a brand relates to its position within a single level in the distribution channel. For this reason, we consider the distribution intensity analysis a meso-level analysis.

## Case 8.2 Connecting providers and customers

### The success of Booking.com

Booking.com is perhaps the most famous site for booking hotels and other accommodations worldwide. The site is very user friendly, and as a customer, you actually get all the information you want. The scores and opinions of customers who have already visited the hotels are also important. You can immediately see if there is still room on the days you want, and you will also be presented with alternatives that 'visitors who looked at this hotel also looked at'.

What is also special is that many hotels can be booked without cancellation costs. That makes the threshold for booking very low. Booking.com is gaining more and more power due to the large number of customers. You can even report it immediately to Booking.com if you have a complaint in a hotel, after which Booking.com will contact the hotel. Usually the problem is solved very quickly!

The rates via Booking.com are no higher than if you book directly through a hotel. Naturally, Booking.com receives a large share of the turnover. Due to the great success of Booking.com, hundreds of marketeers and IT specialists work there.

In the context of a distribution analysis, it is important to continue to explore the possibilities and impossibilities of supplying customers directly and to be neither too cautious nor too progressive in the choice of strategy (see Chapter 12).

To determine the desired distribution intensity, a manager must first analyze the past and current distribution intensity. We now focus on the 'offline' distribution of a brand. The reason is that once a retailer has a webshop, the online distribution intensity is by definition 100% (assuming there are no regional restrictions). So, for online distribution only two values exist: 0% or 100%. The review of distribution criteria that follows is therefore in some sense 'old-fashioned'. But it is still important to manage physical distribution as well, also in the light of the findings of Sharp (2010), who demonstrated that availability and visibility strongly affect market share.

To measure the position within the physical distribution channel, two criteria are typically used:

1 *Non-weighted (numerical) distribution*. This is the percentage of stores in which the brand is available
2 *Weighted distribution*. This is the market share in the product group of the shops in which the brand is available; in other words, or the market coverage.

The difference between the two criteria is that the weighted distribution takes into account the size (sales) of the stores. Shops that sell a relatively large amount (from the product group) count more heavily. For the calculation of the size of the stores where the brand is for sale, the following benchmark exists: the *selection indicator*. This is the average turnover in the product category at the stores where the own brand is present, divided by the average turnover in the product category at all stores where brands from the product category are offered. If the selection indicator is greater than 1, the own brand is located in relatively large stores and vice versa. The selection indicator can also be calculated by dividing the weighted distribution by the unweighted distribution.

The aforementioned criteria say something about the distribution position of the brand in the market as a whole. To measure the position of the brand within the stores where the brand is present, a manager can use the metric sales share. This is the market share of the brand within the stores where it is present (own sales or turnover divided by the total sales or turnover in the product category of the stores where the brand is located).

It can be easily shown that the following relations exist:

Market share = weighted distribution × revenue share
Market share = non-weighted distribution × selection indicator × sales share

Another important indicator of the position of the brand in the shop is the *shelf position*. The shelf position has two important aspects: location and amount. Location (low, middle, high) cannot be quantified. Amount can be expressed in *facings*: the number of visible products. The number of facings is often related to the market share: the bigger the brand, the more facings are given by the retailer.

We have summarized this schematically in Figure 8.1. We illustrate this figure and the previous one with a calculation example (see example 8.1).

## 8.4 Distribution analysis at the micro level: retail analysis

We now focus on the relation between a producer and retail brands. Retailers are in fact the customers of the producer. So, for a producer, an important issue is to anticipate the retailers' needs. The final distribution goal is to obtain a good location on the shelf as well as a lot of positive attention from the sales staff of retailers in terms of personal sales to the final customers (consumers). Important tools in this context are the margins on products and promotional activities in collaboration with the retailer. The concept

## Example 8.1 Position of the brand

Suppose a brand generates a turnover of €500,000 ($B$) on a market size of €5 million ($T$). The brand is located in 100 ($n$) of the 500 ($m$) stores where the product is offered. The turnover in the product category of these 100 stores amounts to €2 million ($W$).

The unweighted distribution is then:

$100/500\ (n/m) = 20\%$

The weighted distribution is:

2 million/5 million ($W/T$) = 40%. The selection indicator is:

$(W/n)/(T/m) = (2/100)/(5/500) = 2$

This was also seen by dividing 40% by 20%.

The turnover share is:

$B/W = 500,000\ /\ 2,000,000 = 25\%.$

The market share of the brand is:

$B/T = 500,000\ /\ 5$ million = 10%. This is indeed equal to $20\% \times 2 \times 25\%$.

The conclusion is that the brand has a low degree of distribution and is mainly located in large shops (measured in sales within the product category). The shops where brand A is located depend on that brand for 25% of their sales in the product category.

The results of distribution analyses are of direct importance for the use of market instruments. For example, if a company wants to increase its weighted distribution, it can choose to encourage retailers to include the brand through extensive advertising and sales staff visits. If the turnover share is disappointing, this means that the position of the brand in the stores where it is located is weakened, for example, due to insufficient support in the store. A strategy in which the retailer is rewarded more for support (push-strategy) is then obvious.

Finally, we mention again the limitation of the previous analysis in that it pertains to the physical (offline) distribution.

of *relationship management* has a central focus: The manufacturer attempts to realize its goals (and those of the retailer) through an optimal relationship with the retailer. Insight into the wishes and desires of retailers is the most important information source in this area. For that purpose, individual retail brands must be examined. Therefore, this involves a distribution analysis at the micro level (distributor analysis).

At the most disaggregated level (sales outlets), a manufacturer may be dealing with many hundreds of 'customers'. By far the largest proportion of them is in one way or another involved in joint collaboration. Thus, in reality, the 'salesperson' of a manufacturer (the sales manager) has to deal with a significantly lower number and often with only a few buyers.

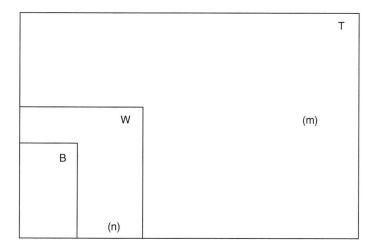

B = sales of brand

W = category sales of 'own' retailers

T = sales total market

B/W = sales share

B/T = market share

W/T = weighted distribution

(W/n)/(T/m) = selection indicator

n/m = numerical (unweighted) distribution

So: weighted distribution = numerical distribution x selection indicator

**Figure 8.1** Summary of distribution measures

For the purpose of organizing the analysis of a distributor, it is important to determine which role the retailer actually plays for the producer. As already mentioned, the retailer is a *customer* that 'resells' the product to final users. Yet in the food industry, retailers increasingly are also *competitors* of producers as a result of the *own brands* of those distributors (*distributor-owned brands*).

Therefore, a distributor analysis is positioned between a customer analysis and a competitor analysis (see Chapter 6). For each retailer, insight should be obtained into the following:

1   The importance and role of the retailer (Section 8.4.1).
2   The position of the manufacturer's brand at the retailer (Section 8.4.2).
3   The objectives, strategy, and wishes of the retailer (Section 8.4.3).
4   The strengths and weaknesses and the expected strategy of the retailer (Section 8.4.4).

### 8.4.1 The importance and the role of the retailer

The importance of a retailer may be measured by its sales in the product category. For the food products industry, relevant data can be obtained from Nielsen, IRI, or GfK. For markets for durable consumer goods, the position of retailers (e.g., the position of Megapool in the market for white fabrics) should be estimated. In addition to sales, the margin is essential. For a manufacturer, the profitability of a 'relationship' is ultimately what matters.

With regard to the role of a retailer, the easily answered question is whether it is only a 'customer' or also a competitor. The retailer is a competitor if it carries its own brands (distributor brands, or D-brands), a situation that occurs in many markets for fast-moving consumer goods. In addition, it is important to determine the degree of freedom in brand supply for a retailer: Does the retailer have a 'preferred supplier' – a manufacturer within the product category that is preferred?

## 8.4.2 The position of the manufacturer's brand at the retailer

Measures of the position of the manufacturer's own brand at the retailer include the shelf position, the number of facings, and the sales of the manufacturer's brand at that retailer in relation to other sales outlets and/or in relation to other retailer brands. Shelf position and facings are tools of the retailer. Another tool is the personal sale, especially in lines of business that are not related to the food products industry. All these tools have an impact on brand sales. Relatively low brand sales may indicate insufficient attention to the brand on the part of the retailer; that may indicate an inadequate marketing policy of the producer toward that retailer.

The other way around it can be argued that for the retailer the producers' brand might also be important. This is especially true if the producers' product contributes to the turnover of the retailer, if the margin is sufficient, if it meets needs of consumers, and also if it helps the retailer to differentiate from competitive retailers.

So, there is a mutual dependency between producers and retailers.

## 8.4.3 The goals, strategy, and wishes of the retailer

*Objectives* involve issues such as satisfaction of the retailer (and therefore the results until the present time) and ambition (limited or fast growth, growth with existing or new activities, etc.). Strategy here involves the implementation of the marketing strategy (positioning and choice of the target audience): On which consumers does the retailer focus? For a manufacturer, it is important to choose a retailer with a marketing strategy comparable to its own. In addition, the use of the four Ps by the retailer should be examined. The 'P' of product in this regard is actually related to the wishes of the retailer: How wide is its assortment; which product categories are in the shop with how many varieties; and what proportions of those are A brands, B brands, and retailer brands? Other relevant questions include the following: To what extent and how does the retailer implement its own communication policy? How does the retailer handle promotional campaigns? In general, to what extent is the retailer willing to collaborate with the manufacturer?

The answers to all these questions will need to be provided, based mostly on observation and experiences with the relevant retailer. It may be expected that an account manager or another representative of the manufacturer will gain insight, through regular contacts with the buyers, into what the retailer does or does not want and how it behaves. All these issues are part of what is called *trade marketing*: the marketing of a producer to the retailer.

## Case 8.3 Strategies of a retailer

## Primark chooses for bricks only

Budget fashion chain Primark, which has shunned the extra cost of home delivery, could add click-and-collect services to its revamped website over time but still sees new stores in markets such as Italy and the United States as its main growth driver.

The chain, whose trendy clothes at rock-bottom prices have taken British and European shoppers by storm over the last decade, will launch a new website in the United Kingdom by the end of March and across its 13 other markets by the autumn. That will better showcase its 10,000 products, provide customers with near real-time information on product availability by store, and enable Primark to mine the data of its over 24 million active 'engagers'. 'We're making the digital move forward in a very big way in both the UK and the rest of Europe. That will generate sales and profits for us', John Bason, finance director of Primark's owner, Associated British Foods (ABF.L), told Reuters. 'Does this give us a capability to move further forward? Well let's have a look at that', he said in an interview.

'If there was an e-commerce opportunity for us, it will probably be more in the area of click-and-collect', he said, referring to products ordered online and picked up in store.

But Bason said home delivery remained off Primark's agenda, as the economics don't stack up for its low price points.

'You can't get our value by delivery to home, it's as simple as that'.

Source: Reuters.com, 11 March 2022

### 8.4.4 The strengths and weaknesses and the expected strategy of the retailer

Finally, an attempt is made, based in part on the foregoing steps, to deduce the strengths and weaknesses as well as the expected strategy of the retailer.

In terms of the strengths (and weaknesses) of a retailer, two types may be distinguished: strengths that are interesting to any manufacturer (e.g., high sales per customer, friendly staff, and short waiting times at the cash register) and manufacturer-specific strengths. After all, for a manufacturer, the issue is to choose a retailer that fits with the target audience and the positioning of the manufacturer's products. Characteristics of the retailer that are congruent present opportunities for the manufacturer (such as a good fresh produce department, high-quality positioning, and a large staff).

Weak points of an existing retailer (e.g., low sales per customer) may be an occasion for more intensive collaboration with the manufacturer (e.g., joint promotions).

The expected retailer strategy also may present opportunities (or threats) for the manufacturer. Expanded support and growth of the retailer's brands may have important implications for the manufacturer. Potential options vary from strengthening the position and positioning of the producer's brands to starting to produce retailer brands.

Just as in Section 8.4.3, statements can only be qualitative in nature and assumptions probably will have to be made if insufficient information is available.

## 8.5 Analysis of the suppliers

This section provides a brief introduction to the analysis of suppliers. For more extensive descriptions, the reader should refer to the literature on *purchasing* and *business marketing* (marketing from a company to another company).

Purchasing occurs in many areas, such as the purchasing of the following:

- Supportive goods and services (office furniture, financial services, online support services, advertising agencies, etc.).
- Means of production (labor and capital goods).
- Semimanufactured articles and raw materials.

A good relationship with suppliers can be a source of a competitive advantage. This applies to all types of purchasing. For example, a good website which is easily found and has a strong 'call to action' may be very important for success. Good housing can have an impact on staff motivation. The usefulness of qualified personnel (labor market) is evident. Good and reliable machines determine the quality of production. Certainly in the case of semifinished products and raw materials, savings in purchasing may be 'channeled' to the consumer. The requirements for purchased semifinished products and raw materials depend on the chosen value strategy. A company that chooses customer leadership (*customer intimacy*) and direct delivery will require flexibility (many varieties) and reliability (timely delivery) in the deliveries. The strategy of *product leadership* requires a high and constant quality of the purchased products. A company that chooses a low price within operational excellence will have a strong need for inexpensive purchasing, for example, through agreements about quantity discounts.

## Case 8.4 Relevance of suppliers

### Marketers have a duty to please suppliers as well as customers

The essence of marketing is pleasing customers. But is this currently still the case? Who needs customers nowadays? Marketing's longstanding obsession with the demand side of the equation – pandering to consumers, diligently working back from their ever-shifting needs, obsequiously striving to 'surprise and delight' – is beginning to look overdone. Shortages of staff and raw materials mean marketers must influence how suppliers perceive them and ground product development in supply chain reality. So, the goal of marketing should be much broader nowadays.

Source: adapted from Marketingweek.com, 5 December 2022

Whichever demands are made for whichever type of purchasing, it will be easier to comply with those demands if good relationships are built with the supplying companies. Therefore, an analysis of current and potential suppliers is important.

Purchasing by a company is in essence no different from purchasing by a consumer: there is a need that is satisfied through purchasing and/or acquisition. The most important differences are the following:

- In purchasing, the need is 'indirect': It depends on the requirements that are made of the products, which in turn depend on the final needs of the final customer.

■ The purchasing process is different and more complicated: Typically, a single person is not responsible for purchasing; instead, there are *decision-making units (DMUs)*. In this situation, various people in a company are responsible for the final purchasing decisions.

In a supplier analysis, the following questions are answered:

1   Which needs within the company have to be met? The analysis of suppliers depends on the need that must be met. Therefore, an internal analysis to define that need is important. For example: do we need a new website? Should we search for more sustainable suppliers?
2   Which supplier can best provide for that need? To arrive at a selection of potential suppliers, the company will have to examine the expected achievements of the suppliers in the following areas:

■ Quality: the concrete characteristics of the products
■ Price (potential discounts, etc.)
■ Sustainability
■ Service

The service component is very important in business markets and includes both components such as warranty, repair service, and reliability and additional service components such as training and information.

To be able to evaluate suppliers on these factors, information from the company's own purchasers is important: they know the market like no one else. In addition, suppliers may be asked to make 'bids'. This may occur through a call for tenders (e.g., construction combinations needed to create and present a building scheme), pitches (advertising agencies that need to write a campaign proposal), or normal quotes. Because trust plays an important role in purchasing markets, issues such as reputation, experience with suppliers, and personal contacts often are decisive in making a choice. This implies that branding and communication are also relevant in a business market. Therefore, in a supplier analysis, these qualitative elements play an important role.

## Summary

An analysis of the distribution and suppliers is important since building relations with retailers and suppliers may lead to competitive advantages. A distribution analysis is performed at the macro level, the meso level, and the micro level. At the macro level, the distribution structure is mapped out. Clearly, nowadays, multichannel strategies are often applied int the sense of offline as well as online. An analysis is made of which levels are used and to what extent and how many sales are made in the category through which channels. A specific point in that regard is what the potential development of online sales might be. The elimination of intermediary links is a way for manufacturers to avoid the increasing power of retailers. At the meso level, the power of the retailers is analyzed, along with the position of the brand at the various retailers. At the micro level, individual retailers (chains) are analyzed; an important point is to discover how the best possible relationship with the retailer can be built. For that purpose, an understanding of the retailer's goals, strategy, and wishes is required. The company's account managers are an important data source for this largely qualitative analysis. For a supplier analysis, the goal is also to build relationships. An analysis will focus on the question of which purchasing needs the company has and which supplier can best meet those needs. The company's own purchasing needs will depend on the chosen positioning. Selection of a supplier is becoming increasingly important, also given the importance of sustainability in climate and in relation to personnel.

## Challenges in food distribution: the Barika story

### An African perspective on distribution

Sub-Saharan Africa is often heralded as an important future growth area. With the rise of an African middle class, spending power also increases, creating growth opportunities that are increasingly difficult to reach in the saturated European or American markets. But, in order to be successful, knowledge of distribution structure is of the highest importance: in order to sell, it is essential to reach the consumer!

The Western shopper is used to buying food in supermarkets, operating under familiar names like Wal-Mart, Carrefour, or Tesco. This is where we spent the bulk of our money. But we easily forget that this pattern isn't the same everywhere. In sub-Saharan countries in Africa, big chains have a substantial lower relevance, often being virtually non-existent.

Nielsen retail sales data show that some 40% of African consumers shop in small, local grocery stores, or 'dukas'. These dukas account for nearly 50% of consumer goods spend. The average duka, often only a few square meters, is loaded with a wide variety of goods and often forms the center of a community. But this is not even the most relevant channel. The most common African shopping channel is the table top: a stall set up at the side of the road or in the local market to capture local and passing trade. In a recent Nielsen study of sub-Saharan countries, it was found that 80% of consumers shopped from table tops. For instance, in a country such as Nigeria, there are no less than 200,000 table tops. At the duka, Africans tend to spend a lot more than during each visit than at the table-top. But this doesn't make the duka more relevant. An important factor is the frequency of visit: consumers tend to shop less frequently in dukas, as stores can be hard to get to without transport. In contrast, they often visit a table top or kiosk daily for smaller, top-up quantities, buying basics like toilet paper or bananas. Shopping patterns also differ by country. In Madagascar, a Nielsen survey showed consumers went shopping 70 times a month on average – this is more than twice a day! – while in Kenya, the average was 38.

At the table top, consumers are familiar with both the vendor and the products, and the products are helpfully sold in decanted or single servings and in rounded denominations (e.g., 100 shillings in Kenya or 1,000 CFA francs in Burkina Faso). So while the shop itself may be no more than a table or countertop, its products unbranded, and the product range small – many might sell no more than four different items – these outlets perfectly meet consumers' needs. They offer familiar goods at the desired price and size, they offer convenience, and they are trusted.

Numbers give an average picture. Companies need to identify the best channels and retailers for their product category. In Lagos (Nigeria), for instance, Nielsen found laundry detergents in distribution in no less than 100,000 outlets, an impossibly large number to reach. But further analysis showed that 80% of the sales value came from just 35,000 of those outlets and a full 50% from a more manageable 10,000. Similarly, in the same city, beverages are sold in 61,000 outlets, but only 24,000 of those outlets generate 80% of sales.

But still, how to reach even the most effective dukas and table tops in an efficient manner? Getting close to the retailer in order to build distribution to support sales in such a fragmented retail market is a huge undertaking, particularly for international manufacturers lacking in local knowledge. Moreover, it is only the final stage of a meticulous process. First manufacturers need to understand who shops where and for what; then they must identify the best retail outlets for a given product, and then they can turn to helping retailers build demand.

Companies also need to consider how to help build demand in an environment where consumers on limited budgets are ultra-cautious about trying new products. Consumers continue to show a powerful preference for products they know, have tried before, or have had recommended to them – not surprising in an environment where budgets are tight and a disappointing purchase is an expensive loss.

But the creation of brand awareness and familiarity, a crucial step in introducing new products to the market, is a huge challenge. Small retailers have little or no display space, shopper loyalty is often to local manufacturers, and premium-priced branded packages are often split open and sold in unbranded singles or servings to meet consumers' needs. So, in a market where brand familiarity and recommendations from others are strong purchase drivers, how can you start with a new product that by definition does not have any familiarity or recommendations?

A close understanding of how smaller, traditional retailers operate is key for the right approach to building sales. For instance, a table-top vendor selling a small range of everyday basics will often stock only a very narrow range of products. With no transport and limited or no storage, the vendor will probably not visit even one distributor or wholesaler. Instead, everything is brought to the stall either on a bicycle or boda boda (cargo-carrying motorcycle), in a motor vehicle, or perhaps even on a pushcart or by foot. Sometimes it is a wholesaler who drops off supplies, sometimes another retailer; often, there is no record of what are all cash transactions. Airtime, cigarettes, and sodas may be delivered as often as three to five times a day. Other goods, such as gum, sweets, biscuits, or analgesics, might be delivered every three days.

The vendors are masters at adapting their offerings to meet consumers' immediate needs, which change at various points during their day. In the morning, the commuting consumer may stop for breakfast – ready-made tea served from a flask, freshly squeezed juice, slices of bread, a cooked sausage, a single teabag, and a serving of sugar – even super glue for fixing a broken shoe. All of this must be understood by a manufacturer that wants to introduce its product to the table top market and develop its success, particularly because it is the vendor and not a wholesaler intermediary that will make the ultimate decision. Meeting consumers' needs in this environment means not only being timely but also thinking about the required pack size, format, affordability, and denomination. If a branded packet is too expensive, the retailer may open the pack, split it into smaller ones, and sell it unbranded, resulting in profit for the manufacturer but weaker brand identity.

Sometimes, it's the small things that have the potential to drive success. A number of these small suggestions to stimulate brand identity in the African market:

- Repackaging and branding products into single servings or at least smaller sizes
- Providing branded packaging such as wrappers or sachets that retailers can use if they spilt up larger portions
- Branding the selling vessel, for example, the basin from which water sachets are sold
- Providing branded cooler boxes for table-top vendors to sell products which require refrigeration
- Providing small, portable display stands for kiosk vendors to stack products and add visibility
- Branding re-usable product packaging or containers for top-ups and repurchases
- Providing free samples appropriate to the time of day and the way the outlet is used. Each table top can be seen as a location to trial new products with no risk to either the vendor or the consumer.

## Barika

Barika is a medium-sized distributor in Burkina Faso, a francophone country in Western Africa. The company profiles with the following mission statement:

African urban societies are experiencing a social change that is reflected in a more individualized food experience. Styles and aspirations are diversifying while traditional community channels are showing more and more their limits. In order to overcome these changes, Barika proposes to facilitate access to quality essential products in partnership with local actors and committed suppliers.

According to its website, Barika offers an innovative distribution network based on:

- a triple principle of modernity, accessibility, quality
- a wide range of products, emphasizing attractive products with social impact
- a brand that caters to all, including the low-income segment
- innovative products, previously unavailable on the market, to enrich the local offer
- collaboration with a wide variety of fully involved stakeholders

The company promises a quality commitment:

- a guarantee of quality to give consumers the assurance of healthy products
- a stable price guarantee
- support to suppliers in improving their local distribution
- quality of service: personalized support for customers in the choice and use of products

And proposes to work with a network of partners

- committed suppliers
- local stakeholders in the field of health, childhood, and so on
- animation offers proposed in collaboration with our partners

### Interview With the Strategic Manager of Barika

**Question: Can you tell me something about Barika?**
Barika is a brand specialized in distribution of innovative products. We aim at good products that are not too expensive. With a focus on local quality products. We get our products directly from the producer, or through an intermediary. Barika has its own shops, 2 boutiques located in Ouagadougou (the capital of Burkina Faso). We also distribute to a number of small shops and table-tops. These small shops and table-tops currently account for most of our sales. We serve them with two sales people, but many owners of shops and table-tops come to our boutiques to buy the goods they want,

**Q: What is the role of the Barika store?**
A strong local store is a proof of quality. We want to use the shop to increase the awareness of the Barika brand, so that the owners of the small shops will come to us.

**Q: But why do you prefer the small shops to come to you? Wouldn't it be better if you go to the small shops?**
A push strategy seems to make more sense than a pull strategy in our market. Going directly to the small shops and the table-tops is very hard work as they

are disseminated all over Ouagadougou with approximately 3 000 selling points. Currently, as I mentioned before, we have only two sales people in our own service. That is why our primary focus is on making Barika a strong and trusted retail brand. Then the shop- and top-owners will come to us, instead of we to them!

**Q: How important is relation management in the Burkina Faso market?**
Very important. Work is not efficient without good relations. There is also a strong hierarchy issue – people are not really saying what they think: they will say yes in order to keep the relation, even if they mean no. The ideal sales person is someone that used to be a respected retailer with a well-established network. We are still looking for the ideal.

**Q: I want to talk about one of the products you distribute: Grandibien. Can you say something about the product?**
Grandibien is a product against chronic malnutrition. It targets pregnant women, as well as young children, in a couple of age categories. Awareness of the Grandibien brand is still limited. The target group doesn't know it too well. Currently it is available in 150 shops, mainly smaller ones. But there is a potential of 3000 sales points for this type of product in Ouagadougou and way more in the whole country, so there is still a lot of work to do.

We found that kids like Grandibien. The sales price is relatively high, due to the high quality ingredients. It pays off, as a healthy diet prevents medical costs due to malnutrition issues. But it's hard to convince our target of the importance of prevention of malnutrition. Prevention awareness is a global issue in the world anyway.

**Q: African consumers are known to be ultra-cautious about trying new products. What is your experience with Grandibien?**
Yes, consumers are very faithful and loyal. They trust big brands such as Nescafé, but above all they trust the person that sells them the product. But consumers here are also curious. We noticed that they try Grandibien, but we need to create more awareness around the brand and the benefits of prevention to create a rebuy.

## Questions

1   Draft a global distribution structure for a consumer product in the sub-Saharan market, for instance, for a product such as laundry detergent in the Nigerian market.
2   A distribution analysis can be executed on three levels of aggregation. For which of these levels does the Barika interview provide useful information? Explain your answer.
3   Is Barika a wholesaler or a retailer? Explain your answer.

4   The manager states that 'A push strategy seems to make more sense than a pull strategy'.
    a   Explain what the manager means with this statement.
    b   Do you agree that in the sub-Saharan market, a push strategy makes – in general – more sense than a pull strategy? Explain your answer
    c   What is your opinion on the solution of the push/pull issue as proposed by Barika?
5   The choice for a focus on the Barika shop (a choice on macro level) seems to be partly driven by issues in the salesforce (micro level). Do you agree that micro-level issues should drive macro-level choices? Why (not)?
6   A distribution channel can be long, short, or direct. How would you describe the distribution channel in which Barika is operating?
7   Describe the current distribution intensity of Grandibien.
8   Consider the information about Grandibien: which distribution intensity would you advise for Grandibien?
9   How would you advise Barika to realize this distribution intensity for Grandibien?

# Chapter 9

# SWOT analysis

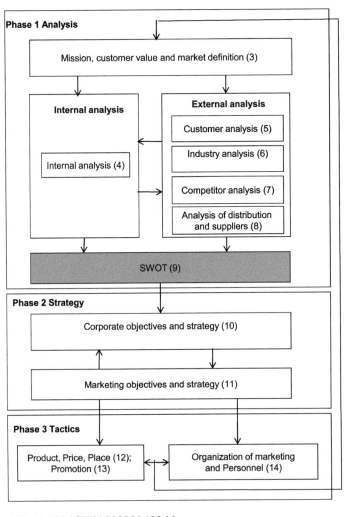

**Phase 1 Analysis**

Mission, customer value and market definition (3)

**Internal analysis**

Internal analysis (4)

**External analysis**

Customer analysis (5)

Industry analysis (6)

Competitor analysis (7)

Analysis of distribution and suppliers (8)

SWOT (9)

**Phase 2 Strategy**

Corporate objectives and strategy (10)

Marketing objectives and strategy (11)

**Phase 3 Tactics**

Product, Price, Place (12); Promotion (13)

Organization of marketing and Personnel (14)

DOI: 10.4324/9781003381488-11

## Key points in this chapter

- Know the steps in a SWOT analysis
- Be able to summarize a situation analysis into a focused problem statement
- Discuss alternative positioning options

## Introduction

In the earlier phases of the strategic marketing planning process, an internal and an external analysis were completed. This is called a situation analysis. In this chapter we describe how the insights from the situation analysis can be summarized and what steps can be taken to come to strategic decisions. The tool reviewed is the SWOT analysis, where SWOT stands for *strengths, weaknesses, opportunities*, and *threats*. This chapter is structured as follows:

1   Definitions and forecasting (Section 9.1).
2   Summarize the situation analysis in a SWOT list (Section 9.2).
3   Formulate a vision of the environment and the core challenge (Section 9.3).
4   SWOT matrix and options (Section 9.4).
5   Selection of a marketing strategy (Section 9.5).

## 9.1 Definitions and forecasting methods

Before moving on to the steps in SWOT analysis, let's discuss two general guidelines: the need for clear definitions and the need for a future perspective (and forecasting methods).

### 9.1.1 Definitions

First we define what should be understood by strengths, weaknesses, opportunities, and threats. A good definition of this is necessary, because otherwise determining it can lead to misunderstandings. We focus on three properties:

1   *The difference between strengths and weaknesses on the one hand and opportunities and threats on the other*. Strengths and weaknesses are internal: they relate to the brand for which a marketing plan is being made. Opportunities and threats are external: they relate to the environment and would exist even if *the brand in question were not there*. For example, a 'good image (measured with customers)' is a strength and, despite the fact that it comes from the customer analysis, is not an 'opportunity'.

2   *The difference between an opportunity and a threat*. The difference between an opportunity and a threat is that a opportunity is a positive development *with unchanged policy* and a threat a negative development. We add the condition of unchanged policy, because, as is often said, 'there are no threats because a company can respond to anything'. If the company opts for this – in itself justified – starting

point, there is no tenable distinction between opportunities and threats, and it is better to speak of issues or external points for attention. So we do make a distinction. For example, a downturn can be an opportunity for a quality product if the brand is able to lower the price. Nevertheless, we regard this as a threat, because if *policy remains unchanged*, there will be an unfavorable impact.

3   *The difference between opportunities and strategies.* One difference between opportunities and strategies is that a strategy is something a brand *does* and an opportunity is not. For example, 'developing a peanut-flavored beer for young people' is not an opportunity but a possible strategy. The underlying probability may be: 'expected growing demand among young people for specialty beers'. Another example: 'rejuvenating a brand' is not an opportunity but a response to the weakness 'old-fashioned image'. The latter often goes wrong with SWOT analyses: all kinds of ideas are called 'opportunities', which is actually incorrect: they are 'options'.

Finally, in this book we sometimes used the terms *relative* strengths and weaknesses, by which we mean that they are strong or weak not only in general but also with respect to the competition: that is, comparatively. Relative strengths can be determined by comparing the 'absolute' strengths and weaknesses (partly derived from the internal analysis) with those of competitors (derived from the competitor analysis).

## 9.1.2 Forecasting methods

A marketing plan, by definition, concerns the future, for example, for one year or, if it concerns a strategic marketing plan, for example, three years. This means that a manager must identify *future* opportunities and threats. Developments that have occurred in the past are not really important. One problem is that no one knows for sure what will happen tomorrow. A manager will still have to make her own predictions. She can often make use of forecasts from research agencies or government institutions.

A manager should not only predict environmental developments. Forecasts of sales should also be made so that financial projections can be incorporated into the marketing plan (see Section 14.3). Because predictions in a marketing plan are important, we now provide some guidelines for choosing a forecasting method. We base ourselves largely on Armstrong (2001).

There are two types of prediction methods:

- *Objective forecasting* methods. Forecasts are calculated in one way or another so that if someone else applies the same method, they will also get the same result (replicability). These methods require quantitative data (data) and sometimes some statistical knowledge. Examples: trend extrapolation and causal regression models.
- *Subjective prediction* methods. The best possible prediction is made 'in the head' of a researcher/expert or customer. Hard, quantitative data can also be used, but this is not necessary. The essence is that a prognosis is arrived at in an 'implicit manner'. In fact, it involves two methods: 'opinion research' (expert prediction) and 'intention research' (asking customers in a sample of how likely it is that they will buy the new product). Examples of intention research outside of marketing are political polls: research into who voters intend to vote for. In everyday parlance this

is often referred to as 'opinion polls', which is very confusing because voters are not 'experts' but 'consumers'. Subjective methods are not replicable. One day an expert or a consumer with the same information can give a different opinion than on another day. Repetition does not therefore give exactly the same result.

A lot of research has been done into when which methods are best. For example, an important factor is whether 'circumstances are expected to change significantly'. Objective methods are by definition based on patterns from the past and therefore seem less suitable for predicting trend breaks, for example. However, subjective methods are not always suitable either. For example, people have a natural tendency to *anchoring*: sticking to familiar situations and underestimating what can change (see Case 9.1).

## 9.2 Step 1: summary of the situation analysis

In principle, the situation analysis produces a large list of strengths, weaknesses, opportunities, and threats. Some of them are important, others less important. In addition, some are related. To keep the follow-up analysis clear, the situation analysis should be *summarized* in a limited number of strengths, weaknesses, opportunities, and threats. We provide the following practical tips (Dibb et al., 2003):

- Include only the most important factors (*issues*). Always limit the number to a maximum of five (so a maximum of five strengths, five opportunities, and so on).
- Rank the points in order of importance.
- Ensure that there is sufficient supporting evidence (research) for each point.
- Strengths and weaknesses should preferably be relative, that is, in relation to competitors.
- Do not confuse strengths with opportunities, threats with opportunities, or opportunities with strategies (see definitions in Section 9.1.1).

The most pronounced issues therefore form the starting point for the further SWOT analysis. The choice of what is relevant requires a high degree of attentiveness and creativity – attentiveness because one can certainly assume that competitors also signal the most obvious opportunities, and the difference can be precisely in less obvious 'brackets'. Creativity is also important: one must be able to sense what an opportunity might be. Actually, the goal of the entire SWOT analysis is: to find a 'golden hook'. Popularly speaking, a 'big idea' can be enough for a profitable strategy. That hook or idea can often be found by listening very carefully to customers and not only paying attention to things that customers like but especially to what they don't like. Figure 9.1 summarizes the result of this sub-step and follows the guidelines from Section 9.1.1 (we use the abbreviation SWOTs).

## 9.3 Step 2: vision of the environment and core challenge

After and in addition to the summary of the situation analysis, a further reduction of the situation analysis is desirable. The reason for this is that the company can then make even

## Case 9.1 Prediction is also difficult for experts

## Major forecasting errors leading to global changes

It would be no exaggeration to say that 2016 was the year in which global opinion polls plummeted. Not only was Brexit not predicted at the time, a flaw in the forecasts was also the completely surprising election of Trump as president of the United States. Besides the difference between intent and behavior, another cause of these massive forecasting errors is that the sample in polls does not always closely match the actual voting population. For example, a relatively large number of votes against (i.e. for exit) showed up for Brexit, and it was easily demonstrable afterwards that the result would have been the other way around if the voter turnout were representative. In the meantime, in 2023, it has been shown that Brexit was indeed harmful for all stakeholders. In any case, this is an important disadvantage of referenda: the result is strongly influenced by mood swings and the associated turnout. A referendum is therefore very popular with the more populist parties and should therefore be abolished as a democratic instrument.

> For marketing purposes, the conclusion is that with consumer behavior becoming increasingly erratic, predicting consumer behavior is becoming increasingly difficult.

Another problem with prediction (especially with subjective methods) is that there is often a difference between intention and behavior. We already mentioned this in Chapter 1 under sustainable behavior. People say they want to behave sustainably but often don't. And the political predictions mentioned previously often go wrong as well. A factor here is that people ultimately make choices based on feeling and 'unconsciously', which can be different than if you ask 'rationally'.

A general conclusion from research into the correctness of forecasts is that combining different forecasting methods yields the best prediction (this is called eclectic research). Armstrong (2001) therefore recommends that instead of putting a lot of energy into one method, it is better to put less energy into a few methods. Preferably, therefore, both an objective and a subjective method should be used.

Finally, the question is how a researcher should come to one prediction if he uses different methods. This point has also been examined in the literature. The surprising conclusion is that simply the (unweighted) average gives the best result.

We end with an example. Suppose an entrepreneur has an idea for a new product. Before taking out a loan to the bank, she must show a forecast of the expected sales over the next five years and must in any case be able to estimate the market potential. Then she could apply the following steps:

1   She conducts an intention survey in which she asks a representative group of men and women how likely it is that they would buy the described product for a certain price. For both segments, she takes the 'will definitely buy' category and calculates the number of buyers accordingly.
2   Benchmarking: she looks at how comparable products have performed and uses this as a basis for a forecast. The problem here is always the degree of comparability.
3   She makes expert forecasts (opinion research). She is looking for four carefully chosen objective external experts and asks them to make a prediction.
4   She combines the three predictions by calculating an average.

Certain future developments may be very uncertain and at the same time very decisive. In the example of the entrepreneur, this could be the possible arrival of a competitor with the same product. In that case, *scenarios* are used. A scenario is a description of a possible environmental situation. For example, the entrepreneur in the example formulates two scenarios: 'there will be no competitor in the next five years' and 'there will be a competitor from the start'. The most likely scenario is chosen, and the alternative can be included in an appendix to the plan. A scenario is not a forecasting method: it is a way of dealing with uncertainty.

| Key Strengths and Weaknesses (SW)* | Key Areas of Interest (Future OTs )* |
|---|---|
| S1 Strong position among professionals | O1 Increasing need for quality photos |
| | O2 Economic growth |
| S2 Good at quality and innovation | O3 Customers rely more on in-store advice |
| S3 Many possibilities | O4 Cameras still pay little attention to style |
| S4 Good relationship with shops | O5 Competitors are not specialized |
| S5 Specialist in photography | |
| W1 High cost and price | T1 Improvement photo quality smartphones |
| W2 Low market share among consumers | T2 Growing need for convenience |
| | T3 Growth of Instagram |
| W3 Brand awareness relatively low | T4 Stronger competition in user - friendly cameras |
| W4 Not very easy to use | |
| W5 No brand extensions | T5 Competition (e.g. Canon) has much wider range (printers, PCs, cameras and so on) |

**Figure 9.1 Selection SWOTs (example digital camera manufacturer)**

* In total, a maximum of 10 internal and 10 external items

better choices with regard to what is or is not important. What really matters here is that the company develop a view on the environment, that is, a short and concise statement about what management considers important in the environment of the brand. For this, a manager can refer to the format of the external analysis:

- the customer analysis
- the industry analysis
- the competitor analysis
- the distribution and supplier analysis

For each of these components, the question is: which future development or trend does the manager consider most important? This is often related to the customer analysis. Does management think there will be more or less need for simplicity in cameras in the future? Such an opinion has major consequences for the strategy choices.

To achieve the best possible focus, it is advisable to draw some kind of conclusion about the problem and the cause from the situation analysis. A marketing goal can also be set, for example, a market share to be achieved. If that goal is then compared to the situation of 'no change in policy' and a gap is expected ('gap analysis'), then something has to change in a company's strategy.

The performance analysis (see Section 4.2) has given a first impression of where possible problems lie. For instance:

- that the marketing objective (such as a certain market share) of a new brand X has not been achieved
- that this was mainly caused by a disappointing percentage of repeat purchases
- that the cause should not be sought in the *implementation* of the planned strategy, because there was no significant difference between planned and actual implementation

This problem recognition is obviously not enough. The question remains: What are the specific causes of the disappointing results? Or, more broadly formulated: For which '*core* marketing problem' should this marketing plan provide a solution? The answer to this question is best given as the capstone of the summary of the SWOTs. After all, all possible relevant internal and environmental factors have been analyzed in this phase. Problems are often a combination of internal and external factors. As a matter of fact, we already point out that the problem conclusion is presented much earlier in the marketing plan itself, namely in the first plan chapter (see Section 2.5). A solid foundation is important for the core problem.

An example of a core problem in practice is that brand identity and brand image do not correspond: the brand wants to have certain associations, but the target group does not see them. This happens a lot, sometimes more than managers realize. For example, it is often said that a brand is 'very strong, because the reputation is enormous'. But image is also important. If an image moves in the direction of 'trusted, known from the past', there is a danger (prognosis) that it will move in the direction of 'old-fashioned, old-fashioned'. Does the company want that or not? A critical interpretation of the situation analysis is therefore desirable.

In this phase, a forecast can also be given of what is expected with unchanged policy: a forecast of sales and profit if nothing is changed in the strategy. Naturally, subjectivity also plays a major role here, and the marketing plan to be developed will have to lead to a better result. An advantage of such a prediction is that it can underline the need for change. Incidentally, this is also often stated in the context of change management: the first step in a change management process is awareness of the need for change. And the best awareness is the belief that if the company continues on the same footing, it will lead to disastrous or at least unsuccessful results.

If we combine this with the vision of the environment, we can give an example for the manufacturer of photo cameras (Case 9.2).

## 9.4 Step 3: marketing strategic options

The aim of this crucial third step of the SWOT analysis is to arrive at possible strategies ('options') from the SWOTs. Here, therefore, a connection is made between the analysis and strategy phases. Although a SWOT analysis is well known in itself, authors use different methods to make this connection. We come up with our own way of doing that in this book.

First, we argue which choices we make in this phase. Next, we'll work this out for the example of the digital camera manufacturer.

### 9.4.1 Features of the SWOT approach in this book

We make the following choices in the SWOT analysis:

1  The goal in this phase is to define marketing strategic options and not to come up with all sorts of tactical ideas.
2  It is important to be innovative and also to be able to think out of the box.
3  Because of the necessary mental space to be creative, we allow sufficient freedom in the connection between analysis and options and therefore do not come up with a detailed weighting method to 'calculate' an option.

## Case 9.2 Development of a vision on the environment and core challenge

### Vision of camera manufacturer

In the market for cameras in Argentina, we see our market share fall to 2.1% in 2022. The main cause of this is the competition with increasingly good cameras in smart-phones. Our goal is to increase the market share to 2.4% over the next three years.

We expect that the need for quick photos via social media will continue to grow and that our competitors will respond well to this. Our image is that we deliver top-quality cameras, but also that our user friendliness is not as good as that of the competitors. If policy remains unchanged, our market share will continue to fall.

### 1 Think in terms of marketing strategy

A central point in this book is that choosing a brand positioning is the core of the marketing strategy. So it makes sense to focus on that right from the SWOT. In marketing practice, people often take too little time to think carefully about brand positioning. And it is precisely the brand positioning that should be the reason people buy one brand and not another. This part of the brainstorming process is therefore very important. When applying the SWOT analysis, it is tempting to immediately brainstorm about tactical ideas. Suppose a weakness is: 'little presence on social media'. How logical is it, then, to consider that an option is: 'become more active on social media'? But such choices can only be made after the formulation of the marketing strategy. For a practical example, see Case 9.3.

## Case 9.3 Strategy development

### How to develop a positioning for Lipton in Asia

Although a long time ago, this interview with Tex Gunning of Unilever Foods Asia at the time says a lot about strategy development in practice.

'We now conduct all major market research in large collective processes. The numbers come back and then we lock ourselves up for three or four days. Then we work our way through all the ups and downs of such a process, but after that it is also a collectively supported positioning. It produces a lot of frustration, but you end up with a conclusion that you would never have come up with one or two other smart people.

Consumers and their relationship with a brand are so complicated that as a marketer you cannot do it alone. We are going to think about that every time with ten, twenty or thirty people and we are going to work on it. And we'll do it again in four months until the positioning of the brand is clear and relevant'. Gunning gives Lipton tea as an example. 'Sounds simple, but everyone sells tea in China. I've been working on it for two and a half years and it's only been two weeks since we think we've really got it. What we're sitting on with Lipton is this: Young Asians know the future is theirs. Those economies are so big and the political influence of the Chinese is growing so fast that the collective self-consciousness becomes infinite. You get a whole group of young people who want to ride that wave. With that in mind, we positioned Lipton as: *bright and vital outlook on life*. That means you have to do more than just sell tea'.

## 2 Be creative and innovative

It is advisable in this phase when formulating ideas not (yet) to be completely guided by existing preconditions, such as the company's vision or financial constraints. In the first instance, any strategy is possible, including outside the current activities. It is very important to be creative. Of course, it must then be examined whether a strategy is realistic, but that is part of the last fourth step of the SWOT analysis.

Creative thinking can be performed in different ways. Aaker (2013) provides the following guidelines for creativity:

1   Do it in groups, because diversity increases the number of different ideas.
2   Do 'warm up exercises' before you start the creative session, for example, taking turns making up a sentence in a story.
3   Define a clear goal of the session, such as finding a suitable extension for the brand.
4   Do not pass judgment on ideas, but generate alternatives.
5   Try to think laterally, for example, by asking the question 'What do we need to do to achieve . . .?' instead of 'Yes, but that's not feasible because . . . '
6   At a later stage, judge the ideas not only factually but also based on feeling.

The brainstorming phase of the SWOT analysis is crucial and therefore requires an important degree of creativity and empathy. The ideas that are conceived must be as concrete as possible. For example, it makes little sense to include vague ideas such as 'increase market share', 'better respond to customer needs', 'diversify', 'reposition', and so on. At the very least, it should be added how exactly the company could do that. To get as many ideas as possible about possible strategies, it is advisable to organize brainstorming sessions. Various representatives from the company should be involved: designers, production personnel, intermediaries (such as sales representatives), and top management. A brainstorming session can consist of the following steps:

1   The participants are first informed about the results of the SWOT analysis itself (the most important Ss, Ws, Os, and Ts).
2   Then they think along about possible strategies. From a marketing point of view, the most important discussion point to address is brand positioning. Questions that can be asked are:
    ■   What is the brand awareness like and what are the brand associations that the target group has now?
    ■   To what extent is this in line with the brand identity?
3   Then they try to come up with a few alternatives, for example, three. For each alternative, the internal and external issues on which the idea is based are indicated in brackets. It does make a difference whether one thinks from a strength or weakness point of view. Strengths provide starting points for a competitive advantage; weaknesses are more likely to result in a defensive (defensive) strategy. Incidentally, that does not necessarily have to be the case; even a weakness can be quickly eliminated by cooperating with a strong partner, thus forming the basis for an offensive strategy.

## Case 9.4 Innovation

### Product innovation or marketing strategy: What comes first?

'Innovate or die' is a phrase often used to describe the approach brands must take to stay ahead in an ultra-competitive market characterized by rapidly changing consumer demand. However, the way companies go about driving new product development depends very much on their structure, priorities, and where marketing sits within the innovation journey. Marketing's influence is key to ensuring new offerings fit with a strategy determined by customers' needs, so companies aren't stuck trying to sell something for which there is no demand. But brands have to balance being insight driven with being able to launch products that no focus group would ever think to suggest. FMCG companies such as Unilever perform all kinds of qualitative and quantitative research and use these as input in product innovation.

Innovation is central to marketing's role within any organization, according to HP global chief marketing and communications director, Antonio Lucio. But he recognizes the approach differs depending on the category. So while in FMCG, the fundamental premise is that the 'customer is king', in a technology business like HP, the goal is to create products consumers have never even dreamed about.

This means marketing is responsible for bringing invention to life from a consumer experience standpoint.

Source: Adapted from *Marketing Week*, 15 May 2018

The following applies at every step: be creative and interpret each signal carefully and based on your own possibilities.

Being innovative also means taking possible new activities into account as much as possible. It is true that these may fall outside the existing market, but signals for this can certainly be obtained from an analysis of the current market. Following the example of the digital camera manufacturer (Case 9.2 and Figure 9.1), examples of signals that could lead to innovations are:

■ Unmet needs: wishes and desires of *existing customers* that cannot be met with the current products. An analysis of complaints can also be helpful here. The main source of ideas is: listening to customers creatively! Example: developing a digital camera that does have a good battery, including an indicator that – when the battery is almost empty – does not jump from full to empty in one go.

■ *New customer* groups that are currently not being targeted. Example: children's cameras.

■ Developments in the *macro environment* that could have a favorable impact on other markets. Example: the aging population, which can be a reason to produce extra-convenient cameras.

■ The expected development of *substitute products* within the industry structure factors. Example: the emergence of mobile telephones with a camera function, which may be a reason to become active in that market as well.

■ What are *competitors doing* outside their core activities? Example: producing copying machines.

In order to make the best possible selection process possible, it is advisable to come up with not one but, for example, three possible alternatives. Then, of course, one must be chosen. Formulating a number of options explicitly, instead of opting for a strategy at a certain level 'at once', based on a situation analysis, has the following reasons:

■ It forces the manager to think about paths other than those already taken.

■ If only one option is presented, it is more difficult to gain support in the company for the 'choice'.

### 3 Make a flexible connection with the SWOTs

The ultimate connection between the SWOTs and the strategic options should be replicable and provide sufficient creative scope. We consider the latter more important than the former.

What almost all authors agree on is that there should be a *confrontation* matrix: in a 2 × 2 matrix, the Ss and the Ws, are in two rows and the Os and the Ts in two columns, and in the four quadrants (SO, ST, WO, WT) come ideas/strategies.

Weihrich (1982) also makes a matrix and proposes numbering all strengths, weaknesses, opportunities, and threats (for example, S2, O3) and then generating ideas per quadrant, indicating which SWOTs are appropriate for each idea. The beauty of this is that it is traceable which SWOTs are linked to which strategies (and vice versa).

Other authors link general directives to the four quadrants as 'attack' (SO), 'defend' (ST), 'fortify' (WO), or 'withdraw' (WT). There are also approaches that go even further in structure. For example, it is sometimes proposed to first insert an intermediate phase in which, for each combination of an internal and external point, it is indicated with pluses and minuses how promising that combination is. Subsequently, it can be 'calculated' what the most promising combination is, after which ideas can be devised that fit it (see, for example, Hummel, 2012). A disadvantage of this method is that in our opinion it is 'too analytical': it is suggested that a strategy can be logically 'derived' from the SWOTs.

This does not work in practice, and we observe that a manager never chooses a mechanical method for strategy development. In general, a situation analysis is carried out, but one never works with weighting of opportunities and so on in order to arrive at a strategy choice. What does happen and is sensible is brainstorming: empathizing with and understanding the results of the situation analysis, discussing, brainstorming, thinking, brainstorming again, and so on (see also Case 9.3). This approach is considered fruitful and has the advantage that it can be carried out by a number of people at the same time.

What we propose is a variant of Weihrich 's approach, with two changes:

1   Ideas are not searched per quadrant but across all SWOTs. After all, it may be the case that both strengths are available for a certain positioning and that weaknesses need to be strengthened. In short: we let go of the quadrants, also because of the next point.
2   The recommendation is to arrive at a coherent marketing strategy and not with various other tactical recommendations.

## 9.4.2 SWOT matrix

Figure 9.2 shows the proposed approach. Our approach may not be exactly a matrix, but for convenience, we'll call it a SWOT matrix anyway.

Figure 9.2 shows an elaboration for the positioning. An elaboration is also possible towards segmentation and target groups. Suppose the segmentation analysis (see Section 5.2) shows that six segments can be distinguished, each with its own wishes and preferences. Then three alternative target groups could be mentioned here, for example:

■   segment of professionals
■   segment of children and young people up to the age of 20
■   segment of the elderly over 65

With a choice for one of these groups, the T of STP ('segmenting, targeting, positioning') is fulfilled.

As the last step in the selection process, a choice must be made.

## 9.5 Step 4: selection of a marketing strategy

In this section we discuss three steps. Section 9.5.1 deals with assessing options on the basis of a number of criteria. Subsequently, in Section 9.5.2, we look at the forecasts

| | O1 Increasing need for quality photos<br>O2 Economic growth<br>O3 Customers rely more on in-store advice<br>O4 Cameras still pay little attention to style<br>O5 Competitors are not specialized | T1 Improvement photo quality smartphones<br>T2 Growing need for convenience<br>T3 Growth of Instagram<br>T4 Stronger competition in user-friendly cameras<br>T5 Competition (e.g. Canon) has much wider range (printers, PCs, cameras and so on) |
|---|---|---|
| S1 Strong position among professionals<br>S2 Good at quality and innovation<br>S3 Many possibilities<br>S4 Good relationship with shops<br>S5 Specialist in photography | **Alternative marketing strategies for the next three years**<br>• Repositioning towards user-friendliness (W2, W5, T2, T4)<br>• Strengthening quality aspect (S1, S2, S3, S5, W1, O1, O2, T1)<br>• Introduction of a user-friendly and stylish sub-brand (S4, W4, O4, T2, T4, T5) | |
| W1 High cost and price<br>W2 Low market share among consumers<br>W 3 Brand awareness relatively low<br>W4 Limited distribution<br>W5 No brand extensions | | |

*Figure 9.2* SWOT matrix

and considerations in the option choice. Finally, we show how the net present value of a strategy can be estimated (Section 9.5.3).

## 9.5.1 Criteria when assessing options

In an approach that is as systematic as possible, ideally each option should be assessed against a number of criteria. Each company can choose its own criteria. Ultimately, expected profit is, of course, a very important one. But that is often difficult to predict. It is also important whether a strategy is feasible. Finally, a strategy must fit within the company's DNA.

Figure 9.3 shows possible criteria for each alternative that can be taken into account when selecting a strategy. This is followed by an explanation of these criteria.

**Criterion 1: fit with vision**
Does the option match the vision ( value strategy ), is the core problem solved?

**Criterion 2: feasibility**
Is the option feasible internally? (preconditions FOETSLE)

**Financial**: to what extent are there sufficient financial resources to implement the strategy?
**Organizational**: does the strategy fit into the organization? Is implementation organizationally possible?
**Economic**: is the strategy in line with the company's economic objectives?
**Technical**: is the implementation of the strategy technically possible?
**Social**: is the strategy socially acceptable? In this context, the company's social objectives should also be considered.
**Legal**: are there no legal problems to be expected (e.g. in the context of trademark law)?
**Ecological**: is the strategy ecologically sound (environmentally)?
**Ecological**: is the strategy sustainable?

**Criterion 3: results and risks**
Expected achievement of the objectives: are the results acceptable to the internal stakeholders (in particular: expected profitability, payback period and associated risks)?

*Figure 9.3* **The selection process of the marketing strategy**

*Suitability*

An initial assessment of the strategic options concerns the extent to which an option fits:

- the higher levels of strategy (vision, corporate strategy)
- the solution of the core problem (if not already done)
- the most important issues in the external and internal environment

For example, a company may have come to the conclusion, based on customer research, that there is a market for significantly cheaper products. However, if the company has not opted for the low price *brand benefit*, offering low-cost products may not fit the brand identity. In that case, the company is not doing what some customers would ideally like. This is in line with our understanding of the role of *marketing as an intermediary between the customer and the brand*.

From the assessment of the appropriateness of options, it may be concluded that various options are satisfactory (see Figure 9.4).

*Feasibility*

Each option that may be suitable is then compared to a number of internal preconditions. Testing on the basis of the seven preconditions (FOETSLE; see Figure 9.4) provides insight into the feasibility: is it possible to implement the option in question?

| | Suitability | Feasibility | Expected profit and risk |
|---|---|---|---|
| Option 1 | ... | ... | ... |
| Option 2 | ... | ... | ... |
| Option 3 | ... | ... | ... |
| Choice: | | | |

*Figure 9.4* **The selection of a marketing strategy**

## Results and risks

The company must make a choice from the options that remain after selection based on the preconditions. This selection is done on the basis of objectives. These can be business or marketing objectives. Business objectives are usually financial in nature (profit, payback period, etc.; see Section 10.1); marketing objectives often relate to sales or market share (see Section 11.1). Profit and market share are not always aligned: with a high marketing budget, a high market share can be 'bought'. Also sustainability goals should be considered.

Which of the objectives is decisive depends on the internal and external situation in which the marketing plan is written.

## 9.5.2 Forecasts and considerations in the selection process

When market share or sales is the selection criterion, one must make a forecast of the expected sales for each option. Although this forecasting always remains a highly precarious business, the forecasting methods we described in Section 9.1 can be helpful in this respect. The option with the highest expected market share is then chosen.

Often, however, financial objectives are decisive: the option that is expected to earn the most money is preferred. A financial selection criterion implies that the profit contribution of each option must be predicted over a range of years. This means that the sales forecast referred to previously must be supplemented with (assumptions about) the required investments, among other things. Because this can in fact only be done after, for example, a communication plan has also been made, we (also) pay attention to this in the last chapter of the book (see Section 14.2). In addition to the expected revenues and costs, the expected risk plays a major role.

In the eventual choice of options, the company must therefore weigh up the expected returns, risks, and investments required immediately and investments required in the long term. Crucial in this list are the expected returns: forecasting methods are needed to determine these. When it comes to financial objectives, a commonly used simple criterion is the payback period: how quickly are the investments required 'now' recovered? The management can also set a maximum for this, for example, four years.

A somewhat more advanced way of comparing alternatives is the *shareholder value analysis*, a method of determining the 'present value' of a strategy. The idea behind the shareholder value analysis is: a strategy can be regarded as an investment that produces a certain future cash flow. If one calculates the expected cash flow back to the point in time 'now' by means of discounting, the expected shareholder value can be calculated. The selection criterion that is used here is therefore entirely financial in nature and actually relates to the value that a strategy has for the shareholders. After all, shareholders can choose from various options when investing capital, and they will in principle opt for the option with the highest cash value. An important advantage of the shareholder value analysis is that it establishes a link between the functional areas of marketing and financing: the strategies are evaluated on the basis of financial measures.

### 9.5.3 Estimating the net present value of a strategy

To calculate the present value, the same formulas may be used that are employed in the investment realm. The present value of a strategy is the sum of the discounted future cash flows (calculated back to point 'zero' in time) plus the discounted residual value at the end of the duration of the strategy. To calculate the *net* present value, the investment made at point 'zero' in time should still be subtracted. The formula is as follows:

$$NCW = \sum_{t=1}^{n} \frac{CF_t}{(1+r)^t} - I$$

in which:

$NCW$ = net cash (present) worth of a strategy
$n$ = planning period (e.g. three or five years)
$CF_t$ = predicted cash flow in period $t$ ($CF_n$ also contains the residual value of the strategy)
$r$ = discount rate
$1/(1 + r)^t$ = discount factor
$I$ = investment amount

The variables mentioned here are calculated as follows:

- The *cash flow* is calculated in the usual way: expected annual sales times gross profit margin less taxes, increases in fixed costs (advertising, R&D) and investments in working capital.
- The *discount rate* is the average cost of capital for the company. If a certain strategy has a relatively high risk, the discount rate can be increased by a risk surcharge.
- The *residual value* of a strategy is the value at the end of the planning horizon. This seems difficult to determine. One approach is to assume that net receipts will continue forever or change by a certain percentage through the end of the planning period.

In choosing a strategy, this procedure should be performed for the situation of 'unchanged policy' and for the options to be considered. The difference between the net present value of an option and the net present value of an unchanged policy is the value of the strategy.

Figure 9.5 contains a calculation example. The most convenient way to do the calculation is to start from the expected *differences* between the strategy to be considered

| | Current values | Forecasta of differences between strategy and unchanged policy | | | Residual value |
|---|---|---|---|---|---|
| | 2023 | 2024 | 2025 | 2026 | 2027 ff |
| | (t = 0) | | | | |
| Cash flow [a] (annual growth 10%) | 100 | 10 | 21 | 33 | 46 |
| Discount factor (r = 15%) | | 0.87 | 0.76 | 0.66 | 3.81 [b] |
| Present value of cash flow | | 8.7 | 16.0 | 21.8 | 175.3 |
| Total cash value | 222 | | | | |
| Investment amount | 150 | | | | |
| Net present value strategy | 72 | | | | |

***Figure 9.5* Example of calculation of present value for a strategy**

a  For examples of how cash flow is calculated, we refer to the literature.
b  Eternity assumption: discount factor/discount rate = .57/.15.

and 'unchanged policy' in one go. Figure 9.5 is based on the assumption (prognosis) that with the chosen strategy (investment amount 150) the cash flow will increase annually by 10%, while a stable cash flow (of 100) is expected if policy remains unchanged. In the example, the strategy should be executed.

An advantage of the shareholder value analysis is that the financial expectations of a strategy are summarized in one key figure. This makes it easier to compare strategies. An additional advantage is that one is forced to explicitly describe all expected returns and costs of strategies. Drawing up financial indicators is always a necessity in a marketing plan.

The shareholder value analysis stands or falls with the reliability of the predicted results. So, as we noted earlier, mapping future returns is a tricky business.

## Summary

The SWOT analysis forms the link between situation analysis (internal and external analysis) and strategy formation. Ideas for possible strategies are generated from the results of the situation analysis. It is important to do this creatively, critically, and in a customer-oriented way and to make a clear choice. The four steps are:

1   Reducing the situation analysis to a limited number of Ss, Ws, Os, and Ts.
2   Reaching a 'conclusion' of the SWOT analysis: key point and future expectation, goal and expectation if policy remains unchanged.
3   Devising marketing strategic options using the SWOT matrix, with sufficient room for creativity.
4   Choice of a marketing strategy.

Various criteria can be used in choosing the best option, such as the FOETSLE criteria and the expected cash flow.

We end this chapter with an important caveat. We indicated earlier that a strategy cannot be 'derived' from a SWOT analysis. For that reason, a certain degree of freedom was chosen in step 2.

But also in this chapter, a systematic approach to selection has been discussed. In step 2 it is recommended to come up with alternatives and then to arrive at a substantiated choice in steps 3 and 4. However, it is an illusion to think that a strategy can be chosen objectively. For example, it is virtually impossible to predict what the future annual returns of a strategy will be. In practice, therefore, a suitable strategy is often developed 'in one go' in step 2.

## Pepsi Cola in the United States: strategic choices

The American market for (non-alcoholic) beverages has traditionally been dominated by soft drinks, especially cola. However, the position of soft drinks has been under pressure for years, partly due to the pursuit of a healthy lifestyle and continuous attention to the dangers of obesity. The need for functional foods is also reflected in the market: consumers are looking for hydration, a good energy balance, or strengthening the immune system. Other product categories, such as sports drinks, fruit juices, and bottled water, are therefore on the rise. The following segments can be distinguished in this market:

- (Carbonated) soft drinks
- Bottled water
- Ready-to-drink (RTD) tea (such as iced tea)
- Energy, health, and sports drinks
- Juices

### Carbonated soft drinks

Sales of soft drinks have been declining for years. Consumers are increasingly buying drinks such as mineral water, fruit juice, and sports drinks instead of soft drinks. The downward trend continues: in 2021 there was another 5% decrease, to around 40 billion liters on an annual basis. In monetary terms, soft drink sales in the United States stabilized around a total of $136 billion. We are still talking about a lot of consumption: the average American drinks more than 120 liters per year.

Initially, companies such as Pepsi and Coca Cola tried to counteract the decline with Diet or Zero Sugar variants such as Diet Pepsi or Coke Zero. But these drinks are also under pressure, partly because sweeteners such as aspartame are also in the news negatively because they are said to be bad for health. And besides, if you really want to live a healthy life, you drink water, not a weak decoction of cola. That is why producers are increasingly trying to turn the tide by innovating and launching soft drinks with stronger flavors or other additives. Experiments are also being carried out with new taste concepts. Coca Cola Zero Sugar Byte is a sugar-free cola that should taste like pixels; Coca Cola Dreamworld is, according to the company, 'a soda meant to capture technicolor tastes and surrealism of the subconscious by inviting drinkers to dream with open eyes'. Pepsi's new Nitro Pepsi is 'creamy, smooth and has a mesmerizing cascade of tiny bubbles topped off by a frothy foam head'. Consumers' search for new experiences and the functional food trend will continue to stimulate these kinds of innovations in the coming years, if only to stop the declining trend in soft drink sales.

## Bottled water

Bottled water benefits greatly from increasing health awareness. While soft drinks are increasingly seen as artificial and sugar laden in the eyes of consumers, bottled water seems to benefit from its clean, pure image. In 2021, sales of bottled water in the United States grows by approximately 8%. The average American drinks nearly 180 liters of bottled water per year. Incidentally, there is an important difference between European mineral water and American bottled water. In Europe, mineral water comes from natural sources, contains all kinds of minerals, and has an image of 'pure nature'. The bottled water sold in American supermarkets usually does not come directly from nature and often has hardly any natural association. It is filtered and distilled water, cleaned of potential germs through a process called reverse osmosis.

Trends such as wellness are creating all kinds of product innovations in the field of bottled water with added vitamins and minerals so that consumers can get their daily dose of vitamins by drinking bottled water. Product innovations continue to drive consumption growth. The European idea of mineral water from natural sources is also an innovative element in the American market.

## RTD tea

Manufacturers of RTD tea have increasingly positioned their products as functional drinks, mainly due to the addition of beneficial antioxidants. Recent product introductions with the addition of green tea leaf extracts benefit from the increased interest in green tea. Specialty teas such as kombucha and yerba mate are enjoying increasing interest. This is partly stimulated by home delivery services such as UberEats; apparently home (or office) delivery stimulates the choice of surprising flavors. Sparkling tea is also on the rise. Due to all these developments, RTD tea remains in the spotlight: the RTD market grew by about 3.6% in 2021 to a total of $2.3 billion. Translated into liters, however, this hardly means an increase: RTD tea contains sugar, and health awareness also influences sales here.

## Juice

Fruit juices are healthy, but they also contain sugar. Partly because of that sugar, the sale of fruit juice in the United States was under pressure for years. But the turning point came in 2020 with the COVID-19 pandemic. The balance then tipped towards the healthy appearance of fruit and therefore of fruit juice. Fruit juices gave consumers a short escape from the lockdown by letting them enjoy a glass of pure nature. Some fruit juices also claim to support the immune system and prevent disease, which also boosts sales. The refrigerated fruit juice market increased by a whopping 7.8% in 2020 to a total of nearly $8 million.

## Sports drinks continue to grow

The sale of sports drinks has risen sharply in recent years due to product innovations and a repositioning in which the link between sports and health has been strengthened. All kinds of viral marketing aimed at students, for example, in combination with 'traditional' campaigns via radio and TV, have stimulated the sale of functional drinks such as energy drinks and sports drinks. As with fruit juices, sports drink sales were also boosted by COVID. The current emphasis on fitness and health will continue to reinforce this growth in the coming years. The growth of sports drinks in 2020 was no less than 15%. Growth opportunities also seem to lie in the field of personalized solutions. The CEO of Gatorade says: 'We see great opportunities for creating personalized advice for athletes and their hydration and nutritional needs during exercise'.

## Pepsico

Pepsico is one of the leading food and beverage companies in the world. Pepsico's product portfolio includes Frito-Lay (snacks such as Lay's chips, Doritos, Cheetos), Quaker Foods (Quaker Oatmeal and other nutritious (breakfast) products), and Pepsico Beverages (brands like Pepsi Cola, Mountain Dew, Aquafina, Tropicana, Gatorade).

Pepsico sees a number of important trends for its markets:

- Retail dynamics, in particular the growth of e-commerce as a distribution channel for food and beverages
- Society is increasingly focusing on the values and ethics of a brand
- Continued consumer interest in health, wellness, and functional foods
- Consumers are looking for 'experiences', also with soft drinks

The company has split its portfolio to benefit from these trends:

- Good-for-you (Tropicana, Aquafina, and Quaker Foods). The Quaker brand is one of the most important brands that Americans associate with healthy food.
- Better-for-you. Diet Pepsi can be considered 'better for you' than 'regular' Pepsi
- Fun-for-you: snacks and soft drinks

The key drinks in Pepsico's portfolio are (figures are for the United States, 2021):

|  | Pepsico's brands | Sales in billions of liters (1 liter is approx. 0.25 gallon) | Market share | Competitors | Market share |
|---|---|---|---|---|---|
| Soft drinks | Pepsi | 11.8 | 9% | Coca Cola | 40% |
|  | Mountain Dew | 9.5 | 7% | Dr. Pepper (Cadbury Schweppes) | 8% |
|  |  |  |  | Sprite (Coca-Cola Company) | 8% |
| Sports drinks | Gatorade | 6.7 | 68% | Powerade (Coca-Cola Company) | 14% |
| RTD-tea | Lipton | 0.9 | 39% | Arizona (Arizona Beverage Company) | 26% |
| Bottled water | Aquafina | 1.0 | 9% | Dasani (Coca-Cola Company) | 8% |
|  |  |  |  | Private labels | 25% |

Pepsico's mission seems to be based on a people-planet-profit idea (source: www.pepsico.com, September 15, 2022):

Create more smiles with every sip and every bite:

- FOR OUR CONSUMERS:
  By creating joyful moments through our delicious and nourishing products and unique brand experiences.
- FOR OUR CUSTOMERS:
  By being the best possible partner, driving game-changing innovation and delivering a level of growth unmatched in our industry.
- FOR OUR ASSOCIATES AND OUR COMMUNITIES:

By creating meaningful opportunities to work, gain new skills and build successful careers, and maintaining a diverse and inclusive workplace.

■ FOR OUR PLANET:
By conserving nature's precious resources and fostering a more sustainable planet for our children and grandchildren.

■ FOR OUR SHAREHOLDERS:
By delivering sustainable top-tier TSR and embracing best-in-class corporate governance.

Pepsico is active in convincing young people about the importance of fitness and a balanced diet, for example, by sponsoring sports activities for children.

Young people are important to the company. Pepsi focuses more than Coca Cola on young people: millennials and Gen Z. Pepsi believes that if the company manages to persuade these young people to adopt Pepsi, they will have a customer for life. Pepsi also profiles itself differently than Coca Cola. Brad Jakeman (marketer at Pepsico) once said that

> Coke represents happiness and moments of joy, while it preserves culture and maintains the status quo. Pepsi, on the other hand, creates culture and embraces individuality. For Pepsi loyalists, leading an exciting life is much more important than leading a happy one.

This insight led Pepsi to opt for a positioning in which the 'excitement' of the here and now is central. The brand thus seems to aim at a target group that has high expectations of life and is very mobile and active. In their lifestyle, they pick the day (Carpe Diem). With the slogan 'That's what I like', Pepsi tries to connect to this lifestyle. The Coca Cola strategy is different. This is clear from campaigns such as 'Always Coca Cola' or 'Open Happiness'. The traditional values of the product are central here. The new tagline 'Taste the Feeling' aligns the brand with an overall sense of happiness and focuses less on an 'experience' than Pepsi.

The position of private labels in the soft drinks market in the United States is getting stronger but is still a far cry from the position of private labels and discount brands in some European countries. In the United States, consumer choice is driven more by image than by price. But a growing awareness of the American consumer could make US consumers more price sensitive, especially now that the US market is ravaged by raging inflation and declining purchasing power.

Pepsi has spent a lot of money on marketing and distribution and will continue to do so in the future. It has created a young and dynamic image. But continuous competitive pressure and the increasing importance of healthy consumption limits the growth perspective. Consumers seem to consume less and less cola. And competition with Coca Cola is also not leading to the desired result: Pepsi's market share has been declining for years. It's a very slow decline, but still, it's falling.

So . . . What should Pepsico do with the Pepsi brand?

## Questions

1   Create a graphical representation of Pepsico's business, using the method described in Chapter 3.

2   How is it possible that volume sales of soft drinks, expressed in liters, fall but sales in terms of dollars remain the same? Mention at least two reasons.

3   An industry can be described by using Porter's five-forces model. Run this model for the US soft drinks market. Draw your conclusions about the attractiveness of this market.

4   Apply the product lifecycle concept to the US soft drink market. Try to include the following product categories in your product lifecycle:
   ■   Soft drinks
   ■   Ready-to-drink tea
   ■   Sports drinks
   ■   Bottled water

5   Markets can be analyzed by using a portfolio analysis (the theory on portfolio analysis is covered in Chapter 10).
   a   Create a portfolio analysis for Pepsico Beverages USA, using the Boston Consulting Group approach
   b   Provide strategic recommendations for Pepsi based on your portfolio.
   c   Assess the portfolio methodology: Do you agree with the recommendations arising from the BCG matrix?

6   Create a SWOT matrix for the Pepsi brand in the United States.

7   Analyze the strategic problem Pepsico faces with the Pepsi brand.

8   What should Pepsico do with the Pepsi brand?
   a   Define strategic options for the Pepsi brand by using the information in the case description and the SWOT matrix you created in question 6.
   b   Develop a strategy for the Pepsi brand based on your strategic options. Use the strategy selection process to make your choice.

9   Imagine you would like to predict sales and market share for Pepsi for the coming five years (2025–2030). Which method would you like to use for this prediction? Explain your answer.

# Part 3

# Corporate decisions and marketing decisions

In Part 2, we explained the situation analysis. This analysis forms the basis for the decisions to be made (planning). In Part 3, Chapter 10 deals with corporate objectives and corporate strategies. In Chapter 11, we discuss marketing objectives and marketing strategies. Decisions at this level concern the long term; they are thus strategic in nature.

DOI: 10.4324/9781003381488-12

# Chapter 10

# Corporate objectives and strategies

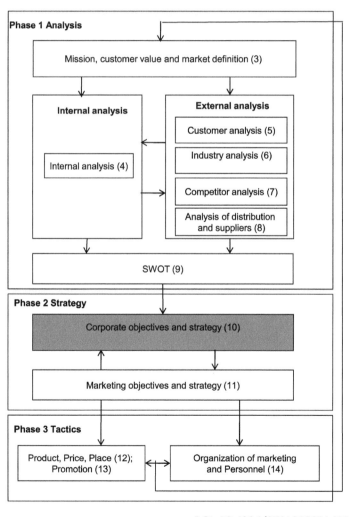

DOI: 10.4324/9781003381488-13

## Key points in this chapter

- Know the difference between corporate strategy and marketing strategy
- Apply a portfolio analysis
- Know the different growth directions for companies
- Know how to relate growth directions to development methods (partnering or not).

## Introduction

In this chapter we discuss the decisions that are made at the top level in the company: the company objective and the company strategy. Chapter 11 discusses the other kinds of decisions: the marketing decisions and market instrument decisions. If there is no difference between the corporate and brand levels (e.g. SMEs), the decisions we describe in this and the next chapter are all determined at one level (the entrepreneur).

Sections 10.1 to 10.4 discuss successively determination of the corporate vision and corporate objectives (Section 10.1), the portfolio analysis (Section 10.2), and then the two components of the corporate strategy, namely the choice of markets and products (Section 10.3) and the choice of possible partners (Section 10.4).

## 10.1 Company vision and objectives

In Chapter 3 we discussed the 'current vision and mission'. Now, after the SWOT, it is time to see if the vision and mission need adjustment.

### 10.1.1 Corporate vision

We have already discussed these concepts in Section 3.1. We provide some summary conclusions.

- A mission mainly reflects the current set of core activities of the company and often also says something about the market in which the company is active. The mission description often also contains the principles that the company stands for. These principles relate to values and norms, such as quality, integrity, and social involvement. Part of the latter is also sustainability. Social goals are sometimes referred to as '*purpose*' and the associated marketing as *purpose marketing*.
- A vision is future oriented: the vision indicates where the company wants to go in the coming years. It reflects the CEO's 'dream'.

Thus, a vision can contain the personal view of top management. This opinion can be about the environment and the role of the company. Because a vision contains a dream (if it's good), it can be motivating for the staff.

A company's vision and mission are often quite general and therefore meaningless. Then they are not benchmarks for the staff. See also Case 10.1.

## Case 10.1 Strategy? Many have no idea

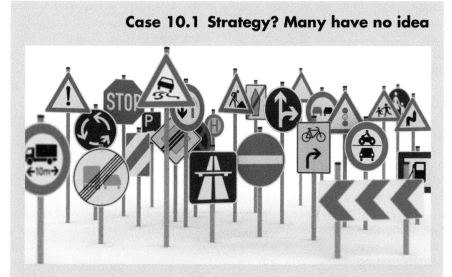

### Use road signs

In many large organizations there is a deluge of documents with countless points of attention that often cause a lot of confusion. This is called 'strategic confusion' and 'strategic overload'. According to a study, 65% of employees of European companies therefore do not know their own organization's strategy. So vague is bad. And wanting too much doesn't work either. The more priorities a company has, the lower the revenue growth. A simple metaphor is: think of your plans and communication as road signs. If you want those works to apply, your signs must be clear at a glance, you must not hang too many of them, they must not be contradictory, and it must be clear which sign is the most important.

Source: NRC, October 15, 2022 (column Ben Tiggelaar)

## 10.1.2 Corporate objectives

In Chapter 4 we set out the general requirements for objectives (SMART) and also indicated that organizations should not only formulate financial goals but also goals related to innovation, customers, internal goals (balanced scorecard), and sustainability. Corporate goals are usually chosen for several years, a minimum of three years.

In fact, when choosing corporate objectives, the following decisions are made:

1  What are the main objective variables?
2  What value of those variables do we want to achieve and when?

Prioritization of objective variables is entirely a matter for top management. This concerns, for example, the question of whether the company wants to emphasize market share or profit. In the specific interpretation of the set goals, it is important that the chosen goals in the organization be supported by those who are responsible for realizing them. This means, among other things, that various sections of the organization must be involved in the realization of those objectives. The balanced scorecard discussed in Section 4.1.2 can be helpful in both decisions (prioritization and interpretation of goals). We already mentioned that nowadays sustainability must also play a role in this and that growth should not always be an obvious objective.

## 10.2 Portfolio analysis

A portfolio is a group of products of an organization. An analysis of this is important to know whether the right markets are still being served and also to know how much to invest in each of the products. One product is more profitable than another.

In Section 10.2.1, we discuss the purpose and content of portfolio methods. We then describe the 'classic' portfolio method (the BCG matrix, Section 10.2.2) and a variant that takes into account more factors (the MABA analysis, Section 10.2.3). Portfolio methods are basically only about existing products in existing markets. In Section 10.2.4, we indicate how new markets can be taken into account (path analysis). Portfolio methods are primarily intended for corporate-level use with different markets. However, often companies have several brands or products in the same market. In Section 10.2.5, we describe 'brand variants' of the portfolio analysis. Finally, in Section 10.2.6, we list some advantages and disadvantages of portfolio methods.

### 10.2.1 Purpose and content of the portfolio analysis

A company that is active in different markets with different products must strive for a balanced combination of its product-market combinations. In this context, balanced means the total use of the financial resources is in balance with – and preferably less than – the revenues of the various product-market combinations. While this may seem like an obvious goal, realizing it isn't easy. Markets and market positions are constantly subject to change, which means that the demand that product-market combinations make on financial resources is constantly changing. After all, a product that people want to grow costs a lot of money. If one wants to keep the market share constant in a growing market, this also requires investments. On the other hand, a product with a large market share usually makes a lot of profit, and products in stable markets require less investment. A balanced 'portfolio' of products may therefore mean that the company has products in different stages of the product life cycle, for example, a product in an introduction stage, a number of products in the growth stage, some in more mature markets, and perhaps some in a downward phase.

The tool that a company has to achieve a balanced portfolio is to set goals for the market positions of the product-market combinations and then try to achieve these goals by investing more or less in the various products.

Portfolio methods are an aid in making a choice about investments in different products. With portfolio methods, the positions of product-market combinations are visualized in a figure or matrix. The two axes are approximations of the following two dimensions:

1   *Attractiveness of the market.* It is based on the hypothesis that more investments should be made in attractive (for example, growing) markets than in unattractive markets. One reason for this is that without additional investments in a growing market, market share will decline, partly due to generally stronger competition. The attractiveness of the market therefore indicates the extent to which cash resources are *needed*.

2   *Market position of the products.* Products with a strong market position have a number of advantages over smaller competitors. These advantages, such as economies of scale, cost advantages due to experience effects (the so-called experience curve), better access to distribution channels, and high awareness, mean higher profitability. The market position therefore indicates the extent to which cash resources will become available.

Based on the visual overview of the positions of the various product-market combinations, alternative investment strategies can then be formulated.

A portfolio analysis can be performed on two levels:

1   *Corporate-level portfolio analysis.* This involves the assessment of positions and the allocation of financial resources across SBUs. This application receives the most attention in the literature and in practice.

2   *SBU-level portfolio analysis.* This involves the assessment of positions and the allocation of financial resources across brands/products. This variant requires a small adjustment of the method.

The two dimensions (the attractiveness of the market and the market position of the products) show that a portfolio analysis links results from the external and internal analysis. For this reason, a portfolio analysis is a logical continuation of a SWOT analysis. Figure 10.1 illustrates the relationship between the SWOT analysis and the portfolio analysis at the *company* level.

Because a SWOT analysis is defined for a market, several SWOT analyses from as many SBUs are the input for the portfolio analysis. The attractiveness of the markets is the result of the industry analyses, while the market positions of the SBUs (the collective position of the brands in a market) are examined in the internal analyses.

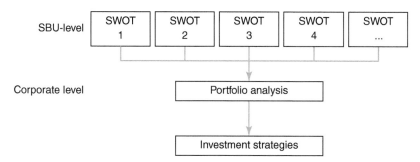

*Figure 10.1* **Relation between SWOT-analysis and portfolio analysis**

Incidentally, countries can also be regarded as segments/sub-markets. A portfolio analysis can therefore be very helpful for a company that has an international investment problem within a market.

Over time, various portfolio methods have been developed. We will discuss:

■   The portfolio matrix developed by the Boston Consulting Group (the BCG matrix; see Section 10.2.2). This is the first and simplest portfolio method, which – due to its simplicity – also has the most limitations.
■   The 'business screen' developed by General Electric (example of a MABA analysis; see Section 10.2.3).

## 10.2.2 BCG matrix

We will successively discuss the content of the BCG matrix, the resulting recommendations, and some points of criticism.

### Content of the BCG matrix

Figure 10.2 contains an example of a BCG growth share matrix. Along the axes are the following two variables:

1   market growth
2   the relative market share

### 1 Market growth

The vertical axis represents the market growth. This axis is divided into two: more and less than 10% growth per year. The variable market growth thus represents the attractiveness of the market. The choice of this variable is partly due to the central role that market growth plays in the concept of the product life cycle (see Section 6.4.2). Another advantage is the easy measurability of market growth.

### 2 Relative market share

The horizontal axis represents the *relative market share*: own market share divided by the market share of the largest competitor. The limit value is 1: a value greater than 1 implies that the company has the largest market share; you are then market leader. The highest value is usually defined on the left and the lowest on the right. The fact that market share and profitability are positively related is partly due to the *experience curve* (or *learning curve*) existing in some industries. This concept means that as a company has more experience in producing a product, the costs per unit of product decrease over time due to various learning effects.

The relationship between market share and profit can not only be reasoned theoretically but is also apparent from many empirical studies. The most well-known studies in this field have been carried out with the PIMS database: a file with financial data of several thousand companies. One of the most remarkable results from PIMS studies is the clear relationship between market share and *return on investment*.

In the BCG matrix, the SBUs are arranged in the form of circles. It is customary for the diameter of those circles to be proportional to the SBU's contribution to the company's turnover.

Depending on the place of a product-market combination in one of the four quadrants of the BCG matrix, we can distinguish four types of products:

1   *Stars*. These are products with a high market share in a rapidly growing market. The used and required cash resources of these products are both high and therefore in principle in balance. When the market's growth slows, the stars can turn into cash cows.

2   *Cash cows*. These are products with a high market share in a market with little growth. Due to the strong market position, they generate a lot of cash, while they require little investment due to the limited market growth.

3   *Problem children*. These products (also called *question marks* or *wild cats*) have a low market share in a fast growing market. As the name implies, they can cause problems: they yield little but require a lot of cash. If they manage to strengthen their position, they can become a star and eventually, when market growth slows down, a cash cow.

4   *Dogs*. This concerns products with a low market share in a market with little growth. They therefore yield little but also require little investment. As with the stars, the financial aspects of these products are in balance. Because many markets are saturated and by definition only one brand can be the market leader, in practice most brands can be characterized as dogs.

In the example in Figure 10.2, the major SBUs are numbers 5 (a *star*) and 6 (a *cash cow*). The company also has a medium-sized *star* and some minor *problem children* and *dogs*.

### Strategic recommendations

Based on a portfolio analysis, the following investment strategies can be chosen:

■   growth (*build*)
■   maintain position (*hold*)
■   harvest/milk (*harvest*)
■   liquidation (*terminate*)

The strong positions of the stars and cash cows should at least be maintained. For the cash cows, part of the proceeds can be used to strengthen the positions of that problem children who have the opportunity to become a star. For some problem children, a growth strategy is therefore used, financed from cash cows. For the other problem children, no investments are made in them: therefore harvesting or liquidation. A problem here is of course selecting the problem children for whom growth opportunities are seen. The choice largely depends on the phase of the product life cycle in which the product is located: the introduction, growth, or maturity phase. A thorough industry analysis is important here.

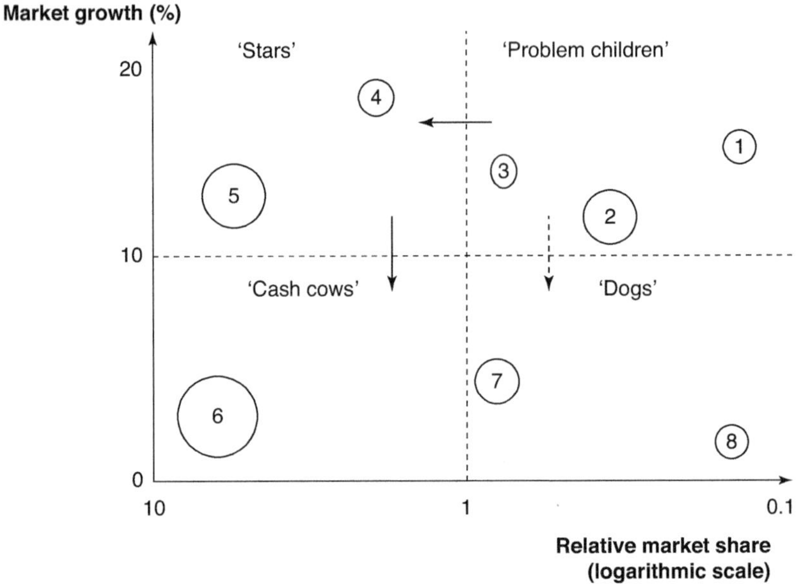

**Figure 10.2**

In principle, the recommendation for dogs is 'milk them out and remove them from the market'. However, if dogs are of a reasonable size, they can be an important part of a company's business. A enforcement strategy then seems possible.

In the example in Figure 10.2, the (sizable) cash cow can be used to collect both stars and possibly a problem. The portfolio of the company in question seems reasonably balanced.

### Critique of the BCG matrix

In Section 10.2.6, we discuss the objections to portfolio methods in general. Here we consider some specific drawbacks of the BCG matrix. As we mentioned, an advantage of the BCG matrix is its great simplicity. However, this simplicity also leads to disadvantages. The main limitation specific to the BCG matrix is that only one variable is chosen for both dimensions, namely *relative market share* and *market growth*. Although these variables are in themselves of great importance for determining market position and market attractiveness respectively, they are only an underlying factor. Other underlying factors should also be considered.

To meet this objection, portfolio models have been developed that take multiple factors into account (see the MABA analysis in Section 10.2.3).

## 10.2.3 MABA analysis

An example of a *MABA analysis* (market attractiveness business position assessment) is the *business screen* developed by General Electric (see Figure 10.3).

Instead of market growth, the vertical axis now shows the attractiveness of the market. This variable is determined by a number of underlying industry factors, such as market

| Market attractiveness | Competitive position | | |
|---|---|---|---|
| | Strong (score > 3.33) | Average (1.67 < score < 3.33) | Weak (score < 1.67) |
| High (score > 3.33) | 1 Invest/grow | 1 Invest/grow | 2 Selective investment |
| Average (1.67 < score < 3.33) | 1 Invest/grow | 2 Selective investment | 3 Harvesting/terminate |
| Low (score < 1.67) | 2 Selective investment | 3 Harvesting/terminate | 3 Harvesting/terminate |

*Figure 10.3* The General Electric business screen

| Competitive Position Criteria | Weight | Value* | Score |
|---|---|---|---|
| Market share | 0.10 | 4 | 0.40 |
| Price competitiveness | 0.05 | 2 | 0.10 |
| Durability | 0.20 | 3 | 0.60 |
| Experience curve effects | 0.10 | 4 | 0.40 |
| Added value | 0.20 | 5 | 1.00 |
| Production device | 0.05 | 2 | 0.10 |
| Production capacity | 0.05 | 2 | 0.10 |
| Quality of the product | 0.10 | 1 | 0.10 |
| Sales promotion | 0.05 | 4 | 0.20 |
| R&D | 0.05 | 5 | 0.25 |
| Labour productivity | 0.05 | 4 | 0.20 |
| Total | 1.00 | | 3.45 |

*Figure 10.4* Determining the competitiveness of a product-market combination
* 1 = low; 5 = high

size, market growth, profitability, intensity of competition, and power of distributors. Attractiveness can be determined by scoring each of the underlying industry factors, weighting each of those factors based on the importance management attaches to those factors, and then calculating an overall score. We have already provided an illustration of how this can be done in the industry analysis (see Section 6.6). After all, the purpose of the industry analysis is to determine the attractiveness of the market. The result of the industry analysis (a attractiveness score) can therefore be used directly as input for the business screen.

Instead of the relative market share, the horizontal axis now shows the competitive position/competitive strength of the product-market combination (relative strength). This variable is also determined on the basis of scores on a number of underlying factors. An example of such a calculation is shown in Figure 10.4.

Based on the scores for the market attractiveness and competitiveness factors, the various product-market combinations are placed in the matrix. The axes are subdivided into three. There are thus nine possible cells (see Figure 10.3). If we take the example of the candy bar market (Case 6.5 in Section 6.6) and declare the position determination from Figure 10.2 applicable to it, the attractiveness score is 'average' (2.95, see the figure in Case 6.5) and the position score 'strong' (3.45, see Figure 10.4). This SBU therefore falls into one of the 'invest/grow' cells of the 'business screen'. Incidentally, when depicting the SBUs in Figure 10.1, as well as with the BCG matrix, the turnover of the SBU can be visualized using the size of the circle that indicates the SBU.

## 10.2.4 Trajectory analysis

For this we have outlined how the *current* set of SBUs (or products within an SBU) can be visualized with a portfolio analysis. A disadvantage of such an analysis is that it does not take any new activities into account. After all, for a new activity, the market share is currently zero by definition, which means that it cannot be included in a portfolio analysis. In order to consider possible new activities for a company (diversification) in a portfolio analysis, a trajectory analysis must be performed (Kerin et al., 1990, p. 53 et seq.). This means that the following three steps are followed:

1   First of all, a manager analyzes the *current position of the SBUs with a portfolio analysis*. The most important question to answer is whether the current portfolio of SBUs is balanced. This involves answering questions such as: Aren't there too many SBUs to invest in? Are there enough SBUs with favorable growth prospects?

2   Subsequently, one must make a *forecast* of the portfolio positions *with unchanged policy*. This should take into account, among other things, the expected growth of the various markets: even without action, the portfolio position of an SBU may change if the market attractiveness changes. Possible actions by competitors will also have to be taken into account: these could affect the market position of the SBUs. In this context, 'success trajectories' and 'disaster trajectories' can be distinguished. In terms of the BCG matrix, a success path that solves a problem child becomes a star through market share growth and then a cash cow when the market becomes saturated. A 'disaster trajectory' is the reverse or if a falling stock turns a cash cow into a dog.

   The expected results with unchanged policy are then compared with the objectives (divergence analysis or gap analysis). If there is no difference, there would be no need to change the existing strategy. If there is a difference – which is usually the case – the next planning step is taken.

3   The company determines the *desired portfolio*. For the existing SBUs, the question is whether the expected positions are acceptable. Growth will be desirable for some (in the eyes of top management) SBUs. For some SBUs in saturated markets with moderate market positions, divestment will be the best strategy. *New activities* can also be included in the desired portfolio. For example, if existing markets are expected to show little growth, new markets may have to be sought for a balanced portfolio.

By establishing the desired portfolio, the development directions of the SBUs (or products) are fixed. This has given substance to the corporate strategy.

### 10.2.5 Brand variants of the portfolio analysis

The portfolio methods outlined above only seem useful for companies that are active in *different markets*. If a company is active in only one market, there is the same market growth/market attractiveness for each product category. The positions of the products (or brands in a market) are then all aligned. Then the market dimension is no longer relevant. However, McDonald (1990) provides an adequate solution for this. He recommends viewing the various products themselves as markets/segments. The rationale behind this is that each brand more or less has its own target group and as such can be regarded as a separate 'market'. With this assumption (in the BCG application) the expected sales growth of the *brand* can be displayed on one axis and the market share (whether or not relative) on the other axis. Figure 10.5 shows this. In this figure, brand 2 is still a small brand, but it has good growth prospects to become a star. Brand 4 appears to be a large established brand with little growth prospects, while Brand 1 appears to be at the end of its product life cycle.

Finally, we make a remark about the use of the two dimensions on their own. Both have to do with the attractiveness of a market for a brand. If there are possible new markets, a trajectory analysis can be applied, as outlined. But a limitation is still that no attention is paid to *barriers to entry*: the barriers that exist to enter a market. Simply put: there may be a very attractive market waiting, but if there is a huge

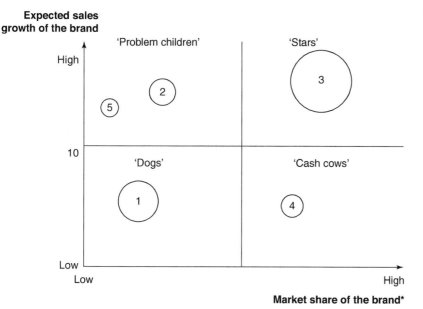

*Figure 10.5*

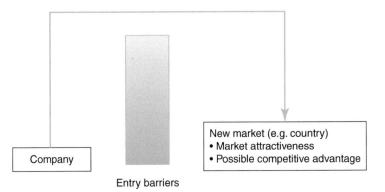

**Figure 10.6**

mountain in front of that market, it is still difficult to choose it. Barriers to entry may include access to distribution channels, minimum brand awareness, physical location, and so on. A somewhat less attractive market with lower thresholds can then be just as attractive. Thus, when thinking about new markets, the recommendations from a portfolio analysis will have to be compared with the resources needed to overcome barriers to entry (see Figure 10.6).

### 10.2.6 Advantages and disadvantages of portfolio methods

Various limitations of portfolio methods have been introduced in the literature (Wind et al., 1983; Schnaars, 1997; Hamermesh, 1986). These are, for example, that the classification of the axes and therefore the designation of the SBUs is rather subjective, which also applies to choosing the underlying factors and giving weights and scores. It all seems 'hard', but it is 'very soft'. And apart from that, the results should not be interpreted too rigidly. For example, an organization can decide to leave a non-profitable product in its range for various reasons, for example, to hold back competitors or because it simply fits well with the rest of the range.

Like many other models in this book, portfolio methods should therefore be used primarily as auxiliary and internal communication tools. In the meantime, don't forget to think creatively and strategically.

## 10.3 Corporate strategy: choice of markets

### 10.3.1 Components of the corporate strategy

In Chapter 1, we explained that at each level, the choice of strategy contains two dimensions: where to compete (markets) and how to compete (competitive advantage)? At the corporate level, the former is the most important. We add a third dimension to this within the corporate strategy: with whom to compete?

We will now first discuss the 'choice of markets' and then the '(possible) choice for cooperation'.

## Case 10.2 Finishing your former core activities

### Lights really go out at Philips: Signify shares in Eindhoven for sale

A historic moment: Philips says goodbye to light. On Tuesday, the ties between Philips and the privatized lighting division will be cut definitively. The company sells all Signify shares. Philips will remain on the lamps on the shelves. But that is all said. Because Philips will sell the remaining part in Signify next week, the former lighting branch of the group. It is no surprise, but it is undeniably a historic moment. For Phillips. For Eindhoven. Because without a light bulb, there would have been no Philips, and without Philips, Eindhoven would never have become the City of Light.

Source: *Eindhovens Dagblad, 20 September 2019*

### 10.3.2 Choice of markets

The core of corporate strategy is *where and to what extent* the firm wishes to compete. In other words: in which markets the company wants to be active and to what extent. In fact, it is about the composition of the portfolio. Depending on the level, this can be the company's portfolio of SBUs (markets) or the portfolio of products/brands. The method that can be helpful in this respect is the portfolio analysis discussed in Section 10.2. In doing so, we advised using a portfolio analysis in combination with a trajectory analysis in three steps:

1 Determination of the current portfolio
2 Forecasting and evaluation of the portfolio if policy remains unchanged
3 Determination of the desired portfolio

In step 3, ideas about new activities should be considered explicitly. This is not possible without creativity, brainstorming, and consultation with lower management. In practice, ideas about new activities will often come from the brands themselves. We have already emphasized the importance of innovation and new activities in the SWOT analysis (Chapter 9).

Generating ideas for new activities actually corresponds to the early stages of what is often referred to in the literature as the process of new product development. Empirical research into the success of new products shows that it often takes dozens of ideas to make one succeed. We note here that the chance of success of a new activity is greater if the new activity is attracted from outside (for example, through acquisition; see also Section 10.4) than if a company decides to develop itself.

If the company is indeed considering entering new markets, it will probably be necessary to carry out a situation analysis of that new market. Then there is a feedback to the situation analysis. Only when the attractiveness of the relevant market outweighs the investments required to enter that market can a decision to enter be made.

By determining the desired portfolio of SBUs, the *development directions* are fixed. The following development directions are possible:

1   Dismantling.
2   Harvesting.
3   Maintaining position.
4   Growth in existing activities.
5   Growth in (setting up) new activities.

The first four directions apply to existing SBUs and the last one to new activities.

Among the five growth directions mentioned, the most attention in the literature is paid to growth with existing SBUs (*expansion*) and growth with new activities (*diversification*). Within both development directions, a total of eight specific growth directions may be chosen (Figure 10.7). These growth directions are based on the well-known Ansoff matrix (Figure 10.8).

### Expansion

There are four types of growth direction by which a company can grow with its existing SBUs:

1   The first and most obvious way of growing is *market penetration*: increasing sales with current products in current markets. In a growing market, an increase in sales can already be achieved by maintaining the market share. In stable markets, an increase in sales can only be achieved if the market share grows.
2   When market saturation occurs, management will explore other growth opportunities, such as *market development*: growth by finding new customers with current products. A well-known form of market development is geographic expansion of the market, for example, through export (see Case 10.2).
3   One can also consider *product development*: new modified products in addition to or instead of the current products for current customers.

| Growth direction | Customer groups | Product [a] | Example rusk manufacturer [b] |
|---|---|---|---|
| **Grow with existing SBUs: expansion** | | | |
| 1  Market penetration | The same | The same | • Increase brand loyalty at the expense of competitors (quality improvement, promotional campaign) <br> • Stimulating the use of current users (advertising: rusks in yoghurt) <br> • Other segments (youth) |
| 2  Market development | New ones | The same | • Other markets (industrial: canteens) <br> • Geographic (export) |
| 3  Product development | The same | Amendment | • Modification: wholemeal rusks |
| 4  Parallelization | The same | Newly related or unrelated | • Related (expansion): rice cakes, (horizontal diversification) crispbread <br> • Unrelated: biscuit tins |
| **Growth with new activities: diversification** | | | |
| 5  Market expansion | New ones | Modification | • Small rusk as 'toast' |
| 6  Vertical diversification | The company itself becomes a customer or supplier | New ones | • Backwards: supplier takeover <br> • Forward: acquisition of retail chain |
| 7  Concentric diversification | New ones | New, related | • Biscuit production |
| 8  Conglomerate diversification | New ones | New, unrelated | • Production candy, detergents |

*Figure 10.7* **Growth opportunities for a company**

a Relationship can be in marketing and/or technology.

b Principle market definition rusk manufacturer: rusk (product) for final buyers, especially women (buyers), for home use (function).

| | Current products | New products |
|---|---|---|
| **Current customer groups** | Market penetration (1) | Product development (3-4) |
| **New customer groups** | Market development (2) | Diversification (5-8) |

*Figure 10.8* **Growth directions in the matrix by Ansoff (1957)**

4   A more far-reaching form of product development is *horizontal diversification* (also called parallelization referred to as): new products for the existing customers (for example, the tea manufacturer who will produce coffee). There is some synergy here (both technologically and in marketing), but there is a limited spread of risk. Incidentally, the name of this growth direction already indicates that due to the strong novelty of the product, this development direction can hardly be counted as expansion anymore.

Case 10.3 is an example of market development through geographic expansion.

## Diversification

When a company expects that it will not be able to achieve its objectives through expansion, it may consider diversification: an exploration of new roads and areas. Four forms of diversification may be distinguished. The choice for one of these forms is determined mostly by the degree of synergy and the extent to which a company remains dependent on a limited number of activities (*risk*).

1   The least far-reaching form of diversification is *market expansion*: reaching new customer groups with adapted products. For this direction of growth, the opposite applies as for the one mentioned under 4: the 'newness' is so limited that in practice this direction is often not referred to as diversification but as a form of expansion.
2   *Vertical diversification* (or *vertical integration*) means taking over links higher (backwards) or lower (forwards) in the supply chain. The main advantage here is greater market power: people are less dependent on suppliers and/or buyers.
3   With *concentric diversification*, new, related products (related in technology or marketing) are introduced to the market for new customers.
4   With *conglomerate diversification*, there is no synergy at all: the company markets new products for new customers.

The last two growth directions show the least or no synergy but the greatest chance of spreading risk.

We note the following about the choices for growth directions in practice:

1   *Be careful with unrelated activities.* Empirical studies have been conducted on the success of related versus unrelated diversification. For example, Porter (1987) analyzed 2,021 acquisitions of 33 highly diversified companies in the period 1950–1980. More than half of the acquisitions had been completed in 1986, while 74% of the 931 unrelated acquisitions had been completed. These and other studies show

## Case 10.3 Market development

### IKEA invests in China, the world's most advanced online market

The Swedish furniture chain IKEA is investing 1.25 billion euros in the further expansion of its activities in China. The investments will allow the group to open an additional number of stores and to expand existing stores. This has been reported by the Swedish group. IKEA has been operating in China for about 20 years. The furniture chain has developed a network of 27 stores there.

In recent years, however, I KEA's growth in the Chinese market has been below expectations. The new investments must provide a solution for this. The chain will also target smaller cities.

Source: nl.express.live, September 24, 2019

that the stranger the activities, the less often the success. The conclusion is therefore that one must be extremely careful when starting up completely new activities and that, if one nevertheless opts for diversification, synergy in, for example, technology or marketing is desirable.

2  *Do additional SWOTs if diversification is being considered.* If a company decides to diversify, there would be a different defined field of strategic activities with different market characteristics, different competitors, different customer needs, and so on. If one wants to be active in such a different market and find a sustainable competitive advantage, then this new market still has to be analyzed in detail. This actually means that an external analysis has to be carried out a second time. Only then can the actual direction of growth be chosen and the next steps in the planning process can be completed.

3   *The stranger the activity, the higher the level of decision.* If we put expansion and diversification side by side, it can be said that the elaboration of the direction of *expansion will take place* more at the *SBU level*, while with *diversification* the involvement of management at the *corporate level will* usually be greater. The elaboration of the direction of expansion (through communication, the price, etc.) will largely fall under the choice of the marketing strategy. On the other hand, setting up completely new activities will require such a commitment that decisions must also be made at a high level. This is also caused by the fact that cooperation strategies are more likely to be considered with diversification than with expansion (see also Section 10.4). An exception to the foregoing is export. Decisions about this geographic form of market development are always made at the company level.

The difference in decision levels does not mean that *ideas* for new activities mainly come from top management. In practice, these come from both the SBUs and the top of the company. It is true that the innovative power of a company is largely determined by the extent to which *top management is* open to new ideas. There are examples of companies where managers from an SBU left the company due to insufficient support for their new ideas and successfully started their own business.

## 10.4 Corporate strategy: choice of partners

'With whom to compete' refers to the choice of partners. That is different from 'competing against whom'. To be discussed:

- Internal or external growth (Section 10.4.1).
- External development: anti-competitive strategies (Section 10.4.2).
- SWOT analysis and the anti-competitive strategy (Section 10.4.3).
- Collaboration in practice (Section 10.4.4).

### 10.4.1 Internal or external growth

If the choice of a grow direction has been made, the next question is whether the company wants to achieve growth through its own development (internal) of through 'others' (external). This decision must be made for both expansion and diversification. There are three possible *development methods*:

1   *Internal development.*
2   *External development through collaboration.* This involves various possibilities, such as joint ventures (joint interest in another company), strategic alliances (long-term partnership), and licenses (approval for others to sell a company's success formula or product).
3   *External development through takeovers* (acquisitions): purchasing new activities.

Internal development carries the most risks: there is no certainty whatsoever about the results. In addition, it takes a long time. But there is more flexibility: everything is in your own hands (see Case 10.4). The reverse of option 1 applies to acquisitions: they can be realized quickly and offer a fair amount of certainty about the result but lead to a decrease in flexibility. In addition, acquisitions usually require a lot of financial resources.

In choosing the way in which it wishes to achieve growth, a company must itself weigh up the advantages and disadvantages. In general, the stranger the activity, the less one has to do oneself (Roberts & Berry, 1985). Export is an exception: this form of expansion can take shape quickly and effectively through mergers and acquisitions of companies that are already active locally.

Because of the great importance of anti-competitive strategies such as cooperation and acquisition, we devote separate attention to them in Section 10.4.2.

## 10.4.2 External development: competition-decreasing strategies

In the literature on corporate and marketing strategies, typically most of the attention is paid to strategies to improve one's own position at the expense of competitors: *position-strengthening strategies* (internal development). The issue here is to claim a position in the market that is stronger than the competitor's position, that is 'beat' the competition.

In addition to a position-strengthening strategy, a company can also opt for a *competition-decreasing* strategy (external development: all forms of collaboration). Examples of such strategies include the following:

■ Strategies in which market concentration is increased through mergers, acquisitions and other forms of collaboration, such as purchasing combinations, franchising, and strategic alliances.
■ Market agreements, for example, price agreements, agreements regarding the division of the market, and cartels.

A competition-decreasing strategy may also be a possibility if a position-strengthening strategy is not feasible: 'If you can't beat them, join them'. It can also be a tool to achieve a desired competitive advantage, for example, a price reduction as a result of important synergistic advantages or a greater focus on sustainability. And also simply wanting to grow quickly is a reason for an acquisition. The choice of an competition-decreasing strategy typically has far-reaching consequences for the entire company. Therefore, decisions in this are made at the corporate level.

There may be circumstances in which it is better to choose to partner with a competitor than to try to 'beat' them. These circumstances can easily be distilled from the situation analysis described in this book. A manager then just has to look at the results of the analysis from a different angle. Particularly in the SWOT analysis, a different angle must be chosen. We now look at that.

## 10.4.3 The SWOT analysis and the competition-decreasing strategy

In Chapter 1 and in the SWOT analysis as described in Chapter 9, we indicated that a company should primarily look for a combination of:

1   A strength of its own that
2   Is a weakness for the most important competitors that

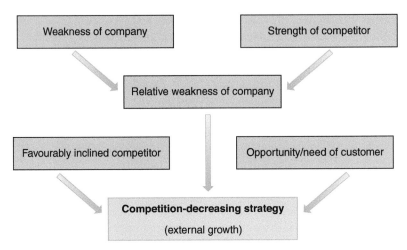

**Figure 10.9**

3 Is difficult to obtain for the competitors and that
4 Is important to the customers.

This combination implies a sustainable competitive advantage.

A competition-decreasing strategy is appropriate when the first two requirements are reversed (Figure 10.9; cf. Figure 2.2):

1 The company has a weakness that is
2 A strength of the competitors and
3 That competitor is favorably inclined and
4 That is important to customers.

In terms of the 'favorable inclination' of the competitor, we note that the same applies to it as to the company that seeks the initiative to cooperate: it is especially interesting if the other party is good at something in which you are not yourself. This means that a relatively weak point of the originator company should preferably be matched by another relatively strong point compared to the competitor. So there must be a *win-win situation*; see also Case 10.5.

Mutual dependence is particularly important if there is an equivalent collaboration (for example, a merger). If there is an unequal cooperation (for example, a company that 'adds' another smaller company to its divisions through acquisition), the requirement of a mutual benefit is less important.

## 10.4.4 Competition-decreasing strategies in practice

In various industries (such as media, banking and insurance, food, aviation, healthcare), there have been 'merger waves'. An important reason for the expanded use of competition-decreasing strategies is undoubtedly the increasing competition resulting from the increasingly open international markets. Particularly when the cooperating companies complement each other's strengths and weaknesses, a partnership can be more competitive than each of the companies alone.

## Case 10.4 Mergers and acquisitions

### So many M&A deals fail because companies overlook this simple strategy

An analysis of 2,500 such deals shows that more than 60% of them destroy shareholder value. Perhaps such deals should come with an official warning: 'Acquisitions can result in serious damage to your corporate health, up to and including death'.

As our research has shown us, the core of the problem is not the high number of M&A deals in itself but rather that too many executives bring insufficient discipline to the evaluation process that fuels these deals – as a result, they often get deals wrong. For instance, despite the importance of accurately identifying and calculating company synergies, diligence work frequently results in an overly optimistic view of the revenue synergy opportunity. Often the weakest assumptions involve estimates of how much additional revenue the companies can generate when combined. This, in turn, leads bidders to overpay.

Ultimately, the key is discipline. By rigorously and relentlessly asking two questions – 'How will the deal help our customers to complete their journey?' and 'How is the deal using our foundational assets to create value in a different context?' – an edge strategy approach to M&A can mitigate the risks of an inherently risky business.

Source: *Harvard Business Review*, 10 May 2016

But there are also dangers of a merger (see also Case 10.4):

■ A merged company is larger and therefore less flexible than a small company, which can make it more difficult to react to current developments in the environment (for example, a competitor's action).
■ If the corporate cultures do not fit together well, there is no balanced fusion. In that case, the merger can lead to large internal problems.
■ Collaboration may make it more difficult to brand the new company. In the case of mergers, an important question is which brand name to use. Often, a new brand architecture is needed (see Chapter 11 about rebranding).

## Summary

In the context of a marketing plan, corporate decisions can in principle be regarded as given. This chapter, after the SWOT, mainly focuses on the choice of markets and related investments in products and brands, and the choice of partners.

A portfolio analysis is an aid to investment decisions in SBUs or in products. In a portfolio analysis, the various SBUs or products are visualized in a two-dimensional space. One axis represents the market attractiveness and the other axis the competitive position of the brand or the SBU. There are several portfolio models, two of which are discussed: the Boston Consulting Group matrix and the business screen. For both methods, quite a few arbitrary assumptions have to be made, which means that the investment recommendations are not always desirable. For new markets, barriers to entry should also be considered.

A company can grow with existing SBUs (expansion). The possibilities are then: market penetration, market development, product development, and parallelization. Growth can also be achieved with new products and services (diversification). This can be done through market broadening and vertical, concentric, or conglomerating diversification.

At the company level, decisions must also be made *with whom* (and not only *against* whom) to compete: alone or in collaboration with others. The latter mainly comes into the picture if the company wishes to add relatively 'strange' activities to the portfolio or if the company wants to grow quickly. Mergers and acquisitions as a form of collaboration involve all kinds of risks that must be taken into account, such as differences in corporate culture.

## Chocolate of Barry Callebaut

Two thirds of the world's cocoa is produced in West Africa. Ivory Coast has the biggest share. The market price for cocoa, like other raw materials for the food industry, is subject to strong fluctuations. The price was under $1,000 for a thousand kilos in 2000, rising to over $3,000 in 2015, and since then has decreased to around $2,800 in 2022. When the price of cocoa falls, a number of farmers in West Africa might turn to lowering production costs by using child labor or even slave labor. The importance of sustainable, 'fair' cocoa may be clear, but an increasing demand for sustainably sourced and 'fair' products does mean that production prices will rise. The unstable political situation in many countries in West Africa also includes a risk for price developments.

In chocolate two important types of companies can be distinguished: the chocolate maker and the chocolatier. The chocolate maker processes cacao beans into basic chocolate. The production of basic chocolate is dominated by two chocolate makers: Barry Callebaut and Cargill. A large part of the chocolate in our world is supplied by one of these two chocolate makers.

Chocolatiers use this basic chocolate to make products (in the form of bars, bonbons, etc.). These are partly large companies, such as Cadbury or Nestlé, and partly small specialized businesses such as certain bonbon makers.

The supply chain is shown in Figure 10.10.

The global chocolate confection market (the sales of all chocolatiers together) is estimated at about 100 billion dollars. The annual market growth is approximately

2.5%. On the one hand, there are the large chocolatiers, with their global brands. Well-known brands are, for example:

- Kraft – Milka
- Nestlé – Nestlé, Kitkat
- Cadbury – Cadbury

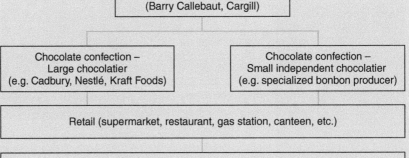

*Figure 10.10* **The supply chain in the chocolate market**

Competition between these companies is intense. Due to the high marketing costs, new brands are rarely introduced. But the importance of private labels of the most important supermarket chains is growing. In addition to these large companies, however, there are also many small, specialized producers, particularly in the luxury segment: for instance, the production of chocolate bonbons and the like.

Many chocolate products are seasonal products. This is mainly due to holidays such as Easter and Christmas. Hot summers have a slightly negative effect on the sales of chocolate.

Chocolate is sold through various channels, such as supermarkets, gas stations, canteens, and so on. In many markets, large retailers account for less than 50% of sales. There is a tendency towards concentration in the retail, but the large variety of channels makes the pressure of the retail sector less strong than in many other markets.

Chocolate is partly bought on impulse. Nowadays the choice for consumers 'on the go' is enormous. This also applies to 'premium indulgence': we can choose from a large amount of luxury snacks.

## Market developments and trends

The chocolate market in Western Europe is mature. However, an important growth segment within the market is formed by premium products. Consumers are also becoming increasingly aware of the effects that chocolate can have on health. This has led to an increase in the sales of organic and dark chocolate with a high content of cocoa. Preferences have shifted to dark, high-quality chocolate: people are looking for a more intense taste experience, and at the same time people are becoming increasingly aware of the positive influence of the cacao bean on health. In addition, the value-for-money segment is also growing. Increasing lack of time leads to more consumption 'on the go'. Chocolate has become a popular snack.

A large growth in chocolate sales can be found in the so-called 'emerging markets'. The increasing relevance of the middle class in Eastern Europe and Russia, but also, for example, in China is responsible for the increasing sales.

The chocolate sector is sensitive to price increases in the raw materials market, in particular, of course, the price development of cocoa. In addition, the following trends can be distinguished:

- Increase of responsible consumption: trend towards sustainable and responsible food patterns
- Growing pressure on margins due to concentration in retail
- Increasing importance of discount retailers in Europe
- Increasing importance of private labels and the resulting pressure on the margins
- Changing consumer preferences: 'diet and health' trends, wellness
- Increased government legislation: food safety, regulations concerning genetically modified products, and so on. This could lead to increasing costs.

For the premium segment, the following trends should also be mentioned:

- *Health: the growing need for healthy chocolate*
  - ☐ Dark chocolate contains more cocoa and therefore more antioxidants. But producers do not rely on only cocoa for the health effects, so healthy ingredients such as acai or pomegranate are added to chocolate.

- *Premium chocolate ('gourmet trend')*
  - ☐ In recent years, the market has been flooded with innovations in the luxury segment. A popular gourmet trend is 'single origin chocolate': premium-brand chocolate that comes from just one source, such as Venezuela, Ecuador, or Vietnam.
  - ☐ Many large producers have called in the help of expert chocolatiers. For example, Nestlé has partnered with the Belgian specialist Pierre Marcolini. Nestlé also invests in its Black Magic products: a luxury indulgence.

- *Ethical chocolate*
  - ☐ Sustainability is also an important trend. Most chocolate makers have promised to buy only 'honestly produced' cocoa.

## Chocolate in Asia

Markets such as China and India, where the economy has grown considerably in recent years, have a rapidly growing middle class. This has led to a significant increase in the total consumption of chocolate. In these markets the middle class is increasingly discovering the western lifestyle and associated eating patterns. Other markets, such as Japan, are more mature but show a clear trend towards premium chocolate. The consumption of chocolate in Asia varies greatly, depending on prosperity, climate, and culture. But even in Singapore and Malaysia, where the bittersweet product is well established, per capita sales are far below the European level. Chocolate consumption in China and India is still low.

Sweet snacks such as chocolate are traditionally unknown in China. But consumption is increasing. 'You used to see people in a Chinese office eat dried fruit, dried fish or dried meat', says the Asia director for Barry Callebaut. 'Now you see more and more yogurt, cookies and chocolate'. The Chinese chocolate market is therefore growing fast. The market is dominated by Western multinationals (Mars, Nestlé, Ferrero): Chinese people have much more confidence in Western producers than in Chinese chocolate suppliers. Chocolate in China is often considered something to give away: especially within the upper middle class, a beautiful box of chocolate is a frequently given gift.

In India the market is growing very fast: in the years 2019 to 2024, an annual growth rate of 10% is expected. With these growth figures, however, we should not forget that per capita chocolate consumption in these countries is only a few 100 grams, compared with 8 to 10 kilos per person in countries such as Switzerland and Germany. So there is still a great potential.

The consumption of chocolate is lower in India than in China: The Chinese market is almost three times as large as the Indian market. In India, however, people are more used to a sweet taste. The market is growing mainly in the big cities; however, there is also potential in rural areas. As in China, Western companies are also dominant in India; the market leader in India is the British Cadbury. However, local brands are gaining popularity in India. Important for Barry Callebaut is that the tendency towards higher-quality (dark) chocolate is already visible in China and India.

And what do people in India say about dark chocolate? Malini Suryananayan, a Bangalore-based baker, says:

> I prefer dark chocolate over mithai (traditional Indian sweets). People here are still worried that chocolate contains eggs or other forms of animal fat. Indeed cheaper chocolate varieties use animal products as emulsifiers. It has been proven that eating dark chocolate releases endorphins into the human brain, and that puts people in a good mood. But dark chocolate works poorly in India simply because we do not accept bitterness as taste experience.

Other observations in the Asian market:

- Chocolate is primarily seen as a Western taste.
- India is a country where the mentality and preferences are as diverse as the country itself; China mainly has a big difference between city and countryside.
- In Asia chocolate often symbolizes parental love: 'The perfect expression that you care for your kids'. Chocolate is mainly regarded as a surprise for the kids.
- Chocolate is seen as a luxury indulgence and not good for health.
- The Cadbury and Nestlé brands are well-established brands among Indian middle-class consumers.

## Barry Callebaut

The almost 200-year-old French-Belgian-Swiss company Barry Callebaut AG is the largest chocolate maker in the world. One in four chocolates eaten in this world was produced by Barry Callebaut. The company has more than 50 production facilities. Some 12,500 people are employed; many of them work in the so-called 'emerging markets'. Annual sales in 2020 amounted to some 7.2 billion Swiss francs, an increase of nearly 5% compared to the previous year.

The vision of Barry Callebaut: 'Heart and engine of the chocolate and coca industry'. The company is the only fully integrated chocolate producer in the world, with a product range varying from 'raw' cocoa to high-quality chocolate bonbons. Barry Callebaut focuses on two market segments:

- Multinationals and other major chocolate brands that use semi-finished and 'raw' chocolate as ingredients for their consumer brands.
- Artisanal and professional users of chocolate, including chocolatiers and bakers, as well as restaurants, hotels, and caterers.

Barry Callebaut's vision reflects the company's core values (annual report 2021):

> Everything we do is rooted in our five core values: customer focus, passion, entrepreneurship, team spirit and integrity. We believe in doing well to do good. This is also reflected by the fact that about 30% of our dividends support the Jacobs Foundation, which is dedicated to education and the future of young people.

The company's business model is full of ambition, according to the 2021 annual report:

> We are the world's leading manufacturer of chocolate and cocoa products, mastering every step in the value chain from the sourcing of raw materials to the

production of the finest chocolates. We are able to provide our customers with value-adding products and services adapted to specific market needs, ahead of trends and at a competitive price. We serve the entire food industry – from global and local food manufacturers to artisanal and professional users of chocolate, such as chocolatiers, pastry chefs, bakers, hotels, restaurants or caterers.

The strategic ambition of the company is described on the corporate website:

Barry Callebaut aims to outperform the global chocolate market. Our long-term strategy is based on four pillars:

- Expansion
- Innovation
- Cost Leadership
- Sustainability

Under the header *expansion*, the company mentions three major growth directions:

- Emerging markets. In addition to the saturated markets in Europe and North America, the company wants to take advantage of the growth opportunities in countries such as China and India.
- Outsourcing and partnerships. The possibilities of outsourcing are described in Barry Callebaut's annual report as: 'Increasing competitive pressure in confectionery opens up interesting doors for our brands, which are now offering ready-to-use concepts and solutions in addition to the chocolate ingredient itself'. In other words: Callebaut not only supplies the basic chocolate but partly takes over the work of the chocolatier by making chocolate products. Shifting part of the chocolatier's work to the chocolate maker is of course in favor of Barry Callebaut. Barry Callebaut itself has a cost advantage by being able to realize economies of scale.
- Gourmet and specialties. With this, the company tries to respond to the aforementioned gourmet trend.

Innovation. Barry Callebaut has played a pioneering role in the trends in the chocolate industry. The company has successfully launched an impressive range of innovative products that meet the demand for better and healthier taste experiences. The company works closely with customers to develop tailor-made products that meet specific customer needs. This takes place in, among other things, so-called chocolate academies, innovation centers where, together with clients, they try to translate Barry Callebaut's expertise into new chocolate products.

Cost leadership is especially important when it comes to outsourcing. By optimizing production flows, economies of scale, and tight cost management, Barry Callebaut tries to become the favorite choice of its customers with respect to outsourcing the processing of basic chocolate to end product.

**Sustainability** is an important issue in the industry. Barry Callebaut believes that it is crucial to pay the cocoa farmer a fair price and encourages the cocoa to be harvested in a responsible manner, with attention for the environment and for the welfare of the workers. To achieve this, the company takes part in all kinds of programs in this area, and Barry Callebaut tries to maintain direct contact with the cocoa farmer himself.

The former CEO, Patrick de Maeseneire, summarizes the strategy of Barry Callebaut in the following way:

The successful interplay of these strategic focal points has convinced multinational confectionery makers to choose Barry Callebaut as their preferred partner. Our wide product range and strong innovation platform are among our greatest competitive advantages. In addition, our global geographic reach allows us to better serve our customers. However, innovation and geographic expansion are only possible if we succeed in maintaining cost leadership in the long term. To achieve this, we are constantly optimizing our cost structure at every step of the value chain, while refining our production processes and technologies and improving our use of energy. This strategy has served us well so far, and we expect to continue to reap the fruits of our investments.

International press release, November 29, 2018
(Source: www.barry-callebaut.com)

Dutch impact organization Tony's Chocolonely, retailer Albert Heijn and chocolate manufacturer Barry Callebaut have forged a strategic partnership to end child labour and modern slavery in the chocolate industry. Together the companies are setting a new industry standard that increases pressure on the wider chocolate industry to drive structural change to work towards a more equally divided cocoa chain.

With a mission to make 100% slave-free the norm in chocolate, for years Tony's Chocolonely has been calling on companies to follow their example for cocoa sourcing based on direct relations with cocoa cooperatives, traceable cocoa and a living income for cocoa farmers. The company shares full details of its transparent supply chain under Tony's Open Chain – an open-source platform where chocolate companies can access all the expertise needed to eliminate social issues from their own supply chain. The platform includes tools such as Tony's Beantracker and the Child Labour Monitoring and Remediation System that has been implemented at all Tony's partner cooperatives.

Dutch biggest retailer Albert Heijn is the first company to sign up for Tony's Open Chain, while world-leading chocolate manufacturer Barry Callebaut has enabled the partnership with its expertise in processing the segregated cocoa to chocolate. 'This is a giant step for the chocolate industry, and an important move towards making sustainable chocolate the industry standard by 2025', says Antoine de Saint-Affrique, CEO of Barry Callebaut. 'It's an amazing opportunity to collaborate with both the biggest retailer in the Netherlands and a company as committed to its slave-free mission as Tony's Chocolonely, and we look forward to expanding this success story through our logistical expertise'.

The partnership between Tony's Chocolonely, Albert Heijn and Barry Callebaut shows it is possible to make a difference on a large scale, and calls on other companies in the industry to join. 'Together we make more impact. I'm thrilled that Albert Heijn and Barry Callebaut are joining us on our roadmap towards slave-free chocolate', says Henk Jan Beltman, Chief Chocolate Officer with Tony's Chocolonely. 'We have always aimed to be exemplary and inspire others to act. Today our impact is bigger than our chocolate alone. We're certain that this is just the first step on the journey to change the industry – together make chocolate 100% slave-free'.

From March 2019 Delicata will hit Albert Heijn shelves with chocolate made exclusively from fully traceable cocoa, bought at a higher price from Tony's Chocolonely partner cooperatives in Ghana and the Ivory Coast. Tony's Chocolonely's five sourcing principles enable cocoa farmers to earn a livable income and remove anonymity from the supply chain, knowing exactly who grows the beans and under which circumstances. According to Tony's Chocolonely, extreme poverty is the main cause of lasting social issues in the cocoa industry, issues which will only be resolved when companies go beyond certifications and are willing to pay a higher price than the certification premium. The three parties unveiled the news of their partnership today at the Tony's FAIR, Tony's Chocolonely's annual meeting in Amsterdam.

Tony's Chocolonely (Source: www.tonyschocolonely.com)

Tony's Chocolonely exists to make chocolate 100% slave free. Not just his own chocolate, but all chocolate worldwide. It is an impact organization that makes chocolate. Tony's Chocolonely was founded in 2005 by three journalists from the Dutch TV show 'Keuringdienst van Waarde' after discovering that the world's largest chocolate manufacturers were buying cocoa from plantations that used illegal child labour and modern day slavery. Since then, Tony's Chocolonely has been working to raise awareness about the inequality in the chocolate industry. They lead by example by building direct long-term relationships with cocoa farmers in Ghana and Ivory Coast, paying them a higher price and working together to solve the root causes of modern day slavery. They want to inspire the industry as a whole to make 100% slave free the norm in chocolate. Tony's Chocolonely has grown into the largest chocolate brand in the Netherlands and is now available in multiple markets such as the United States, Germany, Belgium and Scandinavia.

## Questions

1   Treacy and Wiersema distinguish three value strategies. At Barry Callebaut, elements of each of these three strategies are visible.

a   With the information in the case, show for each value strategy how it has been integrated into Barry Callebaut's activities.

b   According to Treacy and Wiersema, every value strategy must be performed to a certain minimum level, but the company should excel in one of the three value strategies. Explain which value strategy for Barry Callebaut is the 'key value strategy'.

2   The book introduces the Brand Benefitting Model as an alternative to the Treacy and Wiersema model. Which of these models do you consider most appropriate for describing the business of Barry Callebaut? Please explain briefly.

3   Describe the market definition for Barry Callebaut. Make the three-dimensional drawing, and add a brief explanation.

4   Analyze the attractiveness of the chocolate confection market for a large chocolate confectioner (such as Cadbury). Use Porter's five-forces model.

5   a   What is the core competence of Barry Callebaut? Briefly explain your answer.

b   Show the connection between the core competence of Barry Callebaut and the competitive strategy (value strategy) used by this company.

6   Make a SWOT analysis for Barry Callebaut.

7   Indicate how Barry Callebaut could use a portfolio analysis when making strategic decisions.

8   Develop objectives for Barry Callebaut by using the balanced scorecard. Use information from the case, but make your own assumptions where necessary.

9   According to the book, different growth directions are possible for an organization. Which growth direction(s) do you consider most important for Barry Callebaut's expansion strategy? Please explain your answer.

10  a   What is Barry Callebaut's strategic interest in cooperating with Tony's Chocolonely and with Dutch retailer Albert Heijn?

b   Do you consider this a position-strengthening strategy or a competition-decreasing strategy? Please explain briefly.

11  To expand its market, Barry Callebaut considers strengthening its activities in the Chinese and/or the Indian market. Advise Barry Callebaut about this. How should this market development be carried out? Please include in your answer:

■   Internal and/or external growth
■   Target group selection
■   ositioning

# Chapter 11

# Marketing objectives and marketing strategies

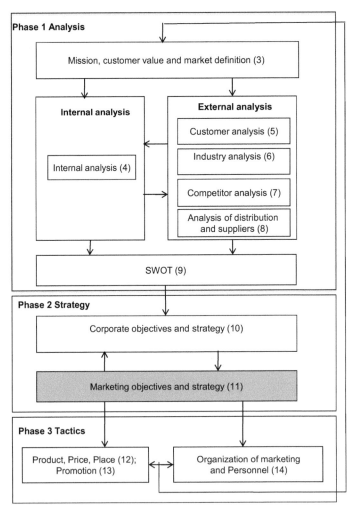

**Phase 1 Analysis**

Mission, customer value and market definition (3)

**Internal analysis**

Internal analysis (4)

**External analysis**

Customer analysis (5)

Industry analysis (6)

Competitor analysis (7)

Analysis of distribution and suppliers (8)

SWOT (9)

**Phase 2 Strategy**

Corporate objectives and strategy (10)

Marketing objectives and strategy (11)

**Phase 3 Tactics**

Product, Price, Place (12); Promotion (13)

Organization of marketing and Personnel (14)

DOI: 10.4324/9781003381488-14

## Key points in this chapter

- Know how to formulate marketing objectives.
- Apply methods for targeting customers.
- Know the principles of and methods for positioning.
- Know the role of the brand.
- Know how to choose a brand name and brand design.
- Apply guidelines for managing brands over products (extensions), internationally, and over time (crisis management).

# Introduction

In Chapter 2, the hierarchy of objectives and strategies within a company was illustrated. In Chapter 10, we took a closer look at the first two stages in that hierarchy:

1 corporate objectives
2 corporate strategies

The result of these steps is, among other things, the choice of markets in which to operate, or the answer to the question: *where are we going to compete?* In this chapter we will discuss the following two phases:

3 marketing objectives
4 marketing strategies (target audience choices, positioning and branding decisions)

These phases mainly answer the question: *how are we going to compete?*

Chapters 12 and 13 are devoted to the decisions concerning the:

5 market instrument objectives
6 market instrument strategies

These phases represent the elaboration of the issue how to compete, or in other words: which instruments do we use to exploit our positioning with the target group as well as possible?

In Section 11.1, we discuss the marketing objectives. Section 11.2 is devoted to the first dimension of the marketing strategy: the choice of target group. Section 11.3 discusses brand positioning. Section 11.4 deals with the brand architecture. Section 11.5 is devoted to choosing the brand name, and Section 11.6 deals with the house style. Section 11.7 covers managing brands over time (including rebranding), across products (extensions), and internationally.

Figure 11.1 shows the relationship between the topics in this chapter and the segmentation topic discussed earlier.

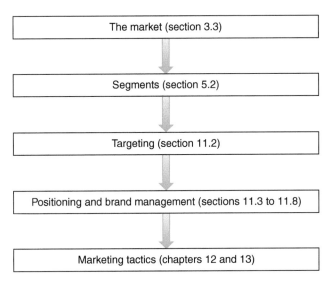

*Figure 11.1* Relationship between the topics market, STP, and tactics

# 11.1 Marketing objectives

Marketing objectives are objectives for which marketing can be held primarily responsible. These objectives can be formulated at different levels: company, business unit and product level. In practice, marketing objectives occur most frequently at product level. Marketing objectives are expressed in measures related to:

1 Customer-oriented variables, such as market share, sales, customer loyalty, and customer ambassadorship. Example: desired market share of brand X on January 1, 2024: 4.2%.
2 Brand-oriented variables, such as brand awareness or the extent to which target groups have certain associations with the brand. Example: aided awareness of brand Y in target group Z on January 1, 2024: 45%.

Naturally, a company will also always formulate profit goals. Those are not marketing goals but corporate goals. Nevertheless, these must be included in the context of a marketing plan, because they are, as it were, a precondition for the marketing goals.

Goals should be specific, measurable, achievable, realistic, and time-bound (SMART) (see Section 4.1.1). The marketing objectives must be in line with and not contradict the organizational goals.

# 11.2 Target group selection

We mentioned earlier the three important STP steps of the marketing strategy: segmentation, targeting, and positioning. Figure 11.2 shows the relationships between these components again.

**Market segmentation (section 5.2: Segmentation research)**

1. Identifying segmentation variables and segmenting the market
2. Developing profiles per segment

**Market target groups (section 11.2: Segmentation and choice of a target group)**

3. Evaluating the attractiveness per segment
4. Selecting the segments

**Brand positioning (section 11.3 thru 11.8: Positioning: managing a brand identity)**

5. Identifying potential positioning concepts for each chosen segment
6. Choosing, developing, and communicating the chosen positioning concept

*Figure 11.2* **Steps for market segmentation, determination of target groups, and positioning**

Segmentation is a form of research in which potential customers are divided into groups (see Chapter 5). Segmentation is the stepping stone for target group choices and brand positioning. The latter two are strongly linked. Because the choice of target groups is also determined by what you can offer them. In practice, the concepts of target groups and positioning are sometimes even confused with descriptions such as 'we focus on people who like non-alcoholic white beer, which generates feelings of friendship'. With such a statement you actually mention the positioning, and your target group is 'people who want it'. That won't help you much in terms of targeting.

This section deals with the following topics:

■ The evaluation of market segments (Section 11.2.1)
■ The selection of segments: target group selection (Section 11.2.2)
■ Inclusive marketing (Section 11.2.3)
■ Loyalty programs (Section 11.2.4)
■ Use of individual online customer data: online behavior targeting (Section 11.2.5)

## 11.2.1 Evaluation of market segments

The result of the segmentation analyses, as reviewed in Section 5.2, is that a manager has divided the total potential buyer group into subgroups (segments). As an example, let's assume a camera manufacturer used two segmentation variables: age and price sensitivity (a customer value). Age is divided into three groups: 0–25, 26–49, 50+. Price sensitivity can be low or high. Combining these two variables, we get a maximum of six segments (see Figure 11.3).

|  | 0-25 years | 26-49 years | 50+ |
|---|---|---|---|
| Low price sensitivity | Segment 1 | Segment 2 | Segment 3 |
| High price sensitivity | Segment 4 | Segment 5 | Segment 6 |

*Figure 11.3* **Example of segmentation result**

The next step is to judge whether this segmentation is useful. To this end, we use the *segmentation criteria* from Section 5.2:

1 *Homogeneity/heterogeneity*: are consumer preferences more or less similar in a segment and different between segments?
2 *Size*: are the segments of sufficient size?
3 *Measurable/identifiable*: can the segments be described?
4 *Accessible*: are the segments easily accessible?

Applying this to Figure 11.3, the following can be assumed:

1 The first requirement is partly met because a customer value has been included: the importance of price. As a result, there is always a difference between segments. The only question is whether the age limit of 50 years is the best split. Perhaps the retirement age is a better limit to describe the differences in photography preferences. It is also conceivable that family life cycle would be a better variable to split the group. When someone has children, the importance of photography becomes significantly higher. And perhaps that also applies to someone who has grandchildren.
2 It is uncertain whether the segments are of sufficient size. For example, it is quite conceivable that among young people who have little money, there are few people who will purchase an expensive camera anyway: segment 4 is therefore probably very small.
3 The segments are measurable and identifiable through research.
4 The segments can also be reached through magazines or online search behavior.

After various possible segments have been identified and described in this way, the manager must make a choice: which segments will we focus on, or what are 'my' target groups in the market?

## 11.2.2 Selection of the target group

Choosing a target group is also known as *targeting*. You do not necessarily have to focus on one target group.

In literature about segmentation, often the following *segmentation strategies* (in fact: targeting strategies) are discussed:

1 *Concentrated marketing strategy (focus or niche strategy)*. This means that one, often not large, segment is chosen. The advantage of this may be that there is little competition in this segment. The disadvantage is the high risk: one is dependent on only one buyer group.

## Case 11.1 Targeting

### 'Thermal tourism' – Greece and Spain say winter holidays could be 'cheaper than putting the heating on'

Tourism operators in Southern European countries are hoping to capitalize on cold winters and energy bills elsewhere on the continent by advertising their warmer climates as winter approaches. Destinations including Greece, southern Spain, and the Canary Islands are taking advantage of 'thermal tourism', a trend in Britain for flying to cheaper, warmer climates to escape the winter and the cost of living crisis in the UK. Greece's tourism minister Vassilis Kikilias told the Observer: 'Our doors are open 12 months round, our friends in northern Europe should know this. They should head here for the winter'. A Greek advertising campaign worth £17.5 million (€20m) will soon be rolled out to the public, featuring the caption: 'Wanna feel 20 again? With warm winter temperatures up to 20C, Greece is the place to be'. Imagery for the campaign shows an older couple on a yacht, drinking from wine glasses and eating fruit.

Source: *The Independent*, 11 October 2022

2  *Selective marketing.* This means that some segments are chosen. The advantage of this compared to a concentrated target group selection is that there will be a lower risk due to the spread of activities. This is common. Examples are car manufacturers with types that differ in price, food manufacturers with various brands, publishers that target different groups, and so on.

3  *Complete market coverage.* A company tries to serve all customer groups in the market. This can be done by marketing a large number of different brands/products.

Examples are manufacturers such as Procter & Gamble and Unilever, which serve the same market with a large number of brands, such as detergents or shampoo. Another possibility is: marketing one or a few products that are intended for a broad target group, as Coca-Cola does.

The name of the segmentation strategy strongly depends on the market definition (see Chapter 3). For example, Mercedes-Benz can be classified as a company with a focus strategy. It is implicitly assumed that Mercedes uses a broad market definition (e.g. the car market) and chooses a segment within it. However, if Mercedes uses a narrow market definition (e.g. top-quality cars) and explicitly adheres to that definition in its situation analysis, then there is full market coverage. The division into strategies is therefore rather subjective.

The choice of target groups is strongly related to the choice of the *brand structure* (see Section 11.4): serving multiple segments can be easier with the help of sub-brands. Furthermore, the choice of the target group cannot be viewed separately from the choice of positioning (see Section 11.3). After all, a positioning describes the properties and personality characteristics of a brand, and these should match the personality characteristics of the target group. In fact, a brand can only have one target group. The only question is how broad that target group can be. Research plays an important role in this. Positioning and target group selection therefore take place simultaneously. It is not necessary to explicitly use one of the aforementioned strategies.

## 11.2.3 Inclusive marketing

At this point we make a comment about what is called *inclusive marketing*. In 2023, inclusiveness, in the sense of giving all types of people the opportunity to 'participate' in and with your organization, is an important social theme, for example, in relation to people who belong to the so-called *LGBTQ groups* or people from other countries, perhaps with a different skin color. Discrimination in the sense of 'excluding groups' or making a distinction at all on the basis of, for example, skin color is often referred to as socially undesirable.

It is good to establish a relationship here with segmentation research and targeting. With segmentation it is sensible and even the intention to look at differences in needs and perceptions of people with different backgrounds. It is also good to take into account differences in people's backgrounds when targeting with the aim of being able to meet the specific wishes of people as closely as possible. So there is nothing wrong with that: on the contrary. And often brands will not want to exclude groups of customers at all in their targeting.

What may be more the case is that brands do not show explicitly enough in their communication that they are also there for multiple target groups. For example, information material from universities and colleges shows that more and more Black students are being accepted along with white students.

## 11.2.4 Loyalty programs

After target groups have been chosen, the next issue is whether the target group should be approached as a whole or one on one. In Section 5.6, we focused on obtaining data

## Case 11.2 Inclusive marketing

## What brands are doing to be more inclusive for people with disabilities

From Asos's wheelchair-friendly jumpsuit to Starbucks opening its first sign language store, brands are making moves to cater for people beyond the mainstream and unlock the potential of the 'Purple Pound'. It is thought that the collective spending power of disabled people – known as the Purple Pound – is worth £249bn to the UK economy. And yet many brands and retailers still don't seem to know how to accommodate the needs of disabled consumers.

Whether down to poorly designed stores, lack of staff training, or simply not offering products and clothes that are disabled friendly or, in many cases, clothes that are far from mainstream fashion trends, retailers are excluding one in five people in the UK who has a disability or impairment – and in doing so missing out on a potentially substantial profit.

But there are signs that these deep-rooted prejudices around disability are, finally, beginning to loosen.

The fashion industry might be quick when it comes to trends, but it has been slow to represent people of different sizes, ethnicities, and abilities. Parents passionately told us that disabilities don't define their children, so the adaptations shouldn't define their clothes.

Rebecca Garner, M&S 2018, however, saw the likes of Marks & Spencer (M&S), Tommy Hilfiger, River Island, and Asos all move in a more inclusive direction – from changes in advertising campaigns to innovative clothing lines.

M&S and Tommy Hilfiger both launched adaptive clothing ranges designed for adults and children with physical and mental disabilities, showing that retailers at both ends of the fashion spectrum are beginning to realize there is a wide audience waiting to be catered to.

Source: *Marketing Week*, 6 February 2019

from individual customers (after approval: *permission marketing*) and selecting the most profitable customers. To strengthen the bond with the most important customers, the company can opt for the use of *loyalty programs* (Dowling & Uncles, 1997). These are programs in which the market instruments are used in such a way that customers are immediately rewarded for loyalty to the brand. In this way, the provider increases the customer's *bond* with the brand and reduces the chance that the customer will switch to a competitor. To do this, an organization must have a database with individual customer data: a *CRM system*, which is the case with online purchases. The next step could be for the provider to actually reward loyalty: a reward for brand loyalty. We count the latter among the loyalty programs. Approaching customers directly and 'editing' in itself (database marketing) is not yet included.

Before a loyalty program can be started, individual customer data is therefore required. This is relatively easy to organize with online sales: after all, people know by definition to whom what is being sold and delivered. In retail, a customer card can also be used for this purpose. A loyalty card can be provided free of charge or for a fee. Free has the advantage of high participation but the disadvantage of low involvement. The opposite applies to a paid customer card ('becoming a member', for example, the Bijenkorf customer card). In both cases, customers must be rewarded with, for example, discounts, being informed about promotions earlier, and/or being sent a magazine.

In our view, a CRM system is not necessarily a loyalty system, although it is often referred to as such. A CRM system can be used to stimulate loyalty. A real loyalty program only exists if loyalty is actually rewarded, that is, if, based on demonstrable brand loyalty (measured by for example, sales), a customer is offered some kind of reward (in the form of a specific interpretation of the marketing mix).

In practice, the following measures are used for customer loyalty:

- How long someone is a paying customer (*customer period*). This measure is often used for magazines: the longer one is a subscriber, the more attractive benefits can be used. This is also used frequently within 'clubs' (whether or not in the non-profit area): the longer the membership, the lower the price.
- The *cumulative purchasing amount*, such as the frequent flyer program of KLM with which points are collected (see also Case 11.3). But the old-fashioned 'stamp cards' of retailers are also an example of this. The 'new' form of these stamp cards is of course the online version. If the online data obtained in this way is then used to give rewards to loyal customers, it is a loyalty program.

The rewards may relate to any of the four market instruments, for example:

1 *Products*. This concerns free *premiums* (extras), service in the form of advice, maintenance and so on.
2 *Price*. That means a discount on new purchases, accessories, and so on. This is the most commonly used form of reward in loyalty programs.
3 *Place*. An example is home delivery for loyal customers.
4 *Communication*. A magazine can be a reward for brand loyalty if non-loyal customers have to pay for it and loyal customers do not pay or less. Targeted information based on customer purchasing behavior can also be called a reward for loyalty.

## Case 11.3 Loyalty program

### The North Face loyalty program

The North Face's XPLR Pass program also offers customers the flexibility to choose how they redeem their rewards points, tailored for its customers' lifestyles. Customers earn loyalty points every time they make a purchase or sometimes by attending events, checking in at certain locations, or downloading the North Face app. When redeeming the rewards, customers can use their points for unique travel experiences such as mountain climbing in Nepal. Apart from such experiences, the North Face also offers many cool benefits for its members like:

- Early access to limited edition collections
- Opportunity to wear test products before they are available to the public
- Product 'field testing'.

Rather than encouraging customers to spend more and get rewards, the North Face gives out rewards that speak directly to its customers. These kinds of unique and curated experiences build up more of an emotional connection with the brand more than standard product discounts.

The rewards can also be increased in stages by letting a consumer choose to move into a 'higher category' (e.g. bronze, silver, gold, or platinum) instead of redeeming the accumulated 'points'. This further strengthens the bond with the brand.

Figure 11.4 captures the essence of a loyalty program. In practice, individual brand loyalty programs are becoming more common due to online shopping.

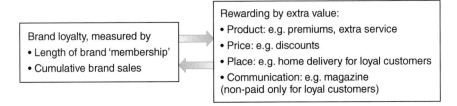

*Figure 11.4* **Characteristics of a real loyalty program**

Based on academic research (Dorotic et al., 2012) about the effects of loyalty programs, it appears that:

1   Loyalty programs often have a positive effect on both attitudinal loyalty and behavioral loyalty.
2   Members of a loyalty program are less sensitive to actions of competitors.
3   A loyalty program is especially effective for 'light' users and less effective for 'heavy' users.
4   Ending a loyalty program give customers a negative feeling.

## 11.2.5 Behavioral targeting

Online behavior enables a new form of targeting, so-called *behavioral targeting* (also referred to as *micro targeting*). A concrete example of this is that based on the search and click behavior of a consumer, this person receives targeted communication messages. For example, when you Google to search information about a new razor, the following day you will probably receive tailored ads about shaving. From a marketing perspective, this is an interesting way of targeting. It fits in nicely with the desire to segment based on relevant behavioral variables and not based on, for example, age or gender (background variables). In principle, it is also positive for consumers because they see relevant communication. In fact, this type of targeting is the main business model for online platforms like Google, Facebook, TikTok, and Instagram.

Of course, privacy is an important concern. According to the platform owners, this is the case because it is 'stated in the terms and conditions'. But that, according to critics, is rather hidden. What has happened in the meantime is that websites are obliged to report that they collect cookies and that a visitor can then refuse to do so.

Because the large platforms are owned by only a few people (Facebook owner Zuckerberg also owns Instagram and WhatsApp and therefore has data from billions of people), it is sometimes said that stricter government control is necessary. All in all, the designation 'micro targeting 'or' behavioral targeting 'has a bad image, while it is an ideal marketing tool if it is used in a fair and transparent way.

## 11.3 Brand positioning

In this key section, we lay the foundation for formulating a positioning for a brand. First, we define positioning and discuss its purpose (Section 11.3.1). Because positioning is all about 'values', we will discuss needs and values in Section 11.3.2. In Section 11.3.3, we present a number of tools that can be used to *choose* a positioning. Section 13.3.4 discusses ways to formulate a selected positioning. Section 13.3.5 contains guidelines for positioning, which we refer to as 'brand laws'. Finally, in Section 13.3.6, we discuss the relationship between positioning and sustainability.

## 11.3.1 Definition and goal of positioning

The word *positioning* has already been mentioned several times in this book and was emphasized by Ries and Trout (1981) in their classic book *Positioning: The Battle for Your Mind*. Positioning means that a company ensures that it obtains a distinctive position in the 'minds' of the target group. Figure 11.5 illustrates what positioning is with the positioning triangle. Central to positioning is *the selection of those 'values' (properties, consequences, and final values)* for which the following applies:

- the *target group* is considered important
- the *own organization* or *own brand* is strong in it
- the *competitors* are less strong at it

A positioning statement is the formulation of a concrete promise that the brand makes. The result of positioning with customers is the image that customers have of the brand (image). Suppose you say 'Volvo' and people associate that with safety; then Volvo has a safe image. So those are the associations. The positioning is part of the *identity* of the brand: what it wants to be and how it wants to come across to the target group.

A brand hopes to achieve that the image of the brand corresponds to the identity, so that Volvo itself also considers safety to be the core of its identity, and not, for example, sportiness.

Positioning is all about brands. A brand (name) can only have one identity and vice versa: an identity must always be linked to one brand (name). This is the same as with humans: a human being also has one personality.

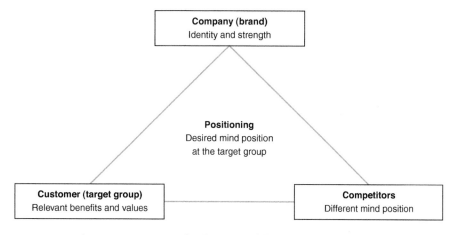

*Figure 11.5* **The positioning triangle: the 3C model**

What is a brand anyway? A brand can be defined from the supply side (the company) and from the demand side (the customer). The supply-oriented definition of a brand is: 'a name, designation, sign, symbol, design, or a combination thereof, intended to identify and distinguish a provider's products and services from competing products and services' (Keller, 2013). So, in fact anything with a name is a brand. A brand may also be defined form the perspective of a customer: A brand is a set of associations linked to a name, mark, or symbol.

Strictly speaking, the latter definition is not a definition of a brand but rather the result of the use of a brand (actually the image). Not only products and services are brands but also retail formulas, people, places, groups of people such as pop groups, events, and ideas. Anything with a name.

Brands fulfill different functions for customers:

1  *Identification.* Brands make products and services recognizable.
2  *Trust and quality.* You know what to expect and who it comes from, and there are no risks.
3  *Symbolic function.* By purchasing brands, people show who they are or want to be.

While consumers in research are less likely to admit that they are strongly guided by brands when making purchasing decisions, research shows that this is in fact the case. The most striking forms of evidence in this regard are blind taste tests. For example, in research by De Chernatony and Knox (1990), 51% preferred Pepsi and 44% preferred Coca-Cola. When tasters were told what they were drinking, only 23% preferred Pepsi and 65% Coca-Cola. In short: branding helps.

Chapter 1 already outlined the basic model of a strong brand by Keller (2019). Keller introduced the concept of *customer-based brand equity* (see Figure 11.6, a copy of Figure 2.3). The basic assumption in the Keller model is that a brand derives its power from the knowledge about the brand that resides in the minds of groups of customers. The more knowledge (awareness), the more brand equity. A second assumption of the Keller model is that positive brand equity leads to more positive reactions of customers to marketing campaigns of the brand. Keller distinguishes two '*sources of brand equity*': brand awareness and brand associations. Those associations must be strong, relevant, and unique.

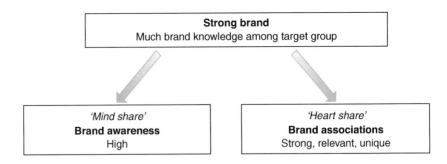

*Figure 11.6* **Sources of brand equity according to Keller**

Unique associations are directly linked to positioning: 'having a good and distinctive image'.

Based on Figure 11.6, organizations should therefore strive for two goals:

1   *Achieving high awareness.* This is called: a strong *mind share*. Mind share is the extent to which the brand is 'top of mind', that is, the extent to which the consumer thinks of the brand (for example, Heineken) when he feels a certain need (I want a beer). The latter (the relationship with a need) means that it is also about *brand relevance*: that the consumer therefore links the brand to his need.
2   *Realizing a distinctive image* (by means of positioning). This has to do with *heart share*. Heart share refers to the extent to which the brand image (image) matches the wishes and preferences of the consumer: do the brand associations strike the right chord with the consumer?

The need for high awareness is in line with research by Sharp (2010), already reviewed in Chapter 1. Keller, as have many authors, explicitly mentions the need for also a clear and unique brand image. The tools to reach that knowledge (awareness and associations) among the target group are (see Figure 11.7):

1   the fixed brand elements, such as brand name and logo
2   the product and service itself and all additional marketing activities (the four Ps)
3   secondary associations that are indirectly linked to the brand by linking them to something else, such as the company name (endorsing), an event, a person, or another brand (*co-branding*).

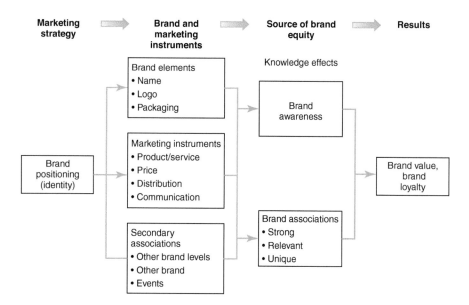

*Figure 11.7* Building customer-based brand equity (Keller)

Figure 11.7 shows that brand equity ('knowledge') should lead to brand loyalty. This is a logical relation: only when there is a clear picture and people are satisfied can a 'relationship' arise in which the customer also feels emotionally connected to the brand. The aim is to create customer loyalty: that customers repeatedly continue to buy the products and/or purchase the services. It is even said that attracting a new customer is four times as expensive as retaining an existing one. But this ratio has not been sufficiently substantiated by research; there are even arguments why an existing customer is 'more expensive' than a new one, such as that he gets used to the quality of the supplier and starts to set higher requirements. Nevertheless, it makes sense to pay sufficient attention to your own customers.

Customer loyalty can also be translated into *brand ambassadorship*. Consumers then recommend the brand to others, for example, by posting positive reviews about the brand on the internet – spontaneous word of mouth.

Having a clear positioning is also important internally in the organization. This has to do with *internal branding* (see Chapter 14).

## 11.3.2 Needs and values

### Brand values

The phrase *brand value* has two meanings:

1 Brand values are the intended brand characteristics, such as cheap, sustainable, friendly, feminine, and honest. In Chapter 4, we explained that there are two levels of brand values: terminal values and brand personality traits.
2 The brand value (without 's') means the financial value of the brand. Measuring the financial value of a brand is important in, for example, acquisitions of brands.

We will now discuss brand values (attributes).

### Means-end chain

For consumers, according to the means-end chain discussed earlier (see Figure 11.8), properties of a product or service lead to *benefits* for consumers, and benefits are seen as more favorable the closer they are to the consumer's values. Values are things that people find important in life. A value is, as it were, the reason a consumer has a certain need. Take toothpaste. If the value 'health' is very important to a consumer, she will find the prevention of tooth decay particularly important and will therefore appreciate properties such as the presence of certain enzymes. But if love and friendship are important values, then fresh breath or bright white teeth can become more important benefits.

### Golden circle

In the famous book *Start with Why*, Simon Sinek (2009) outlines that organizations have a more convincing story if they go into less detail about 'what' they do. In contrast,

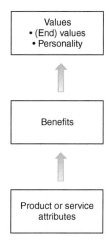

*Figure 11.8* **Means-end chain**

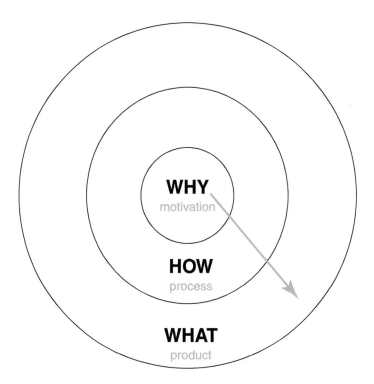

*Figure 11.9* **Simon Sinek's golden circle**

according to Sinek, organizations should mainly focus on the 'how' and even better on the 'why' (see Figure 11.9). Interestingly, this is a similar message to what the means-end chain shows: show your values (which is basically 'why'). In fact, Sinek's golden circle is another representation of the long-known means-end chain. It also ties in with the message that positioning and marketing are primarily concerned with 'how should a company compete?' instead of 'with which products/in which markets'. That 'how' can therefore be deepened with 'why'.

### Positioning strategies

When choosing a positioning direction (particularly functional and/or emotional), a distinction is sometimes made between four positioning strategies. These strategies are based on the means-end chain of meanings. Figure 11.10 shows this chain and the possible positioning strategies.

Four strategies can be used when choosing a positioning, depending on which parts of the means-end chain are considered (see Figure 11.10).

### Informational positioning

In informational positioning the emphasis is on communicating a (concrete) advantage of using a brand, possibly linked to a physical property of the product (*reason why*). Example: Freedent sugar-free chewing gum prevents an 'acid attack' and deterioration of the teeth (*benefit*), because it has a pH-lowering effect (*functional property*). This positioning strategy is widely used for new products (for example, the latest Philips TV) and products with a problem-solving character (for example, detergents, dishwashing liquids, and limescale removers).

Informational positioning is especially effective if there are clear differences between brands, in short if brands have or can claim a *unique selling proposition* (USP). As brands become more and more similar, effective application of informational positioning becomes more and more difficult (Carpenter et al., 1994).

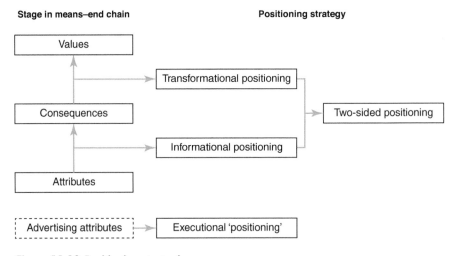

*Figure 11.10* **Positioning strategies**

*Transformational positioning*

In transformational positioning, the emphasis is on communicating the brand personality or end values, possibly linked to the product benefits. Psychosocial aspects play an important role in this form of positioning. This strategy is often used with products that you buy for pleasure (such as soft drinks and beer), with products that differ little from each other (such as cigarettes), and with products where properties do not play a role (such as perfume).

*Two-sided positioning*

With two-sided positioning, the entire means-end chain is used: the product benefits are linked both to functional product properties and to consumer values. An example is Apple, which distinguishes itself through user friendliness and a stubborn character. Many other branches also try to combine rationality and feeling. Think of brands such as McDonald's and KLM. Also, in the fast-moving consumers goods branch, it may be noticed that brands that have had a strong functional position for years (laundry detergents, diapers, feminine hygiene products, etc.) are increasingly working on building a brand personality.

*Execution positioning*

Execution positioning means that the brand is being positioned on the basis of the execution of the campaign. The distinction from the competition is sought mostly or partly from a advertising characteristic. In effect, this is not truly a case of positioning, since advertising associations rather than brand associations are created. The brand or product is linked in the communication to a unique element or symbol.

*Rossiter-Percy matrix*

According to Rossiter et al. (1991), the choice of informational or transformational depends on the category (problem solving or value adding) and on the involvement (low or high). Their recommendations are shown in Figure 11.11.

Our conclusion based on these positioning strategies is that brands should in fact always choose a two-sided positioning: with both a core value and a concrete advantage. Depending on the category and need, the benefit can be more functional or emotional.

## 11.3.3 Tools to choose a positioning

If a *direction* for positioning has been chosen, a concrete need and/or value must be chosen. To this end, we discuss four 'lists' that can be used.

*Brand Benefitting Model*

In Chapter 4 we discussed the Brand Benefitting Model, which is a useful tool to choose a main direction for (functional) positioning. We defined *customer value* as the difference between revenue and cost (in a broad sense) of a product for a customer. And we distin-

| | Low involvement | High involvement |
|---|---|---|
| **Problem solving** | Example: detergents, insurance<br><br>*Informational* | Example: mortgage, healthcare institution<br><br>*Informational* |
| **Adding value** | Example: beer<br><br>*Informational and transformational* | Example: car<br><br>*Informational and transformational* |

*Figure 11.11* **The Rossiter and Percy matrix**

Source: Rossiter et al. (1991)

guished five possible customer values: quality, service/interaction, price, convenience, and sustainability. These five can be regarded as 'needs'.

Furthermore, in line with the means-end chain, we indicated that in all cases emotion will have to be 'added' to the positioning. So, we end up with six values to choose from:

1  quality
2  services
3  price
4  convenience
5  sustainability
6  emotion

With regard to the fifth value (sustainability), later in this chapter (Section 11.3.4), we will introduce a model to choose a specific sustainable value.

### Values from Rokeach

At the highest level in the means-end chain, it is about values that people can have. Various studies have been done on people's value systems. A well-known list is that of Rokeach (1973, 1979), who distinguishes between terminal values and instrumental values (see Figure 11.12). End values are things that someone finds important in their life. It's about things like happiness, friendship, or freedom. Instrumental values indicate how an individual should behave in order to reach certain final values. Examples of instrumental values are honest, ambitious, or obedient. In practice, the distinction between terminal values and instrumental values is sometimes difficult to indicate. A more important problem, at least for the marketer, is the somewhat abstract nature of Rokeach's values. This is because Rokeach defined the values through a survey in which he asked about things that are important to someone 'as a guideline for their life'. This has led to fairly broad and therefore sometimes somewhat abstract formulations, such as 'inner harmony' or 'self-respect'. This can be very important in someone's life, but these kinds of concepts are less useful for the positioning of a brand.

| Final values | Instrumental values |
|---|---|
| A comfortable life | Ambitious |
| An active, exciting life | Broad-minded (open -minded ) |
| Making a contribution to society | Skilled, competent, effective |
| A sustainable world | Merry |
| Peace | Clean |
| A world of beauty | Brave, stand for what you believe, brave |
| Equality | Forgiving |
| Security, happy family life | Helpful (helpful, thinking of others) |
| Freedom | Honestly |
| Luck | Creatively |
| Inner peace | Independent |
| Love | Intelligent |
| National security | Rational |
| Pleasure | Lovingly |
| A life guided by faith | Obey |
| Self respect | Polite, well mannered |
| Respect and admiration from others | Responsible, reliable |
| True friendship | Controlled, disciplined |
| Wisdom | |

**Figure 11.12 Values according to Rokeach (processed)**

### Brand personality dimensions according to Aaker

Where Rokeach developed a list of consumer values, some other authors focus on brand values. Aaker (1997) showed, on the basis of a large empirical study of brands, that brand personality traits can be clustered into five main dimensions (see Figure 11.13). Although Aaker's model has been criticized by other authors (Austin et al., 2003; Azoulay & Kapferer, 2003), it is still a widely used model.

### Value compass by Kostelijk

Kostelijk (2017) showed that brands can better focus on values than on personality when positioning, because values are better predictors of someone's needs. For example, a visitor to Efteling who finds 'safety' important will have different needs than someone for whom 'stimulation' is an important value. Kostelijk researched for a few countries with which values consumers associated a large number of brands. He reduced the set of values to 11 dimensions, summarized in the so-called value compass (see Figure 11.14). Some values in the value compass reinforce each other, while other values entail opposing motivations. This can be seen in the figure by looking at the mutual distance between values. Values with a more similar meaning, such as *attention to each other* and *intimacy*,

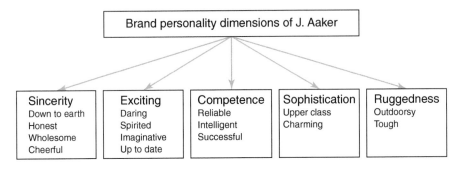

*Figure 11.13* **Brand personality dimensions according to Aaker (1997)**

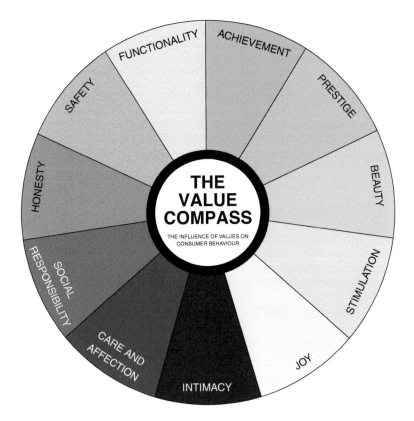

*Figure 11.14* **The value compass**

have been shown as closely spaced or adjacent 'pie slices'. For values that have less in common, the distance between the relevant pie slices in the figure is greater, while values with opposite meanings, such as *solidity* and *pleasure & passion*, are opposite each other in the figure. Brands must therefore choose coherent values.

There is, however, an important caveat here. The lists presented here should not lead to the exact words/values from these lists being used. Often they are quite generic, such as the benefit 'quality', or rather vague, such as 'self-esteem'. The essence is to choose your own words that are close to the words from the lists. So using Google, for example, searching for synonyms of words from the lists can help.

Shifts in the importance of values fall under 'socio-cultural' trends, as we covered in the macro-environmental analysis. This also includes the increasing attention for much more female-friendly behavior (#metoo) by brands (and people); see also Case 11.4.

## Case 11.4 Repositioning

### Goodbye sex bomb, welcome power woman

The lingerie brand Victoria's Secret says goodbye to the supermodel Angels, after years of criticism of the brand's sexism. Not the pleasure of the man but the power and independence of the woman must now be central to marketing. To this end, the brand is entering into a partnership with seven 'successful women' with diverse backgrounds. The new faces include successful American soccer player Megan Rapinoe. The women will perform in advertising campaigns but also think about new collections. The brand is not alone in changing its habits. Calvin Klein, for example, stopped using images of sweating models draped over each other a few years ago.

Source: NRC, 18 June 2021

### 11.3.4 Positioning and sustainability

In this subsection, we discuss three subjects: a tool to choose a certain more specific sustainability goal, 'greenwashing', and some remarks about what intervention methods exist to stimulate sustainable behavior among consumers.

#### SDGs as a tool of making choices

Brands have to be 'sufficient' in the value sustainability and can also try to excel, just as for the other values. In the concrete case of sustainability: an organization can make the choice to make this the leading principle of their business. Many organizations, however, will choose to have a more 'defensive' sustainable strategy and should try to meet a sufficient level.

Another remark is about the value 'sustainability' in itself. This term is very broad and can be interpreted in many ways. In Chapter 1, we mentioned that sustainability can pertain to 'planet' and 'people' and also that this book focuses on 'planet' since it is about marketing and consumer behavior. However in choosing a positioning on sustainability, brands can choose several specific ways to do so. A 'model' of sustainable routes that can be used by brands is the list of Sustainable Development Goals, the well-known 17 SDGs. Figure 11.15 shows that brands can choose a lot of different ways to perform sustainability.

#### Greenwashing

A second decision is whether you, as a brand, will also *communicate* a chosen sustainable value and if so how 'loudly' you will do this. Take Unilever. Unilever has been actively

*Figure 11.15* Seventeen SDGs

## Case 11.5 Improving sustainability: acceptance of LGBTQ groups

### Sustainable models of L'Oréal

For years L'Oréal focused on beauty. In recent years it is explicitly paying attention to diversity, equity, and inclusion (DE&I). Their DE&I commitments to employees, consumers, and suppliers are:

1   Encourage multicultural and socio-economic diversity
2   Accelerate the inclusion of people with disabilities
3   Take into account people of all ages and generations
4   Continue to promote gender equity and foster inclusive environments for LGBTQIA+ people

L'Oréal now uses models who all have some relation to sustainable actions, such as the acceptance of LGBTQ groups or reducing poverty in countries. These are not related to sustainable consumer behavior but might still be an attractive way of positioning because consumers might judge that as a relevant point of difference.

reducing its own footprint for years. But sustainability is not included as a positioning characteristic in their communication by the individual brands. Take on the other hand Shell, who logically has reputation issues concerning sustainability and is doing their utmost to change this. A danger of shouting loudly that you are sustainable is that a brand acquires an image of 'greenwashing': a difference between what the company says it does in terms of commitment to sustainability and what the company actually does, so: 'pretending' (Viererbl & Koch, 2022). This is a difficult issue since it might be that you do tell the truth but that consumers will see this as a way of covering the bad things you do. Since the 20s,

## Case 11.6 Greenwashing

### Shell did not offer $CO_2$-free fueling

In 2021 Shell had a campaign where they communicated '$CO_2$ free fueling'. The reason for this claim was that for every liter, Shell invested 1 Eurocent in planting trees. The Dutch Advertising Code Commission, however, judged this communication as 'misleading' and forced Shell to stop the campaign.

there have been many studies about greenwashing, but the truth about how and when is difficult to point out. There are also discussions about regulations, but it seems inevitable that communication about sustainability should be regulated (see also Case 11.6).

### Influencing methods

Narrowing the gap between a sustainable attitude and truly sustainable behavior can be done in various ways; it is not always just about communication but sometimes also about other market instruments such as price or service. We distinguish the following 'interventions':

1   *Nudging*: facilitating the circumstances to choose a sustainable alternative (see e.g. Byerly et al., 2018). For example: placing sustainable alternatives more visibly or paying more attention to them in advertising brochures. These methods appeal to our unconscious choice processes (system 1). In the short term, this often works. It is unclear whether it also works in the long term.

2   *Making cheaper*: this is also a form of making things easier but is usually not
counted as nudging.
3   *Increasing awareness*: for example, by showing the consequences of climate change.
This is in fact the traditional communication campaign that is the focus of the next
chapter and can be developed in many ways.
4   *Boosting*: making people 'more knowledgeable', for example, with an energy coach.
5   *Transcendental methods*: trying to touch people via their identity and values, for
example, by giving them targeted training and information.

The first three methods can be used by all types of organizations and businesses.
The last two require active participation from consumers and are mainly intended
for organizations that see sustainability promotion as their main task (such as governments).

The choice of which approach is best partly depends on the results of consumer
research, whether or not using the SHIFT model to find out where the biggest obstacles
lie. For example, it makes quite a difference whether the biggest challenges are mainly in
'social', 'habits', or just 'individual'.

## 11.3.5 Tools to formulate a positioning

Once a brand has chosen the desired values, the next question is how to get the positioning 'on paper'. We discuss three ways: the positioning statement, the brand story, and the
brand key model.

### Positioning statement

A positioning statement is a summary of the positioning in the following form: in the
product category . . . brand A is better for target group . . . than competitor B for the purpose
of use . . . because it . . . (benefit). We can prove this because . . . (e.g. property). The core
value of brand A is . . .

So the positioning statement ends with the core value, which is simply the most
important value of the brand. Ries and Trout (1981) argue that a brand should ideally
claim one word. That word must be unique and relevant.

### Brand story

A brand story tells in a coherent way how a brand feels: what is the core of the brand,
as it were, and also why. Aaker and Aaker (2016) speak in this context of *signature
stories*: a motivating and authentic story with a strategic message that is clear about
the brand, the customers, the organization, and the 'business model'. Sometimes it is
first told why the company was founded. But there are also other ways to tell 'your
story'. Aaker and Aaker suggest describing someone (owner, customer, employee)
as a 'hero'. The aim is to inspire employees and customers and to show what your
authentic strength is. There is a lot to read about storytelling, corporate stories, and
brand stories. There are also many agencies that 'offer' these models. There is no
fixed format.

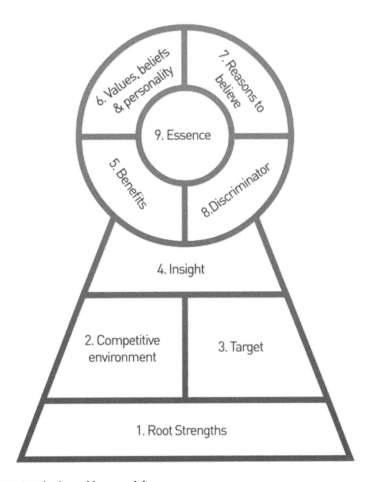

*Figure 11.16* **The brand key model**

## Brand key model

The brand key is a model in which eight parts must be completed (see Figure 11.16).

The bottom part of the brand key (Figure 11.16) shows the most important findings from the internal and external analysis:

1  What about the brand until now: what is our core strength?
2  Who is the main competitor and what is that competitor good at?
3  What is the core target group of the organization?
4  Which core insight is important for the target group, for example, why do customers not buy my product?

The circled upper part of the brand key reads:

5   The benefits: what are the concrete benefits that 'we offer' and which stem from the core values?
6   Values and personality: the major brand personality and values.
7   Reasons to believe (credibility): what is the supporting evidence? Why should anyone believe that we are so expert? Also: why should a customer buy 'us'?
8   Distinctiveness: which of the advantages is unique to us?

And finally:

9   The heart contains the brand essence: what is the core promise, in preferably two or three words? This can also be the start of a slogan.

### Relationships between the models

At the end of this subsection, we show the relationship between a number of models that we have discussed here.

The *Rossiter-Percy matrix* gives direction to the kind of positioning (*positioning strategy*) needed in the category. Assuming that a brand wants to exploit the entire *means-end chain* (two-sided, which is also the essence of the *golden circle*), the *Brand Benefitting Model is* suitable for choosing the central functional advantage (quality, service, price, convenience, sustainability). That model also states that emotional benefits are important. The *Aaker brand personality scale* is a guideline for choosing a brand personality, and the *value compass* can be used for choosing terminal values. For both models, it is not necessary to choose literally the dimensions contained in them, because then there is a risk of a limited or no distinction with competitors. The chosen positioning can then be summarized in a *brand story* (or statement or brand key).

## 11.3.6 Brand laws

In Chapter 4 we laid the foundation for a positioning: searching for the identity (the DNA) of the brand. A positioning should always fit with the current culture of the company. However, this does not mean that nothing can change, nor that there can be no ambition in the positioning. An ambition can also be motivating for employees.

In practice, companies often find it difficult to achieve good positioning. One of the problems is that positioning means 'choosing', and that also means 'choosing what's not important', sometimes called 'the art of omission'. We believe there are four general guidelines for positioning (and communication), which we refer to as the four brand laws (based on Alsem & Klein Koerkamp, 2010). These four laws are shown in Figure 11.17.

### 1 Focus

Managers often want to tell everything about why the company is so good. Focus is needed for two reasons. First, people cannot remember much at once, and a story is easier to remember if there is a clear message. Choose. Related guidelines are simplicity and clarity. A well-known communication principle is KISS: *keep it simple, stupid.* Sometimes 'and repeat' is added to it. A second reason is that it can also be frustrating

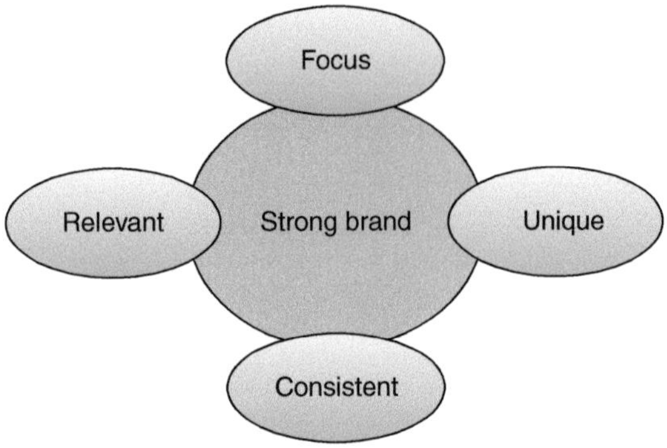

*Figure 11.17* **The four brand laws**

for the employees themselves to be 'good at everything'. Then the company gets 'stuck in the medium'. So brands have to choose. That takes courage.

## 2 Be different

Daring to choose is difficult. In addition, promises are often made that everyone keeps. 'We always deliver the best products and take your wishes into account!' Great, but no one likes it. Everyone says this. What is really distinctive?

Distinction is necessary to rise above the competition. If we limit ourselves to the marketing strategy (brand positioning), then this can be achieved in two ways: first by looking carefully for your own uniqueness and then also naming it. This 'uniqueness' is often easier to find in personality and values than in benefits. This makes it important to have a clear 'why' (Sinek) or – which is in essence the same as 'why' – to have distinctive values. Being different in values implies being creative in communication. A second way to be distinctive is by doing something new, in other words, innovation. This is what Kim and Mauborgne in their well-known book *Blue Ocean Strategy* (2005) termed the blue ocean strategy: create a new ocean without fighting sharks (red ocean). So their well-packaged message is simply: innovate.

## 3 Relevance

Relevance plays at the level of marketing strategy and tactics. At a strategic level, a positioning must be chosen that is relevant to the target group. If customer wishes change, brands can shift their positioning. A positioning, once chosen, does not have to be completely fixed, but the identity that fits with it does. Relevance and brand link are also necessary for the brand elements, such as the house style.

At a tactical level, relevant communication is essential. Relevance relates to content and form. Especially with regard to the form, major mistakes are made, especially in 'ordinary' marketing. The biggest mistake is going too far with the previous guideline: creativity. By overshooting we mean using a creative concept that has nothing to do with the message, brand, or product category. A joke for the joke, for example. Humor that is not substantively linked to the brand is distracting. Then the creative communication can stand out enormously, but if the brand is not remembered, it is pointless. It is about creativity for the benefit and service of the brand.

### 4 Consistency

Building a clear brand image takes time, so patience and consistency are important. Customers must be taught what the brand stands for so that they feel more and more connected to it. That means to persist. A brand cannot show a different personality from one day to the next. That is not credible, and it is confusing. The same applies to

## Case 11.7 Consistency

### Red Bull does everything right with its branding

A good example of applying all brand laws is without a doubt Red Bull. This brand was co-founded by Dietrich Mateschitz, who launched the first drinks in 1987. He had noticed that the drink he had taken over under a different name gave him energy after long flights. With 'Red Bull gives you wings', the brand has started sponsoring all kinds of suitable sports based on its core values of 'action, adventure and adrenaline', including motocross, mountain biking, and exotic sports such as cliff diving. Red Bull also bought a football club and gave it its name (FC Red Bull Salzburg). And with the highest parachute jump (from space), the brand achieved a lot of free publicity. The founder died in 2022, and Red Bull Racing, the team of two-time Formula 1 winner Max Verstappen, paid tribute to him in October.

the portfolio of products: how many different products can you place under a brand? Finally, consistency also applies to communication channels, such as across online and print media.

## 11.4 Brand architecture

Many companies have more than one product or service: a portfolio. New products may be the result of own development but may also be the result of a merger or acquisition. In all of these cases, a company should decide how to name the new products and especially whether to use the existing brand names and whether and how to use brand levels. We first discuss these brand levels, and then we review the choice of the brand architecture.

### 11.4.1 Brand levels

There are different brand levels. Figure 11.18 gives an overview with examples.

The corporate (or company) level refers to the supplier of the brand. A supplier is sometimes part of a larger group. A company may choose to use or not to use the group name in the positioning. In the insurance industry, it can be observed that group names are increasingly being used as a source of trust. This has to do with the expectation that consumers find it increasingly important to know who is behind the brand and how it behaves (socially). A good reputation is therefore very important.

A family brand is a brand used for different product categories. A family brand can differ from the corporate brand.

An individual brand is limited to a product category. The emphasis in this book is on the individual brand. An individual brand has its own image and its own target group.

The lowest brand level indicates the type of product (item or variety).

There is often a relationship between brand level and the type of attribute with which the brand is positioned. At the higher levels, positioning is often done on emotional values. On lower levels, functional benefits are (also) important.

| Levels | Fast moving consumer goods | Durable consumer goods | Services |
|---|---|---|---|
| Corporate brand | Procter & Gamble | Volkswagen (manufacturer) | ING Group |
| Family brand (umbrella brand) | Crest | Volkswagen | ING Financial Services |
| Individual brand | Crest toothpaste | Volkswagen ID | ING Direct |
| Type or variety | Crest Sesame Street Kids' Cavity Protection | Volkswagen ID.3 | Orange Home Loans |

*Figure 11.18* **Brand levels**

## 11.4.2 Choosing a brand structure

Designing the combination of all brands and levels is called the brand architecture. The chosen combinations of brand levels are called the brand structure. The brand portfolio is the combination of brand names and brand levels of a company. There are four possible brand structures:

1  *Monobranding*: the parent brand (often a corporate brand) is used for all products and services.
2  *Branded house*: here the 'parent brand' (the company or family brand) is used as the main name for all products, but the separate products also have their own sub-names (small).
3  *Endorsed brand structure*: two brand levels are used here: the individual brand as the main brand, with the corporate brand as the 'sender'. The difference from a branded house is that the two brand names are used in the opposite way: first the individual brand then the corporate brand. Unilever, for example, applies this way of branding and shows the Unilever logo in ads for their brands, such as Bertolli.
4  *House of brands*: this is a brand structure where only the individual brands are used. This is how Procter & Gamble works: all its brands, such as Pampers, Tide, Bounty, and Always, are communicated without any reference to the mother brand.

In choosing a brand structure, several factors should be taken into account. First, keep it simple. The more names, the harder it is for a consumer to remember. On the other hand, it is sometimes wise to use several names, for example, to provide a quality guarantee as the sender. Another advantage of using two names (*'dual branding'*) is 'cross-selling': the possibility of showing customers that this manufacturer also can offer other brands and products.

A brand structure refers to the combination of brand levels within a company. Combinations of brands are also possible *between* companies. Brands can also visibly collaborate with *other brands*. If both brands explicitly continue to exist in this form of cooperation, it is called *co-branding*. Co-branding therefore means that two 'independent' brands are 'glued' onto one product. The advantage of co-branding is that brands can make use of each other's strengths. Empirical research shows that with co-branding, the weaker brand of the two gains the most advantage in terms of brand image.

A specific form of co-branding is *ingredient branding*. This is the case if a brand presents itself in communication as part of a product of another brand, for example, 'Intel inside'.

A brand can also use a *'quality mark'* (sometimes referred to as 'label'): an independent confirmation of requirements that a brand can meet. This means that the brands meets certain standards, for example, in the area of sustainability. Having a quality mark such as Fairtrade is a guarantee that a brand does not engage in 'greenwashing'.

## 11.5 Brand names

### 11.5.1 Developing a brand name

Suppose you come up with a new technological product to take photos, and you take the brand name Banana. That sounds illogical and unwise. Yet few people think of an apple when they think of the Apple brand name but of something completely different. In short: every brand name can be loaded with associations. And we as customers have to learn those associations. So, does it not matter at all what name you choose for a brand? Yes, it does. Because some names are easier to remember and better to 'load' than others. This section is therefore about brand names.

In many situations, the brand name is already determined. But sometimes, as in the case of introductions, there is a new brand name to be chosen. Mergers and takeovers entail name changes (rebranding), so the question of what name or names should be used arises here. Despite its vast importance, the choice of a name is often poorly thought out in practice. Two dangers in choosing the 'wrong' name are as follows:

1   It is difficult to link the desired associations with the name.
2   The name turns out to be legally invalid.

The brand name is the main bearer of identity. In fact, the same thing applies to people: a person's name gives you a good idea of his or her character. This character (brand personality) is typically learned along with the name over the course of time. Similarly, it is true for people that a name such as Carol, for instance, has different associations than does a name such as Elizabeth. One could say that a name does not have a 'charge' at birth; the charge develops over time. One could also say that each association must be learned for each name; this is partly true. Names may also have meaning built into them. This is true for two reasons:

1   The phonetic characteristics (sound, length, letters) can in themselves lead to associations with a name or word, for example, a word sounding 'Italian'.
2   A name can provide some information about a product; for example, a Duracell battery will probably last a long time.

## 11.5.2 Types of brand names

One can distinguish between the following types of brand names:

1   Functional names
2   Associative names
3   Abstract names
4   Abbreviations or numbers

### 1 Functional names

A functional name is a name that literally describes what the brand is about, a descriptive name. Examples of functional names are the University of Groningen, the *Journal of Marketing*, and the *Northern Gazette*. A special category of functional names includes questions, sentences, and specific promotions such as www.iwantacheaperloan.us. Clearly, an advantage of a functional name is that it is easy to learn what it is about. A disadvantage is that it has a higher risk of being confused with competitors; this often happens in health care, for example, where many organizations 'explain' in their name that they are in health care. Another disadvantage of a functional name is that it is more difficult to stretch the brand into new categories.

### 2 Associative names

Associative names are names that provide some information about the brand without literally saying what it is, for example, by providing information about the category or brand, such as Transavia, Facebook, and Microsoft.

### 3 Abstract names

Abstract names are names that do not provide any clue about the brand. These names can be existing words (word names) or new words. Perhaps the most famous example is Apple. Apple has shown that using a 'random' word can be very successful: no one thinks about an apple when he or she thinks of the brand, even though the name and the logo are still literally an apple. An abstract name can also be a name of a person, for example, Heineken. Abstract names can also be new words, without any information about the brand, such as Sony. Many brands have abstract names. Initially, the names do not have any link with a brand (they are existing or new words, not linked to a brand), but after a while, the target group begins to associate the name with something.

### 4 Abbreviations or numbers

Examples are KLM, HP, TNT, and 501. These names work similarly to the way functional names work: it is difficult to create emotional distinctiveness. Another disadvantage is confusion: abbreviations are easily confused with each other, for example, KPN (telecom) and the paper manufacturer KNP. Companies considering a name that is longer than two words must take into account the fact that people will abbreviate it even though the company does not. This may be a reason to keep the name short.

Which names are the most common in practice? Probably that is abstract names. Figure 11.19 contains the list of the ten most valuable brands in 2022, with an indication of the name itself.

## 11.5.3 Criteria for choosing a name

There are four criteria that should be taken into account in choosing a brand name:

1   Fit with marketing strategy
2   Meaningfulness
3   Distinctiveness
4   Protectability

### 1 Fit with marketing strategy

The name should fit, or at least not be in conflict with the marketing strategy of the brand: targeting and positioning. This means, for example, that for a typical local product, an

| Brand | Name |
|---|---|
| 1. Apple | Abstract |
| 2. Amazon | Abstract |
| 3. Google | Abstract |
| 4. Microsoft | Associative |
| 5. Walmart | Associative |
| 6. Samsung | Abstract |
| 7. Facebook | Associative |
| 8. ICBC | Abbreviation |
| 9. Huawei | Abstract |
| 10. Verizon | Abstract |

**Figure 11.19** Top brands, 2022, and name category

Source: www.visualcapitalist.com/top-100-most-valuable-brands-in-2022/

international (sounding) name will not be logical, or that for a health care provider, a very fancy name will be chosen.

## 2 Meaningfulness

Research shows that the meaningfulness of a brand name is affecting the speed of acceptance (Kohli et al., 2005). This is quite logical: if a name has some meaning, people can easily recognize what it is and thus easily adapt the brand.

## 3 Distinctiveness

A brand should be different than competition. This is perhaps the essence of branding in general. So, preferably also the name should be really different than that of the competition. A related issue here is that the URL (including the countries' extension) should preferably be available. If the countries' extension is not available, name.com can also be chosen depending on how international the brand is.

#### *4. Protectability*

From a legal perspective, virtually all visible distinguishing characteristics of brands (names, logos, symbols, colors, and packaging forms) are considered 'brands' on their own and may be registered as such within the framework of trademark law. Because of the strong associative role of brand names and signs, it is indeed important for companies to register them. Without registration, a competitor can easily misuse the brand signs of another company. For registration, the registration office (in Europe, the Office of Harmonization for the Internal Market [OHIM]) strongly looks at the distinctive power of a brand sign. For example, the color combination yellow-blue of the Swedish IKEA was judged to have too little distinctive power to be registered as a 'brand'. The same holds for the names 'Super Champion' for computer games and 'Fitline' for clothes. Philips successfully registered the form and varieties of this form of its coffee machine Senseo.

Some long-existing brand names are so successful that people start to use them as category names (for example, Luxaflex, aspirin, spa). A risk of using a brand name as category name is that it loses its distinctive power and cannot be legally protected. Recently Jacuzzi dealt with this problem where a holiday park used their names for bubble baths of another brand. Being a market leader might lead to a branding problem . . .

A related issue is whether the URL is available (see also the previous criterion). This is easy to check using specific apps.

When we have a look at the four criteria, it can be seen that they are not independent from each other. There is a trade-off between meaningfulness and distinctiveness/protectability: the more meaningful and thus descriptive a name is, the less distinctive it will be and the less easy it might be to find a free URL. Since it is possible to link any association to almost any name, the recommendation could be to use own, new words. On the other hand, for finding a website, it is easy to have a simple, logical name. In current practice, it is quite common to choose an associative name, for example, CompliMints. Another solution is to choose a name that is in some sense associative, but is 'misspelled', for example, Greetz for a website to send cards.

### 11.5.4 Brand name process

The same thing applies to coming up with a brand name for developing an advertising campaign: First, a briefing must be drafted with the following major points: the vision on the environment, the product, the target group, and the brand positioning. If these points need clarification, it is not yet time to be considering a name. The reason for this is the name should fit with the marketing strategy.

There are three ways to come up with a new name:

- *Invent it yourself.* This is the quickest and least expensive method but typically produces the worst names. The problem is that managers often cannot step outside themselves and may have trouble imagining how the name will go over with the customer.
- *Hold a competition among personnel and/or customers.* The biggest advantage here is that a foundation is created for the name or name change. Personnel and customers must

## Case 11.8 Disadvantage of a functional name

### Oatly loses trademark battle against UK oat milk brand

Oatly has lost its legal battle against PureOaty in the UK after a judge ruled there was no evidence of trademark infringement. The Swedish oat milk brand claimed PureOaty's brand name and packaging were similar to Oatly's and would confuse consumers. It also accused the owner of PureOaty – Cambridgeshire-based Glebe Farm Foods – of 'passing off' the product as Oatly. A court has dismissed these claims, though, describing the visual similarities as 'very modest'. The judge also pointed out there was no evidence of confusion among consumers. Philip Rayner, Glebe Farm's owner and managing director, says: 'It is enormously gratifying that the judge has ruled in our favour, and to see that smaller independent companies can fight back and win. We can now forge ahead with PureOaty and our oat milk enterprise'. Glebe Farm, which rebranded the product as PureOaty in 2020, had net assets of less than £5m for the year to March 2020. Oatly, which listed on the New York stock exchange with a market capitalization of $10bn, had been looking to stop sales of PureOaty plus damages and costs. Oatly says it accepts the court's decision and won't be appealing.

Source: *Marketingweek* 2 August 2021

learn to accept and spread the name, so it is wise not to surprise them with it. The disadvantage is that only obvious, bad names come out of the box. You can hold a contest, but it should be explicitly stated that it is not guaranteed that one of those names will be used; they will be submitted to a professional agency for assessment, for instance.

■   *Use a brand name agency*. There are a few agencies that specialize in this service. Enlisting the services of an agency is typically the preferable course of action, possibly in combination with a contest.

A brand name agency usually takes the following steps:

1   Request a briefing from the client. There must be complete clarity with respect to various strategic decisions in addition to brand levels and use in other countries.
2   Come up with a large number (approximately 50) of names. These names are submitted to the client. The agency learns from the feedback what appeals to the client and what does not. This may also include names from a contest.
3   Submission of a smaller quantity, including old and new names. Using the same process, an attempt is made to narrow the list to three names.
4   Test the three names with the target group. This is not necessary, but it is recommended if quick acceptance is important to the manager.
5   Conduct a connotation and legal study of the three names. A connotation study attempts to determine whether a name creates undesired associations in another country. For instance, a detergent was introduced to the market in Spain that denoted the Spanish word for a whore. A legal study attempts to determine whether the names are already in use elsewhere (and are registered) and, for instance, whether the corresponding web site is still available. For domain names, registration is a common problem. Sometimes large companies have to fight in court for their domain names.
6   Selection of the name by the client.

## 11.6 Design and logo

Because the design and logo are strongly related to brand positioning, we discuss these elements not under the marketing instrument product in Chapter 12 but in this chapter on marketing strategy. Design relates to the design of all external appearance forms of the brand: the logo (form, color, etc.), brand signs, and packaging. Since these product elements are directly linked to the brand, they are important carriers of the brand personality. A logo should be an extension of the brand personality. A good example is the logo of the Rabobank: a person in the middle of a circle who portrays the positioning of the Rabobank: 'you as customer have a central place and we as bank are located in the middle of society'. However, in the case of more abstract logos, a manager should be aware of the spontaneous associations a logo has. In practice, logos are often dealt with too lightly. Often it is said that a certain logo 'is outdated' or 'not appealing enough' and that the 'house style' therefore should be modified. Then a new logo is designed, and if the management likes the new logo, a new house style is born. However, this approach ignores the function of the logo as the carrier of the brand personality. A new logo can be designed only after a discussion has taken place about the brand personality: What does the brand or company want to represent? A similar issue applies to brand signs.

## Case 11.9 Logo

### Logo Twix has a nice surprise

Twix isn't just an example of a rebrand. They also have a consistent campaign story with the 'left and right Twix' and have an up-to-date joke in their logo because the dot on the i is two simple lines that of course represent both Twix bars in a pack but also nicely represent a 'break moment' in which you are equally beautiful . . .

Brand signs are symbols, colors, spelling, and the like that are 'own' to the brand, for example, the special way in which the name Coca-Cola is written or the color 'canary yellow' associated with Post-It from 3M. Brand signs are, just like logos, strongly connected to the brand personality. For example, colors have their own radiation: blue is perceived as mild, red as lively and fierce. Colors are important for the brand and for varieties. For example, colors play an important role in the recognition of coffee varieties (red brand, gold brand, silver brand, etc.).

Packaging obviously plays a functional role but also has strongly communicative one. The packaging design therefore has a relationship with the brand and subbrands.

Not only for products but also for retailers, design is important, perhaps even more important. The house style of a retailer is literally the style of the house/the shop, which determines a large part of the shopping experience of customers. And with the growing competition of online shopping versus offline shopping (clicks and bricks), realizing a good shopping experience is increasingly important. Kotler (1973) already spoke about the atmospheric elements (such as color, lighting, smell, and music) that should stimulate the senses. This is part of *retail marketing*. Optimal design and decoration of the retail space should lead to offline retailers also offering sufficient added value in competition with online shopping. Central is the *experience* (Verhoef et al., 2019). The challenge for a retailer is to align the range, the shopping experience, and the service and expertise as closely as possible with customer wishes and their own identity. That extras compared to web shops can be in:

- personal advice and service
- more confidence through direct contact
- sensory stimulation and experience

Especially the latter (experience) is often mentioned as added value of an offline store. Then retail design is of great importance (including color). Not only does the design of a shop affect the experience but also the scents and the sounds and, of course, the products and the service.

## Case 11.10 Retail design and the message of a color

Tony's Chocolonely uses a clear retail design

In 2021, Tony Chocolonely opened its first travel retail store at Schiphol Airport Amsterdam. The color red is dominant, signaling values like 'energy', 'passion', and 'action'. A range of chocolate, gifts, and items such as t-shirts and tote bags is on offer at the store, along with the brand's new travel retail exclusive range, including a 320-g Tiny Tony's Pouch Pack and the new 240 g bar in a range of flavors.

## 11.7 Managing brands

Brand values have to be managed over time, over products (extensions), and over countries. Specific issues related to this include:

- repositioning (Section 11.7.1)
- rebranding (Section 11.7.2)
- crisis management (Section 11.7.3)
- extensions (Section 11.7.4)
- internationalization (Section 11.7.5).

### 11.7.1 Repositioning

At a certain moment a company might want to change the main communication message of a brand. Changing a communication message can pertain to:

1  The level of positioning, so a new positioning (*repositioning*)
2  The execution of the communication, for example, the creative concept.

One of the brand laws is about consistency. A repositioning looks dangerous because the brand is claiming to change its core message. This might not be credible for customers. In practice, there are examples of beer brands (that are strongly dependent on building image) that changed their brand personality from one day to another. Clearly, such an action lacks credibility.

One the level of specific messages, changes are not necessarily a problem.

This also pertains to changing in execution, although consistent execution leads to easier recognition of the brand. For example, a simple piece of music consistently linked to a brand may lead to spontaneous associations for customers who just hear the music. Execution can thus be a kind of a fixed part of a brand. However, a disadvantage of consistency in execution is that attention will decrease. Research about the effects of TV advertising shows that regular changes in execution lead to an increase in market share (Lodish et al., 1995a). Probably this is caused by higher attention for new advertising. A risk of new, attention-attracting executions is the lack of a logical link with the brand. In that case, no name or the wrong brand name will be remembered. The conclusion is that changes in execution may be good for the brand as long as there is a link with the brand.

### 11.7.2 Rebranding

Rebranding means changing the brand name. This is a more narrow interpretation than is sometimes used, since sometimes repositioning is also called rebranding.

Changing a brand name is a rare occasion. That is logical since the name is the most important carrier of the brand knowledge people have. And this brand knowledge is, according to Keller, the essence of 'brand equity'. Changing a brand name does not imply that the brand knowledge with customer is lost. Only the link changes, which still is a big step.

Reasons for rebranding include:

1 *Mergers and acquisitions*: in these situations, sometimes brands disappear and become part of another brand
2 *Legal problems*: a new name already used by another might lead to a new rebranding
3 *Crisis*: a brand can have a severe image problem and for that reason decide to rebrand
4 *Efficiency*: international companies might rebrand products to have the same name in different countries
5 *Marketing strategic motives*: a company might want to reposition the brand or want to be able to internationalize and change the name (Case 11.11).

What is the best way to organize rebranding? First, it is important to be clear in communication about the motives of rebranding. Information facilitates acceptance. This is investigated for extensions (see Section 11.7.4) and is probably also true for rebranding. Then there are still two possibilities:

- Slow change. In this case, first a new name will be put on the product next to the old name, or the new name will be announced on the old product. After a while the

## Case 11.11 Rebranding

Enie becomes Soly

The Dutch company Enie.nl, founded in 2013, is about sun energy. The company has grown and is wanting to become an international player. A big international competitor of Enie is Engie.com, with almost the same name, sometimes leading to confusion. So, a rebranding was necessary, and agency n8w8.nl was asked to do this. The agency developed the new (associative) name Soly, coming from solar energy. In the middle of the 'o', a dot was added representing the classical symbol of the sun.

old name disappears. The advantage is that the target group can get used to the new name. A disadvantage is higher marketing costs and perhaps some confusion with the two names.

■ Change at once. With a 'big bang', the company is clear: the name is changed due to specific reasons.

## 11.7.3 Crisis management and communication

Another aspect of managing brands over time is dealing with a crisis. This is mostly about communication, but because the reputation of the brand is strongly involved, we discuss this issue in this chapter. There are different forms of a crisis. Ndlela (2019) distinguishes between three types of crises:

1  *victim crises*: non-organizational causes such as COVID, earthquakes, energy crises
2  *accidental crises*: accidentally caused by an organization, such as pieces of glass in beer bottles, spinach with poison, an insurance company that sends sex films instead of information films
3  *preventable crises*: intentionally caused by the organization, such as the diesel scandal (Volkswagen), discrimination or inappropriate behavior

From a marketing communication point of view, those mentioned under 2 and 3 are the most interesting (despite the fact that *victim crises* have the greatest social impact).

Failing to deal adequately with such a crisis is very detrimental to confidence in a brand and the company and is therefore detrimental to brand equity (and brand value). How should it be handled?

The first guideline has to do with brand reputation or brand strength. A strong brand inspires confidence. If, in the eyes of consumers, an organization does not respond adequately to a crisis, confidence will be dented and brand strength (awareness and associations) will by definition decline. You don't want that. This is also where the proverb comes from 'that trust [and therefore brand image] comes on foot but goes on horseback'. Yet that is not entirely true. Research and practice show that strong brands can take a beating. That's because a strong brand actually has a bowl full of positive associations, which doesn't always or just completely empty in one go. That has to do with two things. First of all, people tend to forget things quickly. There are more important things than brands to people. For example, confidence in the strong Volkswagen brand plummeted after the emissions measurement scandal in which Volkswagen knowingly committed fraud. Interestingly, sales recovered quickly, and a year later there was no discernible effect. Case 11.12 shows another (very old but very interesting) example of handling a crisis.

The second reason a crisis doesn't have to be disastrous for a brand is the way it is handled. Then we come to crisis communication (see, for example, Ndlela, 2019). To regain trust, the guideline for crisis communication is simply 'open, honest, and fast'. To start with the latter: the longer you wait, the more likely it is that unwanted stories will be published in the press (Durst & Henschel, 2022). These days with social media, news moves extremely fast, especially if journalists also pick up cases, so get out quickly. Also make sure to provide as much clarity as possible. Don't talk in vague terms. Also stop

## Case 11.12 Crisis management

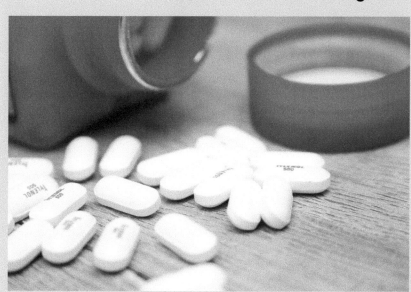

### Crisis handling by Tylenol

It was a crime that forever changed the way we buy over-the-counter medications. In 1982 seven people in the Chicago area died after taking Tylenol capsules that had been randomly laced with cyanide. No one was ever charged with the murders. However, James Lewis was released from prison in 1995 after serving 13 years of a 20-year sentence for trying to extort $1 million from Johnson & Johnson, Tylenol's parent company. About a month after the deaths, Lewis wrote Johnson & Johnson demanding money or he'd strike again. As a result of the case, regulations were adopted that require tamper-resistant packaging. The crime cost Tylenol's makers $100 million for the recall of 31 million capsules. Johnson & Johnson decided to stop all Tylenol advertising until several weeks after the seven deaths. In December 1982 the company aired 'You can trust us' commercials that received high visibility. Tylenol finished third in top-of-mind awareness of all advertising behind Coca-Cola and Burger King that month.

**Source:** Howard, Lucy, and Carla Koehl, 'Release in the Tylenol Case', *Newsweek*, October 23, 1995, p. 8
*'"Trust Us" Tylenol Ads Working'*, *Advertising Age*, December 6, 1999, p. 77.

all your normal communication and any advertising. There is nothing as disastrous as a commercial on TV while you are in the news at the same time. If there are victims, be the first to show your sympathy. In short, think from the customer's point of view and not your own. That is actually the core of marketing.

## Case 11.13 Relevance of customer's point of view

### Heineken's biggest weakness is internal culture

When Russia invaded Ukraine in 2021, almost all European companies withdrew their activities from Russia. Also Heineken promised to do so. One year later, it appeared that Heineken had jumped into the holes that competitors created: they introduced several new brands in Russia. When journalists discovered this, Heineken came up with vague economic motives for their decision. CEO Van den Brink said that there were many 'internal objections' against withdrawal, so he decided not to withdraw. This quote reflects the typical internal culture of Heineken, a culture that also made Heineken so successful: pride, always internally convinced of doing the right things. But in crisis situations, an antenna for signals in society is inevitable.

Source: *Financial Daily*, 15 March 2023, p. 25.

There is one exception to this: inform your own staff as soon as possible about what is going on. As an employee, it is very annoying if you have to hear from others at a party that your company is doing badly in the news. It is better if you know for yourself. More generally: think from the perspective of target groups and not your own! The importance of relationships with all your stakeholders during crises is also emphasized by Bundy et al. (2017) and Ndlela (2019).

In summary: make sure you become a strong brand 'in normal life'; then you can take a beating. And if there is a crisis, react appropriately, and then your image will not go on horseback. Such a communication policy should be organized in advance. Ndlela (2019) talks about crisis *preparedness* (playbooks) and crisis *response* but also crisis prevention and post-crisis management (what can we do better from now on?). The response is, among other things, about 'open, honest, and fast', but above all about having a vision to adopt a customer-oriented approach. So: the core of marketing.

### 11.7.4 Managing brands across products and varieties (extensions)

Many organizations decide to 'hang' new products under existing brands (*extensions*). They hope that this will extend the brand's success to the new product. There are two types of extensions:

1  Category extensions. This means marketing new products under an existing brand name (parent brand) outside the category of the parent brand, for example, a manufacturer of watches that markets cars.
2  Line extensions. These are range extensions under an existing brand within the original category. This involves the introduction of varieties (flavors, shapes, packaging quantities).

The vast majority of new product introductions are extensions; line extensions are the majority. By the way, the definition of what constitutes a category or line extension depends on how the 'product category' is defined. Is Levi's a jeans or clothing brand? See also case 11.14.

Ries and Trout (1981) state that extensions are not allowed. We don't want to go that far. Much research has been done on the success of extensions (for an overview, see Völckner & Sattler, 2006; Peng et al., 2023). This shows that extensions can indeed be successful under a number of conditions. An important research result is that in the eyes of the target group, an extension must fit with the parent brand: there must be a logical fit between the extension and the brand (Aaker & Keller, 1990; Reddy et al., 1994; Kirmani et al., 1999). For example, the extension BIC perfume, in addition to BIC pens, has not proved a success. The extension 7Up Ice Cola (a clear cola from 7Up) has also been unsuccessful for this reason. Research shows that the perceived fit between a parent brand and an extension can be improved through communication (Lane, 2000). Another positive factor for a successful extension is a strong parent brand. The relevance of fit and brand strength for extension success, however, depends on some factors (e.g. age of the consumer) (see Peng et al., 2023).

Furthermore, there is a relationship between the positioning strategy and the possibility for extensions. Brands with an informational positioning are more strongly linked to the product than brands with a transformational positioning and have less room for extensions. In practice, there is a tendency to market many extensions. However, from the point of view of preserving the brand image (also for the mother brand), this is often not wise.

## Case 11.14 Brand extensions

### Levi's sets jeans aside

Levi's no longer wants to rely solely on its iconic jeans. Already 20% of turnover comes from shirts, compared to 11% five years ago. CEO Chip Bergh says he wants to broaden the range even more. For example, the brand also releases bright green-colored jeans jackets together with the Pokémon game brand and the Simpsons brand, remarkable promotions for a brand that is of course known as the number one jeans brand in the world. The danger is that the DNA of this brand will fade, which will reduce customer loyalty to Levi's. With innovations that are increasingly removed from the emotional meaning of the brand, you see it happen more often.

Source: *Dagblad van het Noorden*, 12 February 2021

Managers considering a brand extension should ask themselves the following questions:

- How is the parent brand now positioned?
- Will consumers experience the extension as logical? Which parts of the positioning are stretched?
- Is the part of the positioning being stretched relevant in the new category?
- Is our parent brand strong?
- If there is no logical fit, can communication help to explain?
- What is the effect of the extension on the parent brand and other extensions?

Good market research can help answer these questions. When this happens, brand extensions can be very successful.

If the aforementioned questions indicate that an extension is too risky, a manager may consider rebranding the product and, for example, *sub-branding*.

## 11.7.5 Managing brands across countries

The internationalization of the business world is going very fast. Both retailers and manufacturers and service providers are developing into multinationals. Through mergers and acquisitions, companies seek reinforcement from each other and local brands (brands limited to a country) are increasingly becoming part of international groups that then use these brands for a global brand strategy. Consumers are also becoming increasingly international, both physically (travel) and from the living room (TV, online). In view of these developments, the question is how far an international brand should go in standardizing marketing communication.

An advantage of the same communication in all countries is efficiency and consistency. A disadvantage is that differences between countries are not taken into account. Floor et al. (2020) distinguish four international advertising strategies:

1 *Global strategy*. With this strategy, there is the same positioning, the same creative concept (campaign idea), and the same execution (execution) in every country. This strategy is chosen, for example, by Coca-Cola and Levi's.
2 *Adaptation strategy*. In this strategy, only the execution is modified, usually in the form of a translation (dubbed or recreated). This strategy is chosen, for example, by Philips and KLM. Incidentally, this strategy requires a high degree of coordination between business units and communication consultancies in the various countries. This can be difficult: local companies and agencies often prefer to have more autonomy because they know the local market better.
3 *Differentiation strategy*. The central message of the campaign (proposition) is fixed, but it is left to the countries how the communication is worked out. The advantage of locally devised creative concepts is that cultural differences between countries are taken into account. McDonald's, Pepsi Cola, and all Procter & Gamble brands opt for this strategy.
4 *Local strategy*. Nothing is standardized in this strategy, but positioning, concept, and execution are chosen per country: 'think global, act local'. Many Japanese brands opt for this strategy. A brand like Heineken also seems to opt for this: in the United States, this brand has a different positioning (top-quality imported beer) than in the Netherlands (beer for everyone).

The choice for the degree of standardization depends, among other things, on the nature of the product and the differences in preferences, purchasing behavior, and values between countries. A trade-off will have to be made between the need for a consistent international brand image and the differences in customer values between countries.

A well-known model that visualizes the culture of countries is Hofstede's model (2011). Hofstede distinguishes six cultural dimensions of a country's culture:

1 *Power distance* the degree to which a country accepts that power is distributed unequally. In the Netherlands, this is quite low: managers are often addressed as 'you'.

2 *Individualism* versus collectivism: the extent to which individuals in a society are connected to each other. In individualistic countries, residents have to take care of themselves above all. In collectivist societies, group cohesion is strong and there is more mutual care. The Netherlands is relatively individualistic.

3 *Masculine versus feminine*: this refers to the extent to which traditional male and female roles are followed. A high masculine score means that competition, performance, and success are very important. In a more feminine society, care for each other and quality of life are more dominant. The Netherlands is a relatively feminine country.

4 *Uncertainty avoidance*: how do people in the country deal with the fact that the future is uncertain? With a high score, rules and order are important. The Netherlands scores high on this: a lot has been arranged, and people have relatively many insurance policies, for example.

5 *Pragmatic versus long-term orientation*: the extent to which a society clings to the past and traditions. The Netherlands scores relatively high on this and is therefore quite pragmatic, which means that society is flexible in dealing with changes.

6 *Joy versus self-restraint* (*indulgence*): the extent to which a society values enjoyment and joy. This is relatively high in the Netherlands, which means that a lot of value is attached to free time and there is generally an optimistic feeling. Incidentally, this sixth dimension was only added to Hofstede's model later.

Figure 11.20 shows the scores of the Netherlands compared to those of China. China is very collectivist because of Confucianism and has a large power distance. Chinese culture is also rather masculine. They are, however, very pragmatic, which is reflected, among other things, in following regulations that are issued from above. For example, a few years ago, diesel mopeds were banned in many major cities, and now literally all mopeds in Chinese cities are electric.

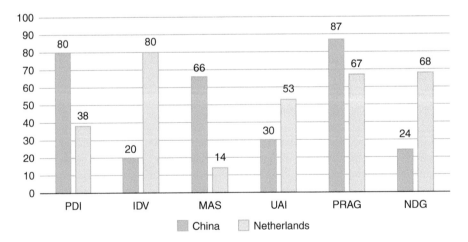

*Figure 11.20* **Comparison of China and the Netherlands according to Hofstede's cultural dimensions**

The model and the scores of the Netherlands and China, for example, show that cultural differences are of great importance in marketing, communication, and sales in and with other countries.

# Summary

Marketing objectives are usually formulated in terms of sales or market share. Target group selection and brand positioning are at the heart of the marketing strategy. Target groups can be chosen after segmentation research has been carried out to determine which target group is most attractive. It must also be determined whether the target group is approached as a whole or in part one on one. In the latter case, loyalty programs can also be used to strengthen the bond.

The brand's positioning is the most important marketing decision an organization has to make. Both functional and emotional values should be chosen. The Brand Benefitting Model can be used for the functional values: quality, service, price, convenience or sustainability. The role of digital marketing and sustainability (in a broad sense: SDGs) should also be considered here. Emotion is also important, with both brand personality and end values being important. Guidelines are focus, distinction, relevance, and consistency.

Once the positioning has been chosen, all brand decisions must be aligned with it. This concerns the choice of brand elements (such as the name and logo), the product/service itself and the other market instruments, and finally the brand architecture and secondary associations. Brand values must then be managed over time (with issues such as repositioning, rebranding, and crisis communication), across products (extensions must fit the parent brand), and across countries ('think global, act local').

## Vorsprung durch Technik

The German car brand Audi is part of the Volkswagen Group, just like Volkswagen, Skoda, and Seat. The Audi brand is looking to its future with confidence. On its corporate website, Audi outlines its strategy.

## Strategy 2020 – the vision of Audi

The company desires to be the largest premium car brand in the world. Its strategic vision is summarized as 'Unleash the beauty of sustainable mobility'.

In its Strategy 2020, the Audi Group emphasizes that it is ready for the challenges of the future. Audi represents values such as sportsmanship, progress, and 'style'. Audi makes technologically advanced cars, but the brand also strives for customer delight in other ways. The brand's recipe for success consists of four key components:

- Focus on research & development. Audi's ambition to deliver high-quality innovative cars is expressed in its German slogan '*Vorsprung durch Technik*'. The brand continues to pioneer with, for example, the use of intelligent combinations of materials, such as aluminum or carbon-fiber reinforced polymers.
- '*We create experience*'. To continuously please its customers, the brand aims to create positive experiences that consumers associate with the Audi brand.
- '*We live responsibility*'. Corporate social responsibility is central to Audi. For example, Audi has already combined its activities in electric mobility in the Audi Q8 e-tron.

■ '*We are Audi*'. The Audi brand continues to pay a lot of attention to product development. Growth is achieved through continuous attention to flexible, efficient production processes, combined with a strengthening of expertise and global presence.

Audi aims for global image leadership. A strong brand is the basis for sustainable success. The Audi Group wants to strengthen the emotional bond with its customers. The image position is constantly being strengthened with a wide and continuously growing model range.

## Audi in Europe

The Netherlands is a relatively small car market in Europe but an interesting one, as the country does not have any 'native' car brands. Consequently, there is fierce competition between all big international car brands to favor the Dutch consumer. And, in creating a strong image position, Audi seems to be in the lead in The Netherlands.

A real ambassador for the Audi brand in this market is Henk de Hooge. He is a man with wide interests. He is online publisher in a number of trendy Dutch blogs such as DutchCowboys and the Blog Idea Factory; he is a marketing strategist and storyteller and refers to himself as a 'digital nomad'. But Henk de Hooge is also a convinced Audi lover. He owns an Audi A4 6-cylinder with seven gears ('fast as lightning and super safe'), but when you put Henk de Hooge in an Audi showroom, he will tell you a story for every model.

I have already had a lot of Audis. The Audi Quattro for example is more than a car, it is an experience. Audi supports the driver with specific training days all over Europe; the car has a low gas mileage. And then that red-lit dashboard, that is so beautiful that is makes really the maximum out of a car experience.

Audi's are modern cars, according to De Hooge.

Many people in the Dutch internet and startups community have an Audi. Audis are also so much more popular than ten years ago. The design says it all. All those models have a completely individual identity. Man, I am in love with Audi.

Audi is the most popular car brand among businesspeople in the Netherlands. But Audi is not only popular with businesspeople. In the annual Dutch election of cool brands, Audi is the only car brand in the top ten, beside brands such as Apple, Google, and Heineken. In a survey among 4,000 Dutch people, the question was asked which car brand they would like to own. Nine percent answered an Audi. None of the other high-end brands, not Porsche, BMW, or Jaguar, nor Aston Martin, nor Volvo could match that. In a brand image survey, Audi stands out as reliable, as classy, as 'pre-eminently business' (no other brand comes even close), as self-assured, and as 'someone who has everything under control'.

An Audi is cool, the car of your dreams. Literally. Because despite all the positive associations, the Dutch roads show a completely different picture. Only 3% of Dutch car owners actually have an Audi. The Dutch mainly drive mid-sized family cars such as Volkswagen or Ford or French brands such as Peugeot or Citroën. But the high desire factor does impact the sales success of Audi in the Netherlands. While the car market was dropping in the past years, the German car with the four Olympic rings seems as recession-proof as the iPhone.

Audi cool? Some people still have to get used to this idea. Not long ago, Audi was a fairly insignificant part of the big Volkswagen group, a brand that was always ranking behind luxury German cars such as BMW and Mercedes. But those times have changed. 'Audi is a sympathetic brand. They do everything right. Product quality, design, image – all of it works very well', according to a brand expert. This is further emphasized in the German home market: 'German prime minister Angela Merkel does not drive a Mercedes or BMW, she consciously chose an Audi. That is a significant signal and has certainly stimulated the brand'.

The management of Audi is making the right choices, according to another marketing expert.

> They have the willingness to cannibalise. Many companies do not dare, fearing that a new model will have detrimental effects on the old models. But if you dare to market models that partially cannibalizes older models, it will only stimulate innovative power. Another plus is the recognizable design. Every model is unmistakably an Audi, but with its own touch. Unity in diversity. That's really important. It gives consumers guidance in creating a homogeneous brand image. A few years ago the design of Audi was still a bit middle-of-the-road. But now they have a line that people find really cool, with which people like to be associated.

## Audi in the rest of the world

Audi does well in Europe. But the Asian market is also of great importance for Audi. In China, German cars represent quality and luxury. In the case of Audi, there is also a distinct kind of prestige: the Audi has been the favorite car of the Chinese party elite for years. A black Audi in Beijing stands for power and status. Someone who drives a black car, of course with tinted glass, gives the signal that he is part of the elite in China. Audi's Chinese sales figures reflect that the Chinese economy is growing less rapidly than before. Despite this, China remains a much more important market for Audi than the United States.

## The visual identity of Audi

It is interesting to read which brand associations Audi aims to evoke with its visual identity. The brand itself claims the following on www.audi.com:

> How does Audi feel? We are a brand engaging in a dialogue, a brand that is not just the sender, but the message itself. A brand that gets involved and at the

same time involves others.

We are very much anchored in the here and now: we are on the move, we think and live digitally. For us, a brand is not a static structure but a living interface.

We offer moments of surprise and inspiration. We share things from the everyday world – but also exceptional experiences. And we always remain clearly identifiable as who we are.

We have structured our visual identity according to the following three design principles: variety, honesty and balance.

These three design principles provide concrete guidance for the implementation of Audi brand design:

### Variety

We are surprising and inspiring. In terms of design, this means more options and fewer rules, ultimately also a much larger and more vibrant range of expression. And more power as a result. From now on there are different options for positioning the rings and aligning text, for example. And diversity is the name of the game when it comes to colors, too. One banner can appear in black-and-white, while in another there may be a predominance of Audi Warm Silver, and a third may feature a striking red accentuation. But all three are correct.

### Honesty

We share the things of everyday life with people as well as fascinating experiences. We communicate simply and directly which is why all our measures have to be easy to understand – and they have to touch people: clear messages conveyed in an empathetic manner. This applies to the rings, which are reduced to the simplest conceivable form of graphic depiction, as it does to our visual style, which avoids any form of artificiality.

### Balance

Overall it is also important to ensure that the various aspects of our creative diversity go together to form a coherent, vibrant appearance. Balance has a key role to play here. It is based on a general sense of proportion and is expressed in the generosity of the design and the consistency of the overall impression. This calm tonality makes us recognizable, thereby giving us credibility, too. In other words: the balance is a gesture of tranquility and of a self-confidence that doesn't require exaggeration.

> Source: Audi's corporate website (www.audi.com),
> in combination with a number of newspaper articles

## Questions

1   Which segmentation variable(s) would you use if you were to segment the market for Audi? Explain briefly

2   Which segmentation strategy is used by Audi? Explain briefly.

3   A brand architecture can be described by using four brand levels. Use Audi as an example to illustrate each of these levels.

4   How would you describe Audi's brand structure?

5   a   Which brand values are emphasized in Audi's strategic vision 'Unleash the beauty of sustainable mobility'?

   b   To what extent do these brand values connect with what's being said about Audi in the rest of the case?

   c   Use the value compass to show whether Audi has positioned its brand consistently.

6   Which of Aaker's brand personality dimensions are used by Audi to profile itself? Explain briefly

7   a   Give an example of how an Audi commercial would look like if informational positioning were used.

   b   Give an example of how an Audi commercial would look like if transformational positioning were used.

   c   What would have your preference for the Audi brand: informational positioning or transformational positioning? Please explain your answer.

8   Use the information in the case to create a positioning statement for Audi.

9   The book distinguishes four types of brand names. What kind of brand name is Audi? Explain your answer

10  The three design principles (variety, honest, balance) guide Audi's visual identity. In what way do these design principles strengthen the brand positioning of Audi?

11  a   Provide an example of a category extension for Audi.

   b   Give an example of a line extension for Audi.

12  The book distinguishes four international advertising strategies. Which international advertising strategy would you advise Audi, given the image of the brand in the Netherlands and in China? Explain briefly.

# Part 4

# Implementation

Following the discussion of the situation analysis in Part 2, corporate and marketing objectives and strategies were reviewed in Part 3. These decisions are strategic in nature and in principle are related to a time frame longer than a single year. Chapter 11 stated explicitly that brand decisions require a long-term vision. Part 4 will focus on the implementation of strategic decisions. We distinguish two phases in the implementation: the elaboration of strategies into tactical marketing decisions and then their execution. The elaboration of strategies in marketing tactics is related to the use of the four P's: product, price, place, and promotion. This is the subject of Chapters 12 (first 3 P's) and 13 (communication). Chapter 14 discusses guidelines for the organization and implementation of marketing.

DOI: 10.4324/9781003381488-15

# Chapter 12

# Choice of product/ service, price, and channels

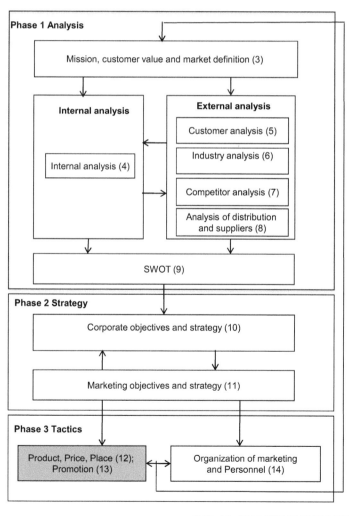

**Phase 1 Analysis**

Mission, customer value and market definition (3)

**Internal analysis**

Internal analysis (4)

**External analysis**

Customer analysis (5)

Industry analysis (6)

Competitor analysis (7)

Analysis of distribution and suppliers (8)

SWOT (9)

**Phase 2 Strategy**

Corporate objectives and strategy (10)

Marketing objectives and strategy (11)

**Phase 3 Tactics**

Product, Price, Place (12); Promotion (13)

Organization of marketing and Personnel (14)

DOI: 10.4324/9781003381488-16

## Key points in this chapter

- See the relationships between a chosen value strategy; the marketing strategy; and decisions about the marketing instruments, product, channels, price, and communication.
- Know which kind of decisions have to be made for the instruments product, price, and channels.
- Be able to strategically implement these three marketing instruments and see innovative opportunities.
- Know key issues about push/pull, intensity of distribution, forms of products, and distribution figures.

# Introduction

Chapter 11 provided an answer to the question: How are we going to compete with the brand? We paid attention to choosing the target audience and the brand positioning on the basis of the value strategy and the competitive advantage the company pursues. The brand elements (name and logo) also were dealt with. The marketing strategy provides the direction for the four marketing instruments (the marketing mix). Figure 12.1 shows the hierarchy of decisions within a company.

In the framework of this book, the review of the four Ps has been limited to a brief overview. For a more extensive description, see, for example, Kotler and Keller (2016). First, we discuss some general guidelines for the choice of the marketing mix (Section 12.1). Next, in Sections 12.2 through 12.4, we discuss all possible decisions that need to be made for three of the four elements of the marketing mix. In light of the important role of communication in building brand and customer loyalty, a separate Chapter 13 is devoted to marketing communication.

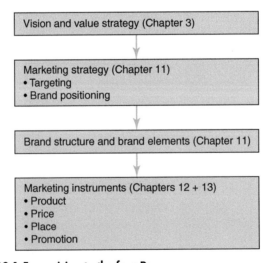

*Figure 12.1* **From vision to the four Ps**

# 12.1 Guidelines for the marketing mix

We propose that companies use three guidelines for choosing the marketing mix (Figure 12.2):

1 Strategic: think from the DNA and positioning of the brand (Section 12.1.1)
2 Innovative: stay ahead of competition (Section 12.1.2)
3 Positive: think in possibilities, not in limitations (Section 12.1.3).

## 12.1.1 Strategic thinking

In the previous chapter, the marketing strategy was formulated. All tactical decisions should be in line with the chosen target group and the brand's positioning (Figure 12.1). This is the only way to create a coherent brand image.

If, for example, a manufacturer of dog food has decided to focus on high-quality food (*product leadership*), the four elements of the marketing mix could be used as follows:

1 *Product*. Goal: quality product. Strategy: quality food in an exclusive and smaller package with a classy name.
2 *Price*. Goal: price. Perception: high price in relation to regular dog food. Strategy: price setting based on the market: higher price than regular dog food.
3 *Channels*. Goal: within half a year a non-weighted distribution spread of 95% in pet specialty stores and 70% in other retail businesses, and also online availability. Strategy: high margin for retailers.
4 *Communication*. Advertising goal: within one year an assisted name awareness of 90% among people with a dog. Strategy: television advertising with the message 'If you truly love your dog, you give it brand X'. In addition, hire three influential vloggers to spread the message online, plus advertising in women's magazines. Action goal: generate 40% 'trial' within half a year. Strategy: an introductory discount of €1.

Thus thinking from the DNA of the brand and consistency is important. However, this does not mean that things never have to be changed: on the contrary.

## 12.1.2 Innovation

To stay ahead of competition and to meet changing demands of customers, it is inevitable to innovate. So, innovation, creativity, thinking 'out of the box': all are part of entrepreneurship. Also from research, it appears that innovation is important. Barczak et al. (2009) shows that successful companies get about twice as much profit from innovations than less successful companies. O'Cass and Ngo (2007) show that an innovative culture has an even stronger relation to performance than market orientation. These authors also show that an innovative culture stimulates a market orientation (Figure 12.2), so innovation has a direct and indirect effect on performance.

Speaking of innovation, one should be clear about what is meant by 'innovation'. The most logical meaning of innovation is 'product innovation'. But there are more forms of innovation. In Chapter 3 we presented the Brand Benefitting Model. Linking the five

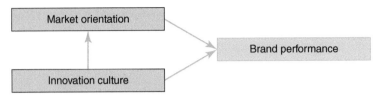

***Figure 12.2* Relation between innovation culture and brand performance**

Source: O'Cass and Ngo (2007)

possible benefits from this model to innovation, the following forms of innovation can be distinguished:

1   *Product innovation*: the 'classical' meaning of innovation: developing, for example, technological innovations to make better products (for example, Apple; see Case 12.1), but new food products are also examples.
2   *Service innovation*: trying to improve the experience of customers, by taking more time, being more customer friendly, providing a better guarantee, and so on.
3   *Cost innovation*: every company wants to have low costs, so striving to optimize the production process to minimize costs is always important. Technological innovations may help but also trying to buy at lower costs.
4   *Convenience innovation*: lowering other 'costs' of customers may also be a source of innovation, for example, lowering waiting times, facilitating availability (online), easier packaging, and so on.
5   *Sustainability innovation*: lowering the 'footprint' of the company or paying new attention to other forms of sustainability (one of the Sustainable Development Goals).
6   *Emotion innovation*: improving 'emotion' is mostly a task of communication, for example, by focusing on other values and by adjusting advertising. Innovation in communication is by definition 'creativity', which we will review in Chapter 13.

In literature, often a distinction is made between product innovation and process innovation. Both forms play a role in the six innovations mentioned. Companies can also choose combinations of these forms. The urgency for innovation and the choice of forms of innovation depends on the chosen customer value of a company. Not every company has to excel in product innovation: companies with quality as focus will especially continuously deal with product innovation.

## 12.1.3 Positive approach

Marketing is about finding and creating opportunities and about making customers happy. This means that marketers should have a kind of positive mindset. What great things is this company about, and how can we involve customers in the nice things that we do? Of course, being realistic is also important, but primarily a marketer will have to see opportunities.

A positive approach can be implemented in at least two ways: focusing on the 'pearls' of the company and creating so-called 9+-experiences.

## Case 12.1 Product innovation

### The power of Steve Jobs

Books have been written about it: the success of Apple and Steve Jobs (who passed away in 2012). Some attribute the success to Apple's marketing, for example, creating scarcity. Or that the products look nice. It is always difficult to pinpoint exactly why one company is more successful than others. The core of Apple's success, in our view, lies in the fact that Steve Jobs instinctively knew what people want 'in the future'. And he made those products. Jobs has never done market research on what kind of devices people want. Justly. Because people don't know that either. They don't know them yet. Product innovation must therefore often come mainly from the creativity of an 'inventor'. The problem with real inventors is that they are often quite technical in nature and have little sense of the psychology of customers. These character traits also lie in two different hemispheres. Normally you can only excel at one of the two. That often makes the combination of technology and marketing in one person difficult. Steve Jobs was an exception. A genius. He combined an incredible sense of estimating what consumers want and inventing the technology to make it happen. This requires 'thinking different'. That's Apple's success. Although Jobs was also (unknowingly or not) good at marketing, Apple's success is, in our view, not primarily a marketing story.

The *pearl principle* means that a company should stress the pearls from the portfolio of products and services. These pearls may be successful products but can also be small successes such as a testimonial of a happy customer. Focusing on these things is not only important for customers but also the staff. Good news stimulates being proud of the company where you work. The pearl principle has consequences for at least two marketing instruments:

- product/service: products/services should be developed to provide customers with the best (9+) experience;
- communication: the best products should receive most attention in communication.

*Figure 12.3* **Guidelines for marketing instruments**

The principle of a 9+-experience is related to the net promoter score introduced in Chapter 5. On the NPS scale of 'ambassadorship', it was noted that according to the theory, only scores of 9 and 10 will lead to 'Promoters'. So, companies should do their best to offer customer the best experiences. This can be realized with unexpected service, for example, a free gift.

Figure 12.3 summarizes this section with guidelines for marketing tactics. We will now go into the four marketing instruments, three in this chapter and the fourth, communication, in Chapter 13.

## 12.2 Products and services

### 12.2.1 Overview of product decisions

A product is an item that is offered in a market to satisfy a specific need. A product may be physical (a good such as a car) but also may be a service (a hairdresser), people (politics), places (vacation country), organizations (an employment agency), or an idea ('a good environment starts with you').

Decisions for the marketing instrument product are made at various levels in the company (Figure 12.4). This is different from the other three marketing instruments that are all real tactical decisions.

We now elaborate on the types of decisions mentioned in Figure 12.4.

1    Product mix decisions: choice of product groups (corporate strategy)
2    Product group decisions: brand portfolio (marketing strategy)
3    Product element decisions
    □    brand elements: name, logo and design (marketing strategy)
    □    product development and product improvement
    □    packaging
    □    services
    □    online products and services

*Figure 12.4* **Product decisions**

### Product mix decisions

Decisions at this level relate to the composition of the product mix (or the assortment) and therefore to the investments in strategic business units and product lines (introduction, growth, maintenance, harvest, elimination). Such decisions are made at the company level and are included in the formulation of the *corporate strategy* (see Chapter 10). Example: the decision by Unilever to stop with margarines.

### Product group decisions

Decisions at this level are related to the composition of the product group, that is, to the introduction, growth, and elimination of brands and/or products. The choice of the number of brands or products within a product group is determined to a large extent by the marketing strategy: the choice of the target audience and the desired positioning. After all, if the company wants to serve several segments, each with its own positioning, it may do this with different brands or products.

Connected to this issue is brand management: the choice of potential line extensions, and so on. Decisions about the composition of a product line and brand policy therefore correspond to a large degree to the *marketing strategy* and are made at a minimum at the SBU level. Example: the decision by Unilever to introduce a new brand in the soup category.

### Product element decisions

This relates to decisions about *individual* brands or products. Only these decisions may be considered *element decisions* with regard to the product, and they typically are the responsibility of a 'product or brand manager'. These decisions include the following:

1   The brand elements: name, logo, and design.
2   Product development and product improvements.
3   Packaging.
4   Service level.
5   Online products and services.

### Brand elements: name, logo, and design

These decisions are strongly related to the brand and are described in Chapter 11 (marketing strategy).

### Composition of the product and product improvements

This involves questions such as the following: What characteristics should make up the product (functional and symbolic)? To what extent should each characteristic be present? Which varieties should be chosen? This decision therefore involves 'technical' product development: the transformation of the product idea into a concrete product. Small product changes (product modifications such as taste alterations) are also included with composition decisions. In addition to decisions about the physical characteristics of a product, decisions about the 'added' characteristics are important, including the symbolic characteristics. All these decisions are closely related to the chosen brand positioning and in principle were determined at that stage. Because new product development is a very important part of product decisions, we deal with this separately in Section 12.2.2.

## Packaging

The packaging has typically been mostly 'technical/functional' in nature: Packaging serves as protection for the product and as such is of essential importance in the logistical trajectory (transport, storage, etc.). However, the increasing importance of positioning and brand policy has led to the process by which a second function of packaging is becoming increasingly important: the *communicative* function. Especially because of the increase in impulse shopping behavior, the external appearance of a product is playing an ever larger role. This applies not only to fast-moving consumer goods such as chips and shampoo but also to the packaging of durable consumer goods such as household appliances. As a result of the communicative role, packaging design has a relationship with the brand and sub brands.

## Service provision

Each product may be perceived as a service. In the context of building customer loyalty, it is desirable to bring about higher customer satisfaction through forms of service provision. This involves not just requested service provision such as giving warranties and processing complaints; it also involves unsolicited service provision with the eventual goal of exceeding the expectations of the customer (9+ experiences). For example, a detergent brand can provide online advice about cleaning. Providing service is strongly related to the personnel of a company: is the staff really customer friendly?

## Online products and services

Online presence is a prerequisite for every brand. Whether a company wants to offer products online (e-commerce) is a strategic decision. Online is a channel and as such part of the 'P of Place' (Section 12.4). But offering a service online also affects the service itself.

## 12.2.2 New product development

New product development is part of product innovation. We already argued that an innovative culture is positively related to performance. But how should a company organize this? Cooper (2008) argues that new product development should be an organized process:

1  The process starts with generating ideas. In this stage as many ideas as possible should be generated. Every idea is welcome and should not be criticized. However,

there should be goals for the brainstorming. Not creativity in general, but in the line of the strategy of the brand.

2   Then the ideas are screened.
3   In the next stage, business plans are made for the remaining ideas. Some ideas will be deleted.
4   Then the ideas are really transformed into products. Also in this stage, ideas can be deleted.
5   Then, some products will be tested; this can be a technical test and a market test.
6   Finally the remaining products are launched.

With respect to the Cooper model, some notes can be made about the way to discover new ideas: the role of the customer and the role of 'coincidence'. In practice, development of new products is often initiated from a technological perspective. Creative entrepreneurs try to figure out which new products can be made. The first thing we want to stress is that a customer orientation, although an important perspective in marketing, cannot always be taken as the starting point of innovation. For customers, it is difficult to imagine things that do not yet exist. Market research many years ago showed that hardly anyone would want to be reachable all the time and everywhere. . . . So, companies should be *inspired* by customers rather than being driven by their needs.

The second note we want to make is that new products can also pop up 'by coincidence'. This is what is called *serendipity*: the fact that researches are looking for new products but that they find other new products than they were looking for. A well-known example is Louis Pasteur, who coincidently found a vaccine against cholera. Serendipity does not mean that innovation should not be organized: knowledge (e.g. about customers) and experience are needed to transform ideas and products into successful innovations.

Finally, we make a note about the testing stage in product innovation. Testing implies making a 'prototype' and finding out whether the prototype works and/or is meeting the customer's needs. In this testing stage, design science can be applied. *Design science* (or design thinking) entails that testing be done in a number of rounds: first a basic version or even a draft of the new product is made and tested, then a improvement version is made and tested (Figure 12.5), and so on, until a product is developed that is convincing enough to launch.

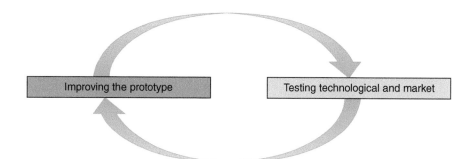

*Figure 12.5* **The principles of design science**

# 12.3 Pricing

## 12.3.1 Pricing decisions

Although price does not receive much attention in marketing literature, it is a vital instrument: Bijmolt et al. (2005) showed that the average price elasticity is –2.6, which is extremely high.

The price is a characteristic of a product. Therefore, the marketing mix element of price cannot be considered separately from the element of product. If the company alters the physical characteristics of the product, this almost automatically will have consequences for the price. There is also a direct relationship with positioning: a quality image often is related to a high price. Conversely, many consumers use price as an indicator of quality: a high price indicates high quality.

Figure 12.6 shows three pricing decisions that have to be made.

### Price policy

Price policy involves the description of policy rules in relation to price. The goal is to create a framework of parameters that the various decision makers in a company can use to make price decisions. In the price policy, items such as the following are determined:

- The relation of the price to that of *competitors*.
- Rules about any *reactions* to price changes by competitors.
- The extent to which price promotions are used.

In Section 7.6, we argued that companies sometimes react too much on each other, leading to too many promotions. We also argued that price promotions may dilute the brand. So, price policies could be more strict on these issues.

### Price strategies

Price strategies involve long-term decisions about the price. These strategies concretely involve decisions regarding the following:

1   Price policy
2   Price strategies
   ☐   Product line pricing
   ☐   Price agreements with retailers
   ☐   Skimming or penetration
   ☐   Dynamic pricing
   ☐   Pricing of sustainable products

3   Determination of the price

**Figure 12.6 Price decisions**

- The pricing of products in a *product line* (e.g., the choice of the price difference between types of video cameras of a single brand or between different types of packaging of one laundry detergent).
- Price agreements with *retailers*: recommended retail price, minimum price, and so on.
- *New products:* using a *skimming strategy* or a *penetration strategy*. In skimming, the company begins with a high price and then gradually drops that price over time. This strategy serves to recover the development costs quickly and is often used for durable consumer goods such as mobile phones. With a penetration strategy, the company starts with a low price that is increased over time. This strategy has the goal of quickly achieving a high market share by simulating trial purchases and is often used for nondurable consumer goods, for example, the introduction of a new snack.
- *Dynamic pricing:* the price can change from one moment to another. This is well known when booking airline tickets. Seasonal prices are also an example. And some supermarkets offer products a bit cheaper when they are almost at the sell-by date.
- *Sustainability pricing:* making a sustainable product lower priced then the non-sustainable alternatives.

## Case 12.2 Economic crisis and pricing

### Consumers switch to private labels

The high inflation stimulates the sales of private labels (retail brands). Retail brands are by definition cheaper than manufacturer owned brands ('A-brands'), and currently consumers do not want to pay more for better quality. According to Nielsen, the financial crises in 2003 and 2007 had the same effect. Marketing professor Steenkamp of the University of North Carolina knows from his research that in many countries the market share of private labels increased during recessions, and that in better times only one third of their loss in market share is restored by A-brands.

Source: *Financial Daily*, 20 March 2023, p. 22.

### Determination of the price

After the price policy and the price strategy have been formulated, the highness of the price should be determined. The definitive price determination is determined by the following elements:

■ The costs (source: internal analysis).
■ The market: What is the status of the price knowledge, price perception, and price sensitivity of the final customers?
■ The prices of the competitors.
■ The price policy and the price strategies.
■ Other factors, such as psychological price borders ($199 instead of $200).

## 12.3.2 Investigating price sensitivity

Since consumer needs are the core of marketing, knowing how customers perceive your pricing is essential. There are various methods for researching the price sensitivity of products, including the following five:

1  *Causal models.* This involves analyzing time series of sales and price (and other elements of the marketing mix) with the aid of *regression analysis*: a researcher tries to find relationships between variables by applying statistical methods. This is the only method that uses actual behavior. A related method is discussed in Section 5.5.5 and entails correlating price perceptions with brand preference. The resulting estimated parameter is a metric for price sensitivity.

2  *Online experimentation.* For online products and services, applying different prices in time (dynamic pricing) provides insights in price effects. But also at one moment in time, different groups can be offered different prices ('A/B testing').

3  *Conjoint measurement (see also Section 5.4.1).* Respondents are asked to arrange a number of 'products' (combinations of characteristics, including, e.g., the price) in order of preference; this is followed by a subsequent calculation of which characteristics are the most important. This can also indicate the influence of price changes on the preference.

4  *The brand-price trade-off (BPTO) method.* In this method, respondents have to choose from several brands at certain prices, after which the price of the chosen brand is increased and the respondent has to make a new choice, after which the price of that brand is increased, and so on. Based on the various choices the respondents make, it is possible to calculate preference shares (a type of market share) of the brands at various prices, which in turn measures price sensitivity.

5  *Price acceptance research.* This involves asking people which prices they consider cheap, expensive, too cheap, or too expensive, after which an acceptable price range can be determined.

A disadvantage of the latter two methods is that respondents are asked more or less directly to indicate the price sensitivity. Such a strong focus on the price apart from other product characteristics may have an impact on the reliability of the results. Conjoint measurement does not have that disadvantage, since it approaches the choice method of consumers closely without placing the emphasis on a single characteristic such as the price. Causal models have the advantage of measuring real behavior but can be used only for markets with sufficient data (especially food products). Conjoint measurements may be used for all product categories.

# 12.4 Distribution

## 12.4.1 Overview of decisions

Channels ('place' or the distribution) form the connection between the company and the final users of the product. Many years ago this was about physical distribution via intermediate stakeholders. The possibility of online shopping changed the world. As we already argued in Chapter 8: make your own webshop (including logistics), and you have a distribution ('reach') of 100%. Having good distribution is very important and may even produce a sustainable competitive advantage. For example, the global and very intensive distribution of Coca-Cola is a clear competitive advantage for this product. Even in remote locations in the Himalayas, Coca-Cola is for sale. From academic research, it appears that the distribution elasticity is large (Hanssens, 2015). This means that sales are strongly affected by the level of (physical) distribution. Figure 12.7 gives an overview of distribution decisions. These decisions will in large part be based on the distribution analysis, reviewed in Chapter 8.

## 12.4.2 Level of availability

An important strategic decision for the marketing instrument distribution is stated in terms of *availability*: 'To what extent and where should the product be available so that those in the target audience are able to obtain it?' So, availability consists of two elements: quantitative (the extent to which; this section) and qualitative (where; Section 12.4.3). The quantitative element may be measured on the basis of the *nonweighted or weighted distribution* (see Section 8.3.2); also, visibility on the shelf is measurable. An example of a distribution objective is: 'With our brand B, we want to increase the weighted distribution from 80% to 90% within one year'.

1. Level of availability (objective)
2. Determining preference for distribution channels
   - ☐ Number and type of channels (e.g. online or not)
   - ☐ Type of intermediate link
   - ☐ Shelf position

3. Management of the distribution channels
   - ☐ Push and/or pull strategy
   - ☐ Collaboration

**Figure 12.7 Distribution decisions***

* We do not include logistic decisions with marketing mix decisions

With respect to the intended level of physical distribution, a distinction is made between three possibilities:

1 *intensive distribution* (as large a number of distribution points as possible)
2 *selective distribution* (a limited number of distribution points)
3 *exclusive distribution* (in a certain region, only a single distributor).

A 'good' distribution does not have to be an intensive one. The intensity decision depends particularly on the type of product that is being offered. In this context, a distinction is made between three types of products:

1 *Convenience goods*. These are products consumers will take little trouble to purchase. Examples are almost all food products. These products should in principle be distributed intensively.
2 *Shopping goods*. The consumer is prepared to make an effort (travel time, collection of information) to purchase this kind of product. This mostly involves higher-priced products such as furniture and clothing. Such products require a selective distribution.
3 *Specialty goods*. These are products with a very high attractive value to the customer. The customer therefore is prepared to make great efforts to purchase them. Examples are exclusive cars and warehouses with a strong attraction. These 'products' can succeed with an exclusive distribution.

For realizing a certain level of (physical) distribution, a company is dependent on other stakeholders. The choice of the intended availability can thus be seen as an 'objective', and with the other decisions (management of the channels; Section 12.4.4), this has to be realized. But first we pay attention to 'where do we want to be available?'

## 12.4.3 Where do we want to be available?

A company should first determine what the 'ideal' distribution picture looks like. Whether this is possible depends partly on the management strategies that will be used in the third step with regard to the distribution channels. In designing the optimal distribution structure, four elements are relevant:

1 *The number of channels*. Especially if a company serves different markets, a choice of several channels is possible. For example, a drinks manufacturer may supply the hospitality industry via the wholesale liquor trade, whereas a food products retailer is supplied with its products via the food products wholesale business. An insurance company may choose more than one channel: direct delivery to customers, via insurance brokers, via banks, and via employers. Clearly, online channels are increasingly used (see Case 12.3). Every company will have to decide on the importance of offline and online channels. Many companies nowadays use both and are thus applying *multi-channel distribution*. However, some companies deliberately choose online only (Case 12.4).
2 *The types of intermediate links and the retail brand*. A food products manufacturer should choose within the group of retailers, for example, supermarkets, discounters,

## Case 12.3 Online shopping

### India aims to 'democratise' online shopping with ecommerce network

India is preparing to launch a government-backed ecommerce initiative to 'democratise' online shopping in an ambitious attempt to challenge the dominance of companies such as Amazon and Wal-Mart-owned Flipkart in one of the world's fastest-growing markets. Open Network for Digital Commerce (ONDC), a non-profit company set up by India's commerce ministry last year, is holding trials in more than 85 cities, including the tech hub of Bangalore, ahead of a nationwide launch next year. While companies such as Amazon run proprietary services controlling everything from vendor registration and delivery to customer experience, ONDC is an 'interoperable' network, where buyers and sellers can transact regardless of the apps or services they are using. The open-source network would allow a customer using one app, such as fintech services provider Paytm, to find and order groceries from a vendor registered to another platform, such as small business hub eSamudaay. This can then be shipped by whichever alternative platform, such as delivery service Dunzo, is able to do it at the fastest and lowest rate. Indian authorities argue that opening up transactions across platforms in this way will create a vastly larger pool of sellers and consumers and result in lower costs and turbocharged ecommerce growth in the country of 1.4 billion. They point to the success of mobile payment network UPI, developed in 2016, as a blueprint.

Source: *Financial Times*, 28 December 2022

neighborhood shops, and specialty stores. Within these types a company should make choices about the specific retailers and also which specific retail brand, such as Wal-Mart. These decisions can be seen as targeting distributors. An example is Unilever, who decided in 2016 to also be available at European discounters such as Lidl.

3   *The shelf position.* The position of a brand on the shelf and the number of *facings* (visible units of the product) may have an important impact on the purchasing

### Case 12.4 Online only

### Picnic: the super market on wheels

Picnic was started in 2015 by some young entrepreneurs. Since then, sales have grown fast. The concept is clear: Picnic delivers your daily supermarket products at home at a lower price than all other (off- and online) supermarkets, including market leaders such as Albert Heijn and Jumbo. Picnic is able to do this, since its DNA is, among others, in big data analytics. Picnic is continuously seeking the optimal model for ordering and delivering, and is, for example, not delivering 24/7. Also, they strongly innovate in their apps to enable simple and personalized shopping for their customers. Finally, they have a less broad assortment than competitors but broad enough to fulfil consumers' needs. Picnic is also active in Germany and France.

opportunity. The optimal place on the shelf depends on issues such as the positioning in relation to competitors that was determined in the marketing strategy.

## 12.4.4 Management of the distribution channels

If an 'ideal' channel has been designed, the next step is an attempt to achieve the established objectives. Since distribution channels consist of companies and people that typically are not under the company's control, strategies need to be chosen for that purpose. This also applies if the company wants to make changes in the existing distribution channel. As a result of the strong concentration in the food retail business in some countries, manufacturers of food products have two target audiences: the distributors and the final customers. In principle, two distribution strategies may be used:

1   *A push strategy*. With this strategy, the company tries to 'push' the product through the channel. Tools that may be used for this include trade margins and trade discounts and the efforts of the sales staff. So, 'push' does not mean 'pushing the consumer' but pushing through the chain.

2  *A pull strategy.* With this strategy, the company tries to 'pull' the product through the channel because an important demand for the product is created at the consumer level. The most important tools here are advertising and promotional actions.

In current practice, push and pull strategies are used in combination: it is important to establish a strategy toward the distributors and also to strengthen and maintain a consumer need. In this area, there is an increasing amount of *collaboration* between manufacturers and distributors. The interests of distributors and manufacturers also are parallel to a large extent: obtaining the highest sales (and profit) possible from the final customers. These objectives can be achieved better through a collective and therefore synchronized effort rather than without consultation. If a retailer is not sufficiently involved in the planning of, for example, a promotional action of the manufacturer, there is a chance that the retailer will run out of stock.

A manufacturer should therefore see the intermediate links as collaboration partners; this leads to a collective effort, and the distribution structure becomes an effective competition tool. In lines of business in which the power of distributors is concentrated (such as the food industry), *account management* is often chosen: an organizational structure that holds individual people at the manufacturer responsible for the relationship with and sales to a single customer (an 'account', mostly a retailer such as Wal-Mart). The relevant account managers then take over some responsibilities from the 'classic' sales managers (sales staff, representatives). In the food industry, the collaboration with retailers is so advanced that some manufacturers attune their decisions about the breadth of a product group (such as new product introductions and their timing) to the wishes of the retailer. This is called *category management*.

The essence of category management is that both the manufacturer and the retailer no longer think in terms of brand and products but instead consider the interest and profit of product groups as a whole. In addition, they need to consider each other's interests. Category management implies that that the manufacturer and the retailer jointly determine and manage the assortment within a product category. The planning of promotional actions is also increasingly attuned to the wishes of retailers. In general, promotions (if paid for by the manufacturer) are an important tool for retailers, especially if the promotions are made exclusively with the retailer.

This section was about the management of, among others, retailers, from the perspective of the manufacturer. A manufacturer has to develop marketing activities towards consumers and retailers. Retailers also have their own marketing to get consumers into their shops and to optimize the shopping experience of consumers. Sometimes the word 'shopper marketing' is used to indicate the combination of both forms of marketing towards shoppers, which is in our view a bit confusing since every consumer is a 'shopper' when he buys something (online or offline).

## Summary

In deciding on the elements of the marketing mix, three principles are important: use strategic thinking (on the basis of the chosen target audience and positioning), be innovative, and be positive (e.g. focusing on pearls). Product decisions relate to decisions about the choice of varieties, the design, and the service. As a result of the necessity of pursuing customer satisfaction, competitive advantages based on products and services are very important. Also the development of improved and new products and thus innovation contributes to better performance. Innovation may focus on the product, service, costs, convenience, sustainability, and 'emotion'.

Price decisions relate to the interpretation of the price policy, price strategies (such as skimming and penetration, dynamic pricing, and sustainable pricing), and price determination. Distribution decisions relate to the required availability, the choice of channels, and the management of channels. Online channels are increasingly important in reaching the shopping consumer. Since in many countries retailers are powerful, a good relation between manufacturers and retailers is important.

## Case Nespresso: exclusive coffee

**Nespresso – 'exclusive coffee' for a mass market – is the first coffee to be presented as a fashion brand: with its own stores and George Clooney as 'Mr. Nespresso'**

No, it was not easy to make a nice cup of Nespresso at home, according to an older lady who tasted a 'new taste' at the bar of a downtown Nespresso boutique. 'Not new taste but variety' emphasizes the girl behind the bar. 'It is not coffee with a taste, it is a bean from the Kivu lake in Rwanda with a subtle refreshing taste and delicate aftertaste'.

'Variety', repeats the sixty-year old lady submissively. Anyway, at first she was struggling with her Nespresso machine at home; she kept pressing the button and there was only a small stream of water. 'The Umutima is a limited edition', explains the barista, imperturbable about the new coffee variety. 'With a fruity initial taste and a full body afterwards'.

Nespresso creates experience. The ristretto or the lungo leggero are not just coffee; they are grand crus. A whole wall of the Nespresso shop is designed to display the grand cru cups. They have their own website, where the terms 'unique', 'sophisticated' and 'precious' dance on the screen. In the slick atmosphere of the Nespresso coffee shops ('Boutiques'), the spicy taste can be tried free of charge. On a regular Monday afternoon, there are already dozens of customers who want to give it a try.

Nespresso is for everyone, and yet there is an aura of exclusivity around the brand. What do you want, with a stylish and politically correct superstar like George Clooney as the face of the advertising campaign, own stores in the world's most expensive shopping streets and prices that are both towering and accessible? Thirty euro cents can be extremely expensive for a cup of home coffee – a basic coffee prepared at home will cost you 2 cents per cup – but still 30 cents sounds to most people like close to nothing, certainly much cheaper than a double latte macchiato in a trendy coffee place.

Democratized luxury is what marketing experts call it: costly, but feasible, just like the Chanel lipstick and the Prada sunglasses for the consumer who buys the rest of his outfit at Zara. It is therefore no coincidence that Nespresso coffee and appliances are marketed as a fashion brand. For example, Nespresso has its own glossy magazine, complete with a Vogue-like appearance in which the 'legendary star photographer' Michel Comte is presented, fashionably posing with his chin in his hands. He prefers to capture 'humanitarian images' in war-torn countries like Afghanistan, but he also signed up for Nespresso's most recent advertising campaign.

Then there are the Nespresso flagship stores. For example, there is a large flagship store of the brand on the Paris Champs-Élysées, right next to prestigious neighbors such as Louis Vuitton and Hugo Boss. More than 1,500 square meters of coffee in shiny aluminum cups, espresso machines – only suitable for Nespresso, of course – and mocha-scented candles at €35, in a decor of gold leaf, mirror walls, and chandeliers. The festive opening a few years ago, in the absence of George Clooney, was cheered up by movie star Sharon Stone and was organized according to the best traditions of the Paris fashion world: flashy cameras, long lines and champagne. 'Brilliant' and 'superslick', applauds a branding expert about the Nespresso marketing strategy. It is 'emotion' and about customers who want an 'experience' instead of an old-fashioned cup of coffee. 'Nespresso radiates: we are unique. Look at the fancy design of the Nespresso boutiques, the colours of the rows of cups. Who wouldn't like to spoil himself with that?'

Nespresso – part of the Swiss company Nestlé, the largest food group in the world, with brands such as Nescafé, Maggi, Buitoni and Perrier – is the European market leader in packaged coffee. It has been growing at a rapid pace for more than 15 years. In 2020, estimated global sales were over 5 billion euros, and the brand aims to grow with a significant percentage for the coming years. The COVID-19 pandemic turned out to be a good thing for Nespresso: the brand offers exclusive delight, even when all restaurants are closed.

The Nespresso club counts more than 5 million members worldwide: customers who order their coffee via the internet or by telephone. Because that's how it works: the coffee-per-serving packaged in an aluminum cap and only suitable for Nespresso machines produced by a limited number of manufacturers including Krups, Siemens, and DeLonghi is not for sale in the supermarket but is delivered at home, or you buy it in the Nespresso stores. With this distribution system, Nespresso keeps the price at a certain level, because supermarkets cannot offer the product at a discount. It can be compared with a box of exclusive chocolate bonbons: not only do people pay 30 euros for a couple of chocolates, they pay the price because they feel that they are buying something special. The price level of the corresponding coffee machines, however, varies as much as the profile of the target audience. Prices vary from the Essenza of less than 150 euros to Porsche designs of almost 1,000 euros. But you can also get them for free: in many subscription plans of glossy magazines, the coffee machines are given away for free. But Nespresso is more than just marketing. Friend and foe agree that you make an excellent espresso, macchiato, or cappuccino with it. Otherwise Michelin-starred restaurants like the world-famous the Fat Duck in London would not offer Nespresso.

The secret is the aluminum packaging, which ensures that the coffee does not lose taste. Coffee that is exposed to the air loses most of the aromas within 72 hours. The disadvantage of all that aluminum is that it is not good for the environment. But there are recycling systems for that, according to Nespresso. In Switzerland, next to practically every glass container, there is a container for the cups. The company also strives for corporate social responsibility in the field of coffee production: 35% of the beans come from the AAA program, which guarantees sustainable cultivation and a good price for coffee farmers. Once upon a time (in the 1970s), Nestlé struggled with an image problem, when the company sold milk powder for baby food in developing countries. Because of the contaminated water on the spot – water was needed to make milk out of the milk powder – breastfeeding was a safer choice. A call for an international boycott was the result. Nestlé never wanted that type of publicity again.

But George Clooney also received some critical questions from the press. How could he justify advertising for a multinational, a journalist once asked. Clooney replied that he works for Nespresso, not for Nestlé. When that turned out not to be enough, he replied, annoyed: 'I am not going to apologise to you for trying to make a living once in a while. I find that an irritating question'.

## The introduction campaign of Nespresso in 2006

Nespresso was launched in 2006. Back then, George Clooney was already the central figure of the brand.

Nespresso hired actor George Clooney for the introduction campaign for a role in the film *The Boutique*. The film lasted 50 seconds and was directed by Michel Gondry (*Eternal Sunshine of the Spotless Mind*).

The film marks the kick-off of Nespresso's first ever celebrity campaign. In the film, Clooney (himself drinking Nespresso, of course) is involved in a comical misunderstanding with two nice ladies in a Nespresso boutique.

The film was shot in Los Angeles, but the production company had the Paris Nespresso flagship boutique on the Avenue Victor Hugo rebuilt on the film set specifically for this purpose. For the realization of the film, a large quantity of coffee, machines, and accessories was shipped, with which 38,500 cups of coffee could be prepared.

Olivier Quillet, international marketing director of Nespresso, explains: 'The Nespresso brand represents a number of values, such as style, refinement and charm. George Clooney also embodies these qualities, making him a perfect ambassador for our brand'.

From May 2006, the film was shown in cinemas and on television throughout Europe. George Clooney could also be seen in the Nespresso print campaign. The photography for the print campaign was in the hands of celebrity photographer Michel Comte.

## Questions

1. Nespresso aims to grow with a significant percentage for the coming years. Is this a corporate, a marketing, or a marketing mix objective? Please explain your answer.

2. The book distinguishes five forms of innovation. As which form(s) of innovation would you label the introduction of Nespresso in 2006?

3. Nespresso is not sold in supermarkets. As a result, supermarkets cannot offer the product at a discount, and the 'sophisticated' image is not affected. Why does Nespresso then allow glossy magazines to offer the coffee machines for free to attract subscribers?

4. Define a price objective for Nespresso.

5. Would you recommend a penetration strategy for the coffee cups when introducing a new taste variant for Nespresso? Why (not)?

6. Which functions does the packaging of the Nespresso cups fulfil?

7. a Does it make sense to define the distribution objective for Nespresso in terms of (weighted or non-weighted) distribution? Explain your answer.

   b Define an appropriate distribution objective for Nespresso.

8. Describe the distribution channel structure of Nespresso.

9. Describe the distribution intensity of Nespresso. How does this relate to the type of product (convenience, shopping, or specialty good) that Nespresso aims to be?

10. Part of the Nespresso image of exclusivity is due to its limited distribution, in which the Nespresso Club and online sales played an important role. Do you think that, nowadays, online sales still contribute to an exclusive image? Explain your answer.

# Chapter 13

# Marketing communications

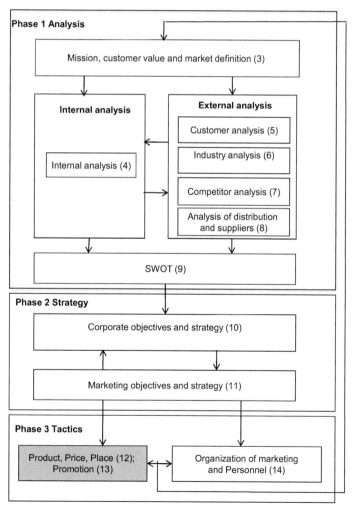

**Phase 1 Analysis**

Mission, customer value and market definition (3)

**Internal analysis**

Internal analysis (4)

**External analysis**

Customer analysis (5)

Industry analysis (6)

Competitor analysis (7)

Analysis of distribution and suppliers (8)

SWOT (9)

**Phase 2 Strategy**

Corporate objectives and strategy (10)

Marketing objectives and strategy (11)

**Phase 3 Tactics**

Product, Price, Place (12); Promotion (13)

Organization of marketing and Personnel (14)

DOI: 10.4324/9781003381488-17

## Key points in this chapter

- See the relationships between the marketing strategy and communication.
- Know how to formulate objectives for communication
- Know the steps in the communication planning process.
- Understand the role of companies and advertising agencies.
- Be able to make a communication plan.
- Know how to measure communication effects.

## Introduction

The 'P' of promotion consists of communication and 'actions' (promotions). Communication then involves informing and convincing the target audience of certain characteristics of the brand; thus, it has not only short-term goals but also long-term goals. 'Actions' (*sales promotion*) refer to all short-term efforts to achieve more sales by making temporary changes in the four Ps. To connect with daily usage, we use marketing communication as an umbrella concept that includes all sale promotion tools. We call the steps that must be taken to arrive at the execution of the marketing communication the communication planning process.

Clearly, the way companies and people communicate has drastically changed since the invention of the internet. So, online communication including social media became an important part of marketing communication and will be treated in this chapter as such.

In the first section we provide an overview of the steps in communication planning. Then in Sections 13.2 through 13.11, all steps are reviewed, and a separate section (13.9) is devoted to online communication.

## 13.1 Steps in communication planning

A well-known principle with regard to marketing communication is the concept of integrated marketing communication. This concept means that a company has all means of communication (such as social media and TV) coordinated in such a way that a consistent and clear message is communicated to the target groups. With good coordination of media, for example, offline and online, synergy can occur: a strengthening joint effect (Naik & Peters, 2009; Pauwels et al., 2017). Today we also often talk about customer experience management (CXM) to indicate that it is about the total experience of customers that 'must be right'. The large difference with integrated marketing communication is that CXM is about the 'integration' of all resources (so, not only communication) from the first contact moment of the customer through his/her entire customer journey.

The implementation of this is quite difficult in practice because there are many channels, often involving several employees. The alignment must also take place with the oral communication, from the first contact of a customer with the company. This chapter is mainly about the creation of a communication plan and/or campaign and what follows here are the logical steps to do so. You could say this more or less more 'precedes' the realization of customer contacts. The closing paragraph pays separate attention to CXM.

**Tasks of the company**

1. Determination of the target audience (section 13–2)
2. Selection of a proposition (section 13–3)
3. Communication objectives and communication budget (section 13–4)
4. Briefing for the communication consulting agency (section 13–5)

**Tasks for the communication consulting agency**

5. Creation and execution (section 13–6)
6. Pretesting (section 13.7)
7. Communication instruments (section 13.8 and 13.9 (online))

**Task of the company**

8. Monitoring and effect research (section 13.10)
9. Customer experience management (section 13.11)

*Figure 13.1* **Steps in the communication planning process**

Organizations can call in all kinds of agencies that deal with communication to help. In this section we therefore assume that a company engages a communications consultancy (also simply referred to as an 'agency'). Sometimes this will not happen, for example, in SMEs. Figure 13.1 contains an overview of the steps to be taken in the communication planning process.

The company (or 'advertiser') has the primary task of choosing a communication target audience and proposition (message) and determining the communication goals and a corresponding budget. In practice, the actual 'imagining' and elaboration of the communication expressions and the selection of the media are delegated to a communication consulting agency (also called an advertising agency). Ideally, the advertiser will to perform the measurement of results afterward. Another task of the company is to integrate all communication and to manage the total customer experience.

## 13.2 Determination of the target audience

The first step to be taken by the company is to define the communication target audience: To whom do we want to tell something? The communication target audience does not have to correspond to the marketing target audience (see Section 11.2). Often the communication target audience is broader: not only should potential buyers be reached but also the most important influencing groups. In this context, it is relevant to know who plays which role within a household in the purchasing process of a product category (initiator, decision maker, etc.). For example, in toys, the mother or father is the final decision maker, and women have a large input into the brand choice for cars. Older people often let themselves be guided by the opinions of their children and grandchildren for certain purchases. Another item that plays a role is whether the goal is to hold onto users or to attract new buyers.

The communication target audience should be described with as much detail as possible so that the advertising agency has as much information as it can have for the development of the campaign. The best results are obtained by describing the target audience as an individual based on the dimensions reviewed in Chapter 5:

■ general background variables
■ product category–related variables
■ brand-related variables.

A different categorizations is more related to communication decisions (Figure 13.2):

1 Strategic dimensions
2 Creative dimensions
3 Media dimensions

Strategic dimensions are dimensions that are related to the actual use of the brand or product. For example, an important choice is whether the manager wants to communicate mostly with users or with nonusers. Creative dimensions are dimensions that in effect relate to customer values: the 'reasons' for brand use. These dimensions give the creative types at the advertising agency an impression of the relationship between the target audience and the brand. The so-called media dimensions refer to the general characteristics of the target audience (independent of the brand): 'hard' background variables such as age and income class as well as qualitative variables such as habits, hobbies, and interests ('lifestyle'). These dimensions are important in the creative process: What kind of person is the average user? This is closely related to the brand personality: an average user can also be described by describing the brand as a person. The second use for media dimensions is related to the formulation of communication objectives and the execution of media planning. For both steps it is desirable to describe the target audience in measurable terms.

Comparing Figure 13.2 with the three categories from Section 5.2.2, it can be seen that in the end the same variables are used.

1. **Strategic dimensions: brand use**
   ■ Users or nonusers
   ■ Trial purchases, habit purchases, brand loyalty
   ■ Preference for our brand or for that of the competitor

2. **Creative dimensions: relationship between brand and user**
   ■ How, when, and where does the target audience use the product?
   ■ What does the brand mean to the target audience?
   ■ What is important to the target audience?
   ■ What are the current brand associations?

3. **Media dimensions: users' profile or "brand personality"**
   ■ What is the demographic and socioeconomic profile?
   ■ What is the "lifestyle" (including media consumption)?

*Figure 13.2* **Dimensions for formulating the communication target audience**

## 13.3 Selecting a proposition

The proposition is the message of the communication: What does the brand or product provide to the consumer to make his or her life a little easier or richer or to solve a problem? The proposition proceeds from the positioning that has been chosen for the brand and is in effect the simplified-language version of the promise that is being made. The proposition may be deduced from this type of positioning. Many designations for the choice of the proposition are used in practice, such as 'advertising strategy', 'copy strategy', and 'creative strategy'. The last designation incorrectly creates the assumption that the proposition has to be created by the advertising agency.

In selecting the core message, it is important to reason strongly from the perspective of the target audience. In effect, only two questions need to be asked:

1    How does the target audience perceive our brand now (*image*)?
2    How do we want them to perceive our brand (*identity*)?

When image and identity correspond, there is no communication problem. However, if there are differences, it is the role of communication to adjust the image. The way in which both questions are elaborated upon depends on the level of customer values that is important in the product category: Is the main focus on instrumental values (physical product characteristics) or on final values (abstract product characteristics)?

Instrumental values are very important in 'problem-solving' product categories such as laundry detergents and feminine hygiene products. Procter & Gamble is very active in these markets. For choosing a communication message Procter uses the so-called Admap (Figure 13.3).

The Admap entails four simple questions that have to be answered:

1    What is the target group currently doing? For example: using competitive brand G.
2    What is the target group currently thinking? For example: competitive brand G removes potato peels better.
3    What should the target group think? For example: our brand X removes potato peels better.
4    What should the target group do? For example: buy our brand X.

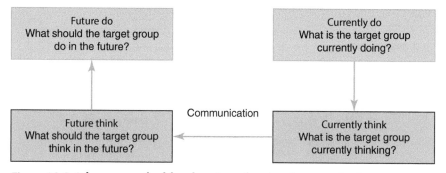

*Figure 13.3* **Admap: a method for choosing a functional communication message**

The gap between 2 and 3 can be resolved through communication (a campaign that shows that potato peels are removed).

This method is suitable for adjusting instrumental values but less suitable for adjusting abstract values. The reason for this is that an abstract image cannot easily be adjusted with communication since a brand cannot suddenly start portraying a different personality (consistency; see Section 11.3.4).

To develop a proposition in which *abstract values* play an important role, the technique of *perceptual mapping* is often used (see Section 5.4.4). In such depictions it is easy to represent a 'desired position' (identity) and therefore include the way the company wants to adjust the image. The fact that this is possible only on a limited scale implies that only limited movements are feasible in such image pictures. The *semantic differential* (Section 5.4.4) is also a useful tool in this regard.

## 13.4 Communication objectives and communication budget

### 13.4.1 Measuring results and effects

A *communication objective* is a desired communication effect. Communication objectives are a tool for the communication planning process. If the requirements for useful objectives are met (specific, measurable, ambitious, realistic, timed: SMART), communication objectives are the standards that can be used to evaluate whether a campaign has been successful. Communication objectives therefore are very closely related to the *measurement of results*. Conversely, measuring results has little value if no objectives have been formulated. Thus, the measurement of results means that a measurement is taken of the extent to which the objectives have been achieved. To make it plausible that the measured results have actually been 'caused' by the communication, *effect research* should be performed in addition to the measurement of results. Effect research generally involves a search for a causal relationship between an 'input variable' (in this case communication) and an output variable (communication goal). Figure 13.4 summarizes these issues.

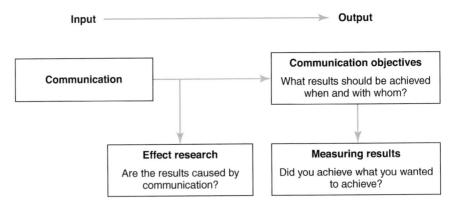

*Figure 13.4* **Measurement of results and effect research**

Although formulating goals and measuring results are necessary from a planning perspective, in practice this is done infrequently. Usually objectives are mentioned, but they are often not quantitative. Sometimes quantitative 'advertising goals' are formulated, but they often appear to be related to coverage. Although coverage is a required condition to achieve real effects, coverage goals in themselves cannot be interpreted as effect objectives. Examples of true communication (effect) objectives include advertising awareness, brand awareness, and brand associations.

## 13.4.2 Choice of communication objectives

In choosing communication objectives, the question is 'What do we want to achieve for whom and when?' We have already discussed the 'for whom' question. We now discuss the question 'What do we want to achieve?'

A goal of communication will always be to achieve more sales, make more profit, attract more visitors, and so forth. Yet goals such as market share are not suitable as a communication objective, since those types of items are determined by many factors besides communication. Sales variables may be mentioned as objectives in communication, but then they should be marketing objectives. 'True' communication objectives are deduced from the marketing goals.

Various diagrams are presented in the literature for the purpose of selecting variables that may be used as communication goals. Most of them are based on the classic hierarchy of communication effects: knowledge (cognition), feeling (affection), and behavior (conation). Quantifying these knowledge, feeling, and behavior effects is very useful, but research shows that a hierarchy of effects cannot be demonstrated (Vakratsas & Ambler, 1999). Another disadvantage of classifications that are based on hierarchical models is that no explicit relationship is established with the input: the communication itself. A diagram that actually does this is the so-called 'advertising response matrix' of Franzen (1998), which is shown (in a revised way) in Figure 13.5.

The advertising response matrix indicates that in effectiveness research (and therefore also in the formulation of objectives), three levels should be distinguished:

1 Communication input.
2 Output at the individual level.
3 Effects at the market level.

### 1 Communication input

The communication input level represents the communication effort. It consists of a qualitative component (category A: the characteristics of the campaign) and a quantitative component (category B: the weight of the campaign). Qualitative aspects are the substantive characteristics of the campaign (e.g., in advertising at McDonald's, a menu or Big Mac in the picture or not, using humor or not) and the physical variables (the length of the advertising spot, using outdoor advertising or not, etc.). Quantitative aspects are the efforts expressed in terms of volume (number of seconds) or money (e.g., the advertising budget portion *share of voice*; McDonald's share in total fast-food advertising expenditures is 50%) or the achieved coverage (e.g., gross rating points [GRPs]: percent viewing

**Communication input**

| | | |
|---|---|---|
| A. | Characteristics of the advertisement (campaign) Choice of media | ■ Rough drafts, creative execution variables ■ Physical variables (length of advertising spot, format, color, etc.) |
| B. | Communication expenditures | ■ Volume: millimeters, seconds ■ Expenditures: money (share of voice: spending share) |
| | Confrontation (exposure) and reach | ■ Reach: absolute or relative [e.g. gross rating points (GRPs): percent viewing figures; unique visitors (online)] ■ Contact frequency |

**Output on the individual level**

| | | |
|---|---|---|
| C. | Communication responses | ■ Communication awareness ■ Communication attitude (likeability) |
| D. | Brand responses | ■ Brand awareness [top-of-mind awareness (TOMA), spontaneous, aided] ■ Brand associations (strength, relevance/ importance, distinctiveness) |
| E. | Brand behavior responses | ■ Purchasing intention ■ Trial purchases ■ Brand loyalty and repeat purchases |

**Output at market level**

| | | |
|---|---|---|
| F. | Market responses* | ■ Sales ■ Market share |

**Figure 13.5 Communication objectives and measurable variables***

\* Not communication objectives but marketing objectives

figures; a campaign of McDonald's has been shown, for example, 20 times in one month with an average viewing figure of 10% and produced 200 GRPs; if the average number of times people have seen the spot was, for example, four [average contact frequency of four], the net coverage is 200/4 = 50%). Online communication coverage may relate to page views and click behavior or the number of unique visitors.

## 2 Output at individual level

The second level is a representation of individual responses, that is, the responses of people from the target audience that the company has to measure itself through market research. These responses consist of three main groups:

1   *Communication respon*ses. These are reactions to a single expression, such as the appreciation (*likeability*; the percentage that enjoyed a particular commercial by McDonald's or the number of likes of a Facebook message) and reactions to a series

of expressions such as advertising awareness (e.g., the percentage of people from the target audience who know that McDonald's has a campaign with soccer teams that are visiting McDonald's).

2   *Brand responses.* This is brand awareness (already very high for McDonald's) and brand associations (percentage of people from the target audience who know that McDonald's offers a soccer menu, percentage of people who consider McDonald's child friendly, etc.).

3   *Brand behavior responses.* These are behavioral intentions with regard to the brand (percentage that expects to be visiting McDonald's within one week), trial purchases, information behavior, purchasing behavior, usage behavior, and brand loyalty (e.g., percentage that indicates recommending McDonald's to friends). Online behavior is, for example, clicking behavior: clicking and ordering. This is called *conversion*: the percentage of viewers taking the intended action. Reactions to online messages are also brand responses. The interesting issue of online media is that reach and responses are easy to collect. In effect, it can be interpreted as *single source data*: a number of data from the same source: for each individual site visitor.

### 3 Market responses

The third level consists of the aggregated effects at the *market level*. This refers to the size and strength of the brand preference in the market, the sales, the market share, the price elasticity, the profit margin, and the cash flow. Both at this level and at the second level, the issue is the effects over time: direct effects (after a single expression), short-term effects (within one year), and long-term effects (after one year).

In terms of the advertising response matrix, market response (sales, category F) is the most important goal that needs to be achieved. However, this is a marketing objective. Individual purchasing behavior (category E) is also a marketing objective. An exception to this is *trial*: Trial purchases are influenced mostly by communication and thus may be considered communication goals. The clearest communication objectives are represented under category D: brand awareness and brand associations. The reason for this is that these objectives are influenced primarily by communication. A second reason is that these are also the sources of *brand equity*, according to Keller (2013). In addition, the communication responses might be presented as communication objectives except for the fact that this is never sufficient: communication is a tool to achieve something with the brand. However, communication responses are very important in pretesting: testing beforehand how an advertisement or commercial comes across to people in the target audience.

In summary, the middle part of the advertising response matrix (categories C, D, and E, with the exception of brand loyalty and repeat purchases) contains all possible communications objectives. Which variables are chosen from this range depends on where the largest bottlenecks are. At this point the 'classic advertising models' are useful. These models assume that consumers progress through three phases: cognitive (knowledge), affective (attitude), and conative (behavior). The oldest model is the *AIDA model*: attention, interest, desire, action. If spontaneous brand awareness is low, there may have to be a campaign to increase it. If the price image is unfavorable, improvement in this regard may be necessary. If the desire is doing well but the trial purchases are not, planning an action is conceivable. Research in combination with the desired proposition will therefore be the basis for the choice of the specific communication objectives. Each campaign will also have a marketing objective, and it is therefore conceivable to incorporate the marketing objective into a communication plan.

To meet the requirements for objectives, the objective should be quantified and should contain a time designation. Examples are as follows:

■ Within half a year, 80% of our target audience (women over age 30) should have heard of our brand at some time (*aided brand recall*).
■ Within one year, the percentage of the 4 million households with a washing machine that identifies brand X as a low-foaming laundry detergent that is effective in cleaning laundry should increase from 10% to 40%.
■ By October 1 of next year, 70% of our target audience should have purchased the product at least once, and the average report mark that the 'trial purchasers' give our product at a minimum should be equal to that of our competitor Q (combined objective).

If a company has different target audiences, the objectives may be summarized as they are in Figure 13.6. This figure also shows that to measure the progress and success of a campaign, a measurement of the variables for the objectives should be taken both beforehand (zero measure) and afterward.

| | Total | | Target audience A | | Target audience B | |
|---|---|---|---|---|---|---|
| | 1/1/23 (current) | 1/1/24 (plan) | 1/1/23 (current) | 1/1/24 (plan) | 1/1/23 (current) | 1/1/24 (plan) |
| Aided advertising recall | __% | __% | __% | __% | __% | __% |
| Top of mind brand awareness (TOMA) | __% | __% | __% | __% | __% | __% |
| Percent of people who associate (aided) brand with "adventurous"" | __% | __% | __% | __% | __% | __% |
| Percent of people who consider brand at purchase | __% | __% | __% | __% | __% | __% |
| Percent of people who purchase brand for the first time (trial) | __% | __% | __% | __% | __% | __% |

*Figure 13.6* Communication objectives for a brand

### 13.4.3 Budget determination

After the communication objectives have been determined, the available budget is determined. These steps are closely linked: Ambitious objectives cost a lot of money. In practice, various methods are used to determine the communication budget. The most common methods are the following:

1  A percentage of turnover (last year's sales or expected sales).
2  Closing entry: what the company can afford.
3  Comparable share to that of competitor.
4  Based on objectives and tasks.

The disadvantages of the first two methods are that reverse reasoning is applied: The turnover determines the sales promotion instead of the opposite. This leads to *cyclical budgeting*. Moreover, the budget then is not based on opportunities in the market and the specific required promotion of products. Case 13.1 shows that companies are better off *not* cutting marketing budget in a recession. A disadvantage of the third method is that it is uncertain whether the competition is doing well. A company is better off looking at its own resources, opportunities, and objectives. Budgeting based on *objectives and tasks* therefore is the best method: What do we want to achieve, and how much does that cost? For that purpose, items such as desired coverage should be determined, and the number of required contacts per consumer should be reached. Since the link between objectives other than coverage and budget is not always easy to indicate, this will require making assumptions about effectiveness on the basis of past experience.

## 13.5 Briefing and requirements for communication

Earlier in this chapter we indicated that an advertising agency almost always is engaged in elaborating the campaign development and media choice. In presenting the assignment, a briefing is used: a description of what is expected of the communication consulting agency. The marketing or brand manager is primarily responsible for this process. After consultation and deliberation with the advertising agency, the agency should declare its agreement with the briefing. The components of a briefing are briefly listed in Figure 13.7. A lot of information for the briefing may be obtained from the marketing plan.

In an introductory section, a description is provided of the company, the brand or product, the characteristics, technical data, and so forth. There follows a reproduction of the objectives and an elaboration of the other Ps: product, price, place, and promotion/communication (to the extent that they have been determined already). A description of the strengths, weaknesses, opportunities, and threats analysis provides the framework within which the campaign is developed. The perceptions of the target group are very important. The core problem often has to do with the difference between image and identity. For the competition, the central focus is the content of their communication, the media allocation, and the budget. The media behavior of the competitors may sometimes be analyzed by the agency on the basis of advertising expenditure figures of Nielsen Media Research (see Section 7.7). Components 1 and 2 form the marketing background of the campaign. Components 3 through 6 are the core of the briefing. First, the communication target

## Case 13.1 Marketing budget

### Don't Cut Your Marketing Budget in a Recession

Most companies reduce spending in recessions, especially on marketing items that may be easier to cut (certainly relative to payroll). This not only pertains to communication budgets but also to investments in R&D and in pricing (so: not lowering prices during recession). In times of the pandemic, advertising agencies were struggling to stay afloat, and Google and Facebook were reporting substantially lower ad revenues as marketing spending dove with the business cycle (cyclical marketing). But that is today's equivalent of bleeding – an old-fashioned but once widespread treatment that actually reduces the patient's ability to fight disease. For example, research in contexts as different as UK fast-moving consumer goods and US automobile markets shows that products launched during a recession have both higher long-term survival chances and higher sales revenues.

Source: adapted from *Harvard Business Review* (online), 14 August 2020

audience is described, for example, based on the dimensions mentioned in Section 11.2. Component 4 is the focused proposition (with any evidence), and component 5 contains the brand personality.

Then there is the communication goal: what does the manager want to achieve with that target audience, and how much money is available (draft budget)? The budget mentioned in the briefing sometimes may be modified on the basis of the creative ideas of the agency.

**Marketing background**

1.   What it is about: company and brand or product
2.   Environment: summary of SWOT analysis and key problem

**Campaign goal**

3.   Communication target audience
4.   Promise and proof
5.   Brand personality
6.   Measurable communication goal and budget

**Preconditions**

7.   Media and resources
8.   Other preconditions (e.g., style and time planning)

*Figure 13.7* **Components of an advertising briefing**

In component 7 (media and resources), the wishes of the company are indicated in relation to any other sales promotion tools (e.g., online) and the media choice. Some companies determine a budget allocation for this (e.g., division print/television); others do it qualitatively or delegate it entirely to the agency.

The last component contains the other preconditions within which the campaign has to be developed, such as necessary elements in the advertising expressions (house style and layout), whether to use humor, and legal regulations. In this component the time planning is also described.

A clear and well-defined briefing is very important for the advertising agency. Advertising agencies often complain that companies do not know how to write good briefings. The biggest problem is that companies cannot or do not make a choice. They want too much. This leads to briefings that are broad and therefore vague. A vague briefing means insufficient direction, which means the advertising agency can go in any direction with the campaign and brand consistency is no longer feasible. The disadvantage of this is that the campaign may go in a different direction different from what was planned originally, and there is also a risk that afterward a lot more work may need to be done if certain designs are rejected by the advertiser. A good advertising agency will therefore refuse to approve a briefing that has not been completed.

At this point, the task of the client is finished and the baton is passed to the advertising firm.

## 13.6 Creation and execution

The simplest way to tell a message is just to tell the message. However, in advertising this mostly does not work, since simply telling the message does not create enough attention. Therefore, creativity is needed. *Creation* involves inventing a 'fun' way to sell the message to the target audience. The goal of creativity (in this context) is to come up with a so called *concept*: an idea to tell the message. The concept is the link between the message and the media (Figure 13.8). *Execution* is the elaboration of that method and the development of the campaign.

We now discuss the creative process. In advertising agencies, usually two people are involved with the creative process: a *copywriter* (text writer) and an *art director* (designer). Sometimes one of them thinks of the idea, and sometimes it is a joint effort. The goal is to find a 'hook' the campaign can hang onto. Few tools are available for the invention of a creative idea. Creation has been called a 'handicraft'. A creative type needs to have a 'feel' for it. One creative type is also different from another. Some advertising agencies are well known for their surprising, innovative campaigns, yet that is not appropriate for every brand. A copywriter mostly will come up with a slogan (if needed). Many brands do not use a slogan, although it is an effective way of summarizing the core value of the brand. Geursen (1990) has developed a 'model' that can be used in the process of creation (Figure 13.9).

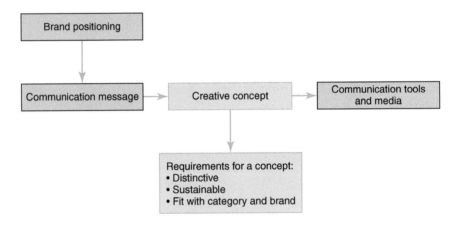

**Figure 13.8 Development of a concept in advertising**

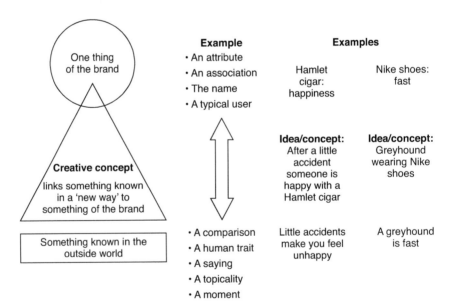

**Figure 13.9 Creation is making one thing big**

Source: Based on Geursen (1990)

Creation starts with considering 'something of the brand' ('Nike shoes are fast'). This 'something' should ideally be invented by the company (proposition), and if it is not, the agency will think of something about the brand. Most often, an advertiser comes up with many 'unique selling points' of the brand, and the agency then has to choose one on which to focus. Agencies have commented that this is simplest when the brand actually has something to say, for example, something new. Research on television advertising (Lodish et al., 1995a) has shown that the effect is the strongest when a brand has something new to announce. If there is no instrumental message, a search can be made for something more abstract (transformational positioning): an element of the brand personality. The creative type subsequently ponders the way in which that can be communicated. The creative idea may be an illustration, a piece of text, a parallel ('a greyhound is fast'), an incident, and so on that can logically be linked to the message and the brand. From this central idea (concept), the campaign is developed (such as a picture of a greyhound with sneakers) and the 'something' of the brand is communicated in an enlarged fashion (hence the triangle).

Figure 13.9 listed the requirements for creative ideas:

- *Distinctive.* Many ads for cars show beautiful landscapes with a car. This is not distinctive and can hardly be called a 'concept'.
- *Sustainable.* This means that ideally the concept can be used in different ways, so with different examples, and also stay interesting in the long run. Ideas that can be developed to go beyond a single campaign into a campaign that will run for years are very valuable. Case 13.2 gives an example of such an enduring concept. Sometimes good creative ideas are thrown out because of imagined 'wear-out'. The true cause of this problem often is a change in managers or advertising agencies. Continuing for a long time with a creative idea requires a long-term vision.
- *Fit with the category and the brand.* There should be a kind of logical relation between the creative concept and the message. This is one of the biggest shortcomings of creative ideas. To be noticed in the enormous amount of communication expressions, agencies continually come up with 'creative' approaches. This makes advertising entertaining, and commercials may hold people's attention. However, the lack of a logical link with the brand leads to a situation in which the advertising is remembered but not the brand. In that case, advertising is by definition not effective. For example, a viewer who watches a television commercial in which a dog with dirty paws walks into the kitchen and a child dries the dog with a towel would not automatically think of candy bars.

## 13.7 Pretesting

There are three forms of pretesting:

1. Qualitative testing of a design for an advertising expression: *concept test.*
2. Qualitative testing of a fully developed advertising expression: *qualitative pretest.*
3. Quantitative testing of a fully developed advertising expression: *quantitative pretest.*

### 13.7.1 Concept test

In the consultation between the advertising agency and the company there is usually a moment at which a design for an advertising expression (based on the 'creative

## Case 13.2 Creative concept

### Sustaining an advertising concept for a long time: Hamlet cigars

An example of a brand that elaborated on the same creative idea for more than 30 years is British Hamlet cigars. The concept (advertising idea) was the accident around the corner: Something went wrong for someone, but by lighting a Hamlet cigar after the incident, the person still developed a satisfied feeling. With the supportive slogan 'Happiness is a cigar called Hamlet, the mild cigar' and always the same music, both an instrumental value (light) and especially a final value (happiness) were communicated; therefore, this was a two-sided positioning. In the years 1961–1994, the company made endless variations on this theme (after that time, television advertising for tobacco products was outlawed), and the Hamlet campaign won many prizes with famous commercials such as 'man in photo booth' and 'free kick in soccer' and was a successful cigar brand for many years. A wonderful example of consistency, creativity, and focus.

idea') is submitted for approval to the advertiser. In print advertising the concept is then an advertising sketch, and for television advertising a *storyboard* is made: drawings of all the scenes with corresponding indications of the audio support (music and text) that is planned. In this phase it may be desirable to ask several consumers for feedback on the design. This could involve questions regarding intelligibility and attractiveness. An advantage of concept testing is that after that stage, it is still relatively easy and cheap to make changes. A disadvantage is that the final expression is different from the concept. Especially in television, advertising this is a problem: A commercial including music, editing, and so on may produce completely different feelings than does a storyboard.

### 13.7.2 Qualitative pretest

A test similar to a concept test may be performed with a ready-made expression. An advantage is that the actual expression is being tested and the respondents therefore receive a faithful image of the advertising. A disadvantage is the high costs of modifications.

### 13.7.3 Quantitative pretest

Quantitative pretests have the following goals:

■   To obtain insight into the expected effects of one or more advertising expressions.
■   To obtain insight into which components of an expression receive the most attention.

Online quantitative pretesting is popular and easy. Simply make, for example, two different websites, banners, vlogs, and so on and track the number of page views and clicks. This is called *A/B-testing*: testing two online communication vehicles. For offline communication, quantitative pretesting demands a bit more effort. The most direct way to do quantitative pretesting is to ask a group of respondents to give their opinion about an expression with the aid of closed questions (e.g., with *Likert scales*: for example, very unclear . . . very clear or completely disagree . . . completely agree). This way of pretesting is used by Procter & Gamble (see Case 13.3).

Aside from questions about the expression to be tested, questions may be posed about the brand, for example, the brand personality. In this way a quantitative pretest can easily be used to perform a 'zero measurement' of the variables included in the objectives.

Some research agencies offer quantitative pretesting tools using *eye movement* analysis. In 'laboratory circumstances', the eye movements of respondents who watch websites, advertisements in magazines, on television, and so forth, are documented. With these data it may be detected which components of the expression are watched the most, how long the expression as a whole is watched, and what the influence of the 'environment' of the expression (the context, such as editorial pages in a magazine) is. The scores are compared with those of competitors and with the medium as a whole. In all of these cases attention is measured, which is not a communication-effect objective, though it is a condition for achieving communication effects.

### 13.7.4 Limitations and use of pretesting

Pretests have two important limitations:

1   *Often no actual circumstances*. With the exception of online A/B testing, pretests are conducted only in research circumstances. The issue here is whether respondents in 'laboratory conditions' will behave in the same manner at home. A danger is that if

## Case 13.3 Pretesting

### Quantitative pretesting at Procter & Gamble

Procter & Gamble is one of the largest advertisers. Procter uses a relatively high amount of TV advertising. Given the enormous investments, it is no wonder that P&G makes sure to pretest the majority of its commercials. The pretesting focuses on three factors: persuasiveness/credibility, uniqueness/distinctiveness, and trial intention. By doing this pretesting for many brands for many years, P&G has compiled a large data file with pretest results. That database also contains the results after the closure of a campaign. By comparing the pretest and the actual results of brands within product categories, P&G gets a detailed insight into the predictive power of pretests. Based on these experiences, standards have been developed that a commercial must meet in a pretest in order to be approved.

respondents know why they are included, advertising expressions will receive too much attention.
2   *Bad predictive value*. Research by Lodish et al. (1995a) demonstrated that the results of quantitative pretests are poor predictors of achieved brand equity and market shares. The results of pretests therefore should not be used in absolute terms, especially not in comparative terms.

In light of these limitations, the question may be raised whether pretesting has any value. The simple answer is that it does. Research by Lodish et al. (1995b) into the long-term effects of television commercials shows that if commercials do not have an effect in the short term, they also do not have an effect in the long term. This implies that it is important from the very beginning to measure the results of a campaign and compare them with the starting situation. If no short-term effects can be detected, action should be taken.

# 13.8 Communication tools and media

A company has a multitude of communication instruments at its disposal to stimulate customers to purchase its products. Figure 13.10 gives an overview. We make a distinction between 'fixed' brand elements, communication in service and promotional communication.

Nowadays, much attention is given to online communication. Companies as Unilever and Procter & Gamble are increasingly paying attention to this. But this does not mean that other ('offline') communication such as advertising on TV is not important anymore. The studies of Sharp, reviewed in Chapter 1, show that dominance in visibility is strongly affecting sales. So, online and 'normal' marketing have to be integrated.

We now analyze the communication instruments listed in Figure 13.10, and we pay special attention to online communication (Section 13.9).

### Brand name, design, and packaging

The brand elements brand name, logo, and design are part of marketing strategy and are discussed in Chapter 11. They are the more or less 'fixed' communication tools that will not change yearly. Another characteristic of brand elements is that some of them can be legally protected since they are legally defined as a 'brand' (such as the name or a logo).

### Brand elements

1. Brand name and name url
2. Design and logo
3. Packaging and location communication

### Communication in service

4   Face-to-face communication of the staff

### Promotional communication

5. Advertising
   - Print
   - TV, radio, cinema
   - Outdoor
6. Online communication
7. Promotions
8. Sales and personal selling
9. Direct marketing communication
10. Public relations
11. Sponsoring and events

*Figure 13.10* Marketing communication instruments

We also mentioned that design in the context of a shop is part of retail marketing and strongly affects the shopping experience of consumers.

Packaging is part of the marketing instrument 'product' and reviewed in Section 12.2.

### Communication in service

Communication in service is the personal contact between an employee and a customer. It can be related to providing information through the telephone, but it can also be the core of the product such as in education, consultancy, health care, and retail. If communication is an important part of the 'product', the quality of the 'product' will strongly be related to how the communication is experienced by customers. For example, the perceived quality of a health care provider is sometimes more affected by how the doctors and other staff members communicate than by the real outcomes of the health care process.

All other communication tools are part of promotional communication.

### Advertising

Advertising includes every paid form of nonpersonal presentation and promotion of ideas, goods, or services by an identified sponsor. Advertising messages are communicated through media: public communication channels. Examples are magazine and television advertising, cinema commercials, outdoor advertising (billboards, bus shelters, etc.), and online advertising. Media themselves are also brands and can also have 'sub-brands' such as TV programs, specific magazines (titles), and websites/platforms (Facebook, Google). Every medium has advertising income. Some media also have income from consumers, such as paid newspapers, magazines, and paid TV channels.

If a company or a advertising agency has developed some kind of communication message and concept, media have to be chosen. The choice of the media strategy is closely linked to the development of the campaign. Some concepts are appropriate exclusively for television, and others primarily for print. In practice, usually a combination of media is chosen. Factors that determine the media choice include the following:

- *Coverage*. Which medium can we use to reach the target audience as efficiently as possible?
- *Communication ability*. Suitability of the medium to the message: Is an explanation required? Does an 'atmosphere' need to be created? Is the message mostly *thematic* (informative) or action-oriented?
- *Contact frequency*. How often can we reach the target audience through the medium?
- *Costs*. What are the costs per 1,000 readers reached (print) or per percent viewing figures (gross rating points: television and radio), and what are the total costs?

For choosing a combination of media (media 'schedule'), software can be used to 'compute' how many people will be reached and how often with different combinations of media. This data is available since in many countries; the coverage of media is measured through panel research: research with a fixed group of consumers who are willing to regularly provide information about what the read or watch (measured online).

## Case 13.4 Media reach

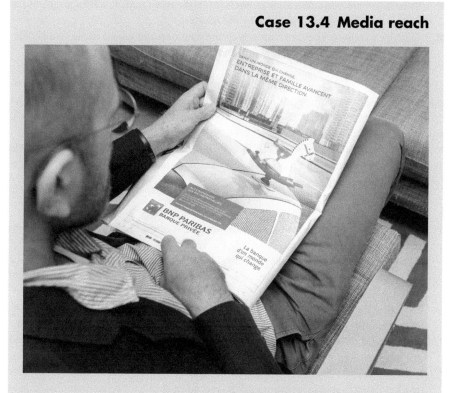

### Nielsen and GfK measure media coverage

Data about the coverage of media (offline and online) is important for companies to plan their media budget. The agencies Nielsen and GfK both claim that they can deliver these data. Both agencies have a large panel of consumers to measure what these respondents 'see'. This is done by a combination of surveys (offline media; for example, whether they read a magazine) and online measuring (what sites they visit, etc.).

**Online communication**
The next section is devoted to online communication.

**Sales promotion**
This includes all short-term actions directly targeted towards stimulating sales. There are three types of promotions (Blattberg & Neslin, 1990):

- *Consumer promotions*. These are promotions by manufacturers aimed at final customers, such as discount actions, money-back actions, and 'premium' actions (a temporary free gift with purchase); these actions are sometimes supported by in-store communications paid for by the manufacturer, such as special article presentations (*displays*).

■ *Retailer promotions.* These are promotions of the retail trade toward the consumer, such as discount actions (paid for by the retailer).

■ *Trade promotions.* These are actions of the manufacturer aimed at the retail trade, such as competitions for the highest sales or temporarily providing bonuses.

In the last few years, there has been a shift in consumer markets from advertising to promotions; increasingly, companies are choosing to stimulate sales in the short term. The causes of this include a greater acceptance in companies of the instrument of promotions, more pressure on product managers to achieve higher sales, and increased competition: more brands that are starting to look like each other. Another factor may be that the availability of more data and more detailed data (scanning) makes it easier to measure the effects of promotions.

Three comments about the use of promotions follow:

1   Frequent use of promotions may have negative consequences for brand equity in the long run: Consumers start to doubt the quality and get used to *brand switching.* Therefore, it is recommended to use mostly value-adding promotions and fewer price discounts. Another recommendation is to have a promotion fit as much as possible with the brand, for example, by offering extras that fit logically with the brand.

2   Effect research into promotions shows that promotions are often not profitable for manufacturers (Van Heerde et al., 2003). Often there is a sales peak during the promotion, but afterward the sales are typically lower (hoarding by consumers), and promotions do not always lead to effects that are favorable for the manufacturer, such as increased sales in relation to the competition and extra consumption. Another market effect is that competitors often react to each other's price promotions, thus decreasing the mutual market share effects.

3   Retailers are often not happy with actions because they lead to irregularities in demand and therefore make extra demands on logistics, inventory, and administration.

Some of these effects are summarized in Figure 13.11, which depicts the price promotion doom loop. Generally speaking, this circle shows the risk of a short-term (cash) orientation of companies instead of a long-term brand and customer orientation.

### Sales and personal selling

Sales is aimed at realizing a transaction. It can be seen as the final step in getting the customer to buy your product, for example, a car. Personal selling is an oral presentation in a discussion with one or more potential customers to generate sales. Examples are representatives, product presentations, company days, exhibitions, and shows. Sales is related to account management. An account is a (large) customer of a company. An account manager is responsible for specific customers and has to take care of good relations with that customer. Account management is used by manufacturers, where the accounts are retailers, such as Wal-Mart. Clearly, to be a good sales manager, personal communication skills are important.

### Direct-marketing communication

*Direct marketing* is a form of marketing that is aimed at obtaining and maintaining a structural, direct relationship between the supplier and the customer. Direct marketing

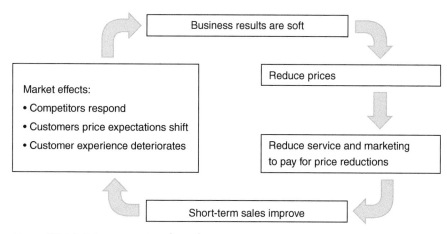

*Figure 13.11* **Price promotion doom loop**

Source: Calkins, T. (2005), 'The Challenge of Branding'. In Alice M. Tybout and Tim Calkins (eds), *Kellogg on Branding*, Hoboken, NJ: Wiley

communication is one-to-one communication that is used for this purpose. The forms most frequently applied are online communication, promotional messages sent directly to people (direct mail), and telephone sales.

### Public relations

Public relations (PR) refers to the systematic promotion of mutual understanding between a company and its public groups. The goal is the creation and maintenance of a positive image in the public groups (customers, employees, suppliers, capital suppliers, shareholders, the government, and the general public). The tools of public relations include press releases, publicity, annual reports, sponsoring, and sponsored media (e.g., magazines of retailers).

PR is aimed at target audiences both outside and within the company. Although it is difficult to include internal PR with marketing, let alone with sales promotion, there is an overlap in activities. Marketing PR entails informing the company about its brands and products and is applied on occasions such as the introduction of new products. In the case of 'calamities', PR is important (see the material on crisis communication in Section 11.7.3).

### Sponsoring

In sponsoring, the sponsor provides money, goods, services, or know-how to the party that is being sponsored, which in turn contributes to the achievement of the communication objectives of the sponsor. Sponsoring is a thematic communication instrument that can be used both for marketing communication and for corporate communication. Among all sponsoring revenues, the majority (70%) goes for sports sponsoring. A goal is that there will be a transfer of associations. It is not clear if this really works. Especially if a brand is one of many sponsors, it is difficult to realize (long-lasting) image effects.

**Events**

*Events* may be organized by the company or may also be sponsored. A distinction has to be made between:

■ Events developed and organized by the company. This can be done by any brand, including small and medium-sized enterprises. The advantage of organizing on one's own is that the brand can be made completely into an 'experience'. The challenge is to get people to go to the event.
■ Sponsoring of/participating in events of others (see sponsoring).
■ Organizing existing events, either limited or big in size.

**Events and destination branding**

Because events are often used for destination branding and because especially mega-events such as the FIFA World Cup receive a lot of attention worldwide, we now make some remarks about the effects of events in relation to destination branding. The goal of destination branding (or city marketing) is to attract visitors, future inhabitants, and/or companies. The emphasis mostly is on tourists. A seemingly attractive way to do this is by participating in or organizing of an event, for example, to 'buy' the start of the Tour de France in your city (does not need to be in France . . .) or to organize the Olympics (Paris 2024) or the FIFA World Cup (Qatar 2022; USA, Canada, Mexico 2026). Policy makers defend the choice of these extremely expensive events because:

1   Events are effective investments to improve the external image of the location and leads to more tourists (transfer of secondary associations).
2   Also the 'image' among current residents improves ('we are proud').
3   Visitors spend a lot of money during the event, leading to an economic impulse.
4   Investments (especially for mega-events) are also useful after the event.

Unfortunately, the effects of events differ from case to case, and literature is critical about effects (Giulianotti et al., 2015). Critiques are about the image of the event itself (corruption in the FIFA, sustainability: climate [Qatar], personnel [Qatar], etc.). But also if the image of the event itself is not negative, the realization of the aforementioned four goals is uncertain. Most audience figures are high. But this does not always lead to better brand associations (showing nice views is not enough) and thus neither to more visits. Also the spending of visitors cannot be compared with the out-of-pocket costs of an event. And often sport stadiums are difficult to make useful after the event. There are positive exceptions: the FIFA World Cup in South Africa led to a significant improvement in its brand image (Knott et al., 2017). This is also because the South African organization combined the event with several supporting activities. Other positive exceptions are cities that were 'European cultural city of the year'. Most of these cities organize new cultural events, which is typically useful for many tourists, thus leading to a significant and long-lasting touristic impulse. In many cases the aforementioned second goal (the image among residents) is also improved. But policy makers trying to organize big non-cultural events should be honest and say that the costs are mainly 'for a local party'.

## 13.9 Online communication

Online communication concerns all communication that takes place via the internet. People can 'consume' online communication through different channels: computer, laptop, smartphone, TV, and so on. The smartphone is often regarded as the most important channel. After corona, the average screen time of people worldwide has increased to more than five hours a day, so you would say there are plenty of opportunities for reach. There are many forms of online communication, often with fancy designations, where it is sometimes unclear what is meant. Moreover, there is often no logic in lists, so the various options become mixed up. We will discuss all forms of online communication in a logical order and then summarize 'digital marketing'. We end with some comments about (online) communication for small companies, because these companies usually have no money or motivation to spend in (offline) campaigns.

### 13.9.1 Forms of online communication

Figure 13.12 shows the different forms of online communication and their purposes. (Google) Analytics plays a role in all these forms: analyzing all online data about reach, number of visitors, page views, click behavior, and so on, so that better performance can be achieved. We now discuss each of the eight forms of online communication.

*Website and content*

A website should of course be interesting in terms of both appearance and content. With regard to the latter (the content), a distinction is made between promotional information, why the brand is 'so great', and more informative content that is not directly promotional. The latter is called *content* marketing: offering relevant content free of charge, where the goal is of course also to get people to your website and indirectly contribute to your image. Examples: a blog (online column) or vlog (online video) about a certain topic, a white paper (downloadable document about a topic) or infographic (a nicely designed overview about a topic). Content can be a nice proof of the positioning of your brand. For example, Pampers can make all kinds of information about babies available.

| Own communication | Methods/Uses | Target |
|---|---|---|
| 1 | Website and content marketing | Building content through website |
| 2 | Search Engine Optimization SEO Search Engine Advertising SEA | Increase site findability |
| 3 | Conversion optimization | Stimulate clicks |
| 4 | Facebook, YouTube, Instagram and so on | Social platforms: own effort |
| 5 | Display advertising | Online advertising |
| 6 | Email marketing | Direct marketing |
| Through others | | |
| 7 | Viral marketing and user generated content | Stimulate reviews and reactions |
| 8 | Influencer marketing | Enable paid ambassadors |

*Figure 13.12* **Forms and goals of online communication**

Content (marketing) is not only useful for a website but also for other online resources such as social platforms. On the other hand, there are of course already all kinds of platforms on specific subjects, which raises the question of what the added value of a content platform of a brand is.

## Website: findability

If you have a beautiful website, it must be found well and therefore visited. Preferably you are at the top of Google when people have typed in certain keywords. But that is very difficult. There are two ways to (try to) get there.

The first is *search engine optimization*, which means that your website appears 'organically' at the top of the search results. But ranking high organically is not that easy, because Google does not disclose exactly on the basis of which criteria and how rankings take place. Of course, the presence of the keyword itself plays an important role. If a site offers 'cheap beer', it makes sense that it counts whether the designation 'cheap beer' is in the name or the URL and also how often it is mentioned on the site. But it's not that simple. It's about much more. Google uses an algorithm that changes regularly, making it a constant challenge to maintain a website properly. For example, relevant content is very important. For that reason, regularly updating a blog or news item is very important. But also the number of links from other sites to your site (*backlinks*), the number of times the site is 'liked' on social media, the structure of the site, working with correct page titles, and so on are very important. Another factor is whether the site is 'responsive', which means that the layout adapts to the device on which the site is displayed. For example, if you click on a site on your mobile phone, instead of seeing the same homepage as on your laptop, but with a small font, you should see a homepage with a modified and easy-to-read layout. There are agencies that specialize in getting websites to appear high in Google, but it often remains *trial and error*.

A second way to be easily found is through *search engine advertising* (SEA). This means that you can have paid search results appear when a keyword is typed into a search engine. The best example of this is Google Adwords. Advertisers can enter keywords into Adwords and indicate how much money they are willing to pay for a click on their site. If a consumer types in that keyword, the paid search results/(mini) advertisements will appear above or next to the 'regular' links. If a consumer clicks on it, costs are incurred (PPC: pay per click). The higher an advertiser's bid, the higher the paid ad will be in the list.

Increasingly, consumers today search by voice ('voice search'), for example, in the car with Siri from Apple, but also at home on devices such as a smart TV, Google Home, your smartphone, and so on. 'Voice search' is not necessarily done with the same keywords as when typing in keywords. For example, more informal language may be used and more often in question form. The strong growth of voice has important consequences for brands to be found on the internet. It means that SEO and SEA will also have to be performed from voice search (Conick, 2019).

### Conversion optimization

Conversion optimization means that as a site builder you design and adjust your site in such a way that people who come to take a look at it actually take the action you want (= conversion). For example, it is important that the 'landing page' (the page on which someone ends up if they come to your site via Google, for example) be clear and inviting. A/B testing is often used to improve conversion on sites, for example, by seeing whether showing a telephone number or a *call to action* ('download this white paper now') on all pages helps.

### Social media: functions

Social media is defined as sources of online information, which are created and distributed by consumers through platforms (Instagram, TikTok, Facebook, Twitter (or 'X' since 2023), YouTube, LinkedIn, Mastodon, etc.) to keep each other informed about all kinds of issues. A point of discussion with these media is whether WhatsApp belongs to social media: there are arguments for (you can share text and images in groups, just like Instagram) and against (it is a direct means of communication without the intervention of third parties).

Much is written and discussed about social media. And in many industries, organizations are wondering how they can or should use social media to strengthen their own brand. A big difference with other media is that social media is 'from consumers': everyone can 'shout' anything. So social media does not belong to organizations. An organization has no control over what is said about it. Social media is in fact a very fast form of word of mouth. There used to be a rule of thumb that stated that one dissatisfied customer can tell ten others. Not fun in itself. But this principle is now outdated. A dissatisfied customer can now tell 10 million others! This goes very quickly when journalists also participate. A complaint can therefore lead to an enormous stream of negative publicity.

Consumer power has increased enormously. Conversely, of course, a very happy consumer can also spread the word.

In our view, a company can use social media in three ways:

1  post messages
2  use others as ambassadors
3  stimulate content and consumer reactions

The last two forms will be discussed later in this section.

### Social media: own efforts

Social media can of course be seen as a new form of media that companies can simply use themselves to convey their message to the target groups. In practice, many organizations have their own Facebook and/or Instagram page, often also a YouTube channel and their own Twitter/X account that broadcasts important information. TikTok is also being used more and more. In this way many followers can be obtained. Consumers can choose to follow an organization themselves. For example, brands such as McDonald's and Coca-Cola each have a few million followers on Twitter.

### Online advertising: display advertising

Display advertising means that you have an advertisement (*display*) placed on a website, app, or social medium. Such an advertisement can take different forms, for example, a 'banner', video, text, and so on. As we mentioned earlier, display advertising can be used very specifically depending on people's search behavior. The number of people who actually click on displays seems to be very low, but a banner also contributes to brand awareness because people do see the banner.

As with offline advertising, the implementation of the display advertising (for example, the format) influences the effect (Tutaj & Van Reijmersdal, 2012). An advantage of display advertising is that it lends itself perfectly to experimenting with different versions of the advertisement (A/B testing).

Affiliate marketing is a form of display advertising but approaches it from the other side: as a website owner, you can advertise for others, where you can receive a share of the proceeds.

### Email marketing

Email marketing is a form of direct marketing (or sales) communication using email addresses. Since the introduction of stricter privacy legislation (General Data Protection Regulation [GDPR]), this is only allowed in a opt-in context: people must give explicit permission to approach them with offers by e-mail; otherwise the sender is punishable.

All the aforementioned forms of online communication concern brands' own communication. The following are two forms of communication *through others* using social media.

## Viral marketing and user generated content

Social media can also be used to encourage others to 'tell you good news'. This can be done indirectly (spontaneously) and directly (paid influencer marketing, to be discussed in the following).

As mentioned, social media is an extremely fast way of word-of-mouth communication. That 'word of mouth' happens very easily without your noticing it. If you 'like' something, it will be visible to everyone by default. You can of course change that so that, for example, only your friends see the 'like'. But then you actually still don't have to 'forward' a message because a like is enough for 'forwarding'. Organizations can do their best to encourage this. A manager then has to come up with a way to 'pass on' a story read and liked. This is called *viral marketing*. Viral marketing has been around much longer than social media but can now be deployed much more easily and effectively and to share.

When creating stories it is important to be creative and to think about what consumers find fun and/or interesting to like. Examples of motives: humour, surprise, recognizability, uniqueness, shock, provocation, and so on. The choice for the type of motif and therefore the content depends on the brand positioning and the target group. Not every brand is suitable for provocation or to be really funny.

Successful viral marketing will also generate all kinds of consumer reactions. This then leads to a lot of *user-generated content*, or a lot of 'content' from consumers on social media about your own content and brand.

A completely different way of viral marketing is to engage people with your brand, for example, by inviting them to take selfies with the logo of the brand or something else and post them on Instagram for a chance to win a prize. The big advantage of this is that the (usually low) brand involvement of people increases. This form of marketing can be combined with influencer marketing.

The big advantage of viral marketing is that it costs little money. SMEs can also use it. The disadvantage is the uncertainty about the effects. Because many brands try to realize viral marketing, sometimes using influencers, it is getting harder to have success. A combination with PR, so getting journalists to share your message, is increasingly important.

## Influencer marketing

Who would a consumer rather believe: a restaurant promoting its food or a good friend telling you to eat there? Obviously the latter because we trust 'the good friend' and we can identify with that friend. That is the essence of influencer marketing: using a 'friend' to promote your brand. Such a 'friend' can be a celebrity with many online followers, in which case we speak of 'macro-influencers' (see Case 13.5). But as a company, for example, as an SME, you can also look for a local influencer, someone who is known in the region, a local hero or a colleague who is known; then we are talking about a 'micro-influencer'. There are four criteria for choosing and using an influencer:

1   *Credibility*: is it credible that the person is promoting your brand? It must be quite logical for the person to do that.
2   *Fit*: does the influencer fit well with you as a brand, in terms of personality? This applies to all forms of communication, of course.

3 *Familiarity*: is the influencer sufficiently known to the target group? That target group does not have to be broad, as is the case with SMEs, so a national film star is not an option and money is wasted.

4 *Interaction*: take care of interaction with the influencer yourself and also let the influencer interact a lot with your target group.

Of course, influencers get paid for their cooperation. They are not 'objective' customers of a brand. For several years now, an influencer's vlog must also include the designation 'advertisement' (or similar). But often that only appears small and briefly on screen, so that a convincing message can still be conveyed in the remaining time. The effects are also quite measurable: if after a vlog the reach of your site skyrockets, and even better the sales of your product, it is clear that it helps.

Said criteria must be continuously tested with a chosen influencer. A celebrity can 'run out', and then an innovation is important. A risk is that an influencer falls out of favor because of an 'issue'; then rapid withdrawal is the only option.

## Case 13.5 Influencer marketing

### Macro-influencer Kim Kardashian

Kim Kardashian is a 'macro influencer' with over 100 million followers. She receives about $25,000 per mail, and she neatly puts #ad in the vlog she does. You have to, because if you don't comply with the rules, you can get heavy fines.

## 13.9.2 Summary of digital marketing

As we have argued several times, digital marketing is part of 'regular' marketing. Digital aspects of marketing have been discussed at various points in this book. To summarize, Figure 13.13 shows which possible aspects and digital activities fall under the three phases of analysis, strategy, and tactics.

We draw the following conclusions from Figure 13.13:

| Planning phase | Digital aspects |
|---|---|
| Internal | Own online performance |
| Customers | Digital consumer behaviour |
| | Big data, Artificial Intelligence (AI) |
| | Behavioral segmentation |
| Industry | Digital distribution channels |
| | Macro environment: legislation |
| Competitors | Digital competitor behavior |
| Distribution _ | Digital retailers |
| | **Strategy** |
| Positioning | Degree of digitization |
| | **Strategy/Tactics** |
| Target audiences | Micro targeting and behavioral targeting |
| | Customer relation management (CRM) |
| | **Tactics** |
| Product | Online services |
| | Online advice |
| | Co-creation / crowdsourcing |
| Price | Revenue model |
| | Dynamic pricing |
| Channels | Online sales and webshop |
| | Delivery options and channel structure |
| Communication | Website and content marketing |
| | Search engine marketing (SEO, SEA, voice) |
| | Conversion optimization |
| | Social media |
| | Display advertising |
| | Email marketing |
| | Viral marketing and user generated content |
| | Influencer marketing |

*Figure 13.13* **Content and aspects of digital marketing**

■ Digital behavior will have to be analyzed in all phases of the situation analysis, so of customers, competitors, retailers, and the organization itself.

■ Precisely because of this digital behavior, a great deal of detailed, person-specific data is available ('big data').

■ The most crucial strategic, digital decision an organization has to make is to what extent it wants to position itself digitally.

■ Subsequently, an organization will have to choose how to approach the target group.

■ Subsequently, for each of the four market instruments, it is necessary to consider how 'digital' the interpretation should be. Nowadays, communication will always be partly digital, even if the positioning is not.

### 13.9.3 Communication for small businesses

Small and medium-sized enterprises often do not have the necessity or money to use the 'classical' offline communication channels. Online communication can be very helpful because it is very cheap and can be directed towards specific target groups. Some possibilities are:

■ Be authentic in your story.
■ Start with a easy-to-find (SEO) website.
■ Use social media to tell your story.
■ Organize an event relevant for the target audience.
■ Try to find a (local) journalist to write a story (PR).
■ Find other SMEs as partners to jointly communicate.
■ Stimulate customers to post news about your brand (ambassadors).
■ Stimulate reviews and react quickly on negative reviews.
■ Use influencers.
■ Use email marketing.

These are some possibilities that are affordable for small business. A challenge is that the owner of the SME should be able to do this or at least have someone in the company motivated and able to do this. For start-ups, this is mostly not a problem; for older SMEs (and owners), it might be necessary to ask others to help.

## 13.10 Monitoring and effect research

### 13.10.1 Monitoring

After all plans have been implemented, the company must verify whether the set goals have been achieved. To this end, measurements must be made of the objective variables (*result measurement*). This is part of the PDCA cycle. By measuring results you know whether you have achieved your goal. In communication, and certainly online communication, it is often said that it was 'very effective because we had (for example) 800,000 views!' Views and expressions are certainly necessary for the effect but say nothing about the actual effectiveness of the campaign. In the end it all comes down to the behavior of the customer.

What you still don't know is why: you don't know whether your effort, for example, in communication or promotions, is responsible for the result. Especially for the use of market instruments, decision-makers often want to know whether they will lead to a sufficient effect. This is most evident in communication: does a planned advertising campaign of, say, 1 million euros lead to a sufficient increase in sales? So can the campaign end? But it also applies to, for example, a price drop, temporary discount, or other promotion: does it generate net money?

### 13.10.2 Effect research

There are two ways to actually conduct effect research for a brand, that is, to find out whether certain results were also caused by your own marketing. These methods are:

1  Regression analyses/causal models
2  Experiments

#### 1 Causal models

'Causal models' may sound complicated, but in fact, it is not. It simply means that you have data both on the possible cause of results, such as communication, and also on those results themselves, such as market share. By linking those time series together statistically, you can see if there are any possible connections. Officially you don't really show 'causality' but 'coherence'. This causality can be demonstrated by means of advanced statistical methods.

#### 2 Experiments

The purest way to demonstrate effects is to set up experiments. As a researcher, you 'intervene' by exposing different (but comparable) target groups to different 'interventions' and then measuring the differences in behavior such as purchasing a product. Such

## Case 13.6 Single-source research and modelling

### Effect research at GfK

GfK is a well-known market research agency. Among many other things, GfK also provides insights into the relation between media (and other marketing instruments) and sales. For fast-moving consumer goods, it has a large consumer panel, where, on the level of individual persons, data about sales and media contacts are collected. This is a nice example of single-source research and can be seen as a kind of experimental research. For tech and data, GfK has a retail panel where retailers share data on sales on the store level as well as data about media investments (including GRPs, impressions, clicks), prices, promotions, and distribution. By relating the data statistically ('modeling'), GfK gets important insights for the manufacturers and retailers about the effects of price changes, promotional actions, and changes in distribution.

an intervention can be part of a website (this is called A/B testing), an online promotion, the creative expression, the time allocation of the advertising budget, whether to display in the store, and so on.

Causal models and experiments can be used for several market instruments, but we will now focus on communication.

### 13.10.3 Measurement of results and effects of communication

As indicated earlier, the advertising response matrix is a tool for choosing communication goals. That means that this matrix may also be used for measuring results. Figure

| | | Communication input | | |
|---|---|---|---|---|
| A. | 1. | Characteristics of the advertisement (campaign) | ■ | Company's own evaluation and judgment by experts |
| | 2. | Choice of media | ■ | Company's own measurements and data Nielsen |
| B. | 1. | Advertising expenditures | ■ | Nielsen Media Research |
| | 2. | Confrontation (exposure) and reach | ■ | Various agencies |
| | | | ■ | Single-source research |
| | | | ■ | Google analytics |
| | | **Output on the individual level** | | |
| C. | | Communication responses | ■ | Pretesting |
| | | | ■ | Communication tracking |
| D. | | Brand responses | ■ | Brand-tracking instruments (monitoring) |
| E. | | Brand behavior responses | ■ | GfK consumer panel |
| | | | ■ | Single-source research |
| | | **Output at the market level** | | |
| F. | | Market responses | ■ | Nielsen, IRI and GfK store panels |

*Figure 13.14* **Communication objectives and information sources**

13.14 shows which data sources are available to obtain insight into the various components of the matrix.

Of course, a brand has insight in their own communication input, for example, by Google Analytics. If a brand also wants to have insight into competitors' communication efforts, data can be bought from agencies. Measurements of advertising expenditures (B1) are available at agencies such as Nielsen Media Research and GfK. Coverage figures (B2) are collected in many countries by various organizations.

Category C contains items such as pretesting, which was discussed in Section 13.7. Communication tracking (C) and brand tracking (category D) means that communication and brand responses are measured continuously and consistently. Those responses are related to awareness and associations. Brand tracking therefore continuously measures the sources of brand equity, which immediately indicates the advantages of tracking.

Category E relates to the purchasing behavior of individuals. For online purchases, this data is available for the company. Also, GfK collects data for markets for fast-moving consumer goods through a consumer panel. An advantage of GfK is that the company receives data on the purchases made from competitors.

*Single-source research* means that within a panel of households, for each individual household ('single source'), it is documented what that household purchases (this occurs through *home scanning*; the consumers scan bar codes of products at home with a hand scanner) as well as what television programs the members of the household watch. Since per household, the viewing behavior (category B2) and purchasing behavior (category E) are known, single-source research is particularly suitable for effect research.

Category F relates to sales data (marketing objectives). The supplier has data regarding its own brand in its own files. Sales of competing brands may be obtained from Nielsen, IRI, or GfK for markets of fast-moving consumer goods.

In terms of the advertising response matrix, several applications of causal models are possible.

- The best-known application is the one in which a relationship is made between B and F in Figure 13.14: whether advertising has an impact on sales. In doing this, it is important to include not only advertising expenditures as an explanatory variable but also other marketing mix elements, such as price and distribution. When all relevant elements of the marketing mix are included, it may be determined whether the sales are influenced by the advertising expenditures. If that is the case and there is a reasonable presumption of a causal link, it is confirmed that the advertising was 'effective' in the sense of being connected to the sales.
- In addition to the connection between advertising expenditures and sales, the relationship between advertising expenditures (category B2) and brand equity (category D) can be examined. For this purpose there should be time series available for the sources of brand equity, for example, brand awareness. If a company uses brand tracking, it will have those time series.
- A third application of causal models is to examine the relationship between brand equity (category D) and sales (category F). In that case, as many explanatory variables as possible should be included. Such research indicates which components of brand equity (e.g., a specific image aspect) contribute to the achievement of sales and to what degree.

Experiments are used regularly in marketing science, for example, for finding out how sustainable eating behavior can be stimulated (Van Ittersum & Wansink, 2012). An example related to advertising effects is a study by Lodish et al. (1995b) of the long-term effects of television advertising. To research that issue, those authors exposed a research group to additional television advertising for one year. During and after that year, the purchases of the research group were documented, as well as those of a control group that had been exposed to less television advertising during the research year. After the research year, the advertising pressure was the same for both groups. The measurements of purchases during the research year and the two subsequent years showed the following:

- If TV advertising has an effect in the current year, that effect will double in the two subsequent years.
- If TV advertising has no effect in the current year, there will be no effect subsequently.

In marketing practice, experiments are not used very frequently, although online experiments are increasing, for example, testing two different websites ('A/B testing'). A reason for the limited use of experiments may be that managers are hesitant to deviate from their preference policy in the area of, for example, communication. For example, it is conceivable that it will be difficult to use an experiment to persuade an advertiser that is convinced of the benefit of television advertising to allocate part of the television budget to the magazine advertising it considers less effective. However, such an experiment could provide support for the advertiser's assumption about the effectiveness of television advertising (or the reverse, which would be equally important to know). Another barrier relates to the implementation. The reliability of an experiment depends on its structure, and a thorough preparation and a well-considered 'design' therefore are necessary (Malhotra et al., 2017).

*Split-cable research* is a specific application of experiments. This type of research uses single-source data and involves two separate target audiences that are brought into contact with television advertising in different ways (e.g., a difference in advertising pressure); the research focuses on determining the differences in purchasing that may result. Studies of Lodish et al. (1995a, 1995b) are based on split-cable research. This kind of research currently can be implemented in only few countries because single-source data is not available in every country.

We conclude this section about communication with a few final remarks. In comparison to expenditures on advertising, companies spend only a little on communication research. It appears that people prefer to increase the media pressure rather than allocating a portion of the budget for effect research. Apparently, the benefit of research is not sufficiently appreciated. It might be a task for marketing science to demonstrate the added value of applied research. The following arguments might be used:

■ Planning cannot occur if objectives have not been set and the results of communication are not measured subsequently. Without planning, providing direction is also difficult.

■ In practice it is often argued that it is impossible to determine the separate effect of communication because so many other factors also have an influence on sales. However, earlier in this chapter we described methods (causal models and experiments) that can be used to determine the separate effect of communication.

■ It is also often argued that even when it is known whether a campaign succeeded, it still is not known why the communication succeeded and therefore it is also not known what should be done differently in the future. In this context it is often said: 'We know that half the communication expenditures are effective, but we do not know which half'. This is an argument for doing more experimentation, since experiments can be used to examine the effect of each form of input, including, for example, two different creative expressions, such as a more informational versus a transformational communication expression.

## 13.11 Customer experience management

An important goal of marketing is to satisfy customers, preferably leading to a certain degree of customer loyalty. In this context, it is therefore also important to provide customers with the most pleasant possible experience or customer experience (CX) during their 'customer journey '. In some organizations separate functions are created for this under the name customer experience management. A CX manager is then made responsible for optimizing the customer journey. The customer journey encompasses all moments that the customer is in contact with the organization. That 'contact' can be personal and direct but can also take place online in a non-personal way, for example. In fact, this is very close to what has been called 'integrated marketing communications' for many years. Nowadays this is often also online, but the intention is always to have consistent and 'pleasant' communication with customers.

## Case 13.7 Customer experience management

### At Malaysia Airlines creating a seamless customer experience is key

Malaysia Airlines flies 40,000 guests daily to more than 50 destinations worldwide. Customer satisfaction and experience is a key priority for the airline. Using ServiceNow, employees are at the center of their IT services, back office services have been simplified, and employees are now served by a single window of service. At Malaysia Airlines, digital transformation is critical to creating a seamless customer experience.

Abdul Rahman Mohamed, head of information technology at Malaysia Airlines, explains how technology plays a key role in differentiating the airline. 'We want to introduce new and better ideas fast in order to distinguish ourselves from other airlines', says Abdul. 'Our aim is to drive automation, personalization, and innovation through digital transformation. Ultimately, the aim is to deliver seamless services to our passengers'.

Airline staff focus more on passengers with a unified and streamlined employee experience.

To achieve this, Malaysia Airlines is adopting a mobile-first and cloud-first strategy while automating back-office systems and processes. It has broken down internal silos by creating a company-wide destination where employees can request all the services they need and track the status of their requests. This approach also allows Malaysia Airlines to standardize its back-end service fulfilment processes and drive continuous service improvement.

According to Abdul, 'We can now worry less about accessing what we require to meet our objectives and instead focus on delivering high-quality, personalized services to our passengers'.

The tasks of a CX manager are partly similar to those of an 'ordinary' marketing manager:

1 Analyzing the current customer journey.
2 Setting goals and determining the strategy for that customer journey.
3 Ensuring that the customer journey is optimized.

We have already discussed what was mentioned under 1 in Chapter 5. For example, you should consider choosing the desired brand values in that customer journey. It is about providing the customer with a 'brand-worthy' experience by organizing 'back stage' that all contact moments deliver a good feeling among the customer. The idea is that if the contact moments are optimal, the customer will reflect a high net promotor score. In practice, there is often a discrepancy between what 'brand managers' do and what CX managers do (Alsem & Van Slooten, 2021). This is, of course, not necessary.

The daily task of the CX manager is the third task and is illustrated in Case 13.7.

# Summary

In the communication planning process, a company should determine the target audience, the proposition, and the communication objectives as well as the communication budget. Communication objectives should be specific and measurable and may relate to brand awareness (knowledge), brand associations (attitude), and purchasing intention (behavior). The choice of the objectives depends on where problems are located (image versus identity) and on the chosen proposition. Based on a clear and focused briefing, the advertising agency develops a creative concept that may be pretested with a target audience. The best creative ideas are ideas that are strongly linked to the brand, entertaining, distinctive, simple, and applicable in many variations.

The message may be communicated through an increasing range of media. Online communication including social media is increasingly important, because people look at their mobile phones for several hours a day. Online channels can be used for your own communication but also to encourage others to talk about the brand so that word of mouth is created. In building a strong, relevant, and distinctive brand image, communication remains the most important means, and brands will therefore have to use the various offline and online media resources in a creative and integrated manner. To generate brand awareness and to be able to convey emotion, advertising via TV or outdoor, for example, remains important.

Companies should continuously and consistently measure factors such as brand knowledge and brand associations and customer satisfaction (tracking) much more than they have done in the past. If such a result measurement yields time series, causal models can be used to investigate whether, and if so why, communication has been effective. The effects of communication can also be investigated by means of experiments. This is quite easy to achieve online through A/B testing. The ultimate goal of all communication is that the customer go through the customer journey in a pleasant way that fits the brand. The coordination of all this falls under customer experience management, which is close to integrated communication.

## Vans: genuine commitment with its fans

A cultural connection with the target group gives a brand meaning. The success story of the shoe and clothing brand Vans is a good illustration.

In 1966, Paul Van Doren started selling vulcanized rubber-soled sneakers with canvas tops from a small shop in front of his factory in Anaheim, California. Paul began distributing his sneaker, known to this day as the 'Authentic', to local retailers in California at an affordable price.

It wasn't until 1974, when a group of surf dudes from Santa Monica, California, adopted the shoe, that the company found its connection with this specific target audience, says Doug Palladini, Vans global brand president.

> These were kids who could be found on their surfboard every day. But on windless days they wanted to do something different. So they tried on their skateboard, on concrete, to imitate what they were doing in the water. They loved Authentics, because of the vulcanized rubber bottom. It gripped the board really well, but they could still feel it under their feet, which is important in skateboarding.

From these humble beginnings, Vans has grown into a global trend-setter that remains culturally connected to the countless generations that have made the brand great, with sales exceeding $4 billion in more than 90 countries. How did the brand do this? How does Vans stay authentic for all of its fans?

### A brand with a purpose

Vans wants to do more than just sell shoes; the brand wants to create a community. That's why Vans looks at its higher purpose. At Vans, that is 'creative self-expression'. 'Creative self-expression is such a powerful part of who we are as human beings', says the global brand president. 'Our goal is to make that possible for people all over the world. That's why creative self-expression is at the heart of Vans'.

By building a community around creative self-expression, Vans is able to act purposefully and deepen the connection with its target group. Due to its strong purpose, the company has maintained authenticity and credibility. 'We are guided in our self-expression by the trends and the people in four domains: art, music, action sports and street culture', says Palladini. 'That has enabled us to stay true to ourselves'.

Many companies make the mistake of hijacking the culture of the target audience. Vans' strategy was to invest in communities that use the brand as the brand wants to be. This strengthens the positioning of the brand. Vans is transparent about what it stands for. 'That's why the target group comes to us', says Palladini. 'Everyone is welcome, but we don't suit everyone'.

> It doesn't matter where you come from, what language you speak, what color you are or who you love. It's all good for us. There may also come a time when you decide that Vans is not the right brand for you. And that is OK for us: Vans is part of a lifestyle, we are not everything to everyone.

## Youth culture of today and fans of the past

It's hard enough to really connect with one age group, but Vans seems to appeal to today's generation as well as generations back then. Today's digital youth are often suspicious of marketing. How can a company as large as Vans, with such a broad target group, still generate consumer goodwill?

Vans is not a company that buys a Super Bowl ad; it wants to build a relationship with the customer. 'We believe "Off The Wall" is a state of mind', Palladini says of Vans' long-standing tagline. 'That connects our target group, regardless of age. We get a lot of information by listening to our fans and communicating openly'.

Vans doesn't want to be everything to everyone. Hence the focus on purpose, facilitating self-expression in actions sports, music, art, and street culture. That also means that not everyone feels at home at Vans; for example, the brand does not do basketball.

Essentially, the 'Off The Wall' mentality allows Vans to position its products but also to develop new products for different areas of interest in different countries. For example, Vans still works with Metallica – an icon for the older part of the target group – but the brand also joins forces with small streetwear brands and social influencers that are popular with young people. Vans also connects with young people through collaborations, for example, with the Simpsons cartoons or through Checkerboard Day. Each year on Checkerboard Day, Vans donates a substantial amount to a number of carefully selected institutions dedicated to the arts, sports or youth. 'It's all about the creative self-expression that is so important to our fans', explains Palladini.

Another example of the importance of self-expression is that Vans is big among chefs. Palladini:

> Many chefs enjoy skateboarding, but this is about mentality. The culture in the kitchen is very similar to that of skateboarding; it's black and white, you have your own style, a chef has a drive, is creative. And as our way of saying thank you to chefs for being fans, we made them special Vans shoes: Vans for the Makers. This is how our brand evolves and how we stay connected with our subcultures.

Vans is selective in the choice of its ambassadors. Celebrities or other influencers must prove genuine affinity with the brand. 'The organic connection is paramount. It has to fit the way we tell stories', says Palladini.

Data-driven insights influence brand strategy, also at Vans, but companies should also listen. 'Many of us have long since outgrown youth culture', says seasoned surfer Palladini. 'Give a voice to the emerging talent in your organization, not just the executive team. Give a voice to your community and listen to them. Go out into the world and experience it for yourself'.

Before COVID-19, Palladini could sometimes be seen chatting with the kite surfers on the beach, going to concerts, or taking part in street culture events. That still happens, of course. But now he and his team are also paying close attention to what their fans are doing on the socials. 'We try to be part of the world we want to represent', says Palladini. 'You can't hire an external agency to tell you what's cool about Gen Z while you sit at your desk answering emails. You have to go see for yourself'.

That understanding and connection is also the foundation of Vans' digital and social media initiatives. 'The depth of the connection with a fan is more important than the number of fans. We want to connect with people who are inspired and give us inspiration'.

## Custom-made design

Another example of that creative self-expression is of course the fact that you can design the Vans shoes yourself. 'If you design something yourself on your phone and then wear it, we win as a brand. If a brand is part of someone's character, then we have done well'.

According to brand experts, it is special that Vans has found such a broad target group while the brand is still popular with its original supporters. 'You can see a twenty-year-old, but also an eighty-year-old walking with a shirt or a pair of Vans. They did a great job', said a brand expert. He explains that most brands that move from niche to mainstream lose relevance for the insiders. 'You can only achieve that by staying very authentic. Vans did this'.

Examples that show that Vans is not aiming for the masses is that the brand makes careful choices in their collaborations. Consider, for example, the collaboration with the Netflix series *Stranger Things*, including a special Hellfire Club edition. The brand expert says: 'They make the right choices, by working with parties that match with the Vans culture'. Self-expression is also central to this. A good example is also the collaboration with cartoonist Denzel Curry, perhaps not a big name, but someone who is loved by the target group. 'That is only possible if you understand which subcultures you have to embrace. They actually build it from the bottom up and that is special'.

## Stakeholder engagement during COVID-19

Vans' commitment to fostering meaningful relationships was also evident throughout the pandemic, for employees and for fans:

- Caring for employees: When COVID-19 hit, Vans put people first. 'We had to make sure our employees were okay', says Palladini. Working from home and zoom meetings therefore became the norm.
- Taking care of the fans: After Vans took care of its own employees, Vans reached out to its fans. 'We needed to let you know that we care about you, even if you're not buying from us right now, and that we're working together to get through this'.

To stay in touch with customers, Vans invested in its digital community, for example, by offering fans a distraction while they were in quarantine, with engagement campaigns such as Bouncing Off The Walls, a content series about how fans of the brand are engaged at home. Another notable initiative was the Shoe Box Challenge. Vans invited consumers to take an old Vans shoebox, transform it into something artistic, and share it online with the hashtag #VansShoeBoxChallenge. Selected winners received a code to personalize a pair of Vans for free.

Also noteworthy during the pandemic was the support for retail partners. 'We connect with the best boardsport shops, music venues and art galleries in the world. This is our extended family. They run on passion, not on cash flow', says Palladini.

For example, Vans invited its partners to collaborate with local artists to create limited edition shoes. Vans then donated the revenues to participating retail partners. 'Best of all, local communities revived as we supported those stores', said the global brand president.

## Black Lives Matter

Vans is also committed to Black Lives Matter. The brand shows solidarity through social media. And not only with words. Vans also donates money to organizations like NAACP (National Association for the Advancement of Colored People) and Color Of Change. 'We believe that Black Lives Matter. If you don't, we respect that you have your own point of view, but we disagree with you. Vans is not the best brand for you then', says Palladini.

By listening and taking action, the company is showing up for what matters. That said, Vans admittedly has internal work to do to further its anti-racist stance. 'We have not been where we need to be in terms of diversity', Palladini reflects. 'We have to be honest with ourselves and take a sober look at what we are committing to internally and externally'.

## Sustainability at Vans

Sustainability is not a priority in Vans' positioning, but the brand is taking steps to be more environmentally friendly. 'When we talk about sustainability, we do it through the lens of our four pillars: art, music, action sports and street culture', explains Palladini. 'A great example is our longstanding partnership with the Surfrider Foundation. It's about keeping the oceans safe and clean so we can continue to use the waves for what we want to do: with surfing'.

Under the leadership of its parent company, VF Corporation, Vans also sets concrete goals to reduce the brand's environmental footprint. The brand is also looking for greener alternatives to the vulcanized rubber that is so important in the shoes.

Source: *Forbes*, Sept. 24, 2020

## Questions

1   For Vans, it is important to foster a community around the brand.
   a   Use this case to best describe the Vans community.
   b   Within the Vans community, several stakeholders can be distinguished. Which stakeholders are these?
2   The first step in communication planning is the formulation of the communication target group. It is important to describe this target group as well as possible.
   a   Choose one of the communication target groups of Vans. Describe this target group as best as possible. Create a persona for this target group.
   b   In Chapter 5 of the book, several segmentation variables are mentioned. Which variable(s) are most important in your description? Explain your answer.
3   Brand values are an important starting point for designing a good proposition.
   a   What is/are the Vans brand values?
   b   Are these instrumental values or final values?
   c   Design a proposition for Vans.
4   How does the Vans slogan (Off The Wall) align with the Vans proposition you designed in the previous question?
5   The choice of the right objective is of great importance in communication activities.
   a   Create a (SMART) communication objective for the Vans brand.
   b   At what level of the advertising response matrix is this objective? Explain your answer.
6   According to this case, what are the most important marketing communication tools used by Vans?
7   Vans does not invest in Super Bowl advertising or other mass communication media. Do you agree that Vans should not invest in mass communication? Explain your answer.
8   Do you think viral marketing plays an important role for Vans? Why (not)?
9   Corporate social responsibility refers to the three Ps: people, planet, profit. Which of these three do you think is/are central to Vans? Explain your answer.

# Chapter 14

# Organization and execution of marketing

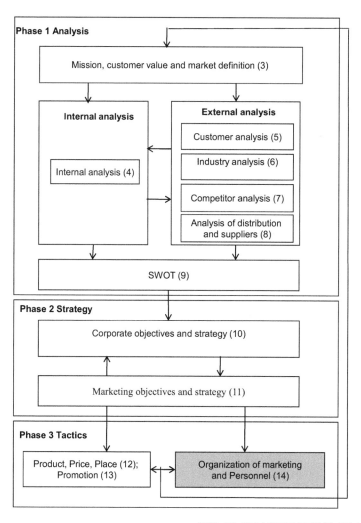

**Phase 1 Analysis**

Mission, customer value and market definition (3)

**Internal analysis**

Internal analysis (4)

**External analysis**

Customer analysis (5)

Industry analysis (6)

Competitor analysis (7)

Analysis of distribution and suppliers (8)

SWOT (9)

**Phase 2 Strategy**

Corporate objectives and strategy (10)

Marketing objectives and strategy (11)

**Phase 3 Tactics**

Product, Price, Place (12); Promotion (13)

Organization of marketing and Personnel (14)

DOI: 10.4324/9781003381488-18

## Key points in this chapter

- Know how to organize marketing and communication in a market-oriented organization.
- Know what motivates people in an organization.
- Know how to stimulate innovation.
- Be able to sell a marketing plan.
- Know the main pitfalls in planning.

## Introduction

Chapters 3 through 11 detailed the various phases of the process of strategic marketing planning. Chapter 3 began with the vision and the identification of market boundaries. Chapters 4 through 9 were dedicated to the internal analysis and the external analysis. Chapters 10 through 13 were about planning (decisions). At least of equal importance is everything a company has to do to implement the plans properly: the organization and the implementation (execution). A marketing plan can be successful only if the people involved in the implementation (often the entire organization) are motivated to implement the task.

This final chapter is dedicated to the organization and implementation of marketing. First, Section 14.1 will discuss the relation between marketing and personnel. Internal branding is one of the issues. Next, Section 14.2 will deal with the organization of marketing and communication. Section 14.3 is about securing a foundation for a marketing plan, including making a financial performance timeline. Section 14.4 provides guidelines for the implementation of the planning. We complete the book with tips for strategic marketing.

## 14.1 Marketing and personnel

### 14.1.1 Relation between marketing and personnel

There are three reasons there is a strong relation between marketing and human resource management:

1. The core values can only be realized if the whole staff knows what these values are and is also acting as such.
2. Plans initiated from top management can only be realized if they have support from the staff.
3. In every company, some level of innovation is needed, which requires input from all staff members.

It is for these reasons that the P of personnel is often indicated as the fifth P of marketing. In every company, marketing and HRM should closely work together. Glassman and McAfee (1992) even suggest that the marketing function and the personnel function should be integrated.

The importance of personnel seems logical, yet it is not always emphasized strongly. In the literature and practice of strategic management, the triad of 'strategy, structure, people' often is mentioned; this means that after the choice of a strategy has been made, a suitable organizational structure is set up, after which the focus is on the completion of the personnel policy. In our view, the sequence of these steps should be altered to 'strategy, people, structure': There is a group of people who are responsible for the execution of the strategy, and those people should be optimally motivated to tackle the task. Then they are surrounded by and supported with a structure that, among other things, should serve to motivate them optimally.

## 14.1.2 Internal branding

The first of the three reasons mentioned previously is related to the issue of 'internal branding'. Internal branding means that all staff members are participating in delivering the chosen customer and societal value (the positioning) (Figure 14.1). This might suggest that realizing the desired behavior of staff members is a top-down process. But of course, this is not the case. This is because the core values are formulated by looking at the current culture and behavior of the staff (see Chapter 4). At the moment the DNA of the company is formulated, the chosen positioning should be the driver for the staff members including getting new personnel (Figure 14.2).

Determining the DNA does not mean that the core values cannot be changed. A company that is too strongly supply oriented can go through a turnaround process to turn into a more customer-oriented organization. This is about *change management*.

In defining the core values of a company, it is important to find values that lend themselves to translating them into *job descriptions*. A value of 'personal attention' is difficult to use for selecting staff members. A value of 'down-to-earth' is related to how people communicate and can be used in a job description.

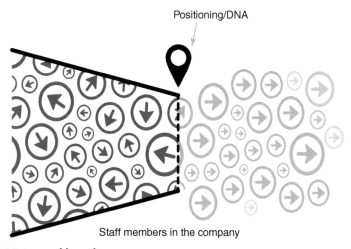

*Figure 14.1* **Internal branding**

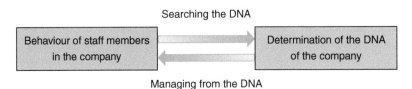

**Figure 14.2 Cyclical process of defining the DNA of the company**

### 14.1.3 Leadership

A good implementation of a strategy is essential for success. Managers can make excellent plans, but a plan will be effective only after a good implementation, and that implementation is done by the employees. Employees perform best when they are motivated, that is, when they are proud of working for their organization. A generally accepted starting point for getting employees motivated is team building. Implementation will be successful if the organization operates as a team of people working on shared goals. Therefore, a good implementation requires motivated and involved staff who are impressed with the necessity of marketing and customer-oriented thinking and also has good relationships with other functional areas within the company. Best is that the employees are proud to work for the company. Because leadership is essential for realizing this, we pay (little) attention to leadership. For more information about leadership, we refer in general to the many books about leadership.

A goal of leadership is to influence individuals to reach a certain goal. Often, that person is the leader. But also non-leaders can influence group behavior. Sometimes a distinction is made between leaders and managers. Leaders are inspirational, innovative, have ideas, and motivate staff members by their inspiring stories. Managers are more oriented toward processes and day-to-day operations and take care of the 'technical' aspects of managing people. In practice it is often hard to make a distinction between 'leaders' and 'managers'. Ideally, both things are present in a company.

The difference between 'leaders' and 'managers' is reflected in the two forms of leadership:

- *Transactional leadership.* This form is based on 'exchange': the leader uses rewarding and 'punishing' as main instruments of motivating people. This form of leadership is closely related to 'management'.
- *Transformational leadership.* This form assumes that behavior is not only affected by rewarding but also by the process itself: motivated by the work in itself and by an inspirational way of management. Transformational leaders should not only have a clear vision but should also 'know their people' and thus have empathy.

In the literature there are many other classifications of leadership styles. Two (related) dimensions often play a role:

- The level of directive behavior: much control versus 'participative': giving responsibility to the people.

■ Being more task oriented (giving clear instructions and checking whether tasks are realized) versus people oriented (motivating people and giving them 'space' to do their job).

Which leadership is best? In our view, the following aspects are important:

■ Clear vision including sustainability
■ Innovation and starting small
■ Open communication
■ People orientation
■ Low level of control and hierarchy
■ Rewarding innovation

### Clear vision including sustainability

In Section 10.1, the importance of a clear vision was argued. It is essential to be clear about the desired future position of the company. A common vision is generally seen as the most important direction for a team. Peters (1994) refers to the 'WOW! factor', in which a vision requires that top management dare to choose and therefore also dare to choose goals it does not want to achieve. This is all related to the positioning of the company/brand and should as such also include attention to sustainability.

### Innovate and start small

In order to stay different, innovation is important. The leader should stimulate employees thinking out of the box. It can also be helpful to reward innovation, as we already discussed in Chapter 4 when talking about the balanced scorecard.

A guideline in innovation could also be to 'start small'. In making a number of small steps instead of trying to make large steps:

■ it is easier to start something new
■ a company gets experience with the new innovation, can evaluate things, and is also able to communicate results internally, thus realizing support for continuation.

### Open communication

Marketing implementation is more successful if leaders create an organizational culture that is characterized by *open communication* between personnel and managers. Conversely, it has been shown that bad internal communication in an organization is one of the most important reasons for bad implementation. Two forms of internal communication play a role: communication between top management and employees and communication among employees. A leader should provide a good example and pay attention to individual personnel. Another principle is that people should be used as much as possible on the basis of their strengths. Therefore, it is important in terms of motivating people to understand the characteristics of individual people and then engage them as much as possible on the basis of those characteristics.

Another important issue is informing personnel about policy measures. Top management should try to be close to the personnel and therefore not regularly announce one-sided top-down measures. A problem that might develop in this regard is that the organization will be less battle ready: endless deliberations and democratic processes may make it impossible to lead an organization and become a barrier to prompt action. However, that does not have to be the case. Obviously, top management should also be able to execute unpopular measures. However, when that happens with a direct and open information supply, the foundation for support is increased.

### People manager

Ideally, the leader should also be a 'people manager', someone who stays close to the personnel, shows that he or she understands them, and knows what matters. The reason for this is that otherwise the 'boss' ends up being detached from the personnel, and there is a risk that the personnel will separate itself from upper management, for example, during changes. A leader should show a good example and pay attention to employees.

Another principle is that employees should be stimulated to use their own strengths. A manager should find out what staff members are good at and exploit the different strengths.

### Low control and hierarchy

Motivation and innovation grow best in organizations where employees have room for own responsibilities. Motivation is higher because employees have more control in their job. A lack of control often is an important cause of stress in a job. And creativity only works where staff members have room for thinking outside the box. Companies with a strong hierarchy often have less room for own ideas of employees. Large organizations can try to give responsibilities to lower-level managers.

## 14.1.4 Labor market communication

The previous chapter was devoted to marketing communication. In some companies labor market communication is insufficiently related to marketing communication. A reason for this is that different functions in the company are responsible. This can lead to a situation where the form and the content of both forms of communication are not aligned, risking a situation where different messages about the brand are communicated. A future employee can also be a customer and the other way around. There is also a more proactive reason for aligning labor market and marketing communication: a message on LinkedIn or in a newspaper is also an opportunity to say nice things about the brand. So, both marketing and labor market communication are to be in line with the core values/positioning of the company. Currently, sustainability is important, also and perhaps especially among youngsters, so this is an important value to attract new, young personnel (see Case 14.1).

## Case 14.1 Labor market

### Shortage in the labor market requires sharp positioning

In 2022, there was a shortage of personnel in many industries due to various causes. This offers opportunities for job seekers such as young graduates to choose an organization where they really feel at home. At the same time, these organizations should do their best in their labor market communication to attract the right employees. More than in the past, young people are looking for a job that is in balance with their private life. And sustainability is also important to them, matters that organizations must therefore pay a lot of attention to.

## 14.2 Organization of marketing and communication

This section reviews how marketing (Section 14.2.2) and communication (Section 14.2.3) should be organized within the company ('structure'). But we start with stressing the importance of marketing as a culture (Section 14.2.1).

### 14.2.1 Part time marketer

As we argued in Chapter 1, marketing is primarily a culture: a company should be customer and brand oriented. A company or organization is by definition a group of people, so this means that all employees in a company should be customer and brand oriented. This is the principle of the 'part time marketeer', introduced many years ago by Gummesson (1987). The principle means that marketing is not restricted to employees working at the

## Case 14.2 Marketing and digital

### Kellogg's uses mixed team for marketing

Kellogg's uses hybrid teams. Because even Kellogg's head of digitization, Julie Bowerman, argues that FMCG manufacturers should not focus too much on the digital landscape. 'E-commerce is often either part of marketing or sales, but it is part of both. You need a vision that includes both. You also have to hire the right people'. Her team also includes both the more traditional marketeers and the more tech-oriented employees. 'The most important thing is the culture and teamwork'.

Source: Marketing Week, *November 18, 2019*

marketing or communication department but that the whole staff is involved in improving customers' experiences. Sometimes it is said that having a marketing department might even lead to a simple excuse of staff members for not being involved in improving customers' satisfaction. Customer orientation concerns the entire organization. The reverse also applies: A customer-oriented organization does not necessarily have to have a marketing department. Especially in smaller companies, there is often no marketing department, but this kind of company may in fact be customer oriented.

So, marketing is relevant for all employees in a company. Nevertheless, it is also useful to have people in house who really know how to do and organize marketing, since implementing marketing demands doing all kinds of specific activities such as advertising or social media. The next section review how marketing can be organized.

### 14.2.2 Organization of marketing

The first thing that is important for organizing marketing is that marketing knowledge is present in *top management* in an organization. Without support from top management, marketing will not have enough 'power' to realize successes. A common misunderstanding is that top managers think that having communication managers is enough and thus lack knowledge about the differences between marketing and communication.

Now we discuss several ways how marketing can be organized.

### Forms of organization

To know how marketing activities should be organized within a company, it is important to establish what those activities are. This includes all activities that concern the analysis of the environment (*analysis*), the making of marketing decisions and the drafting of a marketing plan (*planning*), the implementation of the decisions that are made (*implementation*), and the checking and evaluation of the results (*control*). The most important choices regarding these decisions are the choice of markets and target groups and the distinguishing power. All these marketing activities show that there must be a direct link between marketing and upper management. Moreover, marketing must be 'on equal terms' with departments such as finance, personnel, and research and development. This is the case because marketing decisions can be implemented only in close cooperation with other 'functions' within a company.

How can marketing be organized? The following are the main options:

1  *Functional* organization.
2  *Product* organization.
3  *Customer-oriented* organization and account management.
4  *Regional* organization.

We now explain each of these options.

1  *Functional organization.* Many companies opt for an organizational form in which the various basic functions are fulfilled by separate departments. In this case, a company may have a purchasing department, a production department, a personnel department, a finance department, and a marketing department. The marketing department may include tasks (and subdepartments) such as market research, sales, product development, and communication. An organization in which the tasks of the employees are grouped on the basis of company functions is called a functional organization. A division based on functions is the most common and is a simple system. The disadvantage is that no one is responsible for a particular product or particular customer groups (segments).
2  *Product organization.* Companies with different products or brands often opt for the *product management* or 'brand management' system. Separate managers are appointed who are responsible for a certain product (e.g., the diapers) or a certain brand (e.g., Pampers). Managers in these positions must collaborate extensively with each other within the company to be able to set up all the activities they want to undertake related to their brand (e.g., innovation, price setting, research) in a well-coordinated way.
3  *Customer oriented organization.* Another way to organize the marketing function is as a *customer-oriented organization*: a division according to markets or customer

groups. This kind of division is particularly useful if a company is clearly servicing different target groups, such as consumers and organizations (business markets). The *account management system* is a variation of the buyer-oriented organization. An account manager is a person who is responsible for a client (account). This system is increasingly common among food manufacturers that often have only a few clients (distributors: food retailers) that are all quite large. The task of the account manager is to ensure that the relationship with the distributor remains optimal.

4    *Regional organization.* A fourth form is *regional organization*, in which separate managers are responsible for the turnover in regions (parts of a country, countries, or combinations of countries and/or parts of the world).

### Toward a customer-oriented organization

Forms of a 'brand management' organization are both useful and logical in many companies. It is handy if there is one manager and one group of people responsible for a brand. The danger is that too much focus is placed on the brand and/or product and too little is placed on the customer. It is often said that 'brand management is dead'. This does not mean that brands are not important but rather that a strong organizational focus exclusively on brands is not wise. Because of the vast importance of customer-oriented business, it is important that another buyer-oriented organizational form always be chosen as well. An example could be a consumer variant of account management: the appointment of a customer manager within the company who is responsible for a certain target group (e.g., young people). This manager knows the target group well and tries to promote its interests within the company. The goal is *not* to sell as much as possible. A customer manager is not a salesperson but certainly is suited to coordinate *complaint settlements*. If there are different target groups, there can be different customer managers. If this system is combined with a brand management system, the customer managers will negotiate regularly with the various brand managers to ensure that the target group is served in the best possible way. With a customer manager, the company brings the customer in house, as it were (Figure 14.3).

In practice, one of the forms outlined in the figure may not be used; instead, there are combinations. In these cases, the *formal organization* (the structure) becomes more complicated. Therefore, the importance of good *informal organization* increases. Informal organization concerns the rules of conduct within a company that are not established formally but are customarily followed. Examples include 'dropping in on each other' and drinking coffee together. Informal communication in an organization is very important for the ability to react quickly. Organizations that work only according to established hierarchical systems are often not very flexible and are not able to react quickly to changes in the environment.

## 14.2.3 Organization of communication

All forms of communication of a brand (or company or product) influence the brand image for the target group. A strong and positive reputation is very important for success. This can be achieved only with communication that is organized and implemented professionally. Chapter 11 stated that agencies must be contracted for the development of

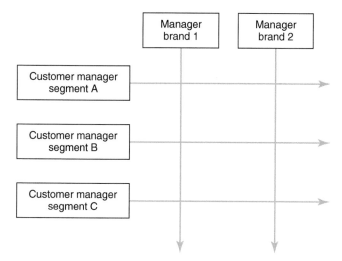

*Figure 14.3* Customer-oriented organization in combination with brand management

a campaign. Creative communication and creative and efficient media planning require independent expertise. However, this does not negate the fact that the responsibility for communication lies entirely with the brand and that there is still a huge amount of communication to be done and arranged by the brand.

There are two major preconditions:

1  A *clear image* should be communicated consistently.
2  This image should be communicated in a *creative way* that *fits* with the brand.

These preconditions can be satisfied only if upper management emphasizes their importance and is therefore prepared to accept their consequences.

The following factors are important in fulfilling these preconditions (see Figure 14.4):

1  *Management from the top of the organization.* The image to be communicated is determined in the vision on brand positioning. This is a matter for upper management. The 'leader' of the company plays an important role in communication, but many others participate as well. This can lead to a consistent image only if an intrinsic top-down management system is already in place. Therefore, there must always be a 'hotline' between the head of communications and the head of the company. The head of communications can also take on the job of 'reputation watchdog' (Alsop, 2004). For instance, if there is a crisis situation (e.g., poison, unsafe products, personal scandals), it should be dealt with quickly and adequately.
2  *Continuous fine-tuning of all forms of communication.* In light of the previous point, all forms of communication must be well attuned to each other. In large companies, there generally should be different departments and persons who are concerned with communication (public relations, sponsoring, advertising, design, personal sales, direct marketing, personnel, etc.), and the primary danger is that they will work

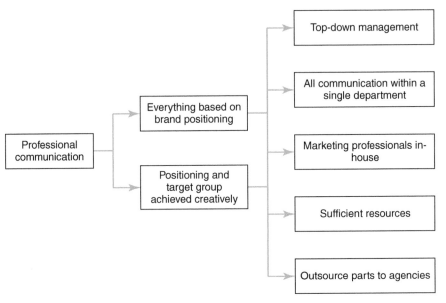

*Figure 14.4* **Factors that promote professional communication**

counter to each other and go their own ways. Organizations often decide to choose another logo without bringing that choice in line with the brand positioning, or a different image may be given in personnel advertisements than is used in advertising. Optimal alignment can be achieved if all communications activities are organized in one large department. In this department, the specializations mentioned above can be defined and the heads of those subdepartments can regularly confer and drop in on one another and on the head of communication. This, in combination with the previous point, provides a picture like the one in Figure 14.3.

3   *Personnel with marketing and communication knowledge.* A great deal of knowledge is needed for professional communication, and so people have to be taken on for this purpose. It is sometimes thought that only people originating from the relevant sector (financial services, universities, health care, etc.) are in a position to run these marketing and communication departments. This misconception leads to the idea that only people with an understanding of that market will work in communication. This has two big disadvantages: The people in question often have little understanding of marketing, and they lack a fresh external perspective. A good communication strategy can ensure good communication in every market and for any company.

4   *Sufficient support and resources.* It takes time and thus money to change images. One-time communication or only a bit of communication is too little. Being modest doesn't help either: Even with a good product, word-of-mouth advertisement and public relations unfortunately do not get the job done today. The competition will do more and do it more professionally. You may be the best, but if nobody knows that, you have a problem.

5   *Support from professional communication agencies.* As stated, even with good communication knowledge in-house, assistance from agencies is often required. Matters

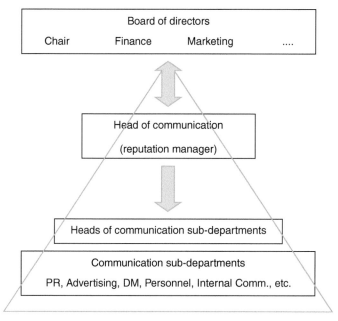

*Figure 14.5* **Organization of communication within a company**

related to communication that can be outsourced include creation (translation of brand positioning into communication), media planning (both through a communication consultancy bureau), brand name development (name agencies), and design (design firms).

## 14.3 Performance projection and selling the plan

### 14.3.1 Performance projection

The first thing the plan should show is that the marketing objectives will be achieved. This implies that marketing expenditures will be paid back in an acceptable time frame and/or that profit will increase, depending on the performance objectives. A challenging goal of an increase in market share of 15 points will demand a higher marketing budget than will an increase of 5 points. Thus, it is critical to make a credible performance timeline. Figure 14.6 provides an example.

Figure 14.6 shows the predicted performance of a high-priced personal computer (PC). The main marketing objective of this brand is to increase market share (in terms of revenue) from 2.2% in 2023 to 2.4% in 2026. Market growth is predicted to slow from 20% to 14% in those years. The underlying marketing strategy is that the brand will focus on the advantages of having a PC at home in combination with a laptop and that Orange has the unique selling proposition that the communication between these computers is the most reliable among all brands. This decision is accompanied by a large campaign in 2014: The marketing budget increases from $15 million in 2023 ('current') to $25 million in 2024. It is projected that sales per customer can increase since more customers

| | Current | Predicted | | |
|---|---|---|---|---|
| | 2023 | 2024 | 2025 | 2026 |
| Market size (units; 1000) | 17,930 | 21,157 | 24,543 | 27,979 |
| Market growth (percent) | 20.3 | 18 | 16 | 14 |
| Market share (%) | 2.1 | 2.2 | 2.3 | 2.4 |
| Sales (units; 1000) | 377 | 465 | 564 | 671 |
| Market size (€ million ) | 17,571 | 19,888 | 22,579 | 25,181 |
| Market share | 2.2 | 2.3 | 2.4 | 2.5 |
| Turnover (€ million ) | 387 | 457 | 542 | 630 |
| Sales growth (%) | 8.0 | 18.3 | 18.5 | 16.2 |
| Average market price (€) | 980 | 940 | 920 | 900 |
| Average price Orange (€) | 1,027 | 983 | 960 | 938 |
| Number of customers (1000) | 270 | 300 | 330 | 360 |
| Revenue per customer | 1,432 | 1,525 | 1,642 | 1,749 |
| Margin (excluding marketing) | 15 | 15 | 15 | 15 |
| Gross profit (€ million excl. marketing) | 58 | 69 | 81 | 94 |
| Marketing budget (€ million ) | 15 | 25 | 20 | 20 |
| Net profit (€ million ) | 43 | 44 | 61 | 74 |

assumptions:

- Consumers appreciate the innovative communication between laptop and Orange PC.
- Competitors are unable to develop a comparable communication technique.

*Figure 14.6* **Example of a marketing performance plan for the personal computer brand Orange**

will buy a PC and a laptop in one transaction. Net profit will be stable in 2024 but will increase in 2025 and 2026.

Making 'wonderful' estimates such as those in Figure 14.6 is not enough; the main thing is they should be credible and sufficiently substantiated. In addition, two kinds of support are necessary:

■ Support from top management, to get money to implement the plan (the next section)
■ Support within the whole organization to fulfil the promises and to facilitate the implementation (Section 14.1)

## 14.3.2 Selling the plan: internal marketing

Managers who make plans have been known to complain that upper management does not have any money for their great ideas. Discontented, they ask themselves how they 'can carry out marketing with almost no money'. This answer is that they were evidently not in a position to sell the plan well internally. If a plan is really good and is sold internally in an attractive manner, the money will be there. There is always money for a good plan. All that is necessary is to convince upper management that the plan will pay for itself. The internal selling of the 'product' marketing plan is called *internal marketing* (Piercy & Morgan, 1991). In big companies, upper management often has various plans under review for which a limited budget is divided. The idea is to sell your plan better than others in the company sell theirs.

The following factors increase a plan's chances of acceptance (Figure 14.7):

1  *Convincing reasons the plan will succeed.* For an upper-level manager, only one thing counts: being convinced of the predicted success. What is the creative discovery, the innovation, the *consumer need* that makes the plan so good?

2  *Good base of support.* Every plan claims that it will pay for itself in no time, but upper management knows that there is always uncertainty with respect to the future. The most convincing plans are those which have the strongest base of support. Research plays a key role here. It is powerful to assert that 75% purchasing intent was attained on the basis of research rather than on the basis of your own estimation. It is also more honest to indicate explicitly the assumptions of the plan than to have upper management find them out during the discussion. That will make them suspicious.

3  *Show the alternatives that were not chosen.* Many managers have a tendency to present a single idea without showing why alternatives were not chosen. A disadvantage of this is that it puts upper management on the spot. There are no choices apart from yes or no. If a comparative perspective is used, the listener can help decide, as it were. This boosts your chances of acceptance. 'Unrevised policy' is always an available alternative, and it definitely helps if you can forecast what 'disastrous' results will occur if this alternative is chosen.

4  *Convincing presentation of the plan.* A convincing method of internal communication of the plan helps enormously: videos, Web sites, oral presentations – anything goes. Some companies are very strong in this area: As soon as a certain idea has the necessary internal base of support, a whole battery of creative tools is put into action

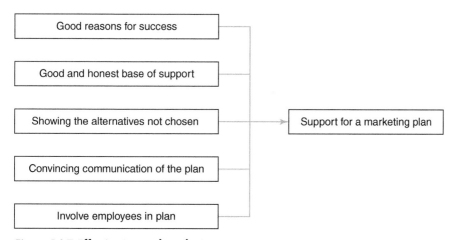

*Figure 14.7* **Effective internal marketing**

### 1. Introduction

In the introduction, the most important items from the executive summary may be shared: the core of the plan, the opportunity that is being responded to, expected revenues, and the budget. In effect this is a short summary beforehand that also immediately gets the attention of and stimulates the curiosity of management.

### 2. Why this plan will succeed

This part contains the situation analysis and the research performed. It ends with the core problem and the most important opportunities and threats, as well as the objectives. The most important message of this part of the presentation is why this plan will succeed (while others fail).

### 3. Strategy and tactics

This part contains the marketing strategy and the marketing implementation of the plans (such as the communication plan).

### 4. Assumptions, prognoses, and financial information

This part contains all assumptions (required to be able to discuss uncertainties and risk), the relevant prognoses, the project planning, the profit and loss pictures, and how much money is required and when.

### 5. Conclusions

Here the most important opportunity is repeated: why the plan will succeed, the required money, and the expected return on investment.

***Figure 14.8* Structure of the presentation of a marketing plan**

Source: Cohen, W. A. (1998), *The Marketing Plan*, 2nd ed., New York: Wiley

to achieve that goal. Figure 14.7 gives guidelines for the oral presentation of a plan. It is important to tell a convincing story in a short period of time. This means that the arrangement of the presentation does not have to follow 'scientific standards' such as slowly and meticulously building up to a conclusion. This kind of arrangement is generally considered boring by managers and is therefore not suitable for selling a plan.

5   *Involving internal target groups in the process.* If other internal target groups are involved in the development of the plan, this will increase the chances of acceptance as well as cooperation and motivation during the implementation phase. This 'involvement' can vary from participation in decision making to keeping up to date (communication). The advantage is that coworkers do not feel ambushed later and can have the feeling of being co responsible.

One might have the impression that upper management will be 'disobliging' and that it will be very difficult to get it to extend its support. This is not the case. The interests of everyone in the company are the same: collectively deliver good performance and thus (for the most part) earn money. Of course upper management is critical to all plans within a company, but the board must also extend a lot of support to marketing plans.

This involves not only money but also attention, information, and the active stimulation of the making of the plan. Upper management must also recognize that not every plan will pay for itself in no time. Especially for brand investments such as advertising, it is not always sufficient to demonstrate that an investment will quickly produce profits. It takes time to build up a brand, just as it does to win loyal customers. Upper management and other investors (such as shareholders) should therefore not always work from a short-term perspective (as with sales promotions) but take a long-term perspective (as with thematic communication).

## 14.3.3 Template for marketing plan summary

In Chapter 2 we already described the content of a marketing plan. All kinds of templates for marketing and business plans can be found in the literature, such as the well-known CANVAS model. The latter model visually summarizes a number of things but uses different concepts and not the order we propose in this book. For this reason, in Figure 14.9, we present our own representation of the core of a marketing plan as we see it before us.

In this figure are:

- the core strengths, weaknesses, opportunities and threats in column 1
- the strategic choices in column 2, including attention to sustainability
- the market instruments and personnel in column 3
- the expected results in the bottom row

| Strengths | Target groups | Products and services |
| | | Price |
| Weaknesses | Positioning and message | |
| | | Channels |
| Opportunities | Partners | |
| | | Communication |
| Threats | Society: sustainability | Personnel |
| Turnover | Costs | Profit |

*Figure 14.9* **Visual marketing plan summary**

## 14.4 Implementation of the plans

### 14.4.1 Guidelines for implementation

We now give a few guidelines for the eventual implementation of these plans.

#### Trigger

A plan will be more successful if it has a 'trigger': someone who feels that she or he is in charge of the plan.

#### Tasks

It is important that people know what is expected of them. Therefore, the formulation of clear tasks is vital. In relation to the targets, agreements must be reached about who is responsible for what. The marketing plan should also indicate in detail what is expected of each person.

#### Interim measurements

A marketing plan is normally drafted once a year. Typically, there is also an annual measurement of the results. However, interim measurements are recommended to enable timely adjustments. For instance, customer analyses can be conducted almost continuously. Customer satisfaction studies, advertising, and brand tracking should be a normal part of the monitoring. This approach requires extensive data collection and therefore an information system that is adapted to this process. In practice, it seems important to appoint a single person to be in charge of keeping the necessary information up to date.

#### Good process evaluation

If the measurements show that the goals have not been reached, a good process evaluation is important. A thorough process evaluation is necessary to avoid altering a strategy or product that is essentially good; the problem is related not to the product but to the implementation. In this context, four possible combinations of strategy (good/not good) and implementation (good/not good) can be distinguished (Figure 14.10).

In the most positive situation, strategy and implementation are both good. In all other cases, the diagnosis of disappointing results is a challenge. If both are bad, it is a failure in any case, but it is unclear whether it is related to the strategy because it was not implemented well. However, if the strategy is good but is implemented badly or vice versa, a risky situation develops. With a bad implementation of an excellent strategy, there is a risk that management may conclude that the strategy is not good. If the strategy is changed unnecessarily, the company moves to the cell at the bottom right in Figure 14.8, where it becomes a failure. With a good implementation of a bad strategy, there are two possibilities. If management concludes that the strategy is not good and alters it, there is still a chance for success (a move to the left in Figure 14.8). However, if management

**Strategy**

|  |  | Good | Bad |
|---|---|---|---|
|  | **Good** | *Success*<br><br>Objectives for growth, market share, and profit are achieved. | *Rescue or ruin*<br><br>Good implementation may soften bad strategy and allow management some time to make corrections, but a good implementation of a bad strategy may speed the decline. |
| Implementation |  |  |  |
|  | **Bad** | *Problems*<br><br>Bad implementation disguises good strategy: Management may conclude that the strategy is not good. | *Failure*<br><br>Cause of failure is difficult to determine because bad strategy is masked by bad implementation. |

*Figure 14.10* **Strategy and implementation: problem diagnosis**
Source: Bonoma (1984)

does nothing, a good implementation of a bad strategy will lead to 'ruin'. In following the results of the chosen strategies, explicit attention should be paid to the question of whether the chosen strategy was implemented well. Only after that step should any changes be made in the strategy itself.

## Flexibility

Finally, we advise against implementing the overall plan too rigidly. Marketing planning must not lead to a bureaucratic budgeting and prognosis system. It also should not lead to only once-a-year thinking about the strategy. Strategic choices have to be made continuously. Furthermore, flexibility and room for creativity should be monitored and safeguarded. Balance must be achieved between strong control of the system and freedom to innovate.

## Differences among companies

For all the guidelines given, there are differences between large and small companies. In small companies, the owner/director is usually very much involved in marketing and planning and there are not many other people in the organization involved in the planning process. In this case, the degree of formulation of the planning and the extent of the marketing plan may be more limited than they are in large companies.

| 1. Clear vision | Choose a point at the horizon; that is motivating. |
|---|---|
| 2. Use insights | Analyse yourself, the environment, and the customer systematically. |
| 3. Positive | Think positive: everything can be an opportunity. Focus on the pearls. |
| 4. Empathy | Think about everything concerning the psychology of the customer; demonstrate empathy for the customers. Also talk with them (qualitative research). |
| 5. Focus | For building relationships a clear brand image is needed. What is your key promise to the customer? Dare to choose: "specialize." |
| 6. Start small | Make small steps. Internally communicate successes. |
| 7. Innovate | Be innovative; think outside the box. One "big idea" can be enough. |
| 8. Patience and consistency | Do not focus on the short term: Building brand reputation and customer loyalty takes time |
| 9. Marketing in home | Make sure there is marketing knowledge in the company and a marketing culture in top management |
| 10. Delegate | Your employees determine the product and service quality. Reward this and delegate responsibilities.. |

*Figure 14.11* Ten tips for strategic marketing

## 14.4.2 Concluding tips for strategic marketing

In this last section of the book, we come up with a number of tips for effective strategic marketing (Figure 14.11). We believe our set of guidelines will leave the competition in the dust.

## Summary

A company or organization consists of people. And these people will have to execute the plans. This means that the values of the company are to be realized by and thus supported by the staff. Providing customer and societal value should be the goal of the whole organization. This makes internal branding important. Second, employees should be motivated to execute the plans and should have an open mind for innovation. A clear vision with attention for sustainability, a leader who is an inspirer and a people manager, collective goals, open internal communication, an open learning environment, and customer-oriented rewards stimulate team building.

The last part of a marketing plan is a forecast of the financial results. A marketing plan must be sold internally to obtain as much support as possible and the necessary resources. The plan should therefore be financially sound, clearly indicate why it will succeed, be grounded in research, and be contrasted with alternatives such as unrevised policy. All other departments should be involved in the development of the plan. Finally, creative internal marketing must be introduced for the plan: the internal selling and presentation of the plan, for example, to upper management.

Successful implementation of a customer-oriented strategy requires a good organization and places high demands on marketing and on the people in an organization. The introduction of a customer management system has the advantage that the customer is brought in-house, so to speak. For communication, it is important that this process be managed and coordinated from the top of the company or the brand. Successful implementation of a plan is facilitated if there is a 'trigger' for the plan, personal tasks are clearly indicated, and there are not only annual but also interim measurements of targets. If a target is not reached, a good process evaluation is needed: is it because of the strategy or because of the implementation? If adjustments are needed, flexibility is needed to leave room for innovation.

# Unilever: business with a purpose

The Unilever group was formed in 1930 by the merger of the English company Lever Brothers Limited and the Dutch company Margarine Unie. The company has since grown into one of the largest producers of fast-moving consumer goods in the world. The turnover is more than €50 billion per year.

Until 2020, the organization had two parent companies, Unilever NV in Rotterdam and Unilever PLC in London, which were linked by a number of legal agreements. As a result, the company was both British and Dutch. In 2020, this structure was simplified and London became Unilever's headquarters.

Unilever's activities are grouped in three divisions:

- Beauty & Personal Care; with brands such as Dove, Axe, and Rexona. This division stands for: 'To be the most positive beauty business in the world for people and the planet'.
- Foods & Refreshment; with brands such as Knorr, Becel, Magnum, and Unox. The motto: 'To be a world-class force for good in food'.
- Home Care; with brands such as Omo, Cif, and Muscle. Home Care stands for 'Making people's homes a better world, and our world a better home'.

Unilever operates globally; there are regional groups around the world that carry out Unilever's activities in their own areas. For example, Unilever Benelux is responsible for marketing and communication in the Netherlands and Belgium. Within the regional groups, product managers are responsible for the individual brands, such as the product manager Unox within Unilever Benelux.

Unilever is best known as a food and detergent group. We are all familiar with products such as Magnum, Lipton, or Ben & Jerry's, next to more local brands like the Dutch Conimex (oriental spices), the Australian Bushel's (tea), or Delma margarine in Poland. But Unilever is also increasingly becoming a personal care company, with again strong local brands such as Andrélon shampoo in The Netherlands, Wheel detergent in India, or Elidor hair care in Turkey, in combination with international brands such as Dove and Axe (Lynx in the UK). Personal care is now the group's largest activity, with global turnover of over € 20 billion in 2021. Beauty & Personal Care's strategic goal is to create competitive products that contribute to the company's growth objective. Focus on innovation and solid investment in marketing communication resulted in a worldwide increase in turnover of 3.8% for the Beauty & Personal Care division in 2021. An important challenge of marketing communication is dealing with the increasing complexity in the communication channels, with an increasing emphasis on 'digital'.

| Turnover per business category in 2021 (in billion euro) | |
|---|---|
| Beauty & Personal Care | 21.9 (+ 3.8%) |
| Foods & Refreshment | 20.0 (+ 5.6%) |
| Home Care | 10.6 (+ 3.9%) |

Under the leadership of former CEO Paul Polman, Unilever has been working on a new strategy: bringing new products to the market in several countries in combination with cost savings and margin improvements. Innovation is important to Unilever, as illustrated by the following quote from an annual report from a few years ago: 'We need to improve our innovation cycletimes and ensure we roll out innovations faster and to more markets. To that end, we have set ourselves some challenging objectives on innovation'. But innovation is not only about new products but also about new marketing. Unilever's Axe brand is a good example. 'Axe has been around for a long time', said a Unilever spokesperson, 'but marketing has made it huge. It targets young men, just look at those names: Cool Metal, Shock, Dark Temptation. And speaking of innovative: new Axe fragrances are launched on the market every year'.

Since 2019, Unilever's CEO is Alain Jope; however, the company's strategy remains broadly unchanged.

As early as the 1980s, Unilever started to build a division that was initially called Cosmetics. The group bought together numerous famous brands, such as Calvin Klein, Fabergé, and Elizabeth Arden. But about ten years ago, the insight broke through that expensive perfumes is not Unilever's cup of tea. Unilever focuses on mass markets. All brands that do not lend themselves to being sold in supermarkets were divested again. In recent years, Unilever has invested heavily in the Beauty & Personal Care division. For a group that wants to have global brands, personal care is more interesting than food. Food is very regional, often even local. An Indian curry is hard to sell in Europe, and Unox frankfurters have no business in Vietnam. But Dove is sold all over the world.

Emerging markets have also become increasingly important for Unilever. After all, there is still a lot of room for growth here. In 1990, Unilever generated only 20% of its turnover from emerging markets; now they account for more than half of its turnover. In emerging markets, as in Europe and North America, the emphasis is on the masses. However, Unilever uses other techniques to reach the masses. In India, for example, door-to-door sales of Unilever products by rural women is an important means of strengthening market position.

The employees are crucial to Unilever in achieving the company's objectives. Under the heading 'Our People' the 2021 annual report states:

> Our people are the heartbeat of Unilever – when they thrive, our business thrives. We believe that when employees are clear on their purpose in life and how this connects to the work they do, they're more engaged and willing to go the extra mile.
>
> Working with purpose is at the heart of our culture. This also helps us attract the very best people, as evidenced by our status as number one FMCG employer of choice for graduates and early career talent in over 50 markets. We see a human, purposeful and accountable culture that is rooted in our values as essential to our purpose-led and future-fit organisation. Using our future-fit plans, our people are shaping development and career plans based on

their purpose. We're creating a culture of learning across Unilever, upskilling and reskilling our people for jobs of the future.

We also want to be a workplace in which everyone feels they belong and are able to thrive. This means creating an inclusive culture free from the barriers that limit people in reaching their true potential.

It is evident that Unilever looks beyond its own business: 'Our business will not prosper without a healthy planet and society'. Unilever considers sustainable business the core of its activities. For example, the annual report specifies 'climate action', where Unilever specifically states that the company aims for 'net zero emissions across our value chain by 2039'. This is operationalized in various ways. For instance, recycled plastics are increasingly used as packaging material. And that is important: a lot of plastics are necessary for packaging consumer products such as shampoo, toothpaste, or detergents. Reducing the footprint also takes place by paying attention to the raw materials, for example, ensuring that no rainforest is sacrificed when cultivating the palm oil or soya beans used in Unilever products. Attention is also paid to 'fair' wages for employees worldwide. The company cooperates with local unions or suppliers to ensure that Unilever employees but also the employees of suppliers around the world are treated fairly, respectfully, and with dignity. Unilever's purpose statement clearly shows how corporate social responsibility is integrated into the company's business. The text below comes from Unilevers's website.

## Our purpose

Our purpose is to make sustainable living commonplace. It's why we come to work. It's why we're in business. It's how we inspire exceptional performance.

We believe that the winning businesses of tomorrow will be those which anticipate and respond to the huge changes shaping people's lives across the world. The businesses that will have the greatest success are those which capitalise on the power of data and biotechnology; adapt to shifting consumer needs; and contribute to tackling the twin challenges of climate change and social inequality.

## Our vision

Our vision is to be the global leader in sustainable business. We will demonstrate how our purpose-led, future-fit business model drives superior performance, consistently delivering financial results in the top third of our industry.

## Our values

We expect everyone at Unilever to be an ambassador for our high ethical standards – what we call 'business integrity'. Much of Unilever's strength lies in the shared values of our people:

- Integrity
- Respect
- Responsibility
- Pioneering

We want to create an environment where employees not only live our values in their own work, but are vigilant in identifying potential concerns, and confident about speaking up in such situations.

## Our strategy

It is our ambition to be the global leader in sustainable business. We will demonstrate that our purpose-led, future-fit business model delivers superior performance, consistently delivering financial results in the top third of our industry. We're guided in that ambition by five strategic choices

- **Accelerate the development of our portfolio into high growth spaces**. We will build our position in hygiene, skin care, prestige beauty, functional nutrition and plant-based foods.
- **Win with our brands as a force for good, powered by purpose and innovation**. Our brands will be built on advanced science and will grow by delivering functionally superior products, as well as taking action on social and environmental issues that our consumers care about. They will improve the health of the planet, improve people's health and wellbeing, and contribute to a fairer, more socially inclusive world.
- **Accelerate our growth in USA, India, China and key growth markets**. We will sharpen our focus and investment in our key growth markets, while further strengthening our leading positions across growth markets where we are uniquely positioned to win.
- **Lead in the channels of the future**. We will capture the opportunity in eCommerce, pioneering with innovative routes to market, and leading with shopper insights which help to drive our growth and build strong relationships with our customers.
- **Build a purpose-led, future-fit organisation and growth culture**. We will unlock capacity through agility and digital transformation, while building our people's capabilities through lifelong learning. We will be a beacon for diversity, inclusion and values-based leadership.

Source: www.unilever.com, January 1st, 2023

## Questions

1  Based on the information from this case, draw the organizational chart of Unilever.
2  The marketing function can be organized in different ways

   a  Which forms of organization of the marketing function are described in the book?

   b  How is the marketing function of Unilever organized? Explain your answer with information from the case.

3  Illustrate the difference between mission and vision using the information about Unilever's business model.

4  Is Unilever's business model in line with marketing 3.0? Explain your answer

5  Which values are essential for Unilever according to the value compass?

6  According to the book, a vision consists of three components: opinions about where the company believes the market is going, the identity of the company, and the long-term goals of the company. Analyze Unilever's purpose statement using these three components.

7  What is for Unilever the most relevant brand promise of the Brand Benefitting Model? Please explain

8  Describe the market definition of the Personal Care division, based on the three dimensions mentioned in Chapter 3.

9  Formulate objectives for Unilever by using the balanced scorecard. Use the information from the case, but make your own assumptions wherever necessary.

10  Do you feel that the Unilever's purpose is translated to the employees by means of internal branding? Explain your answer briefly.

# Literature

Aaker, D. A. (1991). *Managing brand equity: Capitalizing on the value of a brand name*. The Free Press.

Aaker, D. A. (1995). *Building strong brands*. The Free Press.

Aaker, D. A. (2013). *Strategic market management* (10th ed.). John Wiley & Sons.

Aaker, D. A., & Aaker, J. (2016). What are your signature stories? *California Management Review, 58*, 49–65.

Aaker, D. A., & Keller, K. L. (1990, January). Consumer evaluations of brand extensions. *Journal of Marketing, 54*, 27–41.

Aaker, J. (1997, August). Dimensions of measuring brand personality. *Journal of Marketing Research, 34*, 347–356.

Abell, D. F. (1980). *Defining the business: The starting point of strategic planning*. Prentice Hall, Inc.

Abell, D. F., & Hammond, J. S. (1979). *Strategic market planning*. Prentice Hall, Inc.

Alsem, K. J. (1991). *Concurrentie-analyse in de marketing (Competitive analysis in marketing: Theory, techniques & applications)* [Dissertation, Stenfert-Kroese Publishers].

Alsem, K. J., & Klein Koerkamp, R. (2010). *12 merken, 13 ongelukken (12 Brands, 13 Accidents)*. Noordhoff.

Alsem, K. J., & Klein Koerkamp, R. (2016). *Zorg met liefde en lef (Care with love and gut)*. Profiel Publisher.

Alsem, K. J., & Kostelijk, E. J. (2008). Identity based marketing: A new balanced marketing paradigm. *European Journal of Marketing, 42*, 907–914.

Alsem, K. J., & Van Slooten, S. (2021). Naar een merk-waardige customer experience (Towards a brand-worthy customer experience). *Holland Management Review, 202*, 19–25.

Alsop, R. J. (2004). *The 18 immutable laws of corporate reputation*. The Free Press.

Anholt, S. (2010). *Places: Identity, image and reputation*. Palgrave McMillan.

Ansoff, H. I. (1957, September–October). Strategies for diversification. *Harvard Business Review, 35*, 113–124.

Armstrong, J. S. (2001). *Principles of forecasting: A handbook for researchers and practitioners*. Kluwer Academic.

Armstrong, J. S. (2002). Assessing game theory, role playing and unaided judgment. *International Journal of Forecasting, 18*(3), 345–352.

Austin, J. R., Siguaw, J. A., & Mattila, A. S. (2003). A re-examination of the generalizability of the Aaker brand personality measurement framework. *Journal of Strategic Marketing*, *11*, 77–92.

Azoulay, A., & Kapferer, J. N. (2003). Do brand personality scales really measure brand personality? *Brand Management*, *11*, 143–155.

Balducci, B., & Marinova, D. (2018). Unstructured data in marketing. *Journal of the Academy of Marketing Science*, *46*, 557–590.

Barczak, G., Griffin, A., & Kahn, K. B. (2009). Perspective: Trends and drivers of success in NPD practices: Results of the 2003 PDMA best practices study. *Journal of Product Innovation Management*, *26*, 3–23.

Bijmolt, T. H. A., van Heerde, H. J., & Pieters, R. (2005). New empirical generalizations on the determinants of price elasticity. *Journal of Marketing Research*, *42*(2), 141–156.

Blattberg, R. C., Malthouse, E. C., & Neslin, S. A. (2009). Customer lifetime value: Empirical generalizations and some conceptual questions. *Journal of Interactive Marketing*, *23*, 157–168.

Blattberg, R. C., & Neslin, S. A. (1990). *Sales promotion, concepts, methods and strategies*. Prentice Hall.

Bonoma, T. V. (1984). Making your strategy work. *Harvard Business Review*, *62*, 67–76.

Bonoma, T. V., & Shapiro, B. P. (1983). *Segmenting the industrial market*. Lexington Books.

Borle, S., Singh, S. S., & Jain, D. C. (2008). Measuring customer lifetime value. *Management Science*, *54*, 100–112.

Bowman, D., & Gatignon, H. (1996). Order of entry as a moderator of the effect of the marketing mix on market share. *Marketing Science*, *15*, 222–242.

Brakus, J. J., Schmitt, B. H., & Zarantonello, L. (2009). Brand experience: What is it? How is it measured? Does it affect loyalty? *Journal of Marketing*, *73*, 52–68.

Bundy, J., Pfarrer, M. D., Short, C. E., & Coombs, W. T. (2017). Crises and crisis management: Integration, interpretation, and research development. *Journal of Management*, *43*(6), 1661–1692.

Byerly, H., Balmford, A., Ferraro, P. J., Hammond Wagner, C. R., Palchak, E., Polasky, S., Ricketts, T. H., Schwartz, A. J., & Fisher, B. (2018). Nudging pro-environmental behavior: Evidence and opportunities. *Frontiers in Ecology and the Environment*, *16*.

Camp, R. C. (1995). *Benchmarking: The search for best practices that lead to superior performance*. ASQC Quality Press.

Carpenter, G. S., Glazer, R., & Nakamoto, K. (1994). Meaningful brands from meaningless differentiation: The dependence on irrelevant attributes. *Journal of Marketing Research*, *31*, 339–350.

Cattin, P., & Wittink, D. R. (1982). Commercial use of conjoint analysis: A survey. *Journal of Marketing*, *46*, 44–53.

Christen, M. (2000). Does it pay to be a pioneer? In *Mastering marketing* (pp. 167–172). Financial Times/Pearson Education.

Cohen, W. A. (1998). *The marketing plan* (2nd ed.). John Wiley & Sons, Inc.

Conick, H. (2019, June/July). Optimize your website for voice search. *Marketing News*, *53*, 5–6.

Cooper, D. R., & Schindler, P. S. (2014). *Business research methods* (12th ed.). McGraw Hill.

Cooper, R. G. (2008). Perspective: The stage-gates idea-to-launch process – Update, what's new, and NexGen systems. *Journal of Product Innovation Management*, *25*, 213–232.

Damanpour, F., Szabat, K. A., & Evan, W. M. (1989, November). The relationship between types of innovation and organizational performance. *Journal of Management Studies*, *26*, 587–560.

Day, G. S. (1999). Misconceptions about market orientation. *Journal of Market Focused Management*, *4*, 5–16.

Day, G. S., & Wensley, R. (1983). Marketing theory with a strategic orientation. *Journal of Marketing, 47*(4), 79–89.

Day, G. S., & Wensley, R. (1988). Assessing advantage: A framework for diagnosing competitive superiority. *Journal of Marketing, 52*, 1–20.

De Chernatony, L., & Knox, S. (1990). How an appreciation of consumer behavior can help in product testing. *Journal of Market Research Society, 32*(3), 333.

Dibb, S., Simkin, L., & Bradley, J. (2003). *The marketing planning workbook* (3rd ed.). Thomson Learning.

Dijksterhuis, A. (2007). *Het slimme onbewuste (The smart unconscious)*. Bart Bakker.

Doran, G. T. (1981). There is a SMART way to write management's goals and objectives. *Management Review, 70*, 35–36.

Dorotic, M., Bijmolt, T. H. A., & Verhoef, P. C. (2012). Loyalty programs: Current knowledge and research directions. *International Journal of Management Reviews, 14*(3), 217–237.

Dowling, G. R., & Uncles, M. (1997). Do customer loyalty programs really work? *Sloan Management Review, 38*, 71–82.

Durst, S., & Henschel, T. (2022). *Crisis management for small and medium sized enterprises*. Jumper Link.

Ferrell, O. C., & Hartline, M. D. (2010). *Marketing strategy*. The Dryden Press.

Figge, F., Hahn, T., Schaltegger, S., & Wagner, M. (2002). The sustainable balanced scorecard – linking sustainability management to business strategy. *Business Strategy and the Environment, 11*, 269–284.

Floor, K., Van Raaij, F., & Bouwman, M. (2020). *Marketingcommunicatie strategie (Marketing communication strategy)* (8th ed.). Noordhoff.

Foster, C., Punjaisri, K., & Cheng, R. (2010). Exploring the relationship between corporate, internal and employer surf. *Journal or Product and Brand Management, 19*(6), 401–409.

Fournier, S., Dobscha, S., & Mick, D. G. (1998, January–February). Preventing the premature death of relationship marketing. *Harvard Business Review*, 42–51.

Franzen, G. (1998). *Merken en Reclame (Brands and advertising)*. Kluwer Company Information.

Geursen, G. (1990). *Een hazewind op gympen (A greyhound in sneakers)*. Stephen Kroese.

Ghimire, B., Shanaev, S., & Lin, Z. (2022). Effects of official versus online review ratings. *Annals of Tourism Research, 92*, 103247.

Giulianotti, R., Armstrong, G., Hales, G., & Hobbs, D. (2015). Global sport mega-events and the politics of mobility: The case of the London 2012 Olympics. *British Journal of Sociology, 66*(1), 118–140.

Glassman, M., & McAfee, B. (1992, May–June). Integrating the personnel and marketing functions: The challenge of the 1990s. *Business Horizons, 35*, 52–59.

Gummesson, E. (1987). The new marketing – Developing long term interactive relationships. *Long Range Planning, 20*(4), 10–20.

Gummesson, E. (1991). Marketing orientation revisited: The crucial role of the part-tome marketer. *European Journal of Marketing, 25*, 60–75.

Gummesson, E. (1998). Implementation requires a relationship marketing paradigm. *Journal of the Academy of Marketing Science, 26*, 242–249.

Gummesson, E. (1999). *Total relationship marketing – Rethinking marketing management: From 4 P's to 30 R's*. Butterworth-Heineman.

Gupta, S., Hanssens, D., Hardie, B., Kahn, W., Kumar, V., Lin, N., & Sriram, N. R. S. (2006). Modeling customer lifetime value. *Journal of Service Research, 9*, 139–155.

Hamel, G., & Prahalad, C. K. (1989, May–June). Strategic intent. *Harvard Business Review*, 79–91.

Hamermesh, R. G. (1986, July–August). Making planning strategic. *Harvard Business Review, 64*, 115–119.

Han, J. K., Kim, N., & Srivastava, R. K. (1998). Market orientation and organizational performance: Is innovation a missing link? *Journal of Marketing, 62*, 30–45.

Hansen, E. G., & Schaltegger, S. (2018). Sustainability balanced scorecards and their architectures: Irrelevant or misunderstood? *Journal of Business Ethics, 150*, 937–952.

Hanssens, D. M. (2015). *Empirical generalizations about marketing impact.* Marketing Science Institute.

Hendry, J. (1990). The problem with porter's generic strategies. *European Management Journal, 8*, 443–450.

Hillebrand, B., Driessen, P. H., & Koll, P. (2015). Stakeholder marketing: Theoretical foundations and required capabilities. *Journal of the Academy of Marketing Science, 43*, 411–428.

Hoekstra, J. C. (2003). *Direct marketing* (3rd ed.). Wolters Noordhoff.

Hofstede, G. (2011). Dimensionalizing cultures: The Hofstede model in context. *Online Reading in Psychology and Culture, 2*(1).

Hooley, G. J., Cox, A. J., & Adams, A. (1992). Our five year mission – to boldly go where no man has been before . . . *Journal of Marketing Management, 8*, 35–48.

Hooley, G. J., Möller, K., & Broderick, A. J. (1998). Competitive positioning and the resource based view of the firm. *Journal of Strategic Marketing, 6*(2), 97–115.

Hooley, G. J., Saunders, J., & Piercy, N. (2004). *Marketing strategy and competitive positioning* (3rd ed.). Pearson Education.

Hulbert, J. M., & Toy, M. E. (1977). A strategic framework for marketing control. *Journal of Marketing, 41*, 12–20.

Humphreys, A., & Wang, R. J. (2018). Automated text analysis for consumer research. *Journal of Consumer Research, 44*, 1274–1306.

Jassem, S., Zakaria, Z., & Azmi, A. C. (2022). Sustainability balanced scorecard architecture and environmental performance outcomes: A systematic review. *International Journal of Productivity and Performance Management, 71*, 1728–1760.

Kahneman, D. (2011). *Thinking, fast and slow.* Penguin Books Ltd.

Kalender, Z. T., & Vayvay, O. (2016). The fifth pillar of the balanced scorecard: Sustainability. *Procedia – Social and Behavioral Sciences, 235*, 76–83.

Kaplan, R. S., & Norton, D. P. (1992, January–February). The balanced scorecard – Measures that drive performance. *Harvard Business Review*, 71–79.

Kaplan, R. S., & Norton, D. P. (1993, September–October). Putting the balanced scorecard to work. *Harvard Business Review*, 134–142.

Keiningham, T. L., Cooil, B., Andreassen, T. R., & Aksoy, L. (2007). A longitudinal examination of net promoter and firm revenue growth. *Journal of Marketing, 71*(3), 39–51.

Keller, K. L. (1993). Conceptualizing, measuring and managing customer-based brand equity. *Journal of Marketing, 57*, 1–22.

Keller, K. L., & Swaminathan, V. (2019). *Strategic brand management: Building, measuring and managing brand equity* (5th ed.). Pearson Education.

Kerin, R. A., Mahajan, V., & Varadajan, P. R. (1990). *Contemporary perspectives on strategic market planning.* Allyn and Bacon.

Kerin, R. A., Varadarajan, P. R., & Peterson, R. A. (1992). First-mover advantage: A synthesis, conceptual framework, and research propositions. *Journal of Marketing, 56*(4), 33–52.

Kilbourne, W. E. (1998). Green marketing: A theoretical perspective. *Journal of Marketing Management, 14*(6), 641–655. http://doi.org/10.1362/026725798784867743

Kilbourne, W. E., & Alsem, K. J. (1997). Environmental attitudes and marketing: Attitudes of business students in The Netherlands. In D. Arnott, S. Bridgewater, & S. Dibb (Eds.), *Proceedings of the 26th EMAC conference* (pp. 1805–1813). European Marketing Academy.

Kirmani, A., Sood, S., & Bridges, S. (1999). The ownership effect in consumer responses to brand line stretches. *Journal of Marketing Research, 63*(1), 88–101.

Klemm, A., Sanderson, S., & Luffman, G. (1991). Mission statements: Selling corporate values to employees. *Long Range Planning, 24*(3), 73–78.

Knott, B., Fyall, A., & Jones, I. (2017). Sport mega-events and nation branding. *International Journal of Contemporary Hospitality, 29*(3), 900–923.

Kohli, A. K., & Jaworski, B. J. (1990). Market orientation: The construct, research propositions, and managerial implications. *Journal of Marketing, 54*, 1–18.

Kohli, S. C., Harich, K. R., & Leuthesser, L. (2005). Creating brand identity, a study of evaluation of new brand names. *Journal of Business Research, 58*(11), 1506–1515.

Kostelijk, E. J. (2017). *The value compass: The influence of values on consumer behaviour.* Routledge.

Kotler, Ph. (1973). Atmospherics as a marketing tool. *Journal of Retailing, 49*(4), 48–64.

Kotler, Ph. (1984, September 14). Interview in *Marketing News*, p. 22.

Kotler, Ph. (2004). The role played by the broadening of marketing movement in the history of marketing thought. *Journal of Public Policy and Marketing, 24*, 114–116.

Kotler, Ph. (2011). Reinventing marketing to manage the environmental imperative. *Journal of Marketing, 75*, 132–135.

Kotler, Ph., & Armstrong, G. (2021). *Principles of marketing* (18th ed.). Pearson Education.

Kotler, Ph., & Keller, K. L. (2016). *Marketing management* (15th ed.). Pearson Education.

Kumar, V. (2018). Transformative marketing: The next 20 years. *Journal of Marketing, 82*(4), 1–12.

Lane, V. R. (2000). The impact of ad repetition and ad content on consumer perceptions of incongruent extensions. *Journal of Marketing, 64*, 80–91.

Leeflang, P. S. H. (2003). *Marketing.* Wolters-Noordhoff.

Leeflang, P. S. H., & Wittink, D. R. (1996). Competitive reaction vs. Consumer response: Do managers overreact? *International Journal of Research in Marketing, 13*(2), 103–119.

Lehmann, D. R., & Winer, R. S. (2008). *Analysis for marketing planning* (7th ed.). McGraw Hill.

Lemon, K. L., & Verhoef, P. C. (2016, November). Understanding customer experience throughout the customer journey. *Journal of Marketing, 80*(6), 69–96.

Levitt, T. (1960, July–August). Marketing myopia. *Harvard Business Review.*

Lodish, L. M., Abraham, M. M., Livelsberger, J., Lubetkin, B., Richardson, B., & Stevens, M. E. (1995a). How TV advertising works: A meta-analysis of 389 real world split cable TV advertising experiments. *Journal of Marketing Research, 32*, 125–139.

Lodish, L. M., Abraham, M. M., Livelsberger, J., Lubetkin, B., Richardson, B., & Stevens, M. E. (1995b). A summary of fifty-five in-market experimental estimates of the long-term effect of TV advertising. *Marketing Science, 14*, G133–G140.

Malhotra, N. K., Nunan, D., & Birks, D. F. (2017). *Marketing research, an applied orientation* (5th ed.). Pearson Education.

McDonald, M. H. B. (1990). Some methodological comments on the directional policy matrix. *Journal of Marketing Management, 6*(1), 59–68.

McDonald, M. H. B. (1995). *Marketing plans.* Butterworth Heinemann.

Morgan, R. M., & Hunt, S. D. (1994). The commitment-trust theory of relationship marketing. *Journal of Marketing, 58*, 20–38.

Naik, P. A., & Peters, K. (2009). A hierarchical marketing communications model of online and offline media strategies. *Journal of Interactive Marketing, 23*, 288–299.

Narver, J. C., & Slater, S. F. (1990). The effect of market orientation on business profitability. *Journal of Marketing, 54*(4), 20–35.

Ndlela, M. N. (2019). *Crisis communication: A stakeholder approach.* Palgrave McMillan.

Nederstigt, J., & Poiesz, T. (2022). *Consumentengedrag (Consumer behavior)* (8th ed.). Noordhoff.

O'Cass, A., & Ngo, L. V. (2007). Market orientation versus innovative culture: Two routes to superior brand performance. *European Journal of Marketing, 41*, 868–887.

Oliver, R. L. (1999). Whence customer loyalty. *Journal of Marketing, 63*, 33–44.

Paap, R., Van Nierop, E., Van Heerde, H. J., Wedel, M., Franses, P. H., & Alsem, K. J. (2005). Considerations sets, intentions and the inclusion of 'don't know' in a two-stage model for voter choice. *International Journal of Forecasting, 21*, 53–71.

Parasuraman, A., Zeithaml, V. A., & Berry, L. (1985). A conceptual model of service quality and its implications for future research. *Journal of Marketing, 49*(Fall), 41–50.

Pauwels, K., Demirci, C., Yildirim, G., & Srinivasan, S. (2017). The impact of brand familiarity on online and offline media synergy. *International Journal of Research in Marketing, 33*, 739–753.

Pauwels, K., & Van Ewijk, B. (2013). Do online behavior tracking or attitude survey metrics drive brand sales? An integrative model of attitudes and actions on the consumer boulevard. *MSI Report* (pp. 13–118). Marketing Science Institute.

Peng, C., Bijmolt, T. H. A., Völckner, F., & Zhao, H. (2023). A meta-analysis of brand extension success: The effects of parent brand equity and extension fit. *Journal of Marketing*, online, forthcoming in print.

Peters, T. (1994). *The pursuit of Wow!* Vintage.

Piercy, N., & Morgan, N. (1991). Internal marketing – The missing half of the marketing program. *Long Range Planning, 24*(2), 82–93.

Porter, M. E. (1980). *Competitive strategy*. The Free Press.

Porter, M. E. (1985). *Competitive advantage*. The Free Press.

Porter, M. E. (1987, May–June). From competitive advantage to corporate strategy. *Harvard Business Review*, 43–59.

Porter, M. E., & Kramer, M. R. (2011, January–February). Creating shared value. *Harvard Business Review*, 62–77.

Prahalad, C. K., & Hamel, G. (1990, May–June). The core competence of the corporation. *Harvard Business Review*, 79–91.

Ravald, A., & Grönroos, C. (1996). The value concept and relationship marketing. *European Journal of Marketing, 30*, 19–30.

Reddy, S. K., Holak, S. L., & Bhat, S. (1994). To extend or not to extend: Success determinants of line extensions. *Journal of Marketing Research, 31*, 243–262.

Reichheld, F. F. (1993, March–April). Loyalty based management. *Harvard Business Review*, 64–73.

Reichheld, F. F. (1996, March–April). Learning from customer defections. *Harvard Business Review*, 56–69.

Reichheld, F. F. (2003, December). One number you need to grow. *Harvard Business Review*.

Ries, A., & Trout, J. (1981). *Positioning: The battle for your mind*. McGraw Hill.

Roberts, E. B., & Berry, C. A. (1985, Spring). Entering new businesses: Selecting strategies for success. *Sloan Management Review*, 3–17.

Rokeach, M. J. (1973). In O. Bearden, R. G. Netemeyer, & M. F. Mobley (1993) (Eds.). *Handbook of marketing scales: Multi-item measures for marketing and consumer behavior research* (p. 83). Sage Publications.

Rokeach, M. J. (1979). *Understanding human values, individual and social*. The Free Press.

Romaniuk, J., & Sharp, B. (2015). *How brands grow, part 2*. Oxford University Press.

Rossiter, J. R., Percy, L., & Donovan, R. J. (1991). A better advertising planning grid. *Journal of Advertising Research, 31*(5), 11–21.

Schnaars, S. P. (1997). *Marketing strategy* (2nd ed.). The Free Press.

Schwartz, B. (2004). *The paradox of choices*. The Spectrum.

Sharp, B. (2010). *How brands grow: What marketers don't know*. Oxford University Press.

Sinek, S. (2009). *Start with why: How great leaders inspire everyone to take action*. Portfolio.

Srivastava, R. K., Shervani, T. A., & Fahey, L. (1998, January). Market-based assets and shareholder value: A framework for analysis. *Journal of Marketing, 2*, 2–18.

Steenkamp, J. B. E. M., Nijs, V. R., Hanssens, D. M., & De Kimpe, M. G. (2005). Competitive reactions to advertising and promotion attacks. *Marketing Science, 24*, 35–54.

Tobelem, J. M. (1997). The marketing approach in Museums. *Museum Management and Curatorship, 16*, 337–354.

Treacy, M., & Wiersema, F. (1993, January–February). Customer intimacy and other value disciplines. *Harvard Business Review*, 84–93.

Tutaj, K., & Van Reijmersdal, E. (2012). Effects of online advertising format and persuasion knowledge on audience reactions. *Journal of Marketing Communications, 18*, 5–18.

Vakratsas, D., & Ambler, T. (1999). How advertising works: What do we really know? *Journal of Marketing, 63*, 26–43.

Van Heerde, H. J., Gupta, S., & Wittink, D. R. (2003, November). Is 75% of the sales promotion dump due to brand switching? No, only 33% is. *Journal of Marketing Research, 40*, 481–491.

Van Helden, G. J., & Alsem, K. J. (2016). The delicate interface between management accounting and marketing management. *Journal of Accounting and Marketing, 5*(3), 1–5.

Van Ittersum, K., & Wansink, B. (2012). Plate size and color suggestibility: The Delboeuf illusion's bias on serving and eating behavior. *Journal of Consumer Research, 39*, 215–228.

Varadarajan, R. (2010). Strategic marketing and marketing strategy: Domain, definition, fundamental issues and foundational premises. *Journal of the Academy of Marketing Science, 38*, 119–140.

Vargo, S. L., & Lusch, R. F. (2004, January). Evolving to a new dominant logic for marketing. *Journal of Marketing, 68*, 1–17.

Veldhoen, B., & Van Slooten, S. (2010). *De 9+ organisatie: Van marketshare naar mindshare (The 9+ organization: From market share to mind share)*. Van Duren Management.

Verhoef, P. C., Kooge, E., & Walk, N. (2016). *Creating value with big data analytics*. Routledge.

Verhoef, P. C., & Leeflang, P. S. H. (2009). Understanding the marketing department's influence within the firm. *Journal of Marketing, 73*, 14–37.

Verhoef, P. C., & Lemon, K. N. (2013). Successful customer value management: Key lessons and emerging trends. *European Management Journal, 31*(1), 1–15.

Verhoef, P. C., Lemon, K. N., Parasuraman, A., Roggeveen, A., Tsiros, M., & Schlesinger, L. A. (2019). Customer experience creation: Determinants, dynamics and management strategies. *Journal of Retailing, 85*, 31–41.

Viererbl, B., & Koch, T. (2022). The paradoxical effects of communicating CSR activities: Why CSR communication has both positive and negative effects on the perception of a company's social responsibility. *Public Relations Review, 48*(1), 102–134.

Völckner, F., & Sattler, H. (2006). Drivers of brand extension success. *Journal of Marketing, 70*, 18–34.

Vorhies, D. W., & Morgan, N. A. (2005). Benchmarking marketing capabilities for sustainable competitive advantage. *Journal of Marketing, 69*, 80–94.

Webster, F. E. (1992). The changing role of marketing in the corporation. *Journal of Marketing, 56*(10), 1–17.

Webster, F. E. (2005, October). Back to the future: Integrating marketing as tactics, strategy and organizational culture. *Journal of Marketing, 69*, 4–6.

Wedel, M., & Kannan, P. K. (2016). Marketing analytics for data rich environments. *Journal of Marketing, 80*(6), 97–121.

Weihrich, H. (1982). The TOWS matrix – A tool for situational analysis. *Long Range Planning, 15*, 54–66.

Wernerfelt, B. (1984). A resource-based view of the firm. *Strategic Management Journal, 16*, 171–180.

White, K., Habib, R., & Hardisty, D. J. (2019). How to SHIFT consumer behaviors to be more sustainable: A literature review and guiding framework. *Journal of Marketing, 83*(3), 22–49.

Wind, Y., Mahajan, V., & Swire, D. J. (1983). An empirical comparison of standardized portfolio models. *Journal of Marketing, 47*, 89–99.

Woodruff, R. B. (1997). Customer value: The next source for competitive advantage. *Journal of the Academy of Marketing Science, 25*(2), 139–153.

Yoo, B., & Donthu, N. (2001). Developing and validating a multidimensional consumer-based brand equity scale. *Journal of Business Research, 52*, 1–14.

Zahra, S. A., De Belardino, S., & Boxx, W. R. (1988, June). Organizational innovation: Its correlates and its implications for financial performance. *International Journal of Management, 5*, 133–142.

# Index